THE USC TROJANS

THE USC TROJANS

COLLEGE FOOTBALL'S
ALL-TIME GREATEST
DYNASTY

Revised and Updated

Steven Travers

Taylor Trade Publishing
Lanham • New York • Boulder • Toronto • Plymouth, UK

Published by Taylor Trade Publishing
An imprint of The Rowman & Littlefield Publishing Group, Inc.
4501 Forbes Boulevard, Suite 200, Lanham, Maryland 20706

Distributed by NATIONAL BOOK NETWORK

The Library of Congress has cataloged the hardcover edition as follows:
Travers, Steven.
   The USC Trojans : college football's all-time greatest dynasty / Steven Travers.
      p. cm.
   Includes bibliographical references and index.
   ISBN-13: 978-1-58979-356-9 (cloth : alk. paper)
   ISBN-10: 1-58979-356-0 (cloth : alk. paper)
   1. University of Southern California—Football—History. 2. Southern California Trojans (Football team)—History. I. Title.
   GV958.U5857T73 2006
   796.332'630979494—dc22

                                                                        2006006575

ISBN: 978-1-58979-568-6 (pbk. : alk. paper)

♾™ The paper used in this publication meets the minimum requirements of American National Standard for Information Sciences—Permanence of Paper for Printed Library Materials, ANSI/NISO Z39.48-1992.

Manufactured in the United States of America.

To Terry Marks,
who recited the Lord's Prayer
and became a noble Trojan!

———

Fight on and win
For ol' SC.
Fight on to victory.
Fight On!

"FIGHT ON!" USC'S OFFICIAL FIGHT SONG

———

"'Fight On!' meant no matter the conditions,
no matter the opponent,
you always played your best."

MIKE GARRETT, SPEAKING AT THE MARV GOUX MEMORIAL,

AUGUST 2, 2002

CONTENTS

FOREWORD

Marv Goux and the University of Southern California recruited Charles "Tree" Young out of Fresno's Edison High School in 1969. He was a member of USC's famed 1970 team, which traveled to Birmingham, defeated all-white Alabama, and thus helped to effectuate integration in the American South. He was a consensus All-American on USC's 1972 national championship team, considered by many to be the greatest collegiate football team of all time. A member of the National Football Foundation's College Hall of Fame, Young was a first-round draft choice of the Philadelphia Eagles. He played in the 1980 Super Bowl with the Los Angeles Rams and was a member of the 1981 World Champion San Francisco 49ers. Young's three daughters ("Charle's angels") all ran track at USC. He is an ordained minister in the Seattle, Washington, area.

My friend Manfred Moore e-mailed me about Steve Travers, the author of *Barry Bonds: Baseball's Superman*, wanting to do a story about the 1970 USC football team that played Coach Bear Bryant's Alabama football team in Birmingham. Thirty-six years ago, I was blessed to be an important member of that team. As I look back on the canvas of time, the main hero would be none other than my friend, Sam "The Bam" Cunningham. I was quite honored when Steve called, and we set a time to discuss this historical event. Subsequently, Steve and I became friends. He asked that I write the foreword to this book, which details the entire history of USC football. Steve's books deal with historical events that expose paradigm shifts, cultures, and philosophical changes through the world of athletics. Most people are aware that the University of Southern California builds leaders in all disciplines. USC is on the cutting edge of history, and that is why the great historical civil rights event that I was a part of—the 1970 game between USC and Alabama that helped end segregation—unfolded in our time, and is emblematic of the importance of my alma mater and her football history.

In 1875, the Rev. John R. Tansey, then presiding Elder of the Methodist Episcopal Church, proposed the organization of a college in Southern California, and in 1880, that Methodist College became what is now known as the University of Southern California. I mention this to let you know that some of the early abolitionists were Methodist, and it was only natural that the University of Southern California would be part of this great movement.

Predestination is to foreordain by divine decree or purpose. It is true that the 1964 Civil Rights Act and the Voting Act of 1965 provided a framework for significant changes in American civil rights policy. There were two major aspects of these laws— the adoption of the law and the implementation of the law.

The U.S. Supreme Court issued its ruling in the case of *Plessy v. Ferguson* and established the doctrine of "separate but equal." I told you that the University of Southern California was and is on the cutting edge of historical events. This is History 570, and history is a branch of knowledge that deals with his-story of past events.

On April 11, 1968, the Civil Rights Act was passed with opposition from Southern Democrats. This nation's cities were ablaze, and political leaders were being assassinated. Two years later USC would be playing football in Birmingham, Alabama. A stronghold of the Knights of the Ku Klux Klan, a city that bombed and killed four little girls in church, and had the infamous Bull Connor. What Congress and marching took years to do, USC and the University of Alabama did in a season.

Scripture says, where there is no Vision, the people perish. Coach John McKay and Coach Paul "Bear" Bryant had vision. They set out to change the cultural landscape of a nation. This debate or difference of opinion wasn't acted out on the battlefield of Gettysburg, but on the gridiron of Legion Field. The 1970 Trojans soon became national champions and one of the greatest teams in the history of college football.

A few years later, in 1972, if you examine the members of that team, you would find at least five ministers. Offensive lineman Dave Brown helped to organize the coming together of the faithful believers in God. In my opinion that turned our team around. We were undefeated, untested, and untied; we were national champions! Some of the leading sports experts believe that the 1972 USC football team was the greatest team in college history. But the debate continues.

Coach John McKay said, "It isn't just the players that make a team great, but the mix of those players. How well do they get along? Do they respect each other?" Coach Pete Carroll did a great job of assembling and putting together a great mixture of players: Matt Leinart, LenDale White, Reggie Bush ("Thunder and Lightning"), and a plethora of outstanding players.

In 1972 we not only had tremendous talent; we had the perfect blend of personalities. We had the original "Thunder and Lightning," Sam "Bam" Cunningham, and Anthony "A. D., I can do it" Davis. But, no matter how sophisticated your offense is or who is playing quarterback or tailback, if you don't have a great defensive team, it's hard to be a champion. In my humble opinion, that was where the 2005 team fell short.

Over the last hundred years, the USC Trojan football program has been recognized as one of the greatest dynasties in the history of college football. USC builds leaders.

I'm sure other programs such as Notre Dame, Texas, Ohio State, and UCLA build their share of leaders also. Leaders like Joe Montana, Vince Young, Troy Aikman, and Jack Tatum. But USC has leaders all over the NFL. I'm uncertain, but I think that every Super Bowl played has had a Trojan in the game. Lynn Swann and Ronnie Lott have won four each. In the last seven straight years a Trojan has been inducted into the NCAA Hall of Fame.

A wise man once said, "What you do speaks so well, I need not hear what you say."

Most generations in our times know of the greatest of the Trojan football program.

CHARLES "TREE" YOUNG
USC '73; USC 1972 national champs;
Super Bowl XVI Champs; NCAA Football Hall of Famer

INTRODUCTION: THE UNIVERSITY OF THE 21ST CENTURY

"You're a Bruin for four years. You're a Trojan for life!"

When I entered the University of Southern California, my next-door neighbor remarked that I "would be able to call my own shots," a reference not only to the first-class education I would receive at USC, but also to the fact I would have access to the school's legendary "old boy" alumni network.

Had I, when I was a student at USC, known that some day I would write a series of USC histories; be called by the Annenberg School for Communication and Journalism "USC's athletic department biographer"; make speeches on campus, before SC alumni groups, and at the Pasadena Quarterbacks Club; have all my books prominently displayed at the front of the USC Bookstore; and do numerous signings on campus and at the L.A. Coliseum; well, I would have taken that!

Opportunity is what we make of it, and USC's extraordinary recent success in football, which has made the school hotter and more glamorous than ever, has increased the opportunity for me to write a series of books about my alma mater. In 2006 Taylor Trade published *The USC Trojans: College Football's All-Time Greatest Dynasty*. It was so successful (a National Book Network "top 100 seller" with excellent reviews) that in 2010 Taylor Trade chose to re-publish it in paperback. They asked me to update it as well, so this version includes extended review from 2007–2009.

In 2007 Taylor Trade published *One Night, Two Teams: Alabama vs. USC and the Game That Changed A Nation*. This is the true story of Sam "Bam" Cunningham and the 1970 USC-Alabama game, which helped pave the way for the end to segregation in the South. *One Night, Two Teams* was optioned by Hollywood producer and USC graduate Kerry McCluggage, owner and president of Craftsman Films. During the process of selling book rights and cutting a movie deal, I attended a meeting at the legendary William Morris Agency in Beverly Hills. There were eight people in a conference room. All were USC alumni.

My old neighbor was certainly right. My USC connections have paid off, but my love of USC and appreciation for its history had been implanted long before I was a student. The seeds for this book started when I was eight years old.

I was a USC fan from the time I was old enough to *be* a fan. My father, Donald E. Travers, taught business law at City College of San Francisco when O.J. Simpson set all the California junior college rushing records there from 1965-66. After his freshman year, Simpson wanted to play at a four-year school, but his grades were inadequate for admission to USC. Arizona State and Utah would let him in, and he was ready to go when USC assistant coach Marv Goux flew to San Francisco. Goux told Simpson that "great things are worth waiting for." This story is a well known one in Trojan circles, but what is not known is that a coterie of "wise men" at CCSF also counseled Simpson to stay and hold out for Southern California. The group included school president Louis "Dutch" Conlan and my father.

O.J. went to USC, and my dad followed him closely. When *I* "came of age," it was the age of the Trojans; national champions, Heisman Trophy winners, All-Americans. To borrow a Rick Pitino phrase, USC was "the Roman Empire of college football."

My dad gave me Don Pierson's book, *The Trojans: Southern California Football* for Christmas. I read it until I had committed all of it to memory. I was an older student at USC. I had wanted to play baseball for Rod Dedeaux's Trojans, but despite helping to pitch my high school team to a mythical national championship my senior year, the scholarship was not offered. I was ready to walk on, but another college offered me a baseball scholarship. I set a number of pitching records and earned all-conference honors, then played a few years professionally in the St. Louis Cardinals and Oakland A's organizations. I still needed two more years to earn a Bachelor's degree in communications. I decided to transfer to the school of my hopes and dreams, USC.

My grades were not quite up to SC standards, but with the help of two great counselors, Dr. Arthur Verge and Delores Homisak, I was admitted under the proviso that I maintain a B average. Ms. Homisak heard in my voice the conviction and love I had for the school. She knew how much I wanted to be a part of the Trojan Family, and she took a chance on me. I am eternally grateful. I was able to skip the kind of "red tape" that is wrapped around most public institutions. I strove for excellence and found a home where I could achieve just that.

By the time I finally matriculated at the University, I felt like those old-time war vets going to school on the G.I. Bill. I also felt like an art student walking around the Louvre. Strolling the tree-lined lanes of the USC campus; studying in Doheny Library; attending events at Bovard Auditorium; and sitting in class, surrounded by fellow Trojans, being taught by top-notch USC professors; all of it was extraordinary. I had to pinch myself to make sure I was not dreaming. It was an honor and a privilege to be there. To this day, it is a thrill just to walk on that beautiful campus. Driving on the Santa Monica or Harbor Freeways through downtown L.A., getting off at the USC exit; each time I approach USC and see its architecture hovering in the distance, I get a sense of anticipation. I love less USC less than my Lord and Savior Jesus Christ, but He *does* have an apartment on West Adams Boulevard!

I made lasting friendships at USC, and have all kinds of wild memories from the times I spent at a dilapidated sports bar. Located at the corner of Jefferson and Mc-Clintock, next to the Bank of America in the University Village shopping center, the California Pizza & Pasta Company, also known by the unfortunate moniker 502 Club, was a hangout for athletes and beautiful Trojan girls. It is only a memory now. A Yoshinoya Beef Bowl sits where the "Five-Oh" once raged.

Being at USC was very exciting. The actress Ally Sheedy was on campus. I was a classmate of Jennie Nicholson, the daughter of Jack Nicholson, as well as James Garner's daughter. Laker owners Jerry Buss, a Trojan, had his daughter, Jeannie, on campus around this time. Ernie Banks's son was at Troy, too. One rumor had it that Tom Cruise was enrolled at USC. Then *Risky Business* became a big hit. Supposedly Cruise withdrew from school to pursue his now–red hot acting career on a full time basis.

There were many exotic students from faraway lands at USC. I befriended one fellow who claimed to be a member of Sudan's royal family; a crown prince, I believe.

Having played professionally, I naturally gravitated to the USC baseball team. When I graduated, I went to work for a company located in the Wells Fargo Building in downtown Los Angeles. My friends Phil Smith and Terry Marks were coaching USC's junior varsity baseball team, known as the Spartans. They asked me to be a volunteer coach. What a treat!

Every day, I could not wait to make the five-minute drive from the 7th and Flower office to the USC campus. I would change from my suit and tie and wear the glorious Cardinal and Gold baseball uniform that I had wanted to don since high school. I got to know legendary former coach Rod Dedeaux, who just called me "Tiger" as he did everybody else, as well as his replacement, Mike Gillespie, who I stayed in regular contact with. Afterwards Terry, Phil and sometimes other baseball Trojans would knock it all off with a couple of beers at the Five-Oh. Great days!

■ ■ ■

Football, particularly the rivalry with Notre Dame, is what put USC on the national map after World War I. There is so much more to USC than just gridiron greatness, however. Hollywood and USC have always had a symbiotic relationship. The school has produced countless actors, directors, screenwriters, producers and agents.

The University itself has long been used for many scenes of campus life. The 1967 classic, *The Graduate*, was supposed to feature Dustin Hoffman pursuing Katharine Ross up at Cal-Berkeley. In truth, it was shot at USC. Ironically, *The Hunchback of Notre Dame* was filmed not at Notre Dame (either the Paris or South Bend versions), but at USC. The Academy Awards have been held at various locations throughout Los Angeles, often at the Shrine Auditorium, located across the street from USC. On a clear day, the Hollywood sign can be seen from the SC campus.

Famous show biz Trojans include ex-Trojan football player John "Duke" Wayne; *Star Wars* director George Lucas; actor-director Ron Howard; former *Three's Company* star John Ritter; *The Breakfast Club* co-star Ally Sheedy; *Boyz N the Hood* director John Singleton; former All-American Aaron Rosenberg, producer of countless 1960s and '70s television shows; ex-*Magnum P.I.* star Tom Selleck, who played baseball, basketball and volleyball at SC; *That Girl!* star Marlo Thomas; producer David L. Wolper; *Forrest Gump* director Robert Zemeckis; *Dirty Harry* and *Magnum Force* screenwriter John Milius; musicians Herb Alpert and Lionel Hampton; and opera star Marilyn Horne.

Many Trojan sports heroes have made their mark in broadcasting. They include: Hall of Fame pitcher Tom Seaver, a former *Baseball Game of the Week* partner of Vin Scully as well as the voice of the Yankees and Mets; Hall of Fame running back Frank Gifford of *Monday Night Football* fame; Trojan and Ram quarterback, Rhodes Scholar, attorney and national college football announcer Pat Haden; Hall of Famer-turned-sideline-analyst (and possible political candidate) Lynn Swann; Olympic Gold Medalist John Naber, a national swimming broadcaster; ex-big leaguer Ron Fairly, who became an Angels and Giants broadcaster; quarterback and Fox Sports football analyst Craig Fertig.

Legendary sportswriters from USC include Mal Florence of the *Los Angeles Times*. National media figures: Kathleen Sullivan and Sam Donaldson of ABC News. Leading politicians, jurists and statesmen are former Secretary of State Warren Christopher; ex-Congressman and current Chairman of the Securities and Exchange Commission Christopher Cox; former California Assembly Speaker Jesse "Big Daddy" Unruh, whose name graces USC's political science school; Congressman and former California Attorney General Dan Lungren; U.S. Congressman Dana Rohrabacher; All-American John Ferraro, a longtime Los Angeles City Councilman; and California Supreme Court Chief Justice Justice Malcolm M. Lucas.

In the 1960s, NASA created what came to be known as "The Bubble," a device that tested the manufactured atmosphere of space. Because of this, many well-known astronauts of the Mercury, Gemini and Apollo space programs earned advanced degrees at USC. The most famed of these American heroes is Neil Armstrong, the first man on the moon.

Other distinguished alumni include architect Frank Gehry; Persian Gulf War commander General Norman Schwarzkopf; syndicated columnist Art Buchwald; as well as top-ranking executives, including Coca-Cola's Terry Marks and Guy Carpenter & Companies' Peter Cooper.

Just like the Trojans of Homer's *The Iliad and the Odyssey*, the modern day version fights harder, has more moral fiber and better character than representatives of most colleges. USC has always been a traditional school that has extolled the patriotic values of God and country. Countless Trojans have fought with valor, and many have died for our freedom, on the fields of our nation's battles.

From its earliest days, USC has been a place of equal opportunity. The first black professionals in medicine, architecture and other fields were trained at USC prior to

4

World War I. Women have prepared for meaningful careers at USC since its earliest days in the nineteenth century. The ridiculous moniker "University of Spoiled Children" was given to a great, conservative university that was opening its doors to all when those hypocritically deriding it were still cloistered all-white boys clubs.

USC was once falsely described by its jealous detractors as a "football school," despite the fact that the ranks of judges, lawyers, doctors, dentists, and other professions in Greater Los Angeles have long been been dominated by "Southern California men and women." At USC the famous phrase, "There are two kinds of people; those who are Trojans and those who wish they were Trojans," may have been uttered with a touch of arrogance but also with a touch of truth.

President Steven Sample carried forth the work done by previous chancellors. Already considered the leading film school and dental school, and among the top business schools, MBA programs, law schools and medical schools in America, USC under Sample has become one of the top twenty academic institutions in the nation. USC was named "College of the Year 2000" by the *Time/Princeton Review College Guide*, and America's "Hot School 2001" by the *Newsweek/Kaplan College Guide*.

"More institutions might do well to emulate USC's enlightened self-interest," read the *Time/Princeton Review*. "For not only has the 'hood dramatically improved, but so has the University."

"Just as East Coast students go for New York and NYU, the West Coast is gravitating to USC in Los Angeles," wrote the *Newsweek/Kaplan College Guide*. "USC has morphed from a jock school to a serious contender for top students."

From the 1960s until the early 1990s, the top four film schools in America were NYU and Columbia in New York, and UCLA and USC in California. Over the past fifteen years, the USC School of Cinema-Television has emerged head and shoulders above the competition. One of the ways they have achieved this is by instituting a producer's division into their curriculum. Instead of simply educating writers, directors, and actors in the art of film (but not the business of it), USC has created a real-world model for Hollywood success.

Directors, writers, and actors network and connect with fellow-Trojan producers and agents. The result is that USC alumni at every level of the business now dominate the film industry.

The School of Cinematic Arts has benefited tremendously from its many successful alumni. George Lucas has donated countless millions to the program he graduated from in 1966, and one of the school's buildings bears his name. Johnny Carson donated money and has a building housing the study of television production in his name. Steven Spielberg actually was *turned down* for admission to USC, but he bears no hard feelings. He has contributed his time, money, and name to numerous causes benefiting the film school.

The music school and the drama school have reaped natural ancillary benefits of a great film school. Former Ambassador to the Court of St. James Walter Annenberg donated $120 million establishment for a world class communications program, which has produced graduates skilled in advertising, public relations, political campaigns, and Hollywood publicity, just to name a few areas of expertise.

Undergraduate applications doubled over the last few years, as the school led a citywide revival following the 1992 riots and a large 1994 earthquake. Bold political leadership under Mayor Richard Riordan helped decrease crime and clean up the streets. Enlightened corporate and auto industry responsibility resulted in a major decrease in L.A. Basin air pollution from the 1970s and '80s to the 2000s.

USC has made a fabulous, bold outreach to its community. Located in one of Los Angeles' oldest (once one of its best) neighborhoods, the University never ignored its responsibilities as that South-Central neighborhood deteriorated. They have been the driving force behind gentrification projects that have created new housing and shopping in the area. Faculty housing has invested USC professors in the neighborhood many of them now live in. New schools and day care centers have been built and run by USC. Excellent outreach programs have provided deserving African-American, Latino, and other minority students from L.A.'s inner city a chance to matriculate at a school that otherwise would only be a "so close and yet so far" dream. Freshmen in local high schools enter a program in which, if they maintain high grades in academic coursework, they are given full scholarships to USC.

USC has one of the highest tuition, is among the richest colleges in the nation in terms of private endowments, and among the top three in athletic financial donations. It is a university that has managed to seamlessly combine social responsibility with American capitalistic principles, in a manner not unlike the way Olympic President Peter Ueberroth was able to make the 1984 L.A. Games the most successful before or since.

Trojan football reached an 82 percent graduation rate, an all-time high, and more than 20 percentage points higher than the average Division I college football average. In 2001, 14 members of the team had 3.00 G.P.A.'s. USC ranks in the top 10 in the number of NCAA post-graduate scholarship recipients (49 as of 2004) and has had 26 first team Academic All-Americans. Three Trojans have earned Rhodes Scholarships. USC athletes are universally recognized for their approachable, media-savvy demeanors. They are considered unusually articulate and intelligent by sports journalists in Los Angeles and nationally. Sportstalk host Jim Rome has repeatedly expressed amazement at how outstanding interviews with USC athletes on his program are.

The University reached 29,000 students, including the Health Sciences Campus to the northeast of downtown L.A., known to soap fans as *General Hospital*. It is the West's oldest private university, with a student-to-faculty ration of 13 to 1. The USC/Norris Comprehensive Cancer is among the finest of its kin in the world.

In 1994, the most academically talented class in USC history entered the University; the same year that professor George Olah won the Nobel Prize in chemistry. Academic standards and achievements of students and faculty alike have only gotten more impressive in the decade-plus that followed.

40,000 people work for USC, making it the largest private employer in Los Angeles. It has one of the most substantial foreign enrollments of any college in America. Because so many USC students hail from the Pacific Rim, the Middle East, Africa and other exotic locales, it proudly claims the largest non-white population in U.S. higher education. Countless foreign dignitaries—political figures, statesmen, business leaders—learned to love California and America at USC. In turn they have helped foster this nation's international friendships with its global partners.

In its early days, USC offered Methodist religious instruction, but quickly became a private, non-denominational institution serving the needs of the broader world community. In 1912, its athletic nickname was switched from the Methodists to the Trojans. In 1929, a statue dubbed "Tommy Trojan": "faithful, scholarly, skillful, courageous, and ambitious," was erected and stands as a campus landmark for time immemorial.

In the late 1940s, bandleader Tommy Walker also kicked field goals for the football team, leading the music in between! According to legend, he may or may not be one of the inspirations for The Who's rock opera, "Tommy." In the 1950s, the band began the tradition of playing the stirring battle cry, "Conquest," originally heard in the 1947 motion picture, *Captain from Castile*. In 1961, Traveler I, a magnificent white horse, made his first appearance. Traveler I's progeny have been riding the sidelines at USC football games ever since.

The fabulous Heritage Hall, housing USC's countless trophies and the offices of its athletic department and sports teams, was built in 1971: half office building, half museum. In 1974, Dedeaux Field became *the* state-of-the-art collegiate baseball stadium in the country. Cromwell Athletic Field, a first-rate track and field facility, was built next to Heritage Hall. The McDonald's Swim Center was created for the 1984 Olympics.

In 1923, the Los Angeles Memorial Coliseum was built, along with the adjacent Rose Garden, in Exposition Park across the street from USC. The Coliseum and the University have together hosted the 1932 and 1984 Games. The Coliseum has been home to USC football ever since. In 1959, the L.A. Memorial Sports Arena was built next to the Coliseum. It was used for the 1984 Olympics, has hosted national political conventions, Final Fours, professional basketball, and Trojan hoops for over 45 years. A new on-campus basketball facility is scheduled to open for the 2006-07 season.

■ ■ ■

While I majored in communications at USC, and put those skills to work in political public relations, I had also taken a number of classes in USC's famed School of Cinema-Television, including fabulous courses taught by the legendary Andrew Casper. I learned the fine art of screenwriting, and after a number of years pursuing politics, the law and sports representation, I decided to pursue my first passion: writing.

This led to the UCLA Writers' Program and several years working in Hollywood. I also started covering prep football for the *Los Angeles Daily News* and the *Los Angeles Times*. Trojan football and the phraseology of "conquest" inculcated my thoughts, my speech and my writings. At a meeting of prep stringers at the *Times'* Orange County offices, however, assistant sports editor Bob Rohwer, a Trojan in his own right, warned us not to use flowery language.

"Just give it to us straight," said Rohwer. "'Mater Dei High defeated Long Beach Poly last night at Veteran's Stadium in Long Beach, 30-something to 20-something, behind the passing of Matt Leinart, who completed 20-something passes in 30-something attempts for 300-something yards.'"

"You mean," I piped up, "if I see any 'Thundering Herds' outlined against a 'blue, gray October sky,' I'm not supposed to report what I see?"

Rohwer laughed because he understood the reference to Howard Jones's dynasty and Grantland Rice's 1924 classic about the "Four Horsemen of Notre Dame." The rest of the twenty-somethings in the room looked at each other like Dumbellionites.

I mostly covered Villa Park High School, and would sometimes call in reports of Redondo Union and Mira Costa High games to downtown main sports editor Gary Klein, who later became USC's football beat writer.

That was 2000. Paul Hackett was in charge at USC. Carson Palmer was a disappointing, overrated quarterback from Orange County. There was no threat of any "Thundering Herds" at USC. However, on the horizon was the future of the University of Southern California. Like Palmer, he was another quarterback from Orange County.

That year, I saw Mater Dei High School of Santa Ana take on De La Salle High School of Concord, California. This was a battle of titans, played at Edison International Field of Anaheim (now known as Angels Stadium) before approximately 20,000 fans. De La Salle was at the height of their glory, which all things considered may be the greatest dynasty in sports history; pro, college or high school. They would go undefeated from 1991 to 2003, 151 comes, good for four national championships. De La Salle had taken some criticism from "experts" who said they played a "soft" schedule, so in the late 1990s and early 2000s they decided to show everybody. They scheduled games against major powerhouses: Long Beach Poly, Honolulu Punahou, Cincinnati Moeller . . . and Santa Ana Mater Dei.

The 2000 De La Salle-Mater Dei game has been described as the "greatest high school football game ever played." I could not disagree. De La Salle upheld their streak (they would not lose until 2004), 31-28, but Mater Dei's quarterback put on the finest prep performance I have ever witnessed. He was 31-of-47 for 447 yards and four touchdowns. He rallied Mater Dei from a huge fourth quarter deficit, and it was only a failed field goal attempt after he had led the Monarchs down the field with no time left that saved De La Salle.

Those who saw Joe Montana lead Notre Dame in a desperate fourth quarter comeback that fell just short against USC at the L.A. Coliseum in 1978 walked away saying, "I don't care where he is drafted, he's going to be one of the greatest quarterbacks who has ever played the game."

Just as Southern California football fans had seen the future in 1978, and his name was Joe Montana, I had seen the future in the 2000 Mater Dei-De La Salle game, and his name was Matt Leinart. The "disappointing, overrated quarterback from Orange County," Carson Palmer, would come under the tutelage of new coach Pete Carroll and offensive coordinator Norm Chow and win the Heisman Trophy two years later. Carroll had observed the prep landscape in 2000. There were other quarterbacks rated as highly as Leinart, despite his performance against the national champions from Northern California. It was Leinart, however, along with Shaun Cody of Los Altos, who was the centerpiece of Carroll's first recruiting class. He got Leinart to join his Mater Dei teammate, linebacker Matt Grootegoed, and they would form the nucleus of the greatest dynasty in college football history.

In the context of Trojan football lore, he was stepping into a situation whereby any glory or accolades that might come his way had been paved for him by decades of legendary athletes.

My father had been watching USC football since Howard Jones's "Thundering Herd." As a child, he enjoyed playing the "Howard Jones Football Board Game."

"What a great, great legend are the Trojans of yesterday I remember so well. Enjoy them all," my dad had inscribed to me in Pierson's book *The Trojans: Southern California Football*. This is USC football in a nutshell. It is a history of excellence, passed down from generation to generation; stories of winners, tales of legendary games that shaped America. In the years since my dad had written those words, USC has added countless more stories and tales to their legend. This book chronicles what they have done leading into the 2006 season, but I am entirely confident that they will add many, many more chapters to their glorious history. Future scribes will no doubt always be kept busy describing those chapters to many more generation of people who know that the University of Southern California is synonymous with American excellence!

Over the years, great announcers have described great teams. Chick Hearn, Mike Walden, Tom Kelly, and now Pete Arbogast have lent their considerable radio talents to USC broadcasts. The venerable Keith Jackson has called so many incredible Trojan moments that he is our *de facto* TV announcer.

A book like this is the product of many things coming together, and I would like to hereby acknowledge some people. I would like to first thank my agent, Ian Kleinart of Objective Entertainment in New York City, as well as Craig Wiley. Also, thank you to my editor at Taylor Trade, Rick Rinehart, and his former and current assistants, Dulcie Wilcox and Flannery Scott.

I want to thank former Trojan football players John Papadakis, Sam "Bam" Cunningham, and Allan Graf. Further thanks to Mark Houska and Petros Papadakis of Fox Sports and movie producer/attorney David Dizenfeld, USC '71.

I wish to thank former University of Southern California sports information director (SID) Jim Perry, who also co-authored legendary Trojan football coach John McKay's successful 1970s autobiography, *McKay: A Coach's Story*. Perry has been an institution for years at Heritage Hall. He was the SID when I worked alongside Tim Tessalone during my brief student internship in the USC sports information office. My gratitude goes out to Tim, who after succeeding Perry has maintained the high standards that Jim set for the office. A further shout-out to Jason Pommier and Paul Goldberg of USC's football media relations, plus Chris Huston, who has helped me many times over the years.

Thank you to the University of Alabama sports information office, in particular Barry Allen and Larry White. Also, thank you to Jan Adams at the Paul W. Bryant Museum, and particularly Ken Gaddy. Thanks go to Winston Groom, author of *Forrest Gump.*

I extend my gratitude to former *L.A. Times* sportswriters, the late Jeff Prugh and Dwight Chapin, two real pros; to current USC beat writer Gary Klein; and ex-*Times* sports editor Bill Dwyre. I also thank the widow of the great Jim Murray, Linda McCoy-Murray; to Tony McEwing; as well as Gene Collier of the *Pittsburgh Post-Gazette.* Thank you to Allen Barra and Keith Dunnavant, who have written extensively on Bear Bryant and Alabama football.

I thank former USC head football coach Pete Carroll. Coach Carroll and I went to the same suburban California high school. I grew up hearing stories about Carroll, who was a classmate of the comic actor Robin Williams. Thanks also to others in that circle, who include Skip Corsini, Jim Peters, Bill Peters, Bob Troppmann, Ken Flower, Phil Roark, and Jess Payan.

Coach Carroll's former assistant, Mark Jackson, and USC athletic director Mike Garrett are in line for acknowledgments as well. Also, thanks go out to Lloyd Robinson of Suite A Management in Beverly Hills. He is an honest man and, in what is also probably not a coincidence, a loyal Trojan. I would also like the opportunity to honor the memory of the late baseball writer Tony Salinn, whose passion and purity, despite what he may have thought, are not forgotten.

Thanks to all the interviewees. I also wish to mention Dale Komai, Bruce Seltzer, Joe Enloe, Brad Wong, Melanie Neff, Lindsay Lautz, Melanie Pedrick and everybody else with the USC Alumni Association; Barry LeBrock of Fox Sports, John Wooden, Dave Daniel and Matt Derringer of *USC Report*, Loel Schrader, Gary Paskiewitz of www.wearesc.com, Andy Bark of *Student Sports*, Bob Rowher of the *L.A. Times,* the late Sam Skinner and Kathy Pfrommer of the *Oakland Tribune*, John Underwood, Wayne Fontes, Dennis Fitzpatrick, Donovan McNabb, Joe Gibbs, the Washington Redskins, Joe Gibbs Racing, Charlie Evans, Rod Sherman of the Trojan Fantasy Camp, Rich Burg, Stu Zanville, Craig Long and the Oakland Raiders, Sharon Gould of the Eagle Rock High School Alumni Association, San Clemente High School, Charlie Weaver, the Detroit Lions, Richmond High School athletic director Roy Rogers, Arizona Western JC, Ray Butcher, Jimmy Jones, the Harrisburg Boys Club, Joe Namath, the African-American Registry, Ken Hall, Mal Moore, Ken Stabler, Kim Bush, Simon & Schuster, Nancy Covington and Mike Neemah of Mississippi State University, Vigor High School, Suzanne Dowling and Chris Bryant of the University of Alabama media relations department, Alabama Booksmith, the University of Alabama Press, Reid Drinkard, Fred Kirsch of the New England Patriots, Mr. and Mrs. Hannah of Albertville, Alabama, the San Francisco 49ers, the Pittsburgh Steelers, Gene Upshaw and the NFL Players Association, the K Club, the University of Alabama Alumni Association, Richmond Flowers Jr., the University of Tennessee sports information office, Jeff Dubinsky of ESPN Classic, Liz Kennedy and Jose Eskenazi of USC, Daniel Hopper and the Department of Intercollegiate Athletics at the University of Alabama, University of Alabama head football coach Mike Shula, John Sciarra, John Robinson, J.K. McKay, Pat Haden, Art Spander, Don Andersen, Mike Walden, Tom Kelly, Dave Levy, Rod Martin, Johnny Musso, B. Green of the Paul W. Bryant Museum, Shirley Ito and Wayne Wilson of the Amateur Athletic Foundation of Los Angeles, and Howard Schnellenberger.

Additional thanks to Art Spander, Clarence Davis, Sam Dickerson, Bud "The Steamer" Furillo, Tom Kelly, Clem Gryska, John Vella, Dr. Culpepper Clark, Keith Dunnavant, Jack Rutledge, John Hannah, Craig Fertig, Christ Vagotis, Scott Hunter, Wilbur Jackson, Sylvester Croom, Wendell Hudson, John Mitchell, Rod McNeill, and Willie Brown. I would like to make special mention of three extraordinary Trojans, who not only gave tirelessly their time, intellect, memory and support, but also formed a bond of Christian fellowship with me: Charles "Tree" Young, Dave Brown, and Manfred Moore. God bless you.

I would like to remember the late Tody Smith and to thank his brother, football Hall of Famer Bubba Smith.

I also thank Cherie Kerr, Earle Self, Bruce H. Franklin, plus Neal McCready and Randy Kennedy of the *Mobile Press-Register*. Thanks also to the National Collegiate Athletic Association.

Since this book is in about the University of Southern California, I want to thank everybody in the extended Trojan family. As it is often said, "You are a Bruin for four years but a Trojan for life!" These are true words. In that spirit, thanks to the late John McKay and the late Marv Goux, who granted me interviews shortly before their respective passings. Thank you also to Goux's lovely widow, Mrs. Patricia Goux, his daughter Linda (who I had a class with at USC), and his granddaughter Kara (who created the inspiring phrase, "Win one for The Goux," at his memorial service).

I would like to extend my gratitude to the past and present pastors, as well as all of my fellow members, at Christ Lutheran Church.

My most sincere thank-yous are reserved for the end. This includes my parents, who gave me encouragement and support, as they always do, and to my sweet daughter, Elizabeth Travers. No acknowledgments are complete without naming my cousin, Bill Friedrichs, and his wife, Jean, whose great help and support over the years can never really be repaid. I also want to thank seven close friends. Terry and Cecile Marks, and Kevin McCormack, are true Trojans. Jake Downey roots for the Bruins but possesses the nobility of a Trojan. Mike McDowd and Don Rasmussen have provided fellowship over the years. Bradley Cole (who comes from a true USC family) and I go back a long way.

Finally, my biggest thank-you is reserved for my Lord and Savior Jesus Christ, who is the source of all that is good, decent, and true!

I welcome feedback, positive and negative, from Trojan fans. I expect to hear the legitimate arguments of Fighting Irish, Crimson Tide, Sooner, Hurricane, Wolverine, Buckeye, Nittany Lion, Bruin and other college football fans. My opinions are mine. I have well thought-out reasons for them, and offer them with respect. Please offer yours in the same manner.

Steven Travers

(415) 455-5971

USCSTEVE1@aol.com

http://redroom.com/author/steven-robert-travers

DYNASTY: THE NEW CENTURIONS OF TROY

*USC football is now history's all-time greatest college football
and athletic tradition*

Toward the end of the Year of Our Lord 1999, every organization imaginable came up with its "lists," "best ofs," "man of the century," "coach of the century," "team of the century," and every other offshoot of our effort to determine greatness. It is the nature of Mankind, and it is particularly true of Americans, that what is "best" be separated from what is second best. On January 1, 2000, the unquestioned "College Football Program of the Twentieth Century" was the Notre Dame Fighting Irish.

The rivalry between Notre Dame and the University of Southern California began in 1926, and by 1930, the question as to what program was the young century's best came down to these two schools: Notre Dame number one, followed by USC (the 1928 national champion) at number two. Alabama, a two-time national champion according to the varied polls and formulas used to determine such a "mythical" thing, would have made a strong argument. The Irish and Trojans, feeding off each other's notoriety, were indeed recognized national powers.

By 1940, the "number one" question was more convoluted. USC had been dominant in the 1930s. So had Minnesota. California and Stanford had reemerged after down years. Alabama and the South—Tennessee and Duke, in particular—rose again. Notre Dame and USC were in a dead heat.

By 1950, Notre Dame had reasserted its position as *the* collegiate football power after an incredible four-national-title decade. The Midwest in particular was the new football capital. Ohio State and especially Michigan were juggernauts. Army was unbeatable for several years. The West dropped precipitously, with Pacific Coast Conference teams losing to the Big 10 in the new Rose Bowl arrangement. The Southern schools became more inward, choosing to play mostly each other, often to avoid increasingly obvious racial situations.

Despite a down decade in the 1950s, Notre Dame still would have emerged as the top dog, but by a slim margin. Oklahoma dominated the decade. Southern teams—Tennessee, Louisiana State, and Auburn—made their bids. Ohio State replaced Michigan as the Big 10's powerhouse. Out west, UCLA was every bit USC's equal, if not its better. Eastern football made its presence known at Syracuse. USC was no longer number two and probably not number three . . . or four.

Everything changed in the 1960s, in America, in society, in race relations; and with a new breed of athlete playing with new equipment under modernized training methods, in college football. The two strongest programs were the two most disparate: Southern California and Alabama.

The Trojans were free, California easy, and thoroughly integrated. Alabama was old school, resisting racial change and clinging to archaic practices. The two coaches? John McKay and Paul "Bear" Bryant were the best of friends.

Notre Dame under Ara Parseghian regained its place, if not at, then near the top. Southern California rivalries with the Irish and UCLA became blood feuds. Texas and Ohio State crowded near the top, as well. By decade's end, USC had put itself back in the century's number two slot. They were essentially "tied" with Alabama, but the edge would go to the Trojans because they played a more national schedule, were integrated, and earned two Heisman Trophies, and one of Alabama's "national championships" had been awarded prior to a bowl loss to Texas on January 1, 1965. Notre Dame was still king of the hill.

The 1970s were basically a replay of the 1960s: USC and Alabama, followed by Notre Dame, Oklahoma, and Nebraska. The Trojans' games with Notre Dame and UCLA were every bit as ferocious as they had been in the '60s. Alabama had finally integrated, along with the rest of the South. It opened a floodgate, to the benefit of Dixie in every way, on and off the field.

By the late 1970s and early 1980s, USC was beginning to establish dominance over Notre Dame. Having won three national championships in the 1970s (and they easily could have won five), the Trojans under new coach John Robinson then defeated the Irish five consecutive times from 1978 to 1982. After the fifth straight win, with Marcus Allen having won the school's fourth Heisman Trophy the previous year, and their record versus Notre Dame almost at the .500 mark, an assessment of the century's best traditions still would have favored Notre Dame, but this time by the narrowest of margins over USC and Alabama.

It was a strong bid, but it would not be sustained. In 1983, USC entered the longest down period in its history, lasting through the 2001 season. They would lose eleven straight games to Notre Dame and eight straight to UCLA.

In the meantime, Lou Holtz returned Notre Dame to the heights of glory, firmly reestablishing South Bend as the Mecca of college football. In the eyes of many, Michigan would be their greatest rival, not Southern California. Oklahoma, Penn State, and Miami (four times) won national championships.

By 1992, if not before that, Alabama would have replaced USC for the number two position behind the Irish. They had beaten USC in the 1985 Aloha Bowl, an insignificant game except for the fact that by so doing, the Crimson Tide passed the Trojans as the winningest bowl team ever. When 'Bama's unbeaten team won the '92 national championship, that sealed the deal.

The rest of the decade was just grist for the mill at USC, where fans of this once-proud tradition watched the collegiate game taken over by the Florida schools, the Southeastern Conference, the new dominance of Nebraska, and Johnny-come-latelies like Virginia Tech. Penn State had maintained its high position in the early part of the '90s. In their own conference, Washington reached for the pinnacle but could not sustain it. UCLA was good but not great. An apparent shift of power seemed to have eventually centered itself in the state of Oregon, where the Beavers and the Ducks were the best hope of a conference and a region that the rest of the nation derided as "soft."

USC's alumni satisfied themselves that while they would never again dictate and dominate in football, the university had under President Steven Sample developed into one of the finest academic institutions in the country. That, it seemed, was the trade-off, and most could live with that.

Notre Dame, who had started the decade riding high, fell off somewhat, its reputation shaken by revelations in Don Yaeger's book, *Under the Tarnished Dome*. Other traditional powers that had fallen were on the rise: Texas, Michigan, Ohio State and Oklahoma, among others. USC just observed it all in spectator mode.

By 2000, Notre Dame was still the "College Football Program of the Twentieth Century." USC may only have hoped they were still third. By season's end, after Oklahoma completed its return to prominence with an unbeaten national championship season, the Sooners could lay claim to USC's old poll position. Troy was lucky to still be in the top five, derided as "Yesterday U.," its glory days relegated to old clippings and grainy prevideo footage. It was like an aging rock star who was unknown to the young girls who preferred Korn and Eminem.

■ ■ ■

Pete Carroll's University of Southern California Trojans completed the most "perfect" season in collegiate football history in 2004 and almost followed that up with an even more perfect one in 2005. They came within one nine-yard touchdown run with nineteen seconds left in the Rose Bowl of entering the new campaign having attained the following "titles": (1) greatest single-season college football team of all time in 2005; (2) greatest college football dynasty of all time, 2002–2005; (3) quarterback Matt Leinart: greatest college football player ever; plus greatest three-year, two-year, short-term, and single-decade dynasties of all time. While the heroics of Vince Young and Texas turned these premises from absolutes to arguments, it is difficult to dispute that Leinart and Reggie Bush replaced Army's "Mr. Inside and Mr. Outside" (Doc Blanchard and Glenn

Davis) as the greatest one-two teammate combo of all time. USC went from easily calling itself the greatest historical college football tradition of all time to making themselves the most likely choice in a still-competitive field, with every opportunity still beckoning them to go after that moniker in the years to come. They are, without much real argument, still the greatest collegiate athletic department of all time.

Lofty titles, to be sure. Controversial and worthy of argument? You bet. Justifiable hype? You got that right, too.

USC was denied the chance to enter the 2006 season one twelve-game regular season away from Oklahoma's all-time modern record of forty-seven straight wins, set in the 1950s. They had been ranked number one a record thirty-three straight weeks in the Associated Press poll (the previous record was twenty by Miami from 2001–2002). The early predictions were that they would likely enter the new campaign holding that spot again.

In light of USC's recent dominance, it is worth considering their place in history. Not just the current Trojans, but USC's football program going back to the beginning of the twentieth century. While the Rose Bowl loss tarnishes their shine ever-so-slightly, it is still time to take the mantle of "greatest program in the history of college football" away from the Notre Dame Fighting Irish, and lay it squarely with the deserving new champions from USC.

THE THUNDERING HERD

The "Head Man," the rivalry, and a great tradition

It is true that Red Grange, the "Galloping Ghost" of Illinois, was a phenomenon in the mid-1920s. Crowds at Illinois, Michigan, Ohio State, and throughout the Big 10 Conference were huge. But Grange's greatest impact is felt on the professional game. It was his presence that translated the enormous crowds of his college career to the young National Football League, thus ensuring the NFL's success.

The college game, however, was turned into a truly national game by the rivalry between USC and Notre Dame, and that rivalry was marked from the beginning by the two coaches, Knute Rockne and Howard Jones.

"SC wanted to get Knute Rockne," said Ambrose Schindler, the quarterback from 1936–1939, "and he said, 'No, but a young man who just beat me is Howard Jones.' He beat Notre Dame 7–6 and Rockne recommended Howard Jones to the university."

Getting Notre Dame to agree to play his team was the task that Jones gave to USC student manager Gwynn Wilson in November 1925. Notre Dame was in freezing cold Lincoln, Nebraska, for a season-ending game with the Cornhuskers. Wilson and his young wife took the Sunset Limited to Lincoln to ask Rockne for the game.

Wilson could not get to the busy Rockne at the stadium or anywhere in Lincoln. Notre Dame's loss had Rockne in a less-than-jovial mood, anyway. He boarded the train Notre Dame was taking back to Chicago. With Rockne "captive" in the train, and able to relax with the game now over, Wilson approached him, got the audience, and made his pitch.

Rockne was respectful and told Wilson the Trojans had gotten a great coach in Jones, but that the administration at Notre Dame was already giving him a hard time about putting the team on the road so much. Notre Dame Stadium was not yet built, and the audience demand to see them play required that they travel. Wilson may have gotten Rockne to agree had he painted a vivid picture of the enormous crowds that would see the teams play at the new Coliseum and at Soldier Field, but Wilson was unable to make the sale. He returned to his compartment, wondering how he would explain his "failure" to Jones.

Enter *Mrs. Marion Wilson* and Mrs. Bonnie Rockne. On a train filled with football players, football coaches, football writers, and football fans, they found in each other women and kindred spirits. Gwynn found his wife engaged in excited conversation with the coach's wife, and was delighted at what they were talking about: shopping.

Yes, shopping, for it was shopping that started the USC–Notre Dame game. Mrs. Rockne liked to shop. She liked to travel. She liked to travel to warm weather places. She had just spent the day freezing her you-know-what off in a town that had no shopping! Mrs. Wilson, bless her, painted a colorful picture of Rodeo Drive, the emerging boutique boulevard of Beverly Hills where the nouveau riche and famous of Hollywood were buying all those fabulous fashions that she saw in the movie magazines. Mrs. Rockne had already gotten a taste of the Hollywood lifestyle when she had accompanied Rock to L.A. for a coaching clinic.

If Notre Dame would travel to Los Angeles and play the Trojans, Mrs. Wilson explained, Mrs. Rockne would have the chance to spend a few days in sunny California—shopping on Rodeo Drive.

At some point, Mrs. Rockne departed and went to see her husband. Her powers of persuasion were certainly better than Gwynn's. She talked Rockne into scheduling the game.

Wilson had achieved his goal after all. Of course, this story has been hyped in the traditional USC–Notre Dame manner. Rockne certainly recalled the promise of a game with Jones that the two had made after Iowa beat him in 1921. No doubt Rockne gave some further, serious thought to the gate receipts at the Coliseum and Soldier Field. He certainly thought about the recruiting value of playing such a national game. It would be a huge publicity boost. This was Jones's feeling, that the game would allow the Trojans to rise above all Western teams in the recruiting battles, compete with the Irish for other players across America, and use the PR value to boost the program and the school, with all the attendant financial value inherent therein. If indeed these were the hoped-for expectations of Rockne and Jones, their expectations came true in wildly successful fashion.

"He told me that he couldn't meet USC because Notre Dame was traveling too much," Wilson once recalled. "I thought the whole thing was off, but as Rock and I talked, Marion was with Mrs. Rockne, Bonnie, in her compartment. Marion told Bonnie how nice Southern California was and how hospitable the people were.

"Well, when Rock went back to the compartment, Bonnie talked him into the game. But if it hadn't been for Mrs. Wilson talking to Mrs. Rockne, there wouldn't have been a series."

Despite the serendipitous nature of the Gwynn Wilson story, it was later revealed that Rockne wanted a game in a big cosmopolitan city on the West Coast, in order to bookend their games in New York. It has even been suggested that the game was a favor offered not by Rockne to Jones, but vice versa, since it was Rock who had recommended Jones to USC. Either way, to quote Vince Vaughn, it's "worked out pretty well for everybody."

In 1926, USC opened the season with a 74–0 thumping of Whittier. Talk of a national championship, capped by a season-ending home win over the Irish, filled the air. The Associated Press would not begin its polling until 1936, but there were various organizations, systems, and formulas used to determine who was, in fact, number one. The Parker H. Davis ratings were devised by a former player from Princeton and coach from Wisconsin. The Dickinson System (1924–1940) was based on a point formula devised by an Illinois professor. The "winner" was awarded the Rissman Trophy. The Eck Ratings System, in place since 1897, was a mathematical formula devised by Steve Eck. The Dunkel System, started in 1929, would be a power ratings index that has been maintained by Dick Dunkel's heirs to this day. There was also the College Football Researchers Association, which went by a vote system.

The Helms Athletic Foundation named their choice for the national championship. The Football Thesaurus began awarding champions in 1927, and the Williamson System came into place in 1931. In subsequent years, various other organizations, systems, and polls were created to "determine" national champions, which in the absence of a "March Madness" or College World Series type play-off system rely on "mythical" rankings.

By and large, between the systems in place, media attention, "people's choices," and common sense, national champions were generally agreed upon, with varying regional differences. Over the years, USC has been named "national champions" sixteen times, but the reality is that they can consider themselves a true, legitimate national champion eleven times. Some of those are shared, or co–national championships. In recent years, the BCS has failed college football in general, but again, common sense and history accord legitimacy to the school's claim on eleven titles.

So it was that in 1926, with Notre Dame on the schedule and a Rose Bowl waiting at season's end, Trojan fans felt that "this was the year." Interestingly, the creation of the USC–Notre Dame rivalry had the effect of ending Notre Dame's participation in bowls. The criticism of the school's schedule, which resembled a barnstorming crew, had helped to dissuade their administration from approving bowl trips after the 1925 trip to Pasadena. The Southern Cal game, to be played at season's end and in California every even year, would be their "bowl game." When Notre Dame Stadium was finally built in 1930, the school was able to schedule their big games at home instead of traveling to New York or Chicago to play in stadiums that accommodated enormous crowds. They would play in Yankee Stadium and other neutral sites in future years, but not in any postseason games until the 1970 Cotton Bowl. Thus, the SC game would take on enormous importance to Notre Dame in their quest for national supremacy.

After the Whittier game, Troy confidently advanced to a 5–0 record. On October 23, they exorcised their greatest demon by defeating Cal, 27–0, before a crowd of 72,000 at Berkeley. Jones's confident team returned to Los Angeles to read their press clippings and think about the future, which looked like a trifecta of victory over Notre Dame and a Rose Bowl opponent, capped by the elusive national championship.

Along came their old whipping boys, Stanford. A crowd of 78,500 fans came to the Coliseum and were stunned to see Stanford win by a 13–12 margin. It was USC's only loss heading into the Notre Dame game, when 74,378 came to see the first-ever game between the new rivals. If the Trojans could win, they would lay claim to a national title with one loss. Notre Dame denied them, winning by the same one-point score as Stanford, 13–12. USC did not get the Rose Bowl invite, having finished second in the Pacific Coast Conference. Notre Dame maintained its status as the elite team in America, though legitimate ranking systems also recognize Alabama as back-to-back national champions of 1925–1926. Certainly the uncertainty of a non-play-off system was leading more and more in the media toward the conclusion that a more "legitimate" poll system be devised. It was very important to colleges to be able to raise their fingers in the air and shout, "We're number one!" As for USC, they were confident that they would be able to do just that in 1927.

The 1926 USC–Notre Dame game was, up to that point, the most ballyhooed college game ever played. It overshadowed Notre Dame's previous encounter with Army at Yankee Stadium, which produced the "Four Horsemen . . . outlined against a blue, gray October sky," as well as the Rockne-Warner Rose Bowl struggle of 1925. Notre Dame's train trips to Los Angeles engendered headlines at every stop. Rockne had learned from the "Gloomy Gus" Henderson playbook, lamenting to a Tucson writer that the 1926 Irish were terrible. This may or may not have been the first time Jones's USC team was referred to as the "Thundering Herd." The *Daily Trojan* had earlier written that "long years of submitting to an oppressive yoke were avenged at Berkeley . . . when the thundering hoofs of Troy's galloping Herd crushed the Bear of California into the turf of Memorial Stadium," and "the Thundering Herd crashed on its way to everlasting fame."

The game attracted what was said to be the greatest array of coaching talent ever assembled in one place. Jones's brother, TAD (the Yale "head man"), attended along with Red Grange's Illinois mentor Bob Zuppke and Stanford's Pop Warner.

In the end, it was a Notre Dame reserve, Art Parisien, who lofted a pass to Johnny Niemec with a mere four minutes left on the clock to give his team the win, despite early heroics from Don Williams and Mort Kaer. Morley Drury and Brice Taylor, both Trojan legends, failed in extra point attempts in the one-point defeat.

"It was a football battle that has never been excelled for brilliance, thrills and pulsating drama and the Irish won because Harry O'Boyle kicked one goal after touchdown while both Brice Taylor and Morley Drury failed in their attempts to shoot the ball between the uprights," read one reporter's "tearful" account.

"It was the greatest game I ever saw . . ." Rockne told Jones afterward. "See you in Chicago."

The game was great in part because it was so cleanly played, a factor that, with very few exceptions, would mark the rivalry to this day. It differentiated it, in some ways, from the rancorous attitudes of Cal and Stanford toward the Trojans. Clean play was Jones's trademark.

"He was highly intense, clean, had great moral values, and was ethical as the devil," said Nick Pappas. "There was no way anybody was going to play dirty football for him."

Jones was extremely intelligent as well as honest. He devised a brilliant system for the card game of bridge, and taught himself to shoot scratch golf. He was innovative when he needed to be as a football coach, but of course was smart enough to let his team's power take over. His off-field personality was somewhat introverted. Unlike Rockne, the media darling, Jones disliked banquets or press conferences. On the field, however, Jones was dynamite, in his element.

"You could always sense the electricity when he came onto the field," recalled Pappas.

Like a later Los Angeles legend, John Wooden, Jones never took a drink and his greatest expletives were "gol darn" and "by gad," with one exception. The Cal Bears took to such dirty tactics and foul-mouthed, unsportsmanlike conduct that Jones, at halftime, said, "These people, are you going to let them come down here and son of a bitch you!?"

Erny Pinckert, a star player, turned around and just smiled at Pappas.

Despite a thick-skinned reputation, Jones could get sentimental. Stanford made such malicious remarks at a pep rally once that, when Jones heard of them, he teared up. On another occasion, he chewed a player out. When the young man cried, Jones was compelled to cheer him up for an hour.

He did have one true vice, however. He was a chain smoker, which probably led to his heart attack and death in 1941. He also was a bit of an absentminded professor when confronted by nonfootball activities, at least during the season. He dressed with mismatched socks and stranded his family, missing appointments. Perhaps it was for this reason that he kept a low off-season profile.

Jones was an aggressive coach who valued mental quickness, and once stated that Morley Drury exemplified these qualities the best of all his stalwarts. He was also a man of Christian charity who, despite his strong aversion to alcohol, was known to come to the aid of drunks in need.

Despite his love of the rough-and-tumble of football, he enjoyed the solitude of fishing in the high Sierras.

"He was a perfect gentleman to strangers," said Al Wesson. "But he never said a kind word to his closest friends. He always told the athletic director that he couldn't prepare a decent schedule, his assistant coaches that they didn't know how to scout, the publicity boy that he couldn't write English, and the team doctors that they were quacks. But they liked to hear the Head Man talk like that, for they knew it was his good-natured, rough kind of ribbing and that out of their presence he swore by them.

"He would hardly glance at a boy coming off the field after playing his heart out. But when the game was over, in the privacy of the training quarters, he'd hunt out every boy who had played, thank him for what he had done, and be sure that any injuries, no matter how trivial, were immediately cared for.

"He never 'treated,' never carried enough money to buy anyone lunch, and always figured on plucking his golf opponents for enough petty cash to almost any charity that sought him out.

"He didn't belong to a church. But he lived every minute of his life according to the Golden Rule."

Great coaches are only great because they coached great players. One of the greatest was a man called "the noblest Trojan of them all," Morley Drury.

In 1927, when Drury ran off the field for the last time in front of 60,000 at the Coliseum, the standing ovation lasted four minutes. Drury "bawled like a baby."

In that last game, a sweeping win over Washington, Drury rushed for 180 yards and three touchdowns.

"It was a nice way to finish," said Drury. Drury had asked Coach Jones to replace him with a backup with the game in hand, but Jones ordered him to the dressing room, via the playing field, knowing that the crowd would give him the kudos he deserved.

"I crossed the Coliseum floor and the ovation lasted until I reached the tunnel," he recalled. "I knew I couldn't hold back my tears."

Drury was a West Coast "golden boy" from 1925 to 1927, and Jones's favorite player. He was aggressive, courageous, and durable. In the prespecialization days, Drury did everything, which included running, punting, tackling, passing, and blocking. In the 13–0 history-shaping victory over Cal, he scored both touchdowns. In 1927 Drury rushed for 1,163 yards.

Nine of the twenty-three All-Americans under Jones were running backs, however. The vaunted USC ground game was a tradition that he most definitely had a large role in starting.

Brice Taylor was the blocker most responsible for opening the holes that Mort Kaer ran through in 1925, when Southern California outscored the opposition 456–55. Taylor was a 1925 All-American. Kaer earned his honor in 1926.

Howard Jones would usher USC into the era of great rivalries, first with Notre Dame but also with UCLA. However, it was Cal and Stanford who were their fiercest competitors when he arrived, and indeed success (or failure) against them was why he was brought in to replace Elmer "Gloomy Gus" Henderson.

THE USC TROJANS

Andy Smith passed away from pneumonia and Pop Warner left Stanford, right around the time that USC was reaching a point of dominance. This caused the old ill feelings to come out, and the northern schools began to infer that USC was not a great academic institution, but rather a "football school." This charge was, over the years, continually difficult to back up in light of the fact that USC consistently produced leaders in politics, the law, medicine, science, the arts, Hollywood, and all other forms of human endeavor. Some of those leaders were ex-football players, but the carping continues to this day.

Great players from Jones's early USC teams included Frank Anthony, Nate Barrager, Charles Boren, Henry Edelson, Howard Elliott, Bert Heiser, Cecil Hoff, Lawrence McCaslin, Don Moses, Russ Saunders, Albert Sheving, Tony Steponovich, Francis Tappaan, Lloyd Thomas, and Don Williams.

Prior to 1928, Jones had three All-Americans. Taylor would be inducted into the USC Athletic Hall of Fame in 1992. A descendant of American Indian chief Tecumseh, he became a teacher in the L.A. City School District and later coached football at Southern University.

Kaer was a member of the 1926 national championship track team, performed at the 1924 Paris Olympics, was an All-American halfback in 1926, and played professional football for a year. "The Red Bluff Terror" returned to his hometown, where he coached and taught at the local high school for twenty-seven years. He went into SC's Hall of Fame in 1997.

Drury, the "noblest Trojan of them all," who did not have his rushing records broken until Mike Garrett came along, was inducted into SC's Hall of Fame in 1997 after having been elected to the National Football Foundation College Hall of Fame in 1954.

THE GREATEST COLLEGE FOOTBALL TEAM OF ALL TIME
(1928 Edition)

USC passes Cal and Stanford as the top Western power

By 1928, it was obvious to the nation that a major power shift had occurred, with the West having overcome the East. Hollywood began to make a big deal over the Trojans, and after Stanford beat Army, the *Evening World* proclaimed that the victory "had demonstrated the futility of the Eastern one-man offense against Western team play."

Still, the hurdle of Notre Dame stood in the Trojans' way. The Irish were down that year, at least compared to their usual standards. Furthermore, Rockne's son was ill in South Bend, Indiana, so the coach's mind was understandably troubled.

The Irish never had a chance. Russ Saunders scored on what was called "the old 21 play," Williams tossed a touchdown to Marger Apsit, and after Johnny Niemec's pass was intercepted by Tony Stepovich, USC led 20–0. Williams later hit Harry Edelson for a score. Hibbs and Williams sustained minor injuries, but their strong play earned them All-American recognition.

With the 27–14 victory came further analysis of the American football scene. Considering the earlier victories of Stanford and Oregon State over Eastern opponents, the question was no longer whether the best football was played in the West or the Midwest. It was definitely *not* played in the East. If Notre Dame was the epitome of Midwest football, then their loss to Southern Cal seemed to cede supremacy to the West, namely to the Trojans. Alabama was the kingpin of Southern football, and to be fair it was the lack of media coverage in that section of the country that cost the region its share of glamour more than any deficiencies on the field of play.

"Southern California all but hugged the life out of the South Bend Irish, and made it harder than ever for the folks back over the Great Divide to forget Los Angeles," intoned the *L.A. Times*. "The tang of the sea and the heart of the desert do not make sissies. Men are not debilitated into softlings in the great open spaces."

Perhaps there had been some talk that warm weather, comfortable surroundings, and the glamour of the movies made football players in L.A. "go Hollywood," but in reality Americans understood the rugged nature of Western individualism, which had manifested itself in the settlers who had forged a nation against obstacles made by man and nature. The more pertinent question may have been whether that "individualism" would lend itself to a team game like football. It was obvious by now that it did not disrupt it, and that good weather not only made for the best playing conditions, but the best year-round training, as well.

Football was not the only sport being played better in California than anyplace else. The state (and USC) was producing the best track stars and baseball players, as well as swimmers and tennis stars.

The Rissman rating system awarded the national championship to the University of Southern California, based on their 9–0–1 record and 4–0–1 PCC mark, earning them the conference title. The glory of the season, however, was disrupted by a season-ending controversy.

Despite their obvious designation as the conference representative in the Rose Bowl, USC turned down the January 1 invite. Officially, they gave the lame excuse that it was based on a policy that "frowned on any games after the closing date of the Pacific Coast Conference season." Supposedly, they would not play any games after the Saturday prior to Christmas.

In reality, a feud with Rose Bowl officials had caused the impasse, for reasons that have never been explained. In the history of USC, it was one of the very few times that they failed to meet an obligation or a challenge, which has always separated the Trojans from various other unimpressives dotting the landscape. It would seem implausible that Jones avoided the game because he had his undefeated season and national title, and chose not to sully it with a potential defeat. However, absent better explanations, it seems to be a possible answer. That said, it does not square with anything Jones ever did, before or after 1928. He thrived on challenges, met them head on at every opportunity. He created a tradition at the school that has always led the team to risk rankings and records in search of greater glory. No team in America has this record, but 1928 is the exception.

If the nation now saw the West as the best, USC's decision diluted this view and gave the South a chance to rise. California, with a loss and two ties, was picked to face the "Ramblin' Wrecks" of Georgia Tech. Fate seemed to enter the picture because in this game Cal's Roy Riegels was misdirected and ran the wrong way on a play that proved decisive in Tech's 8–7 win. Riegels has forever endured the moniker "Wrong Way" Riegels.

Still, the glory of the number one ranking was one worn proudly by the Trojans. One of those stars was Nate Barrager, who would go on to a film career with John Wayne and pro football, too.

Barrager's hard tackling earned him a spot on Walter Eckersall's All-America team for 1929. Also on the team was the great Minnesota running back, Bronco Nagurski. Barrager was Jones's seventh All-American and one of two in 1929. Coming out of San Fernando High School, Barrager had earned a scholarship to USC after turning down other offers. Under Jones, Barrager blossomed.

"He was an outstanding fundamental coach who taught young men how to handle themselves," he said. "He was a taskmaster, a strictly dedicated football coach. Personality-wise, he wasn't a man who had a lot of things to say. He was just very quiet and very dedicated to his work. There was nothing funny about Jones. He was serious as anything. Chewing gum sometimes bothered him."

Jones switched Barrager from fullback, where he had starred in high school and on the SC freshman team.

"But they needed a center in my sophomore year, and they made me a center," said Barrager. Jones was innovative, and had Barrager backing the line on defense, which made Barrager one of the first linebackers.

Barrager starred in the 10–0 win over Stanford in 1928, and in his senior year Jones turned him into a running guard, defensive fullback, and team captain.

"Being captain of the team and playing defensive fullback, you are into an awful lot of things," said Barrager. "You have to be a leader. All the boys on the team are pretty smart, but you have to keep after them."

In the 1930 Rose Bowl game against Pitt, Barrager and Russ Saunders put the clamps on the Panthers' All-American halfback, Tony Uansa, which made the difference in Troy's lopsided 47–14 victory. The score was exceptional, for in those days strong teams usually played defensive struggles.

"We won, and on that particular day we could have beaten anybody," said Barrager.

His final game was one of the few times that Barrager was able to "laugh and enjoy" football under the taskmaster Jones. With Southern Cal winning handily, Jones was ready to bring in his second team, but Barrager was having too much fun. He and guard Clark Galloway purposely knocked a Pitt player into Jones's lap as he sat on the bench. Jones, impressed, told his subs to sit down because "if anyone can play like that, they're on my team."

The Pitt team that had their hats handed to them had five All-Americans on it. This was an obvious example not necessarily of "East Coast bias," but rather because the concentration of media was congregated in this part of the country. USC's plastering of them made up for Cal's embarrassing "wrong way" loss of 1929. Along with SC's beating of Pop Warner and Stanford, as well as Knute Rockne's Irish in 1928, it played a big part in further cementing the Trojans' place in the football hierarchy.

Barrager played professional football, eventually ending up with the fabled Green Bay Packers. He was able to add three NFL titles to his national championship at USC. Barrager was a teammate of the great Don Hutson, who had starred (alongside teammate Bear Bryant) at the University of Alabama.

Barrager also parlayed his football career into acting. He befriended Paramount contract star Richard Arlen while filming *Salute*, which lead to Arlen inviting Barrager to be a part of his New York stage show. They were scheduled for an appearance after a Packers game against the New York Giants. After winning a close one, Barrager, along with teammates Russ Saunders and Marge Apsit (former Trojans), had to herd Arlen out of the Polo Grounds and into a cab—without changing from their game clothes. The show was a big success, and despite being Packers, the uniformed players were given a big ovation.

THE DUKE

USC's Hollywood connection

Nate Barrager went to work for RKO Pictures and became a top production manager on such hits as *The Greatest Story Ever Told* and, of course, John Wayne films like *Hondo*, *The Fighting Seabees*, and *The Sands of Iwo Jima*. He also worked closely with Bob Hope on television specials.

Barrager was part of a long tradition of ties between USC, their football team, and Hollywood. As big a reason as any for this, aside from the geographical proximity, is the fact that John Wayne played football for Howard Jones.

"He had all the football ability in the world," said Leo Calland. "He had savvy, a great build and the equipment."

"Duke was a good guard," said Normel C. Hayhurst, his coach at Glendale High School. "He played a big part in our winning the Central League and the Southern California championship. He was one of seven players selected for a football scholarship at USC. Our 1924 team was a good one."

Others, however, said that Wayne was not as dedicated to football as Howard Jones required his players to be. Photos of Wayne at USC reveal a big, good-looking guy with black, curly hair and a great build who "had to fight the girls off."

The Wayne visage is one of a rough 'n' tough military man or cowboy, more ruggedly macho than handsome, but many film fans are only familiar with movies he made in his forties and beyond. In his twenties, the man was nothing less than an Adonis.

Wayne's teammate at USC was Ward Bond, who would go on to a long film career. His typical roles were of Irish priests or sidekicks, fighting with and against Wayne, usually winding up sharing a shot of whiskey as a conciliatory gesture. Bond had great desire but lacked Wayne's physical abilities. Observers of the two said that if Wayne's talent and Bond's desire could be morphed, the result would have been an All-American.

Gene Clarke, a lineman who played for Jones, claims to have had a hand in making Wayne a picture star. By accident. Wayne was looking forward to being the starting right tackle in his sophomore year.

"Duke and I used to go down to Balboa Beach and ride those big waves," said Clarke. Balboa Beach is in Newport, and those "big waves" are part of the notorious "Wedge," which has produced injured surfers for decades. It is not uncommon to observe wistful men in wheelchairs staring at the ocean wearing T-shirts that read, "Victim of the Wedge."

"One day we're all on the sand with pretty coeds all around. You know how everyone likes to show off, particularly Duke and me.

"These big waves started to come in. We called them, 'butt-busters.' I mean, they were *big*! They were washing the bottom of the pier. Duke says, 'Come on, let's go and ride them.' I said, 'You gotta be nuts, they'll kill us.' He said, 'Come on, you've got no guts!' And I said, 'Dammit, if you're crazy enough, I'll go.'"

Fifteen minutes later, Clarke and Wayne were out past the breakers.

"I warned Duke that the breakers cup hard," said Clarke, but Duke was caught in one. The last he saw was Duke going down.

"He hit the sand," said Clarke, "and if he hadn't pulled his head to one side he probably would have busted his neck. As it was it dislocated his shoulder."

The body surfing adventure had occurred three weeks prior to the beginning of fall football practice.

"He was playing right tackle in the old Howard Jones power plays," said Clarke, "and in this system you used your right shoulder blocking all the time."

Wayne was injured and unable to effectuate the blocking patterns.

"The old man would give him hell for it," said Clarke. "With Jones you slept, ate, and drank football 365 days a year. He wouldn't understand anyone getting hurt in a foolish accident like that. Well, what happened was the old man thought Wayne didn't have any guts. He didn't know about the shoulder injury, of course. So he put him down on the fourth or fifth team. Took Wayne off the training table, and he had to scrounge for his own meals. He owed the fraternity house so much dough that they had to ask him to move out until he could pay. He dropped out of school and went to Fox Studios."

Born Marion Michael Morrison on May 26, 1907, in Winterset, Iowa, the son of a druggist and a mother of attractive Irish pioneer stock, young Marion moved to the California desert with his family when he was six. His father, "Doc" Morrison, had lung problems and improved in the warm climate.

In that environment, Morrison often fantasized that he was a cowboy on a dangerous mission. He rode a horse every day just to get groceries and run errands. He would scare himself into believing he was chasing or being chased by outlaws.

When Doc Morrison's health improved, he moved the family to the Los Angeles area. Glendale in those days was still open country, and Marion lived a perfect boy's life, fishing and swimming. Morrison got the nickname "Duke" from a local fireman because his dog's name was Duke and the fireman did not know Marion's real name. At first he was "Little Duke," but when he grew to 6'4" it was just Duke. At Glendale High, Duke not only starred in football, but he performed Shakespearean dramas. He was an honor student, president of the Letterman Society, senior class president, and a top debater. He loved to dance and girls went for him.

Despite his football scholarship at USC, he needed to earn extra money and became a top scalper. His scalping took him to the Hollywood Athletic Club, and he also did work for the phone company on movie lots. It was Howard Jones, however, who got him started in Hollywood, so to speak, when he arranged for Morrison and Don Williams to "train" actor Tom Mix for a cowboy movie called *The Great K and A Train Robbery*. They conditioned Mix and moved sets for $35 a week.

Morrison met famed director John Ford, who made him a prop man and liked his rugged film presence enough to cast him in 1928's *Hangman's House*.

Ford later made a football movie about the Naval Academy, *Salute*, and wanted USC players for it. He needed them full-time before the end of the semester, and made Morrison his go-between. Morrison overcame major administrative hurdles in granting permission from school officials, which impressed Ford. He led a delegation that trained east in May 1929, amid much fanfare. The players included Clark Galloway, Russ Saunders, Jack Butler, Tony Steponovich, Jess Shaw, Frank Anthony, Al Schaub, Marshall Duffield, and Nate Barrager. The trip did cause some concern that the work constituted professionalism, since the players benefited financially by virtue of the fact that they played football at USC.

Director Raoul Walsh gave Morrison the name John Wayne when he starred in a $2 million spectacular called *Big Trail* in 1929. In 1939 he broke through with John Ford's *Stagecoach*. He was nominated for an Oscar as Sergeant Stryker in *The Sands of Iwo Jima*, and by 1949 was the top box office attraction in the world. His visual appearance, however, was significantly different by then than it had been in the 1920s, when he was more pretty and handsome than rugged. Wayne liked to pull a cork in real life just as his screen characters did, which may explain this.

Other classic Wayne films include *The Quiet Man* and *The Longest Day*. In 1969 he finally earned a Best Actor Academy Award for his role as Rooster Cogburn in *True Grit*.

Even though he left school early without making a mark on Howard Jones's football team, and never graduated (although he was awarded an honorary doctorate), Wayne is inextricably tied to the school and its football tradition. Through Wayne, Jones arranged for USC players to work as extras on movies. Aside from *Salute*, extravagant Hollywood productions of the era often featured Trojan players in the roles of Roman legionnaires, Napoleon's *Grand Armee*, or Biblical flocks. This was prior to the NCAA, and while there was grousing about "professionalism," there never were repercussions.

The Hollywood connection was an enormous recruiting advantage that Jones made use of. Not only did the players make much-needed extra money, but they were introduced to the beautiful actresses. As any recruiting coordinator could tell you, no inducement is greater than pretty girls.

One story that made the rounds and was written about in a late 1990s issue of *Los Angeles* magazine concerned Clara Bow, the "it girl" of the silent film era. A gorgeous brunette, Bow apparently had an insatiable sexual appetite, and allegedly used Duke Wayne to arrange wild orgies at her Hollywood Hills mansion. This was the kind of extracurricular activity that schools such as Iowa or Duke, where Jones had toiled previously, could not offer.

Wayne maintained a strong association with USC until his death in 1979. When he visited his friend Gene Clarke at the Sigma Chi fraternity house, he noticed a derby that had been given Clarke as a member of Southern Cal's 1931 team.

"Don't you wear it?" asked Wayne.

Clarke thought it was silly, but Wayne was so taken with the memento from SC's stirring victory over the Irish that he "wore that derby for the longest time, hardly ever took it off."

Nick Pappas developed a very close relationship with Wayne, and used Duke many times in his role as director of Trojans' Athletic Support Groups.

"He's a fraternity brother of mine, and the night before a big game with Texas in 1966 we were having cocktails together," Pappas said in Ken Rappoport's book *The Trojans: A Story of Southern California Football*. The interview took place prior to Wayne's 1979 passing.

"This is in Austin, see, and he had come in just for the game," said Pappas. "We drank until about four in the morning—Wayne's drinking scotch and soda all this time. All the guys at the party had gone to dinner and come back and then gone to bed, and we're still in there drinking.

"In the course of our conversation, he says, 'Pap, I want to talk to the kids at breakfast tomorrow.'

"I told him, 'You're in, Duke,' without thinking. I hadn't asked anyone whether it would be all right for Wayne to talk to our football team on the morning of the game. It was a big one, a season opener with Texas ranked number one and us number two.

"But I remembered that Coach John McKay loved John Wayne movies. He used to talk about his big evening—sitting home with a peanut butter sandwich and a glass of chocolate milk and watching a John Wayne movie. And he never met him. I also remembered that McKay would awaken early on the day of games, he was always up by six o'clock, and read the papers. Have breakfast, and go over his diagrams. He was constantly working on football.

"So I call McKay and tell him I had a problem. 'Look, John,' I said. 'I was with John Wayne last night. He asked me if he could talk to the kids, and I said yeah.' And before I could finish, McKay says, 'Geez, great . . . bring him down.'

THE DUKE

"The kids are all assembled in the locker room at ten in the morning, and in walks Wayne. Damn, he was fantastic. He walks in with this white 20,000-gallon cowboy hat and black suit—he looked just beautiful. The kids look up, and their eyeballs pop. Here's the *real* John Wayne. And Wayne walks over to the coach and gives him a big hello and squeezes him—you'd think he and McKay were long lost buddies. They had never met before.

"It was beautiful. A former player and all, Wayne gives one of the greatest fight talks you've ever heard—and the kids got all fired up. We win the ballgame 10–6, and back in the locker room after the game, McKay says, 'Hey, guys, how about it? Let's give the game ball to John Wayne.'

"For a moment Wayne stands there—nonplussed. It was probably the first time in his life that he couldn't think of anything to say. Then he looks at the ball for a minute and pumps it like a quarterback. Then he puts the ball under his arm, and the kids break into a cheer, 'Hooray, Hooray.' All the guys joined in. He's still a Trojan."

Mike Walden was the USC play-by-play announcer, and recalls that 1966 Texas game, and Wayne's unique role in the events of that weekend.

"My first game in 1966 was on the road versus Texas," said Walden. "There'd be a press gathering in Austin, what they called 'smokers' down there, where everybody got together. Well, Wayne was down there making *War Wagon* in nearby Mexico, and he shows up with Bruce Cabot.

"'I'm gonna have some whiskey,' Wayne says to the bartender, who pours it, and Wayne just looks at it, shoved it back, and said, '*I said WHISKEY!*'

"Texas had a quarterback they called 'Super Bill' Bradley who was supposed to be outstanding, but SC just controlled the ball and won, 10–6. Afterwards, [assistant coach Marv] Goux came in and said wasn't it great, we didn't get anybody 'chipped off.' Well, Wayne and Cabot were somewhere, and someone got in an argument the next morning and their make-up artist was dead of a heart attack. It was confusing; I don't know for sure what all happened. Wayne and all of 'em were out drinking all night and came in at seven in the morning, maybe it was too much for this guy, but this make-up artist died.

"'Well,' Cabot said, '*We* got somebody 'chipped off,'' after Goux said, 'We didn't get anybody chipped off.'"

Wayne was an absolute Republican and a superpatriot, traits that were fairly common in Hollywood when he was in his prime, but toward the end of his career he found himself increasingly isolated from his fellow actors. In 1968, Alabama's segregationist governor, George Wallace, ran for president as an independent. He asked Wayne to be his vice presidential running mate. Wayne agreed with Wallace when it came to states' rights and fighting Communism, but could not stomach racism. He declined.

Tired of the liberal media spin of the Vietnam War, he made a highly jingoistic film, *The Green Berets*. It was propagandistic in nature and lacked gritty realism, but viewing it today, the film does emphasize military heroism that cannot be denied. It was a huge box office success. That and three 1970 war films, *Patton, Tora! Tora! Tora!,* and *Midway,* all succeeded artistically and financially, showing that the American public was not as widely antiwar as implied by the popular misconceptions of the era.

Wayne's conservatism earned him plenty of critics, but even in 1969, when he won the Oscar for *True Grit,* Hollywood opened its hearts to him without reservation. Others found him to be a celluloid hero who had not served in wars, while real war heroes like Ted Williams were thought to be "the real John Wayne."

Jeff Prugh, the *L.A. Times* beat writer for USC football in the 1960s and '70s, recalls a story from that 1966 weekend in Austin.

"Well, there was this one L.A. sportswriter writer whose name shall remain anonymous," said Prugh. "Everyone is gathered at the bar, and John Wayne's holding court. This old writer is off in the corner getting drunker and drunker. He's liberal and Wayne's an outspoken conservative Republican. Finally, this old writer has had enough, and he approaches Wayne, interrupts him in mid-sentence with all Wayne's pals staring at him.

"'So . . .' the old drunk writer says, 'they tell me, uh . . . they call ya . . . *The Duke!'*

"'Yeah, what of it?' says Wayne.

"This writer just gathers himself," continued Prugh.

"'Waaal . . . *Duke* . . . You ain' *s—t!'*

"Well, it was almost a full brawl right then and there but his pals held Wayne back," said Prugh.

Craig Fertig was a star quarterback at USC and a graduate assistant in 1966.

"One time, the players wanted to go see *Easy Rider,*" Fertig recalled, referring to a "hippie" movie of the 1960s. "Duke Wayne says, 'Don't let the kids see that crap!' So he arranged for 'em to see *War Wagon* instead.

"I'm low man on the totem pole in '66, so I gotta chaperone the team and do bed checks. Now McKay's hosting a party for Wayne."

(This contrasts with Nick Pappas's assertion that Wayne and McKay had not met prior to the morning of the next day's game, but considering that alcohol, old alums, and memories were involved, the discrepancy is a minor one.)

"I finally put the kids to bed, so I make it up to this party, see," continued Fertig. "I see John Wayne and introduce myself to him, and he's like, 'Oh, I saw you beat Notre Dame,' and he's just like my best friend.

"Well, he has Bruce Cabot with him, and this make-up artist, too. This make-up artist's mixing drinks—vodka one time, Bourbon, scotch, right? He's gettin' hammered.

"The next day, I'm assigned to Duke Wayne, 'cause he's gonna speak to the team. Wayne's mad as hell, 'cause his make-up guy's not there.

"'Son of a bitch's never around when you need 'im,' he says. It turns out the man's died during the night, maybe 'cause he mixed drinks and it was too much for his heart? Anyway, I gotta get Duke ready, the job this dead make-up guy usually does."

Apparently, Wayne had not yet learned of the make-up artist's demise.

"'Whadda I wear?' asks Duke. I tell him, 'Everybody knows you as a cowboy, so dress like that.' Ten-gallon hat, cowboy boots, brass belt buckle; I got him lookin' good.

"We're scared sh——s; Texas is number one in the country. So at the stadium he fires up our team. Then he's introduced to the crowd. He comes out and he's in this cart with my dad."

Fertig's father, "Chief" Henry Fertig, was the longtime head of the Huntington Park, California, police department in L.A. County, and a tremendous USC booster.

"He's being driven around the stadium in this cart, and the whole time my dad's pouring whiskey into a cup and Duke's drinkin' out of it," continued Fertig. "Now, the Texas fans, they see The Duke, and he's wearin' this cowboy hat, and most of 'em don't know he's a USC football player. Duke's givin' 'em the 'hook 'em, 'horns' sign with his fingers, and the Longhorn fans are cheering.

"'Duke's a Texas fan,' they're sayin'.

"All the time, Duke's sayin' to my old man, 'F—k the 'horns.'"

All things considered, Duke Wayne cut a swath across the entertainment industry like very few others. In terms of longevity and impact, perhaps only Clint Eastwood has played a greater all-around role in showbiz.

USC continues to be integral to the film industry to this day. The USC marching band actually bills itself "Hollywood's band." They have appeared in numerous movies and even helped cut a gold record, Fleetwood Mac's *Tusk*. USC athletes have made a disproportionately large number of careers in the media.

"Going to school in L.A. is a big advantage," explained former USC football coach John Robinson. "It's a big difference being interviewed by major media there than it is to say, 'yes, sir,' or 'no, sir' to a local sportscaster in Alabama."

Many major movers and shakers in Tinseltown are part of the "Trojan Family." John Wayne would be proud.

USC VS. UCLA

The City Game

When one looks back at Howard Jones's tenure at Southern California, it is impossible not to be struck not just by his astounding success, but at how much better it could have been! In his first four years, Jones's teams were 36–5–2. The five losses were by *twelve points!* In 1925, the Trojans lost to Stanford, 13–9, and Washington State, 17–12. In 1926 they fell to Stanford and Notre Dame by one each (13–12 and 13–12, respectively). In 1927 it was by one again at Notre Dame, 7–6. Both Notre Dame losses came when Morley Drury missed extra points. The ties were against a great Pop Warner-coached Stanford eleven and cheating Cal on a muddy Memorial Stadium field.

With a little luck, Jones could have been riding a forty-three-game winning streak, or at least a nonlosing streak (add to that three straight wins to close out Elmer Henderson's last season in 1924). It is with this in mind that one considers that, while Jones would win three more national championships in the 1930s, his 1929 squad is thought by some to be his best.

They scored 492 points, a school record that stood well into the modern era, and destroyed Pittsburgh in the Rose Bowl, 47–14.

Braven Dyer, in *Top Ten Trojan Football Thrillers*, felt that the team might have been Jones's best. They were not perfect, however, and it cost them the national championship. Cal beat them fair and square this time, 15–7. The fact that Rockne's Irish had what it took to defeat USC, 13–12, in front of 112,912 at Soldier Field, tells much more about Notre Dame's greatness than it does about any failure on SC's part.

The Thundering Herd took care of UCLA, 76–0; Washington, 48–0; Occidental, 64–0; Nevada, 66–0; Idaho, 72–0; and Carnegie Tech, 45–13, to finish 10–2, good for first place in the Pacific Coast Conference. These opponents (with the exception of UCLA), while some are not considered top football schools anymore, were all strong opponents at the time.

Writers gave colorful nicknames to the Trojans, such as "Field" Marshall Duffield and "Racehorse" Russell Saunders. According to Braven Dyer, the Thundering Herd appellation stuck in 1929, but as noted, the *Daily Trojan* and other sources had made use of the phrase in earlier seasons. There may have been multiple sources, which include Maxwell Stiles and PR man Al Wesson. Wesson denied it (although he did write the school song, "All Hail") because he was Jones's mouthpiece. Jones always downplayed his team in order to lull opponents. There is no doubt that part of the nickname's origin comes from the Noah Beery film of the time called *The Thundering Herd*.

"Those 'Thundering Herd' teams didn't throw the ball around much," said Dyer. "They thought that was the sissy way to play the game."

The starting backfield consisted of Saunders, Erny Pinckert, Harry Edelson, and Jim Musick. Their subs were Duffield, Jess Mortensen, Marger Apsit, and Jess Hill. Sophomore Gus Shaver was a quarterback/fullback. Nate Barrager and Francis Tappaan were All-Americans. Jones was sparing in his compliments. Grantland Rice was researching his All-American picks, and Jones wired only that Tappaan is "the best end we have." Wesson insisted on replying to future telegrams.

Pinckert was a bit of a court jester, a favorite of writers looking for quotes. Lord knows Jones was tightlipped about things. Pinckert also had a propensity for playing in great pain—muscle tears, bad ankles. But Novocain was available and it took just enough of the edge off to play hard.

"I've heard him hit guys in a game and make them squeal," one friend said of him. "He just knocked the wind out of them."

When Southern Cal beat Georgia, 60–0, in 1931, Gene Clarke and Gus Shaver visited their All-American end, "Catfish" Smith, in the locker room afterward. His body revealed criss-cross marks and deep, dark bruises, courtesy of Pinckert.

"Man, I ache all over," said Smith.

"We have a pretty tough system here," Clarke told him. "Jones has this power play where we have two of our linemen taking you out of the play most of the time."

"Man, there were only *two*?" was Smith's dazed reply.

Cal's All-American guard, Ted Beckett, was blindsided by Pinckert, leaving him doubled up like Smith. Pinckert just picked him up, slapped him on the back, and said, "Nice going, kid."

Players like Pinckert belied Cal's insinuations that USC's players were thugs and academic rejects. Tough as nails on the gridiron, Pinckert had the soul of an artist. He painted beautiful murals and invented football pads, which brought him a small fortune. In 1930 and 1931, he made All-American.

Famed Pitt coach Jock Sutherland brought his unbeaten, untied team to Pasadena for a repeat of the 1928 Rose Bowl, when they had lost to Stanford, 7–6. Both Knute Rockne and John W. Heisman (another famed coach and namesake of the award) picked Pitt to win. Running back Tony Uansa was a breakaway threat who had run for long touchdowns of seventy yards or more twice against Duke and once against Ohio

State, in addition to a receiving TD against the Buckeyes and three scores versus West Virginia.

Heisman said they were clearly the "class of every other Eastern team." They were playing for a national championship, since both they and Notre Dame were 9–0 prior to New Year's, 1930. By beating the Panthers and knocking them out of the picture, SC was helping themselves, in a sense. The success of each team's rival, making the other look better in the process, would be the unique aspect of the USC–Notre Dame series.

Those "fans" who say, "My favorite team is USC and my second favorite is whoever beats Notre Dame," are adhering to a Chinese maxim that the "enemy of my enemy is my friend." It may apply in war, but usually not in football, and is no more valid (unless conference titles are at stake) with regard to the UCLA rivalry.

The Pitt game swung early when Uansa broke for what looked like one of his long touchdown runs. Saunders, "knocked on his rumble seat," according to Dyer, then picked himself up and gained eight yards on his man, nabbing him at the SC 14.

A Pitt star named Montgomery summed it up to the reporters later.

"What the hell . . . we broke our fastest runner into the clear," he declared, "knocked down your safety man, and then he got up and caught our man!"

Pittsburgh failed to capitalize on deep possession, with Pinckert swatting away a pass. Then Jones really foiled Sutherland. Despite Braven Dyer's assertion that the Trojans felt passing was for "sissies," that was what Saunders did, tossing a fifty-five-yard beauty to Harry Edelson and a twenty-five-yarder to Pinckert.

USC's 26–0 halftime lead was so thorough that recapping it in 2006 reminds one of their equally stunning demolition of Oklahoma in the 2005 BCS Orange Bowl.

"The ease with which the Trojans amassed 26 points in the first half left the capacity crowd (of 71,000) stunned with astonishment," read one report.

The second half was more "showtime": perfect passes, leaping catches, glittering runs. The Rose Bowl crowd and assembled literati had to be scratching their heads, wondering how Cal and Notre Dame had beaten this team. All the pregame predictions left egg on the faces of Rockne and Heisman, but they were not alone.

"Saunders is the greatest back I have seen since Glenn Presnell," said Sutherland. "They rate with the great backs of all time."

Saunders, never an All-American, rates as one of the most underrated players in USC football annals.

"The outstanding lineman on the field was [Garrett] Arbelbride," read one game account, going on to speculate whether the man "had wings the way he came flying through the air."

"The Trojans are the equal of any team in the country," Sutherland said afterward. The Pittsburgh media found a convenient excuse, however, stating that the Panthers were "seduced by Hollywood glitter." It would not be the last time L.A. glamour would be trotted out as a reason a team from the "heartland" had lost, and indeed if the "stars in their eyes" could make football teams lose, it would be repeated many, many times over the years.

Grantland Rice's theory about California athletes being a "hybrid" of "supermen" now gave rise to further analysis, with one reputable man of science declaring that "sunshine and vitamins"—ultraviolet light, California-grown oranges, fruits, and vegetables—provided USC players with "more energy."

While hard to prove, this theory seems to have some validity even to this day, but whatever advantage is gained by the environment, Walter Eckersall nailed it best when he stated, "Better football is played on the Pacific Coast than in any other section of the country."

Walter Eckersall was referring to USC first and foremost; beyond that, California and Stanford seemed to be the only teams other than Notre Dame and Alabama worthy of taking the field against Southern California. Little could anybody recognize that still another football power would rise up out of the land of "sunshine and vitamins."

"Opening the season for the first time in local history with a Pacific Coast Conference game, the Trojans of Southern California and the Bruins of UCLA clash on the Coliseum gridiron this afternoon," read the report. "In years to come this game will probably be one of the football spectacles of the West."

After USC's 76–0 slaughter of UCLA, they wrote, "What this proves, if anything, is not certain." That writer might have said of Custer's "last stand" that defeat at the hands of Sitting Bull was a "setback" that did not "prove anything." He would ultimately have been right. While UCLA has not "come back" to avenge defeat as thoroughly as the U.S. Army did in eventually "winning the West," the big early loss was not a "certain" predictor of the future by any means.

UCLA failed to win a single game in their initial season in the PCC. Jones was by this time a major football figure whose book, *Football for the Fan*, was a best-seller. But UCLA had hired a good coach, a contemporary of Jones at Minnesota when the "Head Man" had been at Iowa. Bill Spaulding had been building his program patiently since 1925.

Forty thousand showed up for that initial game. USC *rushed for 753 yards*. The loss did not deter the plucky Bruins from playing USC the next year. The Southern Campus yearbook of 1930 declared that "the siege of Troy has begun."

Over the years, various analogies and metaphors based on the USC nickname, "Trojans," have tried to compare the events of ancient Greece with modern football, creating various confusing interpretations. UCLA may have wanted to effectuate a "siege of Troy," such as when the city of Troy fell to the Greeks under King Agamemnon in 1184 B.C. Of course, Homer's *Iliad* and *Odyssey* describe the Trojan Army laying siege on Greece. Further references to the Battle of Thermopylae fail to account for the fact that the Trojans were not involved; rather this was a fight between the Persians and the Greeks. The Peloponnesian War is a more appropriate comparison, although this was a fight of Greece not with Troy, but rather with the Spartans. "Spartans" has been the name given to USC's freshman or junior varsity teams over the years.

The sports comparison does gain some credence in light of the fact that the first Olympic Games were held in Athens, in part to celebrate the peace following the Trojan Wars. The good feelings of the Games did not prevent the Peloponnesian War (possibly because they were not open to non-Greeks), although that war did spawn the philosophers Socrates, Plato, and Aristotle. Their attempts to create professional politics and diplomacy as a substitute for war led to democracy.

Despite historical confusion, the two schools again played on opening day of 1930. It was obvious from the beginning that sharing the Coliseum was a disadvantage to UCLA. Against USC, it meant an away game. During other home games, it meant a ten-mile drive to their rival's campus, where their fans were forced to walk across the "hallowed shrine" that was the University of Southern California, replete with all the splendid monuments to the all-conquering Trojans!

Forty thousand Los Angelenos showed up to see "Field" Marshall Duffield score three times and Orv Mohler add two more in a 52–0 rout. Whether giving up 128 points in the first two games or being shut out twice was more devastating was a problematic conundrum for UCLA. Either way, USC looked at UCLA much the way New York Giants manager John McGraw had looked at the American League. In 1904, his Giants were National League champions, but he refused to play the American League title holders because he considered the upstart junior circuit a "busher league." In 1905, when his team repeated, he did agree to play Connie Mack's Philadelphia A's. His haughtiness was justified in an easy win. However, McGraw would be proved wrong, and quickly, since the American League indeed caught up to the senior circuit.

So it was with USC, who decided after the 1930 game that UCLA was not worthy of their schedule. This despite the fact that the Bruins managed to win three games after the 52–0 loss. USC was big business; their games drew huge crowds and everybody wanted a part of it. There was disagreement over whether to play UCLA early or late in the season, and USC felt neither. They replaced UCLA with St. Mary's.

However, Coach Spaulding made UCLA perfectly respectable from 1931 to 1933. His teams were 15–12–1 with wins over Montana, Stanford, and Washington State. When USC struggled to a 4–6–1 mark in 1934, talk revived about renewing the game, and when UCLA had a better season in 1935 than Southern Cal, they decided to start up again, this time in earnest.

JOHNNY BAKER AND THE COMEBACK AT SOUTH BEND

After this game, nothing was ever the same again

In 1931, all the previous highlights of USC football paled in comparison with the spectacular, dramatic events of that season. It is possible that the game played between SC and Notre Dame that year is to this day the most significant in school history.

Gus Shaver, Garrett Arbelbide, Johnny Baker, Erny Pinckert, Stan Williamson, Ernie Smith, and Robert Hall, all Trojan legends, made up that team's incredible roster. A first-year player, Aaron Rosenberg, would make All-American.

The season opener was a scheduled blowout of St. Mary's at the Coliseum before 70,000 on hand for round one of the coronation. Taps were blown for the death of Rockne.

"This may have been an expectant championship year for the Trojans, but they looked anything else but," wrote Paul Lowry in the *Times*.

St. Mary's had good teams and would continue to field excellent ones for more than twenty years after that season. However, their 13–7 victory over SC may be the biggest upset the Trojans have ever suffered, especially considering that 70,000 fans, flush with expectation, were on hand at the Coliseum.

From there, however, USC went on a winning streak. Oregon State, Washington State, Oregon, Cal, Stanford, and Montana fell like Italy, Austria, and Poland under Napoleon. After the St. Mary's game, USC won six straight, five by shutout (Washington State lost 38–6). On November 21, the Monster lay in wait. The Siegfried Line. The Atlantic Wall. Hannibal staring at the Alps.

"Notre Dame is so good that [new coach] Hunk Anderson could lick any team he has played, Northwestern excepted, with his second string," USC scout Aubrey Devine told the reporters. "It is impossible to set a fool-proof defense for the Irish because they are such a versatile squad. Just when you think you have them stopped, they break out in another direction."

Notre Dame had beaten USC four out of the first five times they had met. Jones amped up his practice sessions, and did it in secret.

"There is every reason to believe that the team we buck up against Saturday is much stronger than the one which trounced us 27–0 last year," Jones said. "On the other hand, there is nothing to indicate that my boys are any better than they were that day Knute Rockne's eleven made us look bad."

Notre Dame was indeed the "greatest American football team of the generation" under Rockne, but USC was right on its tail. If USC had beaten the Irish four of five instead of vice versa, the Trojans' record would have put that "title" on them. If the teams had "split," 3–2 or 2–3 either way, the "greatest" description may well have been a split decision. But the Irish had earned the moniker and USC knew it.

The train pulled into Tucson, Arizona. USC held a practice there in the arid desert. Johnny Baker, recovering from a bum knee, had a mental lapse on his defensive assignments. Jones came down on him hard.

"I remember quite distinctly the bawling out which Howard gave Baker," said Braven Dyer, who seemingly was covering the Trojans, on and off the field, day and night, in those years. "Johnny was quite mad about it. Later he told me that he came within a whisker of quitting the team right then and there and heading back to Los Angeles."

(Dyer indeed seemed to be "everywhere" throughout his career with the *Los Angeles Times*. In 1964, while traveling with the Los Angeles Angels, he got into a drunken fight with playboy pitcher Bo Belinsky at four in the morning at the Shoreham Hotel in Washington, D.C. Belinsky punched the then-elderly sportswriter, knocking him out. Despite the fact he was a star at the time, Belinsky found himself traded to Philadelphia faster than he could say, "Braven Dyer.")

The newspapers in South Bend were much more provincial than the Chicago papers. They gave USC very little respect, despite their fabulous record over the past years, and the pounding they had given opponents since the St. Mary's game. Notre Dame was the big time, and when it came to that test, 1–4 said it all! Certainly, playing at South Bend would prove to be an atmosphere that, combined with the talents of the Irish, could not be overcome. The Irish were riding a twenty-six-game winning streak. USC entering the 2005 season with two straight national titles and the imprimatur of invincibility only had a twenty-two-game streak at the time.

Fifty-five thousand (a capacity audience; 50,731 was considered the paid attendance) let USC know what they were in for from the moment they took the field. The Trojans were intimidated by the surroundings. The Irish had them off-balance early when Steve Banas finished off a drive with a four-yard touchdown run. 7–0, Irish.

USC stiffened on defense but could not push the ball at all. They felt lucky to be trailing only by seven at the half, but all seemed lost when the great quarterback Marchy Schwartz took it in from three out in the third quarter to make it 14–0.

"The score looked as big as the population of China," wrote Dyer. "In fact it looked a darn sight larger than that, if possible, because of the consummate ease with which the Irish scored those touchdowns.

"In other words the Irish were in command of the situation, and everybody, apparently, but the Trojans knew it. Schwartz had been whizzing around his own right end repeatedly for long gains. Banas, on a twisting, 32-yard run which ended up on Troy's three-yard line, had made the Trojans look positively silly. And the ease with which Schwartz went over for the touchdown presaged others to come."

USC fullback Jim Musick broke his nose. Orv Mohler replaced him at the position, and it was a Godsend for the Trojans. He and Gus Shaver started making gains in the fourth quarter. Jones's hard practices and conditioning in the California heat began to pay off in the chill of an Indiana November. USC got it to the one, where Shaver bulled in. At that point, a tie seemed the best they could hope for, but when Baker missed the extra point, a 14–6 deficit in the fourth still looked insurmountable.

But USC held Notre Dame, got the ball back, went to the air, and when the Irish were called for pass interference (a brave call from an official in South Bend), they had a first-and-ten on the Irish 24. Shaver and Mohler, fighting for every yard, pushed it to the nine. Mohler lateraled to Shaver, and he went around the left end to score. Baker made the conversion, and at 14–13 the crowd was silenced, the USC cheers rising above their silence. Momentum was in USC's favor, and all that was left was the famed "luck of the Irish." It was not to be.

"The fury of Troy's attack in the second half astounded everybody," wrote Dyer. "No man, unless it be Gus Shaver, stood out. Morley's choice of plays was almost perfect, and the way the 162-pound Orv rammed into the Irish line inspired his mates immensely."

Possessions were exchanged and the clock, Notre Dame's only remaining ally, wound down to four minutes. USC had the ball on its own 27 with time left for one dramatic drive.

Two plays failed, but Shaver made a daring pass after being forced to retreat from Notre Dame tacklers, spotting and hitting Ray Sparling with a diving grab for a first down at the Notre Dame 40 (Dwayne Jarrett, anyone?). This gave life to the Trojans and created a sense of foreboding in the Irish rooters, who by this time were counting on Baker's inconsistency if he lined up for a field goal.

Bob Hall caught a pass and got the ball down to the 18. A penalty moved it to the 13, and Sparling ran into the middle, putting the team into good field goal position while the clock wound down. Some confusion reigned when Jones sent Homer Griffith into the fray with instructions to go for the kick, but Mohler waved him back.

"Cold sweat broke out on his [Jones's] brow, and his assistant coach groaned in anguish," read one report.

(Again, the "confusion" near the goal line in '31 eerily presages what happened in '05.)

But Mohler did call for a field goal. The team caught Notre Dame off guard and lined up for the kick, but it was Baker, he of the missed conversion who had come "within a whisker" of quitting in Tucson, who stood at the ready.

It was in God's hands now.

Baker was straight and true from twenty-three yards out, and now it was 16–14,

Trojans. USC celebrated as if it were Armistice Day in 1918. With a minute and three seconds left, they would have been wise to consider the magic of Notre Dame. USC kicked off, but they were so enthused and Notre Dame so shocked that they simply smothered the Irish on their side of the field until the cannon roared.

"Great. Boy, great! But why did you do it?" Jones yelled at Mohler.

"Baker and I have been practicing that play all year," said Mohler. "I knew if it failed I'd be the goat and we would be licked, but old 'Bake' doesn't miss on those short ones. I knew he wouldn't fail me. Wasn't it a beat?"

Jones restrained himself from punishing Mohler for winning the biggest game of his career, indeed in USC annals and certainly in football history up to that point!

"Notre Dame was far from the Fighting Irish type when Howard Jones' Trojans got hitting on all 11 cylinders in the last period of play," wrote Tom Thorpe of the *New York Evening Journal*. "No one would have thought it possible for any team to tally at a greater rate of speed than a point a minute against a Notre Dame squad. This Southern California did without much trouble.

"Notre Dame has no excuses. The Trojans simply outplayed them during the last 15 minutes in a manner that left no room for alibis. 'Old Rock,' looking down from up above, must have wept with tears of genuine sorrow when he saw his former Irish playmates being pushed around. It has been seven years since any team has been able to manhandle the Irish as Southern California did."

Of course, assuming "Old Rock" is with the Lord, it does not seem likely he "wept" over the loss of an earthly game.

Dyer seemingly lost much of his "journalistic integrity," morphing from colorful sentimentalist to wordy fan in his game story.

"Noah Webster's diction book does not contain enough adjectives to describe the way the Trojans refused to be licked," he wrote. "Until the Trojans get home, you can paste this in your hat for future reference. Nobody ever saw a gamer battle than that which the Southern California players staged against supposedly insurmountable odds this afternoon. It did not seem humanly possible for them to win, but thanks to the indomitable fight of a great gang of kids, plus the cool nerve and steady hoof of Johnny Baker, the Trojans today achieved the greatest athletic triumph in Southern California history.

"Yours truly has run out of paper, his typewriter has broken down completely, and it's getting late. You'll have to wait until tomorrow for more about the stunning achievement of a bunch of boys who were rated no better than a two-to-five bet to upset the mighty Irish."

Dyer's further commentary included the following gem:

NOTRE DAME STADIUM (South Bend, Ind.), November 21
(Exclusive)—When Howard Jones is old and a darn sight grayer than now he will tell his grandchildren about the heroic fight his 1931 Trojans made against the undefeated Irish of Notre Dame. He will tell them how his boys,

with the odds hopelessly against them and with a sound thumping staring them in the face, came back to do the impossible and score sixteen points in the last quarter to bring to an end the sensational winning streak of the greatest team in Irish history. (Braven Dyer, *L.A. Times*)

In addition, the game was broadcast nationally by Ted Husing on radio. Millions of Americans could recall for years afterward being huddled around their radios, listening to the wild descriptions of this event.

Tears of sadness were shed in the Notre Dame locker room; tears of joy on the USC side. Gordon Clark held the game ball for all it was worth.

"I knew they couldn't stop us," Pinckert shouted. "I've waited for two years for this day—but boy, what revenge."

Indeed, it may have been revenge, but the atmosphere was totally different from the cold calculus of Total Victory that had enveloped the 74–0 thrashing of the "poor sport" Cal Bears. A sense of mutual respect pervaded. After losing three times by a point, USC now had the respect of the Notre Dame fans, players, and allies in the sporting press. They were looking at an open road toward Howard Jones's second national title in four years, and were sitting firmly on top of the college football mountain.

USC alumni actually crashed into the locker room to congratulate Baker—in the shower! Trojan fans danced with the naked, dripping Baker.

Jones was beside himself, disheveled and totally beyond his normal reserved persona. He just went about shaking hands and declared that he was too "flabbergasted" to be eloquent.

"But I'll tell you that it was the greatest team in the world," he stated of his club.

Jones had a little time to compose himself when the team boarded the train, but he continued to stay out of character, acting like a "kid let out of school," according to Jack James of the *L.A. Herald*. "The strain and worry of past weeks all fell away from him like a discarded garment the moment the gun ended that game on the Notre Dame greensward Saturday afternoon. From that moment he 'unlaxed' as the saying goes."

At stops, Jones was seen throwing snowballs at the athletic director and his assistants. He brought snow into the train, committing acts of hijinks in order to "get" various players, sneaking into their compartments amid great laughter.

The "special train" was "a regular madhouse" for the three-day, three-night trip back to Los Angeles. Jack James admitted that he preferred "sanity," but if he thought he would find it in the City of Angels, he was wrong.

Three hundred thousand fans met the "men of Troy, conquering football heroes," said the *Examiner*. The cheering came from the rooftops and all about.

"I never saw anything like it in my life," said Ernie Smith. The team all wore bowlers, a style of the day, which were purchased for them in Chicago. Dressed in their best finery with the bowlers, the team was loaded into waiting cars, two per car, for a ride down Fifth Street to Main, then on to city hall.

"There seemed to be a half-million people lining the streets," said Smith. "When we left city hall and started down toward the school, ticker tape came flying out at us. We rode down Spring Street, I remember, and people had torn up telephone books, and they were throwing all this paper out of windows. It was a real thrill—it was unbelievable. For a football team to get this type of reception, I mean it was *really* something."

In the midst of the Great Depression, Los Angelenos had found escape in the exploits of their beloved Trojans. On this day, USC became a tradition in the city. Perhaps the Dodgers would equal the intensity of fan enthusiasm and loyalty a few decades later, but other than that, in the history of Southern California, no team—not UCLA, the Angels, Rams, Lakers, or Raiders—would establish greater tradition than what USC started, and over the years proudly continued to live up to!

"I think Ted Husing's national radio broadcast of the game had a lot to do with that welcome," recalled Al Wesson. "He had built up the last quarter to such a dramatic extent that Los Angeles people were running out into the streets during the game and screaming.

"It was the wildest sports demonstration that the city of Los Angeles ever had. 300,000? I don't know; there were at least 200,000 in the line of march to see the Trojans riding in their cars. Everyone got a helluva cheer."

The team rode "fancy touring cars," open on a mild L.A. November day. People leaned out of office buildings. Streamers and confetti were hurled out of the sky. It was a ticker tape parade that observers said could compare to the one Charles Lindbergh had received on Broadway in New York City after his trans-Atlantic flight in 1927.

"A reception never before equaled for athletic stars turned downtown Los Angeles into a half holiday as the triumphant Trojans rode through the city at the head of a three-mile parade beneath a barrage of confetti and flowers," the *Examiner* went on. "At the first cry of 'Here they come' and the first notes of Harold Roberts' Trojan band, playing 'Fight On!' men and women poured from every building on Spring and Broadway and Hill. . . .

"Bankers and laborers . . . industrial kings and clerks . . . merchants and typists. . . . For a day USC was the adopted alma mater of the city. Through the jammed lanes of humanity, the Trojan warriors who fought the Battle of Notre Dame rode as heroes ride. Police sirens screamed to clear the congested traffic."

The paper went on to state that the team had left as college students and returned as heroes. The cheers of the populace were only the beginning. The student body received them like Caesar returning from victory over Gaul. An "arch of triumph" was fashioned out of chrysanthemums and poppies in cardinal and gold colors. Flowers, serpentine, blossoms, and confetti reigned.

Mayor John C. Porter presided over a city hall welcome with 40,000 filling the area in front of the building, made famous in the 1960s TV police series *Dragnet*. Bishop John J. Cantwell of the Roman Catholic diocese of L.A. and San Diego certainly seemed to favor the locals over Notre Dame despite the religious conflict. Howard Jones stood before a cheering crowd that would not let him speak for several minutes.

The applause could be heard for many, many blocks.

In Los Angeles, writers who had not made the trip got many further recollections, such as captain Stan Williamson saying that Jones had kissed him in the locker room. Williamson kissed the man right back before he realized "it was the 'Head Man' himself."

Garrett Arbelbide had been sidelined and was in the locker room. All he heard was "racket" when the team came in. A movie camera had captured the game, and it was replayed as a full-length feature in L.A. by MGM for a long while, with Dyer providing narration.

It played at Loew's State Theater, the top downtown movie house at the time. It began as the first of a double-bill, but was so popular it ran over and over, breaking all the house records at Loew's.

A strange twist became public when it was revealed that third-string center William Hawkins had been imprisoned, allegedly for leaking team secrets to Notre Dame. Hawkins had missed some practice time, and upon his return inquired of the plays the team was practicing in his absence. Assistant Coach Gordon Campbell suspected that something was amiss. Apparently Hawkins had friends at Notre Dame, and this fact concerned the coaches. After being "grilled" by the rest of the staff, he was placed under the custody of detectives, and spent the week of the game at a mountain lodge in Topanga Canyon, away from his team and his classmates. He missed a week of school and did not even hear the game on radio.

A subsequent investigation exonerated him. His home was searched, he was shadowed, and his Notre Dame friends questioned. In the end, he was found innocent, prompting a genuine apology from Jones to Hawkins and his enraged parents.

USC had gone from football players to movie stars, but it did not go to their heads. Washington fell, 44–7, and when they beat Georgia, 60–0, it stamped the team and the West as the kingpins of the game. It most certainly did not improve the image of the South as it related to gridiron prowess. Alabama's back-to-back national titles and Georgia Tech's "wrong way run" win over Cal two years later (following the 1928 season) had previously elevated Dixie.

Georgia guard "Red" Mattox got into it with Baker on the field, but the thrashing wore him out.

"All I want to know," Maddox told Baker in those Prohibition days, "is where can a guy get a gallon of corn liquor after the game?"

USC went on to play another Southern school, Tulane, in the Rose Bowl. The Green Wave was a very tough challenge, very well coached and the best team in their region at 11–0. Jones's brother, TAD, predicted a close contest. Their end, Jerry Dalrymple, was acclaimed to be the best in the nation.

An overzealous L.A. sports editor misquoted Dalrymple, headlining a story with, "Dalrymple says he'll stop Trojan attack." The article was great bulletin board fodder for the Trojans, who did not know the Tulane man had not said it. The player was distraught, as was coach Bernie Bierman.

The Southern sportswriters had heard tales of the Notre Dame drama, Grantland Rice's 1920s exclamation that California produced "supermen," scientific theories that the sun, the weather, and maybe the gene pool of settlers and Hollywood hopefuls further created "perfect" football players. They expected he-men, brutes, animals, but were surprised at what they found.

"You never saw such quiet, boyish looking chaps . . . polished gentlemen all," wrote Bill Keefe of the *New Orleans Times-Picayune*. "Williamson, a great big kid with a baby face, looks as if his feelings could be hurt with a frown. We expected to see gangs of ferocious, cruel, and twin-headed monsters, but find only a band of fine young chaps. No university ever boasted a more gentlemanly or clean-cut set of boys. Barring Pinckert, Shaver, and Williamson, they are not much bigger or tougher-looking than Tulane."

A great deal of film obviously existed of USC, however, and the more Bierman observed it, the more he realized his team was overmatched. He predicted a four-touchdown USC win. Seven Trojans made All-American. Pinckert was named for the second time, and honors went also to Shaver, Mohler, Williamson, Baker, Rosenberg, and Smith.

The Associated Press declared USC the "outstanding sports team of the year" over the World Champion St. Louis Cardinals. The Rose Bowl parade had a distinctly international theme, and with the Olympics scheduled for that summer, there was a distinct feeling in the air that Los Angeles was now the "sports capital of the world." Radio broadcasts of the game delivered it across the Fruited Plain.

Once the game began, Pinckert took charge, sweeping through Dalrymple to score from thirty and twenty-three yards out. USC led by 21–0. Tulane rallied, but it was too little, too late.

"Southern California had more power than any team I ever saw," said Bierman after the 21–12 defeat before 84,000.

"These players accomplished more throughout the season than any team I ever coached," stated Jones. USC was an undisputed national champion, and the new Knute Rockne Trophy was awarded to the "Head Man" and his team.

Indeed, despite the observation by the *New Orleans Times-Picayune*, USC had a powerful team of 200-pounders-plus. Pop Warner made note of this, assessing that the Trojans had no weak spot and were as strong as any club he had ever seen, which was saying something. Players of that era, when questioned in the 1970s, when the game had modernized in terms of player size and equipment, were still convinced that they could have adapted: diet, weight training, equipment.

"The guys I played with had good athletic ability—and guts," said Gene Clarke.

Chief among those was Pinckert, who often played the full sixty minutes and was given the Douglas Fairbanks trophy as the nation's most valuable player.

Clarke also offered an amusing anecdote, describing some near-fisticuffs involving Tom Mallory and an opposing player in a game USC was winning by five touchdowns.

"'What's the matter with you guys?' the referee says to them. 'Don't you know how to play football?'

"'Don't we know how to play football?' Mallory retorted. 'For Christ sakes, look at the scoreboard, buddy.'"

Greatness also followed the Trojan players in the years after the 1931 season. Ernie Smith went from All-American to All-Pro and then the NFL Hall of Fame. Without his USC teammates, however, "I never would have achieved what I did," he said.

He and Aaron Rosenberg were the great off-tackle blocking combination that fueled The Thundering Herd. Smith also had the utmost respect for Jones.

"He was called the 'Head Man,' and he was that in all respects," said Smith.

Smith, who hailed from Gardena, a small community a few miles south of the USC campus, was an all-around person who played the trombone. He had grown up a USC fan, attending Trojan games, and had seen the Four Horsemen play in the 1925 Rose Bowl when his Gardena High band played at the game. At USC he performed in dance orchestrations. Smith was a good example of why Cal's "professionalism" charges had no merit. He had come to school on a music scholarship!

Once in, Smith worked many jobs to make ends meet, further negating the myth. He did get work through his football connections, however. Smith was a football player, cowboy, and singer in fifty-five movies.

"I worked in all of Will Rogers' pictures through that era," he recalled. "I was a waiter in Charlie Chaplin's *Modern Times*."

In 1932, a movie was made called *The Spirit of Notre Dame*. It was filmed at Loyola College in Los Angeles, and the football sequences were shot using Trojan and Loyola players.

That fall, defending national champion USC played Loyola, and despite their great reputation, the game was a close one, 6–0 Troy. It turned out that the close proximity of the players on the movie had made USC familiar to Loyola; they knew their plays and techniques, and lost their intimidation of them.

In Smith's 1930–1932 career, USC won two national titles, two Rose Bowls, averaged thirty points a game to four for the opposition, shut out sixteen teams, and compiled a 28–3 record.

Smith was also one of those gentlemen that the New Orleans writer had made note of, a true credit to the Trojans and an example of the sense of élan, esprit de corps, and happiness that often marked Trojan football over the years.

1932: UNBEATEN, UNTIED, BACK-TO-BACK NATIONAL CHAMPS

Los Angeles and USC: the sports capital of the world

1932 was the height of the Depression, and Los Angeles was hit as hard as most American cities. However, when it came to the world of sports, and especially college football, L.A. was "fat city." Dean Cromwell's magnificent track program was at full throttle, making the Games, held at the Coliseum, resemble a USC home meet of sorts. A Trojan had earned a gold medal in every games since 1904 at St. Louis. The great Fred Kelly had taken gold in the 110-meter high hurdles at Stockholm in 1912. Charles Paddock, the "fastest man alive," had competed in the famous *Chariots of Fire* Paris Games of 1924, where he came up empty after having earned gold in the 100 meters and four-by-100-meter relays in 1920. Frank Wykoff had earned gold in the 1928 four-by-100 meter relays, and Buster Crabbe had won a bronze in swimming.

The L.A. Games were a Trojan extravaganza, with SC trackmen taking five golds. The great Frank Wykoff took two of those, and Crabbe went for the gold and got one in the 400-meter freestyle swimming event.

Fresh off the glory of the Olympics, which by virtue of its being held at the Coliseum turned the campus into the Olympic Village, showing off the school, the city, and the greatness of its athletes as well, defending national champ USC and Los Angeles itself were flush with success as the 1932 football season got underway.

The participants and fans in L.A. simply had decided not to participate in the Depression. USC became not just a great football school, but a world famous institution, in large part because it was showcased at the Games with Hollywood as its backdrop.

The 1931 team, number one and bathed in glory after beating the Irish and winning the Rose Bowl, were the epitome of college grid excellence. The 1932 team was even better, if that can be believed, than the '31 squad.

A new superstar emerged, Aaron Rosenberg, the All-American defensive guard who powered one of the greatest defensive juggernauts of all times. Eight opponents were shut out (after six had gotten goose eggs in 1931). In 1938, Duke would be unbeaten, untied, and unscored-upon in the regular season. So, too, would Tennessee the following year. Both those teams were beaten and scored on . . . by USC in the Rose Bowl. In light of that, the '32 Trojans must rank as one of the truly great defensive teams ever.

"Aaron Rosenberg is still considered Troy's mightiest guard—on defense he stopped everything that came his way and charged viciously on offense," was one appraisal of the era.

Smith was "headline material," a "hammer-'em-down 200-pounder."

"I give credit to Rosenberg for playing a big part in the success of the team's defense against Notre Dame and Stanford in 1931 and 1932," Coach Jones said. Any fullback he was assigned to tackle, he "cracked him and messed him up."

"The 1932 team was the strongest defensive team that USC ever had," stated Al Wesson. "There were only two touchdowns scored on us all season—and they were both by passes. No one could move, no less score on the ground against us. Smith was one of the greatest tackles we ever had. Rosenberg was a smart, fine athlete. You couldn't buy a yard against this team. I'd say without qualification that the offense of the 1931 team and the defense of the 1932 team were the best produced by Jones."

Captain Tay Brown was an All-American tackle. Left end Ray Sparling made huge plays in crucial situations. New recruits of equal strength, an indication of Jones's enormous recruiting ability, replaced the players from the 1931 champs who had graduated. There is little doubt that USC had gotten to the point where they enjoyed a huge advantage in attracting players to their school, for reasons that went well over and above football. It was also obvious that the modest but steady success of UCLA was not preventing the great stars from wanting to be Trojans.

"If any of these players of prominence show signs of lagging," wrote one football magazine, "Jones will have somebody else in there in a hurry."

Jones knew that team competition was a very good thing that pushed everybody. "Players get one or two chances to make good, and if they fail it is a long time before they land on the first string again," the magazine continued. Shaver was thought to be the player most likely to be missed, and the backfield might "lack cohesion" early.

A new superstar emerged in the USC backfield. Cotton Warburton quickly became a Trojan legend. He was only 140 pounds, but the sophomore from San Diego was a scatback, a term that applied to a number of great runners of the decade. Ted Williams, the great baseball star who also grew up in San Diego, had seen Warburton as a high schooler, would follow his career at USC, and later in his life counted Cotton as one of his all-time favorite athletes.

Warburton scored a touchdown in a 9–6 win over Washington and scored in the 13–0 defeat of Notre Dame. He scored twice in a 35–0 pasting of Pitt in the Rose Bowl.

"I was responsible for the one and only blemish on our undefeated, untied, and almost unscored-on record," Warburton did admit. He slipped in the Cal game and let the Bears score. Against Stanford, Warburton knocked down multiple Stanford passes.

"The USC defensive power was absolutely astounding; their ability to out-dazzle Mr. (Pop) Warner's razzle-dazzle was uncanny," wrote Mark Kelly of the *Los Angeles Examiner*.

USC opened the year with five straight shutouts before Warburton slipped and Cal broke the string in SC's 27–7 victory. Cal was said to be desperate to win, or at least show, against the Trojans. They were perplexed by their loss of football prestige over a decade against the team, USC, that they wanted to beat more than any. Stanford of course is their biggest rival, but USC is the top of the mountain. Perhaps they took some solace in that they ended USC's scoreless record, but the loss was hardly a "show." USC no longer even looked at the Bears as anything more important than the rest of the schedule. Oregon and Washington fell, and Notre Dame came into town.

Warburton returned a punt thirty-nine yards to set up a touchdown pass, and USC recovered an Irish fumble to create another score. The game was not the dramatic extravaganza of 1931, but the Trojans faithful of 93,924 were happy to observe a good old-fashioned whuppin'.

The Pacific Coast Conference champions returned to Pasadena, where Pittsburgh came in hoping for some measure of respect after their 47–14 loss three years earlier. They should have stayed in the Steel City for the holidays.

Colgate was left home. The papers remarked that they were "unbeaten, untied, unscored on and uninvited."

Sophomore quarterback Homer Griffith out of Fairfax High had mostly handed off to Warburton, but toward season's end he came into his own against Notre Dame and Pitt. He hit Ford Palmer for a fifty-yard first quarter touchdown in front of 78,874. Warburton starred on both sides of the ball. He scored twice late.

Pitt went home with their tails between their legs, 35–0. USC was the back-to-back national champion, and at that point if a poll were taken to determine the greatest program of the century up to this season, it would very well have been a tie between USC and Notre Dame, with a slight edge to SC.

Four years later, Pitt returned to Pasadena to play Washington. Coach Jock Sutherland ordered the bus to a stop on the hill overlooking the Arroyo Seco and announced, "There it is. There's the place two Pittsburgh teams were beaten by a total of 68 points."

Some of the greatest legends in USC football history played for Howard Jones's Thundering Herd teams of 1930–1932. Halfback Garrett Arbelbride was an All-American in 1930 who also played on the baseball team. Inducted into SC's Hall of Fame in 1999, he was an educator and rancher.

Quarterback Orv Mohler came to USC from Alhambra High School, made All-American in 1930, also played baseball, was inducted into the USC Hall of Fame (1995), and became an Air Force colonel. He died when his jet crashed in 1949.

Erny Pinckert came out of San Bernardino High School, was a two-time All-American (1930–1931), won the Davis-Teschke Award, is a member of USC's and College Football's Halls of Fame, and played professionally for the Washington Redskins.

Guard Johnny Baker, from the central California valley town of Kingsburg, earned All-American in 1931. A member of the College Football Hall of Fame, he later was the head coach at Iowa State and the athletic director at Sacramento State.

Quarterback Gaius "Gus" Shaver of Covina High earned All-American in 1931, made SC's Hall of Fame, and was a Trojan assistant coach.

Center Stan Williamson, from the Sacramento Delta hamlet of Pittsburgh, was an All-American in 1931 (as well as team captain), and eventually the athletic director at U.C.–Santa Barbara.

Tackle Tay Brown came to USC from Compton High School and made the 1932 All-American team. A College Hall of Famer, he became the basketball coach at the University of Cincinnati and the athletic director at Compton J.C.

"I'd have to say that that all of us hitched our wagon to a star, and Howard Jones was that star," Athletic Director Willis O. Hunter, who had hired Jones in 1925, said of this golden era of USC football. "He made all of USC's later success possible."

NAVE-TO-KREUGER AND A RETURN TO GLORY

The Trojans go to the air and win Jones's last national title

After a series of down years, in 1938 Howard Jones let his quarterback go to the air. By the end of the season, it would be a pass that earned USC not just a Rose Bowl win, but eternal glory for the passer and the receiver.

Doyle Nave became a national hero for winning the Rose Bowl game against Duke. He was named honorary Mayor of Gordo, Alabama. Women wrote love letters from many states. Sick children wanted autographs. An organization of deaf people tried to adopt him as hard of hearing even though he was not.

Nave's touchdown pass rivaled Johnny Baker's field goal. Years later, a magazine poll determined that the Rose Bowl game he won was the most thrilling of all holiday bowls—ever.

"I was nervous when I went in," Nave confessed. Oh yes, he was not a starter. He had played all of thirty-five minutes in the regular season. He was a last-gasp hope against a team that stamped out all hope.

Grenville Lansdell, Mickey Anderson, and Ollie Day had tried their hand as USC's quarterback on January 2, 1939. Their opponents: the Duke Blue Devils. 1938 record: unbeaten, untied . . . *unscored on.* Unlike Colgate a few years earlier, the Blue Devils were not uninvited. The Associated Press had begun their poll in 1936. USC, at the top of college football's mountaintop, had not been ranked in the first two years of the poll. Bernie Bierman, now at Minnesota, had led the Golden Gophers to the pinnacle in 1936, followed by Jock Sutherland's Pitt Panthers in '37 (who won the AP version, Cal was number one in alternate rankings). In 1938, Duke looked to be a shoo-in. Number one.

When the Trojans upended them, 7–3, on January 2, 1938, it knocked them off-kilter. Davey O'Brien and Texas Christian would win it, followed by Bob Neyland and Tennessee. USC was back in the hunt, finishing seventh on the strength of an 8–2 campaign. They would knock a Southern school out of a "sure" national title two years in a row. In so doing, they would return Howard Jones to the heights of glory.

Duke featured Eric "The Red" Tipton, a terrific punter who constantly kept opponents pinned deep in their own territory, whence they never got out. In fact, so good was Tipton, he sometimes punted prior to fourth down because the Duke defense was more likely to make breaks deep in the other team's territory than they were to sustain long drives.

In the Rose Bowl, both teams held the other to zero until Tony Ruffa's twenty-three-yard field goal made it 3–0, Duke in the fourth quarter. The previous quarterbacks were ineffective. Nave was known as a good passer, but lacked experience, knowledge of the first team offense, and technical ball-handling ability. What he did not lack was heart.

Duke fumbled in their own territory, but USC's field goal for a tie missed on a close official's call. It gave them some hope, though. When they got the ball back, they made it to the Duke 34 with two minutes remaining. At this point, Jones made a decision that was either a gamble or a calculated risk, depending on the perspective. He could have tried to stay conservative and play for a game-tying field goal. However, two things dissuaded the "Head Man" from this. First, he was the kind of coach who played to win, not to tie. He had played to ties in the past, with Cal and Stanford. In 1936 the 7–7 deadlock with UCLA was a moral defeat for Troy and a victory for the upstart Bruins.

Furthermore, USC's kicking game was not strong. The kick could miss. Unlike the 1931 Notre Dame game, a kick was not a winner. So, Doyle Nave's name was called.

"Jones gave me a few minutes to warm up," Nave stated, "and I was nervous, I'll tell you." The voices of 89,452 fans filled the air with a cacophony of sound.

Because Nave was not first string, the receiver he was most comfortable with did not start either. He schemed to pass one to "Antelope Al" Kreuger in the game to replace the ineffective first string and because he was Nave's partner.

"I completed the first pass and made twelve yards on a button hook," recalled Nave. He followed that up with a "27," a flair in which Kreuger went down, pivoted, then broke to the outside. The catch went for a first down.

In 1987, announcer Tom Kelly narrated a video called *Trojan Video Gold: 100 Years of USC Football 1888–1988*. Nave and Kreuger were interviewed together. Nave claimed every ball was "right on the numbers" while Kreuger rolled his eyes behind his back, indicating spectacular dives. In truth, the passes were not perfect and Kreuger indeed made excellent grabs, albeit not totally sprawled out. It was a moment of great humor and camaraderie.

"Was I havin' a good time?" Kreuger asked rhetorically. "Why, of course, I was goin' to *SC!*"

With the ball on the far left side of the field in those pre-hashmark days, Nave needed to devise a way to get Al some maneuver room. Nave worked a play toward the center of the field, but his pass was picked up on and Kreuger dropped for a loss after snaring it.

On second-and-twelve, Nave told Al to go for the end zone; there was little time left for anything but heroics. On a "27 down-and-out" Kreuger got away from Eric Tipton while Nave faded deep into the pocket. According to Nave, he unloaded the ball when Kreuger was on the "seven or eight," which had to be an exaggeration. Nevertheless, the ball was thrown for the back of the end zone. With forty seconds left, Kreuger clutched the pigskin to his chest and "we went berserk."

According to Maxwell Stiles of the *L.A. Times*, "strange events" led to the play. Stiles heard of it from Joe Wilensky, a former Trojan guard-tackle who was on Jones's 1938 staff. Stiles and Joe Hendrickson wrote a book together called *The Tournament of Roses*:

> Wilensky was manning the telephone on the bench, relaying the messages of assistant coaches Sam Barry, Bob McNeish, and Julie Bescos, who had been observing the action high above in the press box. Suddenly Wilensky got an idea. He decided to take a chance to do something to pull out victory. He knew that the coaches above had already left the press box and were on their way to join the team. Nobody had scored a point all season against the great Duke line.
>
> "Our only chance is to get Nave in there to pass," thought Wilensky. "He has the arm to hit Kreuger and dent this great Duke defense." Wilensky snatched the phone. "Yes," he shouted so everybody on the bench could hear. "Yes, yes—I get it. I'll tell him right away." Wilensky slammed the receiver on the hook and excitedly nudged assistant coach Bill Hunter.
>
> "The word is to send in Nave and have him throw to Kreuger," said Wilensky to Hunter, who in turn passed it on to Jones. Nick Pappas, who helped Jones with the coaching and today is a member of the USC athletic administration staff, verifies that this is the true story of how Nave got into the game.

Duke had gone into a "prevent" defense, which seemingly to this day consistently prevents the team that uses it from winning the game! With the defenders playing back, Kreuger used his clever breakaway ability to find the seam he needed.

Wallace Wade was Duke's coach. He had led Alabama to two straight national championships in the 1920s, but he had no scouting report on Nave or Kreuger. It cost him. Trojan scout Clifton B. Herd would later say that if they had known the scrub quarterback actually had the best arm on the team, they would have rushed him, getting him to hurry. Wade also had to contend with a running play and the possibility that Jones would not go for broke, instead "settling" for a field goal.

Wade showed no Southern courtesy afterward, prompting criticism that TCU should have been the invitee. He never congratulated Nave even though he had the chance, and slammed the whole atmosphere.

Nave, who was gracious, pointed out that Wade's wife was ill back in North Carolina. During World War II, they exchanged gracious letters and Nave, now serving in the military, was able to visit with him.

Nave actually had not "earned" a varsity letter with one hundred minutes of playing time, but Jones waved that rule.

Jones's analysis of the game did not include the Wilensky story. Instead, Jones said that while Lansdell might have gained rushing yards in a final drive, he knew his "only chance was to pass, and Nave is the best passer." He stated that he "knew" that Nave alone was the only hope, "so I sent him out there and told him to get at least one of them off to Kreuger."

Southern Cal Chancellor Dr. Norman Topping was quarantined in a hospital with Rocky Mountain Spotted Fever, running a 105-degree temperature.

"I was dying, they had given up on me," he recalled. "No visitors, not even my wife."

Barely aware of his surroundings, he had the presence of mind to request a radio.

"They said it was impossible," he said. "I insisted, demanding that they grant my last request."

When Nave hit Kreuger "something remarkable happened. A miracle. It did more for me than any medicine. My temperature immediately started going down."

Dr. Topping did indeed recover to collect on a $50 bet. God works in mysterious ways.

Braven Dyer had actually been advocating that Nave be used throughout 1938. He wanted USC to upgrade its offense to accommodate the passing game. To fail to modernize, Dyer insisted, would set the program back.

"Give my boy Doyle Nave a chance," Dyer had written in an open letter to the coach.

Dyer actually *missed the play* because of a deadline: "Somebody has to get out the paper." Apparently, he needed to beat the always-brutal traffic jam that to this day makes getting not just out of the Arroyo Seco, but out of Pasadena proper, a nightmare. He heard it on the radio along with several colleagues as they drove back to the *Times*'s downtown offices.

Rumor has it that he fainted at the wheel, but Dyer called that a "dastardly report." What he did do was "let out a yell which all but shattered the windshield and promptly began jabbering like an idiot. The 'gridirony' of it all practically slays me."

Dyer noticed when he saw the newsreels just how great Kreuger's catches were, too.

As a Naval officer assigned to an aircraft carrier in the Marianas during World War II, Nave ran into former Duke center and captain Dan Hill.

"When I came into the game," Nave asked him, "did you have any idea that I was going to pass?"

"Hell, no," Hill replied. "we didn't even know who you were."

The 1939 Rose Bowl completed a season in which Troy rebounded from a four-year down period, but it did not start well at the hands of a great Southern school. Alabama put the wood to SC, 19–7. A crowd of 70,000 Los Angelenos came out to see the fabled Crimson Tide, already a power at least the equal of Troy. 'Bama was eager to represent the South after having lost to Cal in the previous season's Rose Bowl. The game would be the first of seven, to date, between two of the most storied programs of all time. Both teams would give as well as take, and to date the Tide, along with Notre Dame, is one of a tiny, select group of schools with a winning record over USC (5–2).

Sportswriters painted a dismal picture of 1938 after the opener, stating that the 19–7 score did not represent the true mediocrity of the team. Two weeks later, though, USC earned a very important win for the program when they made the trip to Columbus, beating the Ohio State Buckeyes, 14–7, in front of 62,778. The season turned in their favor when they defeated Stanford at The Farm, 13–2. Two weeks after that they overtook defending national champion Cal, 13–7, in a defensive struggle before a packed Coliseum audience.

A tremendous downturn occurred in a place that would always be difficult for Troy. The state of Washington tends to get cold and rainy in November, and when USC plays in the Northwest late in the season, it is always difficult. On November 12 in the mud, the Huskies beat them, 7–6, throwing the PCC race into a tizzy.

But in 1938 USC took advantage of their schedule, an opportunity they would get many times in the future, especially in even years. While Cal and Stanford grab the spotlight and would play their Big Game at the end of each season, USC would get *two* big games. In 1938 that meant UCLA and Notre Dame at the Coliseum.

The Bruin game was already an "instant classic," with memories of the two lopsided shutouts of 1929–1930 a distant memory, but in '38 they were no match for USC, 42–7.

A crowd of 97,146 came out for a titanic struggle with the Irish December 3. This was a game that would truly define the program, and answer any lingering questions over whether Jones's team was a major power again.

Elmer Layden, one of Rockne's "Four Horsemen," was the coach of a team riding an eleven-game winning streak with national title hopes. One report stated that the Irish did not know if it was an "earthquake or a shock" in a game in which they were "outclassed in almost every department of play."

It was Al Kreuger, portending things to come at Pasadena, who hauled in the touchdown pass with little time left in the first half to basically win it for USC. The 13–0 shutout was sweet revenge for a four-year winless skein, eliminating number one–ranked Notre Dame's hoped-for national championship aspirations. It also was enough prestige to land the Trojans in the Rose Bowl despite a 6–1 first place conference tie with the Golden Bears. Having beaten Cal in addition to wins over the Bruins and Irish, plus the natural tendency of those years not to send repeat champions to Pasadena, helped USC.

TCU lobbied ferociously for the invite, probably too zealously. In the end, Duke got the nod. While Texas Christian was bitterly disappointed at the financial hit that came with the loss of invite, they gained by not having to face the buzz saw that was Troy on New Year's Day. In the end TCU was named the AP national champions.

The hallowed tradition that is Southern California football has elevated many teams to the status of "legend." Perhaps it was because World War II started right at the beginning of the season, thus engendering grave concerns for other things, but the 1939 Trojans are in many ways a "forgotten" team in Trojan lore. In truth, they are one of the best teams the school has ever produced.

Howard Jones's teams sometimes started slowly. Some of his better squads suffered strange defeats early, or in this case a strange tie (7–7 at home against Oregon). But the juggernaut picked up steam after that, cruising in the style of the Thundering Herd to four shutout wins in five games. Washington State fell, 27–0; Illinois, 26–0; Cal, 26–0 at Strawberry Canyon; Oregon State, 19–7; and Stanford, 33–0.

The Trojans were balanced with the likes of ends Al Kreuger, Bill Fisk, and Bob Winslow; tackles Phil Gaspar and Howard Stoecker; guard Ben Sohn; center Ed Dempsey; and quarterback Doyle Nave. In 1939, Nave demonstrated more all-around ability than in '38.

Cal coach Stub Allison, who had led the Bears back to glory after the death of Andy Smith in the 1920s, called it the "best Southern California team I have seen."

Oregon State coach Lon Stiner stated that he had competed as a player for Nebraska against the Four Horsemen and "seven mules," as well as against the great Red Grange, but Southern California was "better than all these other great ones—the greatest team I ever saw."

Indeed, Stiner saw what Jones had taken some time to finally develop, which was a balance between the pass and the run, thus fully "modernizing" his team's offense. Stiner pointed out that defending the Trojans was in 1939 much more difficult than figuring out how to defend the great-but-predictable 1933 club that the Beavers tied, 0–0.

Howard Jones made what would be his last visit to South Bend, pinning the second loss of the season on the Irish. With the score 6–0 USC entering the fourth quarter, both teams traded touchdowns, but the Irish could not convert point-afters. With three minutes to go, Ambrose Schindler made a tremendous forty-one-yard touchdown run to ice the 20–12 USC win.

USC suffered a scare in barely beating Washington, 9–7, at home, setting up a huge showdown with UCLA before 103,303 fans. The Bruins had built themselves into a major football power by fully integrating their program. Even though the Trojans had starred Brice Taylor in the 1920s, they had not kept up with their crosstown rival's social progress. It cost them athletically. UCLA had the likes of Kenny Washington and future baseball great Jackie Robinson in the late 1930s. Largely through their heroics, UCLA had created parity with USC. In no prior year was this more apparent than in 1939. On December 9, Washington and Robinson led the Bruins into the Coliseum.

"I really was worried," stated Nave, who also played safety. "I was trying to figure what I'd do if they tried a pass to Woody Strode, the big end. He was the man I was assigned to cover. Woody stands about six-five, you know, and I'm under six feet. I couldn't figure any way I could stop him from catching a high pass if they threw to him. Well, I was lucky. They didn't throw at him at all. I sure breathed a sigh of relief when it was over."

(Strode later played the black gladiator who gives up his life so Kirk Douglas can live in *Spartacus*.)

Indeed, so did the entire Trojan team. They were lucky to come out of it with a 0–0 tie. UCLA totally blundered the game by not going for a field goal with the ball on the USC 5 with ten seconds left. Instead, quarterback Kenny Washington passed to Bob MacPherson in the end zone, but Bobby Robertson managed to knock it down. It cost UCLA a $120,000 invite to their first Rose Bowl. Coach Babe Horrell's Bruins had driven seventy-six yards, but play-caller Ned Matthews chose to try for six when three would do. With the ball just a few yards from the goal line, USC's defense stiffened and held the Bruins to a fateful fourth down situation.

In a strange twist of democracy gone too far, five UCLA players *voted* for a field goal try, while five wanted the touchdown. Matthews opted for the latter course and came up snake eyes. The smart play not only would have been to try the kick on fourth, but to try it on third in case it missed, giving the team another crack at it.

Coach Horrell deferred the blame from Matthews, stating that he supported the decision. USC had also missed scoring chances of their own in a game that while slow in terms of defensive dominance and lack of movement, built to a crescendo of pressure in front of the mammoth throng. In the first quarter, Grenny Lansdell, suffering from a hand injury that made it hard for him to grip the ball, fumbled at the Bruin goal. Lansdell fumbled again at UCLA's 22, and a Trojan drive that died at the UCLA 25 was their only other threat. After the game he abjectly apologized to Coach Jones.

USC had their hands full boxing in Jackie Robinson, especially on UCLA's almost-successful final drive. The greatest criticism of Horrell came not from the decision not to kick, but his inexplicable choice not to get the ball into Robinson's or Washington's hands once inside the USC 5.

"It was one of the cleanest, yet most bitter struggles in Coliseum history," wrote Paul Zimmerman of the *Los Angeles Times*. After the game, in what has become tradition, players from both teams, acquainted with each other from high school, four years of rivalry, and sharing the same city, mingled in "the finest display of sportsmanship anyone could ask for," wrote Zimmerman.

USC was outplayed by Robinson, Washington, and the Bruins. There was no haughtiness left, no returning to the days of yesteryear in which they looked down upon the public school from Westwood. They were lucky to be going to the Rose Bowl and they knew it.

UCLA felt no consolation, as they had in 1936 when they were still feeling their oats. They had blown it. Jones offered in his postgame commentary that the Irish and Husky games had drained his team, but to a man Kenny Washington's "hip-wiggling" running style, which portended a revolutionary change in the running back position over the next decades, elicited praise from USC.

Jones made a point to console Lansdell over his fumbles. Grenny had given him all he had. Statements like "those Bruins are a fine bunch" and "give 'em credit" lent to the general feeling that Southern Cal welcomed a true conference rivalry on par with what Cal and Stanford had up north.

The two teams oddly were, and would finish, undefeated. USC was 8–0–2, while UCLA sported an unusual 6–0–4 record. Tennessee was invited to Pasadena in a true national championship game.

Whereas the 1938 game had engendered controversy over the selection of Duke over Texas Christian, with USC coming in as the underdog, the 1940 game promised to be the national battle America longed to see.

Bob Neyland, the Volunteers' coach, may not have been a legend at Jones's historic level, but in his "neck of the woods" you could not win that argument. The Vols, riding a twenty-three-game winning streak, came in with the same credentials as Duke in 1939: unbeaten, untied, unscored on. Unlike the Duke game, which had been a donnybrook, the USC-Tennessee Rose Bowl affair was all Trojans from start to finish. They were bigger, stronger, and faster. Ambrose Schindler had a terrific day. Southern California prevailed by 14–0.

"We weren't stale or off form," Neyland announced. "We were outclassed. We were badly beaten by a superior team, and my hat is off to Howard Jones."

Tennessee quarterback George Cafego had to be removed when he suffered an injury, but offered that he would not have made any difference "against those big guys anyway."

"I remember they [Tennessee] had two All-American guards, a guy named Sutheridge and a guy named Belinsky," recalled Carl Benson in *The History of USC Football* DVD. "These guys just said to me, 'You guys are something else.' I said, 'I can't even make the first ball club, and we're coming right through ya.' And by God we did."

"I said, this is the Rose Bowl and I'll give these people something to think about," recalled Schindler. "It was the perfect play. I lobbed the ball out to Al Kreuger and he turned and there it was. It was real neat."

Newspaper headline: "Tennessee Unable to Cope with Might of Southern California Grid Machine."

"I believe it played the heaviest schedule and accomplished the most of any team I ever coached," Jones said (in archival footage that still exists) when he accepted the national title trophy from Professor Frank G. Dickinson, a respected analyst whose system was considered one of the arbiters of national championship status.

"The Trojans were the best team in the best section . . . and the nation's other top teams did not play as strong schedule as USC," stated Professor Dickinson.

The win improved Jones's Rose Bowl record to 6–0. Their victory also restarted the talk of a decade earlier, when pundits were saying that the best football was played on the West Coast, particularly in the Golden State. Rose Bowl losses by Alabama (1938), Duke (1939), and Tennessee (1940) tarnished the Southern football reputation, especially considering that Duke and Tennessee had looked impregnable playing their regular schedules, only to be exposed by Southern Cal. The South still had its supporters, who pointed out that Texas at least was maintaining standards, what with Texas Christian's and A&M's strong years in 1938–1939. But Alabama had been soundly beaten by California in 1938, the West's supporters pointed out.

"They raise them rugged out here," wrote Henry McLemore, which was an interesting side of the double argument: one that says Californians are indeed "raised rugged" and the other that says they have "gone Hollywood . . . soft," the warm sun creating a population of loafers who had never "walked a mile to school in the snow."

McLemore theorized that "nature" made for a tougher athlete who could "withstand earthquakes." He said it was the water that made for men who were bigger and even had to shave more often!

Jones was back on top, to be sure, but it was his final reach for greatness. If indeed California was the football capital of America in January of 1940, it would not last for long.

In 1940, his team was depleted. For whatever reasons—age, failure to go the extra mile?—Jones had failed to recruit the usual replacements who had fueled his team's long, dominant run. They won only three times. Jones would die of a heart attack on July 27, 1941, making 1940 his last year at SC. Against tough odds, the Trojans played Notre Dame to the wire before going down in his last game.

"With his passing, there ended an era of football in the West," wrote Max Stiles. "No man ever brought so much gridiron glory to the southern section of California. No man ever gave more of himself to the game he loved. To him, football was the first bright rays of dawn, the noonday sky, and the stars that shine by night. To him, football was a creed and he kept it clean and pure. Good sportsmanship and perfect execution of assignments on the field of play were sacred, and woe to any player on his team who failed to measure up to the field degree of either standard."

CONQUEST: THE "LITTLE WHITE-HAIRED MAN" TAKES OVER

The monarchy of John McKay: the first decade of the most
dominant twenty-year dynasty in history

During pregame warm-ups on September 12, 1970, at Legion Field in Birmingham, a white player from the segregated Alabama Crimson Tide approached Sam "Bam" Cunningham, the black fullback of USC's integrated Trojans.

"I bet you're shakin' in your boots havin' to face the mighty Alabama Crimson Tide," he said to Cunningham, trying to shake him up. Cunningham just pointed to John McKay.

"I'm only scared of one thing: the little white-haired man over there," he replied before rushing for 135 yards and two touchdowns to lead his team to a historic 42–21 trouncing.

McKay was a cigar smoking, whiskey drinking, duck huntin', iconoclastic, conservative Republican West Virginia Catholic. He was known for his sharp quips to the media. He was a favorite of the writers who came to him for good quotes. In light of his success and great reputation, it seems incongruous that McKay was not enamored with the "Knights of the Keyboard," as Ted Williams had disparagingly referred to the Boston press.

But McKay did not trust the press. This attitude stemmed from his early experiences with them. When he came to USC, McKay installed a revolutionary new offensive scheme called the I formation. It totally veered away from the age-old concept of a "triple-threat" quarterback/running back. It placed a tailback well behind the line. In the eyes of lesser lights of the press box, the "I" in the I formation stood for "incompetent, intolerable, and ineffective." McKay never forgot the barbs.

There are college coaches who are considered greater legends, among them Knute Rockne, Bear Bryant, and Joe Paterno. This is only because McKay chose to move on to the National Football League when he could have cemented his legacy for another decade at USC.

McKay's Rose Bowl battles with Ohio State's Woody Hayes and Michigan's Bo Schembechler are what makes college football great. The Notre Dame rivalry, which was down because both programs were down prior to their arrival, became the greatest in the nation because of what McKay and Ara Parseghian meant to it. It is always more heated when both teams are at the top, playing for number one. Every season from 1966 to 1974, the game had a major impact on the chase for number one.

The same thing can be said for the UCLA game. The Bruins made a major bid for national supremacy, but McKay's Trojans, with a few exceptions, managed to keep the barbarians from breaking through the gates.

McKay, who would serve for four years as athletic director, led USC to the ultimate heights of football and athletic glory. The period from 1962 to 1981, the last five years in which McKay's handpicked successor, John Robinson, was at the helm, represent the most dominant twenty-year run in the entire history of college football. The Trojans won five national championships and earned four Heisman Trophies. But victories are only part of the story. They also became the team of excitement, of last-minute drama, of ultimate glory, and Hollywood glamour. The prestige of the school itself owes much of that panache to the image created, fostered, and led by John McKay.

McKay would, like John Wooden across town, adapt to a changing game and a changing roster. He always won with great tailbacks, but when football in the Pacific 8 Conference opened up, he never missed a beat.

"He was dedicated to execution and that's what John believed in," said Lynn Swann on *The History of USC Football* DVD. "He believed in fundamental football. He was a very conservative coach with regards to offense, but allowed his defense to be aggressive, and they played with that emotional aggressiveness. He wanted his reins on the offense, but every once in a while, when he needed a great play, he wanted that great receiver who could make it for him. Somebody he could go to."

"He was an extremely competitive man," said his son, John K. "J. K." McKay. "It wasn't that he so much hated to lose, which he did, but he loved to win and he loved to compete."

Furthermore, McKay the Southerner is seen through history as a modern-day "Moses of progressivism" when it came to providing opportunities for black athletes, sometimes at the expense of criticism and resistance from both within and outside the Trojan family. McKay forged a special relationship with Alabama football coach Paul "Bear" Bryant. Between them, they oversaw seminal events that transcend football, changing American society and politics.

McKay was aloof, arrogant, condescending, a smart aleck, and by no means a "player's coach." He instilled fear in his men.

McKay has his detractors, but only grudging ones who hedge any criticism of his communication skills with acknowledgement that his way produced All-Americans, Heisman winners, national champions, first round draft picks. He was laconic, possibly even clinically depressed, subject to wild mood swings. He is credited with saying some of the funniest things in the history of coach-speak, but what only those in the room knew was that his commentary often came affixed with an icy stare and a heaping helping of ironic sarcasm.

Along with Jerry West and the great fighter pilot Chuck Yeager (who broke the "sound barrier"), McKay may well be the most famous person ever to come out of West Virginia, but he was made for L.A.—the perfect press conference sound bite and banquet speaker, a man who conspired with his friends in the media to create an image that is larger than life.

McKay was only 5'9", pleasantly handsome, and a high school football player with enough game to take it to the University of Oregon. McKay was a coach on the field, a description that was also applied to one of his contemporaries, Tom Landy, who was said to virtually call the shots for the famed "New York Giants defense" that he played for in the 1950s.

McKay's future in football was obviously as a coach, although he was a good player. He hooked on with Oregon's staff, and quickly became one of those guys whose star rose, his name bandied about as "the next big thing," the logical replacement wherever a coaching job opened up.

Fate and timing made the University of Southern California the place where his star would shine. Don Clark had taken the Trojans back in 1959, but he had a cloud over his head. He failed to beat Notre Dame or UCLA, cardinal sins at University Park. The "McKeever incident" tarnished him with the reputation of being a "dirty coach," which was unfair, but Clark left. The decision seems to have been a mutual one. He took over his family's business. The fact that he never returned to coaching indicates that he actually did choose to leave the profession on his own. But the brutal USC alumni wanted national championships and victory over their fierce rivals from Westwood and South Bend.

"A couple of bad things happened," said writer Joe Jares of the Clark years, on *The History of USC Football* DVD. "There was a period he got in trouble with the NCAA; it was relatively minor. Don Clark resigned to go into the overall business with his brother. There'd been an assistant on the staff for one year, a former World War II tail gunner and a former Oregon star runner on the same team with Norm Van Brocklin, and his name was John McKay."

"He had a great background, coming from Oregon under a great coach, Len Casanova," said *Orange County Register* sports columnist Steve Bisheff. "It took a while, a couple of seasons, but once he took hold he captivated the town. He was great, wonderful with the media. I always said it was like having George Burns or Johnny Carson as the coach. You didn't have to come up with lines; he came up with all the one-liners; he was very funny."

"McKay had a very tough veneer, a tough exterior, and I had the opportunity to do his coaches' show and I'd ask him a question and it was only a half hour long and he'd still be answering the first question at the end of the show," recalled longtime TV sportscaster Stu Nathan.

"He was fabulous speaking to a room of strangers," said assistant coach Dave Levy. "But to people on his staff or in his inner circle, he felt he had the right to be himself. He could be a dominating person: definite, rude; and then he'd allow you to forgive him and you'd go and have a drink together."

"The first time I met him, I met him at Julie's across the street, which was an old long-time Trojan hangout," recalled offensive lineman Allan Graf, now a movie director who at the time of this writing was developing a film about the 1970 USC-Alabama game. "And he was recruiting me out of San Fernando High School, and I went in there and he was just bigger than life, and I was a big SC fan all my life growing up, and I met him and I sat down and he said, 'You wanna play with the best, don't you?' And I said, 'Yes, sir,' and he said, 'You know where the best are, don't you?' and I said, 'Yes, sir, right here,' and he shows me a '67 national championship ring and he says, 'You want one of those, son?' And I said, '*Yessir!*' and he said, 'The only place you're gonna get it is right here,' and I said, 'Where do I sign?' It didn't take much!"

Howard Jones was the famous Iowa coach who had beaten Rockne, who recommended him. Jeff Cravath had starred for Jones. Jess Hill had been, too, in addition to being a Major League baseball player, a track star, and coach of the two-time national champion USC track program. Don Clark was a Trojan and a pro football player.

McKay had come over from Oregon to coach USC's backfield in 1959. Jess Hill had it in mind that if Clark left, McKay would succeed him. For that one season, McKay was a coaching colleague of Al Davis. They both adhered to the famous "just win, baby" motto.

McKay indeed took over in 1960. He installed the I formation offense.

Frank Broyles of Arkansas and Bear Bryant of Alabama freely admitted borrowing from McKay, even though "I don't think McKay's borrowed anything from us," said Bryant.

Other coaches begged McKay to "help" them install his offensive schemes, but of course he kept his trade secrets at University Park. McKay was a product of his environment, which meant hard work, work hard, and work harder!

Despite the Depression era hardships of growing up in a family of five kids after his father passed away when he was only eleven, and having to work his way through high school, McKay was an honor student. He served in the Air Force during World War II. He claimed that being a tail gunner during the war made him a deep thinker and a cigar smoker.

He was one of those guys who might not have gone to college had he been five years older, but as a veteran he was determined to expand his horizons in the brave new world of postwar America. A West Virginian going to college in Oregon would have been unlikely before the war, but McKay was part of a newly mobilized society.

As a halfback with the Ducks, he played alongside the great quarterback Norm Van Brocklin, a future coach himself.

McKay was an All-PCC selection on a Ducks team that went to the Cotton Bowl. The New York Yankees of the All-America Conference drafted him, but he decided to direct Oregon's offense and pass defense. He also developed a reputation as a master recruiter. He could charm parents with his living room skills.

When McKay was named USC's head coach, he "broke the mold" of what a coach was supposed to be, said Jon Arnett. Coaches were usually alumni, but they also were often dour men, or colorful personalities, or hard-driving taskmasters. Read: Howard Jones, Red Sanders, Jeff Cravath.

McKay was different. He was one of the first coaches who might be called a "politician." His was a new era. His youth, his attractiveness, his media skills, and his lovely blonde wife with the descriptive nickname "Corky," made him one of the New Breed. In New York, the ancient Casey Stengel had worn thin on Yankee management, so he was replaced by a man similar to McKay, Ralph Houk. In McKay's L.A. years, he would stand out from some of the other coaches. Wooden was a sainted figure, but dull. Dodger manager Walt Alston made Wooden look like Casey Stengel. Ram coach George Allen was so consumed with work that he gave the media nothing more than blandishments.

The shame of it was that Sanders had died, never squaring off against McKay. Those two may very well have had a fistfight at midfield if they had coached in all those USC-UCLA games of the 1960s.

McKay had nobody singing his praises in 1960 and 1961. He called them "rebuilding" years, but going from 8–2 to 4–6 and 4–5–1, when viewed through hindsight, has distinctive Tollnerian overtones. Which is not good. There was a glimpse of the future in 1961 versus Iowa, however. The Hawkeyes were a powerhouse. USC was weak. USC trailed 21–0 before rallying for thirty-four points in the 35–34 loss. When USC scored late, they had a choice of going for a tying point-after kick, or a game-winning two-point conversion. McKay, who would be described in later years as "a gunslinger," went for two. The Trojans failed, but the fight of the team, the comeback against considerable odds, and the gutsy choice to make it win-or-else impressed a few of the writers who had been lambasting McKay.

But in 1962, all the demons were exorcised, the past injustices—losses to Notre Dame, *allowing* UCLA to ascend above them, the scandal—all of it was washed away by a perfect 11–0 season and USC's first national championship in twenty-three years.

To Ken Rappoport, author of *The Trojans: A Story of Southern California Football*, McKay said, "I know there are millions of people on this planet who don't even know or care there is such a thing as football." This mirrored his famous 1966 statement, following a brutal 51–0 loss to Notre Dame, that "a billion Chinamen couldn't care less who won" the game. McKay was a philosopher who was influenced by his Catholicism. He was able to separate the "importance" of football from truly meaningful life events, but his profession was coaching. He took it as seriously as a man can—without going insane.

"I never worry about being hung in effigy," he said. "Every season I send my players out to buy up all the rope in Los Angeles."

Of emotion, McKay bluntly stated that if it won football games, he would start his wife, Corky.

THE PERFECT SEASON

A new chapter in the tradition of Troy

In 1962, the Trojans would ascend to the heights of glory. McKay would be vindicated. Hollywood front-runners would show up to cheer them on. The season certainly did not hold high hopes in the beginning, though. A mere 26,400 fans showed up at the L.A. Memorial Coliseum for the season opener against eighth-ranked Duke. A national TV audience was surprised to see the Trojans prevail, 14–7.

The team was just that, a team. There were no huge superstars, no Heisman hopefuls. Terry Baker, a quarterback from the L.A. area, would win it that year for Oregon State.

The captain of the team was Marv Marinovich, and out of this the Trojan family would expand. Marinovich would go on to marry sophomore quarterback Craig Fertig's sister. Marinovich's brother would become the football coach at Bishop Amat High School, where his star players would be McKay's sons, J. K. and Richie, quarterback Pat Haden, and future UCLA Rose Bowl MVP John Sciarra. Marinovich and Fertig's sister would have a son, Todd, who would break all of Haden's California state passing records, and then all of USC's hearts—but not until after he would lead USC to victory in the 1990 Rose Bowl over Michigan.

Fertig was part of a talented trio of signal-callers: Pete Beathard and Bill Nelsen were the others. Somehow, they were able to work together as a unit without problems.

"I remember Pete Beathard and I were the first two quarterbacks he recruited, and he told us we could play baseball," Fertig recalled in *The History of USC Football* DVD. "He's a catcher and I'm a pitcher and like I said, his first year didn't go so well. But his freshman team went undefeated.

"So one day we're on the baseball field and McKay's secretary comes out and says to Coach Dedeaux, 'Coach McKay'd like to see Beathard and Fertig.'

"Well, I just looked at Beathard and said, 'What'd you do?' And he said, 'I'm your roommate; I haven't left your sight.' So we go on up to McKay's office and he's reading the sports section, and all you can see is the cigar smoke comin' from behind it, and he says, 'You guys aren't real good at either sport, *make a decision.*' I cleaned that up for you, too. That's when we decided to be football players."

USC brought an integrated team to Dallas for game two. A mere 14,000 showed up to see them defeat Southern Methodist, 33–3. Ranked number six, they won a defensive struggle over Iowa, 7–0. Cal came to L.A. and lost, 32–6. After winning at Illinois and beating number nine Washington, the peculiar fandom of Los Angeles was aroused.

Ticket manager John Morley found himself rising at three in the morning to meet the demands of alumni he had not heard from "in ten years." Typical L.A. The Trojans realized they had something good going on when they made all three columns of the *Los Angeles Times* in one day.

"We knew we had a good football team," said All-American end Hal Bedsole, "but no one felt that it was a national championship caliber team—you don't think of things like that before a season, anyway."

The Washington victory vaulted them to number two. Wins over Stanford, then Roger Staubach and Navy, had them thinking about it. They were number one heading into the UCLA game. McKay did it in an unusual way, alternating Beathard and Nelsen. Fertig was number three but considered part of the mix, too. As the season wore on, though, Fertig asked and received permission to play some at wide receiver, just so he could get in games.

Both Beathard and Nelsen would achieve success in professional football, Beathard at Houston and Nelsen with Cleveland.

"Beathard was as fine an athlete as played college football," said Bedsole.

The team did not approach games with the expectation of putting a lot of points on the board, although as the offense synchronized, they became much more potent than they had been at the beginning of the year.

"I know we're playing a lot better defense," McKay told the press. "I feel our defense against Iowa forced them into a good many errors. You've got to be stubborn to win against top competition, and stubbornness should begin on defense."

"We beat the Bruins for the Rose Bowl 14–3 with a great comeback," Bedsole said. "They were ahead 3–0 in the last five minutes, and then Brown made a miraculous catch near the goal line and they turned the ball over and we scored again."

A crowd of 86,740 watched Troy earn a trip to Pasadena. Of course, beating Notre Dame was still a task that lay ahead.

"It's like the poker player," McKay told his team. "He's won all the money, and then somebody challenges him to a showdown, all or nothing."

On the game's third play, Beathard swung a pass to Willie Brown who gained thirty-four yards to the Irish 18. Fullback Ben Wilson, weighing 228 pounds, went for eight, then three plays later leaped over the pile to make it 7–0. John Underwood of

Sports Illustrated wrote that the game was USC's from that moment forward. Whenever Notre Dame made an adjustment, USC countered. Notre Dame coach Joe Kuharich's squad kept shooting themselves in the foot with penalties and mistakes. McKay went conservative in the second half.

The 25–0 win set up one of the greatest Rose Bowl shoot-outs of all time. It would be a game against Wisconsin that totally went against the ebb and flow of USC's season. They would be outplayed, according to some, but they would survive and leave with the national championship.

The number two Badgers came in talkin' loud, full of Big 10 bravado. The press was with them, too. Quarterback Ron VanderKelen was the best in the country. It was not a typical bulldozing Big 10 bunch. Wisconsin played pro-style passing football. McKay was scared to death of them, although nobody knew it at the time.

An audience of 98,698 packed the Rose Bowl to see two 10–0 teams. According to Bedsole, McKay's approach to the game was quite extraordinary by today's standards. The team approached the contest "like it was an exhibition. That was the atmosphere . . . a kind of picnic." The team did not use their allotted practice day. McKay, possibly using psychology, said that the honor was just to be there.

After the Tournament of Roses honored America's recent breakthrough in the "Space Race" with the Soviets, USC exploded like a rocket ship. Bedsole made two touchdown catches, including a leaping grab in the corner of the end zone. He also was called for three personal fouls.

"You were supposed to get thrown out after two," he recalled. "For some reason the officials blew it."

Wisconsin was screaming bloody murder as Troy built up a 42–14 lead. On the sidelines, the team was celebrating early.

"Everybody just wanted to know where the party was after the game," said McKay.

Penalties piled up. Marv Marinovich punched a Badger player and was thrown out. Wisconsin got fired up. McKay, a class act who never ran it up on opponents, wanted to lay off. He went to the ground, choosing to let the clock wind down.

"He didn't want to embarrass these people," Bedsole said.

The game would take three hours and five minutes, a long one in those days, and end in darkness. The Trojans had sustained a series of strange injuries prior to the game. While none of that appeared to make a difference in the first half, it all came to roost in the second half.

The defensive line and the secondary were depleted, allowing VanderKelen to make adjustments and pick them apart.

"We had an interior line with no experience, no pass rush, and VanderKelen had all day to throw," said Bedsole. "We got tired . . . and it got dark."

In the fourth quarter, VanderKelen completed eight of ten passes to orchestrate a long drive, resulting in a thirteen-yard strike to Lou Holland. A Wilson fumble gave

Wisconsin the ball on the USC 29. VanderKelen followed with another quick scoring strike. Suddenly 42-14 was 42–28 and nerves were twitching.

Wisconsin held. VanderKelen struck again, only to have Willie Brown intercept him in the end zone. It looked to be over, but USC got thrown for a safety. Two points to the Badgers and their ball, trailing 42–30. VanderKelen led them back, hitting Pat Richter to make it 42-37. Two minutes remained.

The Trojans just barely managed to hold onto the football and run out the clock. Afterward, there were some accusations about Big 10 officials failing to call Wisconsin for holding during VanderKelen's drives. As it was, the game was marred by penalties throughout, as well as fistfights and general bad sportsmanship.

In the locker room, USC filed in silently, with their heads down. It was quite an unreal scene for a team that had just finished a perfect season, clinching the national title.

"Get your heads up," McKay told them.

When Bedsole teamed with VanderKelen on the Minnesota Vikings, the former Badger star confessed that it was only because McKay had called off the dogs that Wisconsin had a chance to get back in it.

"You could have scored fifty or sixty points on our defense," he told Bedsole.

When a reporter asked Brown what happened, the Trojan star replied testily, "We won, that's what happened."

"We came in number one," McKay assessed. "They came in number two and lost. That makes us number one."

The 1963 Rose Bowl was a turning point in the modern development of football. The NFL was still playing a ground-oriented game, resulting in low-scoring defensive struggles. The new AFL was opening up the game, led by genius offensive minds like Oakland's Al Davis, Dallas's (then Kansas City's) Hank Stram, and San Diego's Sid Gilman.

The USC-Wisconsin shoot-out was the college version of the AFL long before anybody called it the "West Coast offense." While Wisconsin's passing schemes were new, so too were McKay's formations on both sides of the ball.

"John started the I formation and made it popular; he revolutionized the game," said former Arkansas coach Frank Broyles on *The History of USC Football* DVD.

"The 'monster defense' was made up by Frank Broyles at the University of Arkansas," said McKay, "and it always had what we call in the terminology a 'strong safety' up one side or the other on the wide side of the field. I said we should get a formation shift away from it and run to the weak side of the defense, which we did in 1962. We won eleven games and won the national championship. In all honesty our guys taught me more about it than anybody else. Our tailback said, 'Put me farther back, I can see better.'"

"Almost everybody on that team was from California," said Assistant Coach Dave Levy. "We spent almost no money on recruiting. No one was from out of state, but that group was a pleasure and we had some super athletes; it wasn't by accident."

"We weren't in the Top 20; we were unrated," said Fertig. "We beat Duke 14–0, beat Hayden Fry; I scored my first touchdown against a young Hayden Fry. We beat UCLA 14–3 to set ourselves up and we still have one other game against Notre Dame, and we beat 'em 25–0, and what a thrill it was to go to the Rose Bowl."

"We had given up fifty-four points in eleven games," said McKay. "So I said after we scored three or four touchdowns, I said, 'This game's over.' We get ahead 42–14."

"John calls me over to the sideline," said Bedsole. "He said, 'Go and tell Pete to run the ball and let's just run the clock out and not embarrass their coach.' Milt Groom was a nice guy he'd known a long time. It backfired and before we know it, they were throwing on every down. They abandoned their offense and we're chasing 'em down."

"One thing that disturbs me is that you'd think from reading articles that Wisconsin won the game, but we beat 'em up for three quarters and totally controlled the game," Beathard said. "But yes, in the fourth quarter we were trying to get on the bus and go to the postgame party."

"For forty years I had to live with the fact that we won but people remember Wisconsin coming back, but we in fact won," said Bedsole. "If we did to them what we were capable of, I think the '62 team would be considered one of the best of all time, not just the team that started the John McKay era."

The oddity of the game was its juxtaposition with the rest of the season. Here was a team that had played conservatively, winning low-scoring games with great defense. Suddenly, they found themselves opening up on offense, but their defense (albeit beset by injuries, penalties, and ejections) was a sieve.

The press made a big deal over USC's first national championship since 1939, and first unbeaten season since 1932, especially in light of the fact that Dr. Topping had upgraded the admissions standards. After the "payola" scandals of the 1950s, a decision had been made to increase USC's academic prestige and not place so much emphasis on sports. Interestingly, this decision would presage the school's all-time greatest sports era, which was a nice testament to college athletics, or at least to the way USC handles it.

McKay had struggled with Clark's recruits. He had fully integrated his program with black players, earning the nation's respect as a recruiter and tactician. He also earned himself a nice contract renewal with a raise. Furthermore, McKay's jaunty personality, which fell on deaf ears when the team struggled, now made him a quipster and press favorite.

McKay was lauded for finding positions for his players, for recruiting for athleticism, not by position. Washington and UCLA also were strong. The scandal was now a thing of the distant past. UCLA had beaten Ohio State earlier in the season. Three West Coast teams ranked in the top eight at one point in the season. Wisconsin held the number two position in the final polls. Bedsole and linebacker Damon Bame made All-American.

The junior Bedsole had come to SC out of Pierce J.C. in the Valley. Nicknamed

"Prince Hal," Bedsole played for the Minnesota Vikings. Bame was another junior college transfer, from Glendale Community College. He was a two-time All-American left guard-linebacker at 5'11", 192 pounds.

Jim Bates was picked by the Bears, Wilson by the Rams, Mike Bundra by the Lions, and Marinovich by the Rams in the NFL Draft. In the AFL Draft, Frank Buncom, Bates, and Wilson went to the Chargers, and Ben Charles to the Bills.

FERTIG-TO-SHERMAN

"84-Z delay" beats the Irish

1964 would prove to be memorable, yet bittersweet. The Trojan quarterback was Craig Fertig, a senior out of Huntington Park High School. Fertig is a colorful figure in Trojan history who would go on to become an assistant coach under McKay, a head coach at Oregon State, a longtime Fox Sports football analyst with Tom Kelly, a fixture on the alumni banquet circuit, and the host of USC campus tours. He is, in many ways, the "face" of USC.

Fertig was always a guy who liked to have fun, enjoyed partying, and had an eye for the ladies.

"Lemme tell ya the difference between the Cal quarterback and the SC quarterback," Fertig remarked, referencing All-American Golden Bear signal caller Craig Morton, a contemporary who also enjoyed a good time. "Well, he had a girlfriend, a really beautiful girl from Santa Monica, a cheerleader. Well, lemme tell ya, the SC quarterback was takin' care of that, if ya know what I mean."

Fertig had waited his turn while Beathard and Nelsen were draped in the glory of a national title. The 1964 schedule was grueling again. A disappointing 39,173 showed up at the Coliseum to see Southern California beat Colorado, 21–0, but USC shocked number two Oklahoma, 40–14, at Tinker Field in Norman. Elevated from unranked to number two, the Trojans could not figure out who they were. Michigan State beat them, 17–7, at East Lansing. Texas A&M fell, 31–7, but number two Ohio State dominated them, 17–0, at Columbus.

They beat Cal but lost to Washington. After beating Stanford they went into the last two games with a shot at the Rose Bowl. Running back Mike Garrett rushed for 181 yards, and Fertig passed for three scores to lead Southern California over UCLA, 34–13.

The stage was set for the anointing of Notre Dame's expected national championship on November 28. The Irish had not captured the crown since 1949. The 1950s and early '60s had been down years in South Bend, although they had given USC all they could handle. But Northwestern's Ara Parseghian took over that year. At first, little was expected of him.

The Irish quarterback was an unknown senior who had not started. John Huarte and his favorite receiver, Jack Snow, had grown up in Orange County, which is "Trojan country," but they had gone to Notre Dame. In the summers they had worked on pass routes on Orange County's beaches. In 1964 they put the practice to good use.

Notre Dame surprisingly went through their first nine games undefeated, earning them the number one ranking. Huarte was just dripping with Notre Dame polish. The best quarterback in America that year was Alabama senior Joe Willie Namath, but Namath injured his knee in the seventh game of the season. That gave Huarte the inside track to become Notre Dame's sixth Heisman Trophy winner.

Up until 1964, USC had not yet won any Heismans. By 2004, Southern California quarterback Matt Leinart would be *his school's* sixth Heisman winner. He would also be the second from Mater Dei High School in Orange County. Huarte was Mater Dei's first. There are only two high schools in the country that have produced two Heisman winners (the other: Woodrow Wilson High of Dallas with Davey O'Brien and Tim Brown). When Leinart won the 2004 Heisman, Huarte, a Southern California businessman, donated his Heisman to Mater Dei for display. Coach Bruce Rollinson was delighted to have the unbelievable recruiting tool of multiple Heismans associated with the Monarch program. Fertig probably was hoping his nephew, Todd, would be one of those Heisman winners, but he transferred out of Mater Dei after his freshman year and never earned the trophy in his star-crossed USC career.

Huarte would also be paid an enormous bonus by the New York Titans (later Jets) of the American Football League. He would not make it in New York. The Titans would pay even more bonus dollars ($400,000) to Namath, who would make it.

But on that November day of 1964, the best quarterback in America was not Huarte, Namath, Craig Morton, or any of the other more-heralded signal callers of the year. It certainly did not look that way at first.

McKay had played it cool with the press, deferring to Parseghian, making pessimistic statements like, "Notre Dame can't be beat," that the best they could hope was to "definitely make a first down."

Notre Dame's 262-pound and 245-pound tackles could not be blocked. A pregame steak dinner was his "last meal." It went on like that. Parseghian would not have any of it. Neither did Fertig, who was just itching to get at these guys. All that Notre Dame glamour was giving the Trojans a bad taste in their mouths.

With his team safely removed from the press, McKay outlined to his team a seemingly odd strategy, based on using Mike Garrett between the tackles. He hoped to block down the tackles and take it to their linebackers, who he saw as their weak links. If Garrett could establish the run, then Fertig would be able to take to the air. If, if, if . . .

USC advance scout Mel Hein had the Irish thoroughly scouted. The unspoken understanding at USC was that the Irish were good but a little overrated. Just being Notre Dame, they were subject to this kind of adulation. They were fourteen-point road favorites, a very high prediction against a good Trojan club, their biggest rival, only two years removed from a national title of their own.

McKay also knew that his reputation would be cemented on this day. Either he could beat Notre Dame or he could not. Beating them when they were ranked number one would prove his place. He had an open date after the UCLA game to prepare.

None of USC's plans or hopes appeared to amount to a hill of beans when Huarte started to shred the USC defense. He hit on eleven of fifteen attempts for 176 yards in the first half. He spotted Snow for a touchdown, a field goal was good, and another drive ended with Bill Worski's run into the end zone.

Despite the 17–0 halftime deficit, Garrett had run well against Notre Dame on the inside. In the history of college football, the greatest *halftime* coach may well be McKay. He had a serene confidence, an ability to make adjustments, a way of conveying calmness to his team that is not matched.

"Our game plan is working," he told the Trojans. "Keep doing your stuff, and we'll get some points."

In the other locker room, Parseghian told the Irish, "Just thirty minutes of football separates you from a national championship." While true, the words conveyed a sense of "running out the clock." Parseghian was one of the best coaches ever, but this kind of thinking, which was exemplified on several high-profile occasions, costs him legacy points.

What McKay wanted was an early third quarter score. Notre Dame had run their schedule with ease. McKay felt that "if we can make this thing close, they might not know how to react."

Garrett was just the tonic USC needed, opening up nice gains behind good blocking, then allowing Fertig to hit wide receiver Rod Sherman over the middle. When Garrett ran it in, the 17–7 score looked a lot different to Notre Dame than 17–0. With 83,840 Coliseum faithful exploding with pent-up emotion, they found their plans taking a turn.

It all may have gone for naught but for a fumble by Notre Dame on the Southern California 9. Notre Dame started to press after that. Penalties went against them, including a touchdown-nullifying flag. Suddenly, they were in "prevent" mode, just hoping to hold on.

Fertig lit up the Los Angeles sky on an eighty-two-yard drive. Fred Hill's catch made it 17–14.

"I knew we had 'em," McKay later said of his attitude at that point. "The momentum was all ours. In a situation like that, the number one rating is a fairly suffocating thing."

Huarte was unable to sustain a drive. Jack Snow's punt to Mike Garrett was returned eighteen yards to the Notre Dame 35. Two minutes and ten seconds remained. The Coliseum was awash in noise and emotion, a cacophony of sound. There are many large stadiums in America. Ohio Stadium. Michigan Stadium. South Bend, Yankee Stadium, Fenway Park. Crowds in these cities are boisterous and crazy. L.A. fans have a well-deserved reputation for being laid back. USC's backers, while loyal and among the best alumni in the world, are often well heeled and quiet compared to the crazies at Florida State, LSU, or any of two dozen other venues. *However*, with that being said, those who have experienced the Coliseum at full throttle, when all is on the line usually against Notre Dame or UCLA, these people describe a tidal wave of sound and excitement that matches if not exceeds any atmosphere in America. So it was that day in '64.

A field goal, of course, would tie. Many coaches in the days before overtime play were rightfully criticized for "playing it safe." Two years later, Parseghian would do just that against Michigan State. His career is tarnished by it. McKay never thought about ties. On this day, he further calculated that he needed a win, even though the game was not conference action, in order to sway the league into choosing his team to represent them in the Rose Bowl.

Garrett carried for nothing. Fertig called time. McKay called Craig the "best pure passer in college football," a huge compliment for a man whose contemporaries included Morton, Huarte, Namath, and Roger Staubach. Maybe McKay was a little biased, but the point is that he had confidence in the guy who was "like a son" to him.

When action resumed, Fertig nailed Fred Hill on a down-and-out pattern for twenty-three yards. With a first down at the Irish 17, anything could happen. For the Trojans, a field goal was not an option.

After another time-out, Fertig hit Garrett, who stopped the clock when he went out of bounds at the 15. Fertig then went for broke, appearing to have Hill in the end zone, but the receiver was ruled to have caught it out of bounds. A third down try missed, so now the world was on Fertig's shoulders. Forty-three seconds remained. The field goal unit was noplace to be found.

Sherman told McKay he wanted to try "84-Z delay." He would split wide to the left, delay one second after the snap, sprint ahead for five steps, fake outside, then cut sharply down and across the middle. Fertig would just have to avoid a sack, trusting that his man would be where he was supposed to be.

"I watched the way their halfback reacted and I figured that I could beat him," Sherman said.

Sherman juked Tony Carey and Fertig hit him chest high. Fifteen yards. Touchdown. The Coliseum exploded. Sherman and Fertig would live off this moment for time immemorial.

"Beat Michigan" in the Rose Bowl was scrawled on the locker room blackboard when the team returned full of triumph. USC and Oregon State had identical conference records of 3–1.

"We beat the number one team in the country," Fertig said, "and Oregon State, God bless 'em, beat Idaho, 7–6, so they went."

News of the decision hit McKay at a postgame celebratory dinner. Silence ensued, until Jess Hill announced, "As far as I'm concerned, this is one of the rankest injustices ever perpetrated in the field of intercollegiate athletics."

Fertig the witticist tried to get up a pool so the Trojans could go to Oregon and play the Beavers.

MIKE GARRETT: POET-WARRIOR

*USC embodies a new era and the Heisman finds a home
at University Park*

Growing up on the tough streets of L.A.'s Boyle Heights, Mike Garrett knew that his key to success would be football, but that it was a means to an end that would be the *real* key to his success: education.

"If it hadn't been for football, I'd have been a bum," he said. Listening to tapes of a young Garrett speak, one finds this hard to believe. Even as a youthful football player, he was comfortable with the press, speaking articulately while handling himself with class. By no means did he ever give off the aura of some guy who could play sports but was out of his element in an academic atmosphere. Garrett was a guy with a social conscience and a slightly rebellious streak.

The first Super Bowl, known then as the AFL-NFL Championship Game, was held at the Coliseum in 1967. It has gone down in history as a big moment in pro football history, and one of the most well covered by the media. Old footage of the game and surrounding events survives in countless NFL Films archives. Some of that footage is of a half-dressed Kansas City Chief rookie, Mike Garrett, lamenting his team's sound thumping at the hands of Green Bay. Garrett appears to be thoughtful, gracious, and conciliatory. Five years removed from Jefferson High and one year removed from USC, it is *not* the image of a man who would ever have become "a bum."

"I had a long conversation with Garrett and Willie Brown," said former USC assistant coach Dave Levy, who had been Brown's coach at Long Beach Poly High before coming to USC. "I told them that they owed it to other black kids to make the most of the opportunity football gave them, through education, to pave the way for others."

Garrett then decided he wanted to live off-campus. He wanted to rent an apartment in Pasadena. Pasadena was the hometown of Jackie Robinson, but the city—at least the section where Garrett wanted to live—did not "rent to blacks," according to Levy. Garrett vented to his coach.

"I just told him that instead of getting mad at white people," Levy said, "he just had to stay with it, to give people a chance to change, and in time it would happen. He nodded and came to agree with that."

Garrett was also a baseball star for Rod Dedeaux's team. He would play briefly in the Los Angeles Dodgers organization. At USC, he roomed with a young pitcher from Fresno named Tom Seaver. Seaver had been unrecruited out of Fresno High, so he joined the Marines, where he grew in height and in physical strength. After the Marines, with his newfound physical maturity, he had starred at Fresno City College and with the Alaska Goldpanners, earning a baseball scholarship from Rod Dedeaux.

The friendship of Seaver, the mentoring of Dave Levy and Marv Goux, the father figure John McKay; through these experiences and associations Mike Garrett's manhood was formed. He was a man who took the team on his shoulders, too.

After USC beat Colorado, 21–0, in 1964, Garrett made a point of apologizing to his linemen for missing holes they opened for him. Garrett might have been described as a scatback because of his size, speed, and moves, but he was willing to hit and run "between the tackles," which was the key to winning the 1964 Notre Dame game. In three years, Garrett rushed for an astonishing 3,221 yards, more than Jim Brown, Ernie Davis, "Mr. Inside and Mr. Outside" at Army (Glenn Davis, Doc Blanchard), or any other collegiate runner.

Garrett also caught passes for 399 yards, occasionally threw the ball (48 yards), and was a potent threat returning punts and kicks. In 1965 he rushed for 1,440 yards.

"I don't think anything is more exciting than winning the Heisman," he said. It turned Garrett into a prized rookie who weighed competing offers from the Rams, who made him their first pick, and the Kansas City Chiefs of the AFL. Garrett, who had never known his father, and whose mother worked as a domestic while raising her son in a $36 per month housing project, now had the things he had always wanted but never had. Garrett, however, once said, "I didn't know then that I was poor."

Garrett made some runs that McKay said "could (not) be made, yet Mike made it." Garrett was the ultimate team player, too. There was no sense of prima donna to him. He practiced hard, exhibiting leadership qualities as befitting his role as captain. He was not USC's first black captain by any means, however. Willie Wood (1959) and Willie Brown (1962) had helped pave the way for black players like Garrett.

McKay once said that Garrett was a complete football player who would have been his best linebacker or guard and "might have been my best quarterback" if he had been installed at those positions instead. Garrett never would have complained.

The night before the Heisman Trophy winner was to be announced, Garrett lay in bed thinking it over. The more he thought about it, the more confident he became that he deserved it. Early the next morning he got the call congratulating him from USC's sports information director.

Garrett had just the right amount of bravado. When he won the Heisman, he said that the previous black Heisman winner, Ernie Davis, "was a great man." He later stated that winning it is "like winning a Pulitzer Prize. You don't have to worry about anything else once you've won that Pulitzer." But when held to fifty-seven yards by Notre Dame, he said, "All I was thinking about was getting off the ground. That's where I was most of the time." Garrett was always thanking his linemen, a trait that O. J. Simpson learned from him.

Garrett's records would be broken by O.J., but he had broken the marks set by the likes of Morley Drury (1,163 yards in a season, 1927), Orv Mohler (career total of 2,025 rushing yards from 1930–1932), and Jim Musick (219 carries from 1929–1931). Garrett had 3,269 yards in total offense, eclipsing the record set by his teammate, Pete Beathard. He was described as being like trying to tackle "a bowling ball." Against UCLA in 1965 he ran for 210 yards. Like other class acts before and after him, he entered the UCLA locker room to congratulate the Bruins after they won.

"He darn near had me bawling," said UCLA's great halfback Mel Farr.

"He's the greatest runner I've ever seen," said the Bruins' Dallas Grider. The day had been a tough one, though. Despite his yards, Garrett had coughed up the football at crucial times in the 20–16 defeat, costing Troy a trip to the Rose Bowl. It was a disappointing last game for an SC Heisman winner, not unlike Reggie Bush's game (which included a costly fumble) against Texas in the 2006 Rose Bowl.

McKay was near tears himself after the game, one of his all-time low moments. Part of his disappointment was for Garrett. Garrett would be smiling, however, when he became the first California collegiate player ever to win the Heisman.

When Garrett won the Heisman, he said he would invite "every one in Boyle Heights," a gritty midtown L.A. neighborhood, to "come take a look."

Garrett broke the NCAA career rushing record previously held by Ollie Matson of the University of San Francisco from 1949 to 1951. Garrett had taken that tradition one step further. Using McKay's famed Student Body Right and beginning with Garrett, USC truly became "Tailback U."

JUICE

The glory days of the star-crossed O. J. Simpson

In 1966, John McKay was notable—and noble—in defeat. First, after losing to Notre Dame at the Coliseum, 51–0, he told the inquiring press, "A billion Chinamen couldn't care less who won this game." This statement was probably uttered in response to news reports about Red China's rapid population growth in association with Chairman Mao's embarkation of the "Cultural Revolution," a ten-year reign of terror that started in '66.

A little over a month later, McKay went for a two-point conversion against Bob Griese and Purdue in the Rose Bowl. He failed, but received great praise for his "gunslinger" style, choosing to go for a win instead of a tie, which Ara Parseghian had done against Michigan State earlier in the season. McKay would rather have the win than the praise, and in 1967 he brought in a player who would help him achieve that goal.

What is there to say about Orenthal James "O. J." Simpson—Trojan legend, NFL record-breaker, Hollywood celebrity, infamous "criminal"—that has not already been said!?

O. J. is one of those people in American society who is instantly recognizable by his first name—as in *Michael* Jordan—or by his initials, as in his case. That is the way it was when he was a mere college junior. The familiarity reflected nothing but a positive glow on this American icon for decades . . . until June 13, 1994.

O. J. is at once a source of some, if not the greatest, pride in the history of USC sports. For that very reason, his fall from grace caused great anguish, embarrassment, and public humiliation for the school that made him and then suffered because of him. O. J.'s murder accusation and subsequent trial came on the heels of the L.A. riots (1992) and a major earthquake in Northridge (1994). USC's football team had fallen into mediocrity. A stray bullet from a drive-by shooting that struck a player (injuring him but not seriously) in practice just added to the feeling that the paint was peeling on the school and the city.

■ ■ ■

When he carried the football forty-two times, McKay was questioned about it.

"The ball's not heavy," McKay drawled, "and he's not in a union."

It was a more personable variation on Paul Brown's theory regarding Jim Brown.

"When you have a big gun," said Coach Brown, "you shoot it."

"If you don't have O. J. carrying thirty-five to forty times a game," said McKay, "it would be like having Joe DiMaggio on your team and only letting him go to bat once a game."

"He was big, six-twoish, lean, and ran a legit nine-four in the 100-*yard* dash, he was a national class sprinter, a smart runner, durable," said Levy on *The History of USC Football* DVD. "You can't ask for more."

"It's no wonder he fit perfectly in McKay's I formation, carrying thirty to forty times a game, and he was fabulous," said Garrett.

Out of the I formation, Simpson was a whirling dervish who had everything. At 6'2", 207 pounds, he possessed enough size, strength, and attitude to bowl defenders over in Brown's fashion, but he was faster than Brown, with incredible moves both between the tackles and in the open field. Against UCLA he managed to carry four Bruins on his back for the better part of ten yards into the end zone. Simpson's all-time play was called "22-23 blast." It was a quick opener, like most of McKay's schemes not fancy, based on his speedy finding of the hole. He averaged thirty-two carries per game over two years and dealt with pain, but he was tough as nails. He also perfected the art of the slow recovery after the tackle.

Simpson would act like a man on his last legs, meandering on back to the huddle as if unable to walk another step. It was half-real, half-fake. When the next play started, though, he was off to the races.

Simpson led USC to the 1967 national championship. He finished behind UCLA quarterback Gary Beban in the Heisman Trophy balloting, but that was a joke. Beban was a senior and Simpson a junior college transfer, but Simpson stood so far head and shoulders above Beban that it should not have been close.

He won the Heisman in 1968 and set national records for yards gained in a season (1,880 in 1968) and in a career (3,540, more than any three- or four-year careers prior to his). He scored thirty-six touchdowns.

Simpson was an Olympic-quality sprinter on USC's national championship track team, running a spectacular 9.4 100-yard dash. By the time he left, the media was strongly recommending that in the one hundred years that college football had been played through the 1968 season, O. J. was the greatest player who had ever lived. This of course took into consideration such stalwarts as Jim Thorpe of Carlisle, Red Grange of Illinois, Doc Blanchard and Glenn Davis of Army, Doak Walker of Southern Methodist, Billy Cannon of Louisiana State, Roger Staubach of Navy, or a host of other contenders. He was the future of football, the new breed, something never quite seen before.

Opposing players were in awe of his ability but had only praise for his demeanor. He congratulated opponents on good hits, called them by their first names, never spiked the ball, never "got in people's faces."

Sportswriters were equally impressed. Many stated simply that he was the "nicest," the "most gracious," and the "easiest to talk to" of any athlete they ever dealt with. Simpson gave of his time, whether the writer was with the *Los Angeles Times*, *Sports Illustrated*, or the student newspaper of that week's opponent. Despite having grown up in a ghetto, Simpson quickly belied questions of his intelligence, which had been raised because of his mediocre high school grades.

Simpson displayed intellect, articulation, and ease of language. He showed humility and intelligence on a wide range of subject matter. It was a complete reversal of the caricature that USC's detractors had made of him coming in. It dispelled all the myths about his character.

When Simpson won the Heisman, he went above and beyond the call of duty in praising his teammates, his coaches, and, above all else, his *linemen!*

"I want to emphasize that this is a team award, and the guys on the team won it as much or more than I did," Simpson said at his news conference. This is a truer statement than many people realize. The Heisman is very much a team award, and is won by a program. Credit is due even to that school's sports information department. It is much less individualistic in nature than the professional Most Valuable Player awards. The Heisman is a major factor in upgrading a program's prestige among the press, recruits, and the historians judging their place in the pantheon of greatness.

When O. J. was at USC, his initials became a catchphrase. A popular chain of orange juice stores came into being. They made a tasty concoction of oranges and ice cream, calling it "Orange Julius." It quickly was shortened by patrons to "O. J." Whether the store was named after the player or the player was named after the store is a bit confusing to this day, but the "Juice" part stuck. Simpson occasionally signed his autographs "O. Jay Simpson," but newspaper headlines quickly threw in the "Juice" appellation when describing USC's winning ways.

Despite O. J.'s physical stature, he had been sickly as a young boy because he lacked calcium in his bones, possibly suffering from rickets. Another great African American athlete of the era, Cardinal pitching ace Bob Gibson, had dealt with similar disabilities as a kid, but both men had grown to the heights of physical greatness.

It is important to note the importance of sports among black kids, which gets to the heart of why integrating Southern colleges became so important. In O. J.'s case, having grown up near Candlestick Park, he gravitated toward the Giants, a team in the early 1960s known for having excellent black and Latino stars. O. J.'s idol was the great center fielder, Willie Mays. Mays would give of his time to the young black kids hanging around the park. O. J. was one of them.

O. J. had the good fortune of getting good advice. His coach at Galileo, Larry McInerny, talked him into believing he could play college football instead of joining the Army.

"You'll never get anywhere letting people give you stuff," people told him, and O. J. took it to heart.

When O. J. starred at CCSF, Mays got involved.

"You have an unusual talent," he told the kid.

O. J. rushed for 2,552 yards and 54 touchdowns (national records) at City College. He carried 17 times for 304 yards against San Jose City College, with scoring runs of 73, 58, 14, 88, and 16 yards, plus 27 on a pass play!

Marv Goux was straight with him. Despite his talents, Goux did not fawn all over him as so many recruiters did. He recognized O. J. had a sense of pride about his ability to fend for himself, developed on the streets but nurtured by coaches along the way. Goux told him he would have to earn his chance to play at USC. The program recruited superstars from all over the country. Rumor has it that one player from Texas was as talented as O. J. but did not have his drive. According to the story, McKay spotted him picking daisies during an on-field team meeting. The kid, who by then saw that O. J. was "the man," was quickly gone from the scene.

O. J. enjoyed "straight talk," not being "jived to." Goux was the king of straight talk.

Regarding other schools, "they were offering me everything in the world," he recalled. "I'd get this and that, be first string, everything. But Marv Goux, an assistant at USC, made it clear."

"We aren't going to offer you a darned thing," Goux told him. "We'll give you the chance to play for Southern Cal and become a Trojan. I watched you play and if you want you can star there. But you'll have to work. You're the one who has to make it your own way."

O. J. liked what he heard and "when I got there, the fellows I met impressed me. All of them were All-Americans."

"When he first got here and ran inside," said McKay, "he fumbled too often." O. J. was not used to the hot Southern California sun after growing up in foggy San Francisco. He later recalled practices under McKay and Goux as resembling a Marine training camp.

"Two guys held big, five-foot-long bags," Simpson later said. "They gave you a stiff belt as you took off. You banged through with power. Another big bag was about two yards away. Now you must turn light-footed. They then threw heavy air bags at your feet and knees. You learned to hit, elude, and make moves on the defensive backs."

"He kept at and at it, as if to say: 'This is where I am going to make my name,'" said McKay. What McKay and his staff were successful in doing was turning O. J. from a strictly broken-field runner to a power back who could hit the holes.

A 49–0 win over Washington State marked O. J.'s entry into big-time collegiate football.

Simpson's second game had national championship implications when 67,705 came to the Coliseum to watch a night game against the fifth-ranked Texas Longhorns. Texas wanted revenge, for the 1966 loss in Austin and perhaps even for the C. R. Roberts 44–20 game of 1956. Prior to the game, McKay got more involved than the usual impassive, sit-in-the-cart role he normally played. McKay the perfectionist began to see that "perfection," such as it is, could be attained. He pushed the players and his staff hard.

McKay uncharacteristically engaged players on the practice field, shaming some, kicking them off the field for their "failures" to "show" him anything. "Super Bill" Bradley was back. Tailback Chris Gilbert gave McKay cause to worry.

McKay could not help but get excited over what he saw in Simpson. He favorably compared his young tailback to the Bears' Gale Sayers, an unreal act of hyperbole that had the added virtue of being true. McKay told it like he saw it.

"Simpson is the fastest big man who has ever played football," McKay added. "There are some guys for whom they have made up times, but who never could achieve them if they were tested. Simpson is legitimate. "

Of Ron Yary, McKay said he was "as good as I've ever seen," and at 6'6", 255 pounds, Yary was a monster of the day.

McKay switched his psychology on and off each day during the week of the Texas game. He praised and cajoled, yelled and screamed. On Friday night, he switched gears and stated that Texas was "far better." Then he followed that up by stating that while nobody was *supposed* to run on Texas, that was precisely his intention. It was a replay of his reply to Frank Broyles's comment that "you can't run on Texas."

"Yes, I will," was still McKay's mantra.

Texas arrived at the Coliseum like a nor'easter, full of bluster and wind. They scored first, but USC, led by O. J., struck back to tie it up. It was 7–7 at the half. McKay, the ultimate midgame coach, went to the blackboard and diagrammed a more open second half approach utilizing the amazing speed of wideout Earl McCullough, an Olympic-caliber sprinter. First, quarterback Steve Sogge (subbing for the injured Toby Page) drew Texas in with short passes to the tight ends. McCullough could either be thrown to or made into a decoy. Then, what to do about Simpson? George Patton used to exhort his officers during battle to "hold 'em by the nose then kick 'em in the ass." McKay had a similar attitude: "You ran in. They could hardly walk in. Now's the time to put it to them."

It was too much for the Longhorns to handle. Tim Rossovich began to penetrate the Texas line, putting pressure on the Texas backfield. Mike Battle was on their receivers. Sogge was efficient.

O. J. was outstanding, carrying thirty times for 164 yards in a stirring 17–13 Trojan win.

"I doubt if there is a back with more ability than Simpson in the country," said Texas coach Darrell Royal afterward.

In a 30–0 pasting of Stanford, Simpson ran for 163 yards. USC was now ranked first.

"Winning the number one spot was in the back of our minds," said Sogge. "Even though you don't shoot for the national championship, it's always there."

Simpson's legend, like many of Notre Dame's opponents over the years, was made against the Irish. It turned him into an All-American and a Heisman contender, rare for a junior, unheard-of in a J.C. transfer. Despite the hoopla surrounding him and his team, the "intimidation factor" that is South Bend in autumn—with "Touchdown Jesus" framed behind the goalposts, the crowd noise, and the weight of twenty-eight years of bad memories—was enough to make the Trojans the underdogs.

"Intercollegiate football's most colorful intersectional rivalry will be resumed here tomorrow on another of the bizarre notes that have been the rule rather than the exception whenever Southern California and Notre Dame clash," read the *Chicago Tribune*.

"Undefeated Southern California, rated number one nationally, is a 12-point underdog. It could happen only in this computer age."

History looked to repeat itself when the Irish jumped out to a 7–0 lead. Then Simpson entered history. He rushed thirty-eight times for 150 yards in a dominating 24–7 victory that left no doubt.

Early on, the game was tentative and dominated by hard defensive hitting. It looked to be a match between linebackers, USC's Adrian Young and Notre Dame's Bob Olson.

"The burly Trojans were just too fast, too quick and too determined," read the *Chicago Tribune*. "It was a bitter defeat for Notre Dame, made almost humiliating by a genuine Irishman from Dublin, one Matthew Adrian Young. Three times he choked off Notre Dame scoring threats within the 12-yard line by intercepting passes. A fourth threat cracked up on a fumble on the four-yard line.

"In all, Young, born in Ireland and raised in California, made four of the Trojans' seven interceptions (five thrown by heralded Terry Hanratty)."

Indeed, Young made *his* legend that day, too. He *was* a Dubliner by birth and a Bishop Amat Lancer by high school affiliation. The coach at Bishop Amat was Marv Marinovich's brother, Gary. The Catholic school in La Puente would later be the staging grounds for J. K. McKay, Pat Haden, and John Sciarra. It was the top prep football power in California in its heyday.

Young, USC's cocaptain in 1967, would earn consensus All-America honors as a 6'1", 210-pound linebacker. He played in the National Football League from 1968 to 1973, with the Eagles, Lions, and Bears.

Hanratty, who would be Terry Bradshaw's capable backup on the Pittsburgh Steelers' Super Bowl champion team, spent the day clutching his helmet and throwing his hands up before Parseghian in disbelief.

O. J. had dominated the offensive side of the ball with a one-yard bulldozing through the Notre Dame line, then a thirty-five-yard end sweep for a touchdown. His third touchdown run of three yards in the last quarter clinched it. O. J. had really broken loose in the third quarter, eliciting groans and silence from the Notre Dame faithful. Assistant Coach Johnny Ray was heard muttering, "Too many yards, too many."

When O. J. broke free for a long touchdown, Ray just shouted an agonizing, "*Nooooooo!!!!*"

McKay was carried off the field by his players, saying, "This is my greatest win."

"We just had better football players than Ara did and that's why we won," was McKay's blunt assessment. "Southern Cal hadn't won at Notre Dame since 1939, and I was getting awfully tired of being reminded of this."

After the game, McKay noted in his usual dry manner that at the beginning of the contest, crowd noise had resulted in several offsides penalties assessed to the Trojans. After Simpson took over and USC took command, it "had a quieting effect," he stated.

McKay would always say this was his most satisfying victory. It was the great turnaround, the dividing line, the demarcation point of the rivalry, and that first major step toward establishing the University of Southern California as a football tradition that people could look at and argue was maybe, just maybe, equal or even better than Notre Dame's. It was that little extra ingredient that their fans could point to and say, "Well, Alabama's great, and so is Oklahoma, but we play Notre Dame, we beat the Irish at their place, we win Heismans, we've got the edge."

"We had them figured," said McKay. "Our people were able to get in the right places. Hanratty was off, and we got him to throw impatiently on a few occasions."

Memories of the 16–14 victory of 1931 were stirred up. The papers revisited the comparisons in the sweet days that followed.

A classic line was uttered by Notre Dame sports publicist Roger Valdiserri, when he said, "Simpson's nickname shouldn't be 'Orange Juice.' It should be 'Oh, Jesus,' as in, 'Oh, Jesus, there he goes again.'"

"The turning point of the 1967 season was that Notre Dame game," said Sogge, who also starred on Rod Dedeaux's baseball team before becoming a catcher in the Dodger chain. "Southern Cal feels that it has to beat Notre Dame, even though it's a nonconference game. There's a tremendous amount of pride going. Everyone talks about the UCLA game, but I never held UCLA in the same esteem as Notre Dame."

Indeed, something had changed in the 1960s. The UCLA rivalry intensified under Tommy Prothro and his successors in the 1970s. The Bruins were a national power, the City Game almost always was for the Rose Bowl, and usually had national title implications, sometimes for both sides. But the 1963 Rose Bowl win over Wisconsin and the national championship that came with it had upped the ante at Troy.

The "wilderness years" in which USC had always lost at South Bend and never finished number one had lowered expectations. The Trojans had become a program that shot for the Rose Bowl and considered that their ultimate goal. Under McKay, just getting to Pasadena was no longer enough. Now, they had a whole laundry list of goals, which included beating both the Bruins and the Irish, getting to and winning the Rose Bowl, *and* going undefeated with a national championship to top everything off. As unrealistic as these yearly goals may be, it did not take long for USC fans to consider it their "birthright." The fact is, in 1967 there were still plenty of old-timers from the Jones era who still thought it their birthright. Their influence had carried over to younger alums who had never seen Jones's teams. But McKay basically created a football Frankenstein like none other. The 1967 Notre Dame game was its power switch.

The success of the 1967 Trojans was a tremendous accomplishment for McKay. The team was ranked seventh coming in, but they had to replace eleven starting seniors while breaking in a running back. On top of that, they had to break in not one but two quarterbacks fighting for the job. But the fact that a number of players had been ineligible for the one-point loss to Purdue in the previous year's Rose Bowl had, along with the 51–0 fiasco, created lowered expectations. O. J. very quickly had heightened those expectations.

Earl McCullough was a speedster left end out of Long Beach Poly High. Defensive end Tim Rossovich from St. Francis High in Mountain View was a terror. Defensive back Mike Battle, who had played with Fred Dryer at Lawndale High, made up for a lack of great size through sheer football attitude. He and Rossovich bordered on mental instability between the lines (and sometimes off the field). Rossovich was once featured in *Sports Illustrated lighting himself on fire!* Battle was a heavy partyer who tripped the light fantastic in New York with Joe Namath.

Adrian Young was an All-American. Ron Yary came out of Bellflower High School, establishing himself as one of the greatest tackles of all time. McKay did not like to play the "low expectations" game of Parseghian, Rockne, and "Gloomy Gus" Henderson. He called it the way it was. While this was his natural tendency, the reality of the L.A. sports market might have played a factor. A coach at Alabama or Notre Dame could say anything and his season would be sold out ahead of time. McKay needed to build enthusiasm in order to sell tickets.

"We'll be better than last year in all ways," he had said. "Better defense, better offense, better passing, better running, better punting. What else is there?"

McKay's caveat was the treacherous schedule. USC in those days played the toughest one in America.

"It was great to have O. J., not only because he was so good, but because he was so modest," said Sogge. "We all felt very close to O. J., and we were happy that he got such publicity. We never had a morale problem. We were such a closely knit team because O. J. was such a fine, fine person."

The national press took major attention of the Notre Dame game, calling it the "Poll Bowl." They made note of the fact that in thirty-nine meetings since 1926, "the most important rivalry in modern college football" resulted in the winner ending up as "the national champion in somebody's poll 14 times."

As the season went on with USC firmly ensconced at the number one position,

Simpson put up the numbers and piled up the accolades. Pro scouts drooled over his power, speed, and peripheral vision. He was versatile and lacked what McKay called "blinders."

"They see what's in front but can't see what's at the side," he said. "The great ones see the color and numbers of an opponent's jersey. O. J. is the only man I've known who can come back to the huddle and tell who made the key blocks."

THE GREATEST GAME EVER PLAYED
(1967 Edition)

"The USC-UCLA game is not a matter of life or death. It's more important than that."

FORMER UCLA COACH RED SANDERS

O. J. had sustained a slight injury but recovered in time for the UCLA game. In terms of college football games where everything was on the line, the 1967 City Game ranks above all other so-called games of the century. The combination of the pregame hype, the special circumstances, the excitement of the game itself, and the results of the season based on its outcome, makes it probably the greatest game ever played at this level. Few if any pro games match it, for that matter.

In 1949, Red Sanders had said, "The USC-UCLA game is not a matter of life or death. It's more important than that." Some would call this statement overhype. Others, sacrilegious. The City Game is indeed one of the very best college rivalries in the country. Where does it rate?

The USC–Notre Dame game is an entirely different kind of affair. Considering the tradition and sheer importance of the game to college football history, it must rank first. After that, in no particular order, rank the USC-UCLA, Ohio State-Michigan, Nebraska-Oklahoma, Texas-Oklahoma, Alabama-Auburn, and Army-Navy games.

The 2005 Orange Bowl between USC and Oklahoma matched that season's Heisman winner versus the previous season's Heisman winner; four of the five Heisman finalists; the defending national champions, ranked number one from the preseason on, versus a team ranked second from the preseason on; and both teams were unbeaten, untied, and considered two of the most storied franchises ever. It is one of the few games ever to come close to matching the pregame bells and whistles of the '67 SC-UCLA match.

However, USC's thorough 55–19 whipping of Oklahoma ended any speculation that this would rate with the greatest games ever played.

The 2006 USC-Texas Rose Bowl may be the only game that surpasses the '67 SC-UCLA contest. It featured all of the best elements of the previous season's Orange Bowl, including two Heisman winners, a Heisman runner-up, and four of the top ten NFL Draft picks, and, on top of it all, was played in that most venerable of settings, the Rose Bowl.

The 1967 City Game also met all expectations and then surpassed them. The old saw is that "Hollywood couldn't write a better script." The truth is, the script at the Coliseum on November 18, 1967, was Oscar-worthy.

First, there was the Heisman campaign. Gary Beban was the preseason favorite. As a sophomore he had engineered a stirring 14–12 "gutty little Bruin" win over Michigan State in the Rose Bowl. Now a senior, he was the perfect Heisman contender: smooth, polished, poised on and off the field. He was the epitome of what UCLA had become: first class all the way.

O. J. had entered the season a heralded junior college transfer. Heralded, for sure, but still a J.C. transfer. The idea of a J.C. transfer winning a Heisman trophy was, if not ludicrous, certainly never contemplated. In all the years since, it has never happened and no other J.C. transfer has ever even been a serious contender in his first year.

The benefit of 20/20 hindsight now sheds light on the fact that O. J. should have won the 1967 Heisman in a runaway. Juniors had won it before, but the strong predilection of voters then was to award it to a senior. The arguments that say quarterbacks are more favored and that race could have been an issue (Beban is white) do not hold up under scrutiny. Simpson had a spectacular year, but so did Beban. It was UCLA, not USC, who was ranked first in the nation coming in to the game. Beban's thunder was loud and proud!

Folks had not yet seen O. J.'s performance in two Rose Bowls, his record-breaking senior year, or his Hall of Fame pro career. In retrospect it seems impossible that a future NFL "taxi squad" player would win a prestigious award like the Heisman over a legitimate American legend. Of course, voters *did* see what O. J. did that day, which really makes one wonder, "What were they thinking?"

To date, USC has won seven Heisman Trophies, tied with Notre Dame for the most of any college. The fact is, they should have nine. O. J. should have won in 1967, and Anthony Davis in 1974. Furthermore, had the "payola scandal" not hit, Jon Arnett may well have won for 1956. Ricky Bell (1976) and Rodney Peete (1988) seemed to have had a strong shot at it, but in fairness the right player won it over them both years. Peete was in fact the favorite who enhanced his chances in a similar "Heisman game" with Troy Aikman, but Barry Sanders was just too spectacular at season's end to deny him. Tony Dorsett was off the charts in 1976.

Aside from the Heisman race, the 1967 game was for the national championship. Whoever won would be number one; there was no doubt about that possibility. Notre Dame, Alabama, Michigan State . . . the "usual suspects" of the past few years were out of the picture by November 18.

Of course, while it was "for the national championship," that really meant that it would be for the *opportunity* to win the title, and that opportunity would come in the Rose Bowl. This meant that it was for just that . . . the Pacific 8 Conference title and with it the Rose Bowl, too. Then again there were all the usual nuggets of this game: city pride, bragging rights, family versus family, brother versus brother, husband versus wife, office boasts, schoolyard shouts, neighborhood yelling, the whole nine yards. The closeness of two schools in the same city playing for such a thing gave it an aura *unavailable* to any other rivalry. Even if Cal and Stanford played for such stakes (they never have), while they are close geographically within the *region* of the San Francisco Bay Area, neither is *in* San Francisco.

Nebraska and Oklahoma are not close. The Red River connects Oklahoma and Texas, but it is a haul from Norman to Austin. They split it in the middle: Dallas. Alabama and Auburn are in the same state, but hours apart. The fact that two teams in the same city could attract the kind of players to make both national contenders, each with Heisman favorites, says as much about the wealth of athletic talent in California and the L.A. Basin as any other statement. It also demonstrates how, if one of the programs gets the hammer over the other and gets *everybody*, then no team in America can hope to match up with them.

At various times, this has described the situation for UCLA basketball, UCLA volleyball, USC baseball, and USC track. It seemed to be the case for Pete Carroll's Trojan football team, but in 2005 UCLA demonstrated that the *residual* talent available in the region is still good enough to compete at the highest level. But in 1967, the difference between them was as thin as a *Cosmo* supermodel.

"Never in the history of college football have two teams approached the climax of a season with so much at stake," wrote Paul Zimmerman in the *Los Angeles Times*.

"It was not too many years ago the Trojans owned this town," wrote Jim Murray in the *Times* of the fact that UCLA had won eight of the preceding fourteen matchups:

> Cotton Warburton, Erny Pinckert, Johnny Baker, "Antelope Al" Kreuger, Doyle Nave, Jim Musick were heroes.
> There was a time USC used to beat UCLA twice a year.
> When Howard Jones left the scene momentum and the uncertainties of the war years helped conceal the fact USC's athletic program was as bankrupt as Harvard's. A succession of comic opera searches for a coach who could wear Jones' halo ended with the University hiring somebody who was standing there all the time but not before big names were tossed about.
> In 1949 Red Sanders came to UCLA from Vanderbilt and proceeded to show the West how backward its coaching techniques were. He beat Southern Cal 39–0 and later a Rose Bowl-bound USC team 34–0.
> USC hired its own jester type in 1960—cherubic, cigar-smoking Johnny McKay. . . . It was UCLA's move and they brought up Sanders' assistant, Tommy Prothro.

UCLA promptly stopped being the movable object. USC began to look on occasion as the resistible force.

They put on another one of their cobra vs. mongoose matches Saturday. UCLA's will motor eastward from a complex of soaring architecture that looks more like Camelot than a campus. Southern Cal, which has begun to cave in old buildings around its school to drown out its trolley car past, is only a short punt away. More than the Rose Bowl is at stake. The town is. The Trojans want it back.

McKay the brooder also yearned to shut up those critics who had taken to saying that UCLA coach Tommy Prothro was smarter than he was.

"Well, we pushed 'em all over the field in 1965, but we fumbled on their 1, 7, and 17," McKay responded to media speculation that Prothro "had his number." "I guess he planned that."

Prothro, however, was hard to dislike. He was a class act all the way. Before the game, McKay unleashed Marv Goux.

The fiery Goux urged the Trojans to "win one for John." He held up a photo of McKay, dejected as he left the field after losing the 1966 UCLA game.

"Listen, listen," Goux said in fistic rage. "The worst thing in life is to be a prisoner. Never. I would rather die. We've been prisoners to those indecencies over there for two years. Today's the day we go free."

It was almost identical to Kirk Douglas's rhetoric in front of the gladiators whom he urges to initiate a slave rebellion against the Roman Empire in the Stanley Kubrick classic, *Spartacus*. This was not an accident. Goux had played one of those gladiators in the film.

Goux's speech did not center on the so-called big issues of Rose Bowls, Heismans, and national titles. He spoke of pride in the city of Los Angeles. He hit closer to home than he would using any other tactic. McKay countered Goux by telling them that the walk back to the locker room after the game would either be the longest or the shortest of their lives.

Tommy Prothro made no effort to downplay the game's importance or his team's chances behind Beban, who he said could win using the "run, pass, fake or call." Beban was indeed an expert audibler.

"There's something about the way he manages things out there that gives everyone confidence," said UCLA fullback Rick Purdy. "You just know whatever he calls is right."

When asked, however, Beban shrugged and called himself "ordinary."

Pro scouts called him "self-assured" on the field, though. He was a "gamer," not judged by statistics but by wins and losses.

USC's first nine games had revealed that O. J. could run between the tackles, dispelling any question that he was strictly an outside breakaway threat. His pregame comments contained glowing praise for his line.

The game this time would feature plain, old-fashioned football excellence, and none of the hijinks that had marked many USC-UCLA contests. No UCLA students rented a plane to strafe the USC campus with blue and gold paint. Nobody at USC sealed a UCLA sorority's doors with brick and mortar. Nobody at USC planted dynamite in the UCLA bonfire. No nuts planted a bomb under the ground of the end zone, as had happened in a previous year. On that occasion, the police had gotten wind of it and dug it up. It turned out to be a *smoke* bomb. The culprits in that case finally confessed after a yearlong investigation.

UCLA, despite having a Heisman-quality quarterback, won with swarming defense. McKay used a mathematical formula to grade out position-by-position. When he was done he saw that both teams were exactly even.

"It's gonna be a helluva game," he said. Despite UCLA having taken over the number one ranking late in the season, USC was considered a three-point favorite. The "it" factor was their tougher schedule, but the Bruins had beaten Tennessee, who would finish second in the AP poll. They had also beaten Penn State, but the Stanford game had been a narrow margin.

"We've been good when we had to," said Prothro.

"We've had to be good," McKay countered.

Despite Goux's exhortations, UCLA players demonstrated more on-field theatrics, jumping around "like thieves trapped in a corridor," according to one observer. McKay was once described as a man who watched the game looking like "a commuter waiting for the 5:15 to Larchmont." His teams reflected his businesslike demeanor on the sidelines.

A mob of 90,772 packed the old stadium. They enjoyed the added bonus of beautiful November weather. A huge national TV audience got the full treatment of sun, color, and, believe it or not, that season *for the first time*, the USC Song Girls. They have long been regarded as the most beautiful and classiest of college football cheerleaders. Other colleges have taken to dressing their hotties in skimpy outfits that more resemble something worn by strippers or porn stars. USC's girls wore sweaters, not bikinis. They could actually dance. Many public schools like UCLA have tended to take Affirmative Action to the next level, insisting that their cheerleaders include a girl of every race and ethnicity at the expense of sheer attractiveness, which of course is what the (male) fans care about. Not at USC, where "the best girls get to dance."

In 1967, a student vote had been taken allowing for female cheerleaders to replace the worn-out old male yell leaders who had long handled sideline chores. According to unconfirmed lore, USC had never gone to female cheerleaders even though they were popular at high school and college sporting events long before 1967. A wealthy donor had given handsomely to the school under the proviso that the only women allowed on the field would be band members.

Whether that anonymous donor passed away around 1967 or just relented is not known. What is known is that a few years later the USC Song Girls were winning national competitions. USC's women inspired the famed Laker Girls. In 1997 *Sports Illustrated* voted them the best in America. *L.A. Times* sportswriter Lonnie White, a former Trojan football star, said in his excellent book *UCLA vs. USC: 75 Years of the Greatest Rivalry in Sports*, that the Song Girls were the "gold standard" by which all other squads are judged.

When the thing finally started Beban, who had bruised ribs, engineered a long drive topped by Greg Jones's twelve-yard touchdown run. Marv Goux grimaced at the "indecency" of it. UCLA's "swarm" defense trapped O. J. throughout the first quarter. It looked like the Trojan phenom had met his match. If so, then so had his team.

USC's defense saved the day early, though. Pat Cashman stepped in front of Jones, picked a Beban pass, and raced fifty-five yards to tie it, 7–7. Prothro later said it was a new play that he had called. It was a "stupid play," he said, one that he took the blame for because Beban had not practiced it enough. Cashman blitzed Beban in the second quarter, and his painful ribs showed on his face as he made his way back to the sidelines. Still, he had gotten his team into field goal territory, but Zenon Andrusyshyn missed.

A USC reverse handoff to McCullough netted fifty-two yards followed by a thirteen-yard pass to "The Pearl," as he was called (a reference to Baltimore Bullet basketball whiz Earl "The Pearl" Monroe). O. J. ran it in from thirteen out. One writer said the noise was as loud as the Normandy landings.

After the half, Beban was effective, but Andrusyshyn was not. Tall Bill Hayhoe blocked his field goal try. The Bruins held, though, and on the next possession Beban directed a tying touchdown drive, hitting halfback George Farmer from forty-seven yards out.

Cashman had overstepped on the play, guessing Beban would try the same "stupid" pass he had intercepted earlier. He got burned. UCLA controlled the line of scrimmage. Beban probed patiently until he had them inside the "red zone." Then 6'8", 254-pound Hayhoe sacked Beban. Andrusyshyn began to enter the pantheon of all-time goats when his field goal try was blocked.

Beban later said he was confident despite the missed field goals because "we knew we would score again."

He was right. In analyzing this game, one can make a strong case that UCLA was indeed the better team. If they were the better team, then they were the best in the country. That being said, the game often rides on special teams and they were found wanting. They also did not have O. J.

The teams battled in the pits. Then Beban took over again. He nailed four straight passes covering sixty-five yards. Dave Nuttall hauled in the last for the score, but Andrusyshyn was having one of the worst days in kicking history. Kickers dread such a day. They have nightmares about it.

Up 20–14, he kicked a low one. Hayhoe got his hand on it again. McKay told the press that even though Hayhoe was tall, the purpose was to get Andrusyshyn to rush, which he did.

"I call that brilliant coaching," McKay would say.

For every goat, there is a hero. In a game in which O. J. and Beban worked with equal brilliance, and Beban's team was a little better, O. J. was the difference. Amid the tensions and noise of a one-point game in the fourth quarter; with everything that can possibly ride on a college football game at stake; with fans in the stands looking at each other and saying, "This really *is* more important than life or death," O. J. separated himself from normal. He entered the shrine of immortality.

Toby Page was in at quarterback. He was ostensibly the starter, but hurt a lot, so he and Sogge both played. His plan was simple: hand off to O. J. Simpson. The big tailback was utterly winded. He carried twice to little effect, picked himself up, and thought that at least, on third-and-long, he could "rest" for one play.

In the huddle, Page saw O. J.'s hangdog expression. He decided to try something that might net seven or eight yards for a needed first down. O. J. did not seem to have it in him at this point in the afternoon. At the line of scrimmage, Page saw both of UCLA's linebackers eagerly anticipating his predictable play selection. He audibled: "23-blast."

"That's a *terrible* call," O. J. said to himself. But Page had called for O. J.'s favorite play. It meant running between the tackles, not always the best method for gaining eight yards, but it caught the Bruins flat-footed. O. J. took the handoff, hit the line, juked, and *ran to daylight!*

It was the most memorable run of his career, pro or college. It is probably the most famous in USC history, and one of the most well remembered in collegiate annals. Guard Steve Lehner and tackle Mike Taylor opened the hole. Center Dick Allmon knocked down a befuddled Bruin linebacker. O. J. headed toward the left sideline, benefited from *another* block that eliminated two Bruins in one fell swoop, then swerved back up the middle. McCullough hung by his side like the Marines protecting the flank. O. J. was off to the races.

All the commentary about the game could not match Prothro's priceless, exasperated lament to an assistant coach while the play was still in progress: "Isn't but one guy can catch Simpson now," said Prothro as McCullough whizzed by him stride-for-stride with the ball-carrying O. J., "and he's on the same team."

It was a variation on something Phillies' manager Gene Mauch said when Willie Mays had hit a home run over the fence, just beyond the outstretched glove of one of his outfielders.

"The only guy who could have caught it," mused Mauch, "hit it."

O. J.'s dash beat UCLA, 21–20. It ranks with "The Play," the famous returned-kick-lateral-through-the-band run that gave California an improbable 1982 win over John Elway and Stanford. *Sports Illustrated* gave it its front cover: "Showdown in L.A."

"All on one unbearable Saturday afternoon is strictly from the studio lots," wrote *S.I.*

In the locker room, Beban's ribs looked like an "abstract painting," but he had passed for over 300 yards. Simpson's foot was swollen and grotesque, but he had rushed for 177 yards.

"They should send the Heisman out here with two straws," wrote Jim Murray.

Beban graciously visited the Trojan locker room, a practice O. J. also did regularly throughout his career.

"O. J.," he said, "you're the best."

"Gary, you're the greatest," replied Simpson. "It's too bad one of us had to lose."

"Whether that run earns Simpson the Heisman Trophy and moves coach John McKay's Trojans back as the number one team in the nation remains for the voters to decide later," Paul Zimmerman of the *Times* added. "But the witnesses will remember this as one of the greatest."

"Whew!" wrote Murray.

"I'm glad I didn't go to the opera Saturday afternoon, after all. This was the first time in a long time where the advance ballyhoo didn't live up to the game.

"The last time these many cosmic events were settled by one day of battle, they struck off a commemorative stamp and elected the winner President.

"On that commemorative stamp, they can put a double image—one of UCLA's Gary Beban and one of USC's Orenthal James Simpson. They can send that Heisman Trophy out with two straws, please."

While O. J.'s extraordinary record does lead one to the conclusion that he should have been the Heisman winner, Beban, playing in pain and matching Simpson's performance, was enough to sway the voters to him in the Heisman balloting. He would have traded it for the Rose Bowl and the national championship. He goes down in history as one of the worthiest opponents ever to lace up his cleats against a Southern California football team.

"I have always said that the 1967 game was easily the highlight of my athletic career," Simpson was quoted in *UCLA vs. USC: 75 Years of the Greatest Rivalry in Sports*. "It was far beyond even when I ran on the 4x100 world record team at SC and even more than the 2,000 yards. I never felt more elated or joy after any athletic event than I did after that game."

THE PROMISED LAND

McKay's second national championship and O. J.'s Heisman

USC students of the late 1960s and early 1970s would purchase their season tickets before the first game. The package would of course include the home nonconference games and Pac 8 matchups with Cal, Stanford, Washington et al. The UCLA game and the Notre Dame game (in even years) cost a little more than the other games. Then they would notice something really great: a Rose Bowl ticket. Before the season had started.

With McKay, it got to be a running gag. He had the advantage in Pasadena because it was a "home game for USC." It was "on USC's schedule."

From 1967 to 1970, the Big 10 sent Purdue, Indiana, Ohio State, and Michigan. The Pac 8 just sent USC. Pencil 'em in. When USC had lost to Purdue on January 2, 1967, then-recruit O. J. Simpson had remarked to a disappointed player who would be returning, "Don't worry about it. We'll be back next year."

Prior to the 1968 Rose Bowl, McKay was questioned by the sporting press about his tremendous schedule: Texas (national champs in 1963 and '69), Michigan State (Rose Bowl in '65, number two in '66), Notre Dame (defending national champs), Washington at Seattle, and of course number one–ranked UCLA!

"I told my scouts when I saw that schedule to go out and find me someone who was six-foot one-inch who weighed 205 pounds and could run the 100 in nine-four," said McKay.

Simpson scored both touchdowns and gained 128 yards in Southern California's 14–3 win over Indiana. He was named the MVP. His 1,543 yards led the nation. The game clinched another national championship for McKay. The victory had none of the Hollywood dramatics of the City Game.

"The idea is to win, isn't it?" McKay asked rhetorically.

"It was a big deal to us, the players, a feeling of satisfaction of a job well done; having accomplished something like that," said fullback Mike Hull of the 1967 national title, "and even though I have a Super Bowl ring, I wear the national championship ring."

Five of USC's regulars missed the start of the game due to injury. Two more had to be removed during the course of the game. Rossovich and Hayhoe contained Indiana tailback John Isenbarger. Afterward, USC's defense was compared to the Minnesota Vikings' "Purple People Eaters" and the about-to-be three-time World Champion Green Bay Packers. Not bad company for a college team.

In the days prior to the "coming out early" rule that allows nonseniors to declare for the pro draft, Simpson's return for his senior season was a given. He was expected to have one of the best years ever. He did not disappoint.

Against Minnesota in Troy's opening 29–20 victory, Simpson ran for 236 yards and 367 in total offense.

"Don't ask me to describe him," said Golden Gopher coach Murray Warmath. "Everyone already has. There is really nothing more to say."

"Simpson is better than Red Grange," wrote Leo Fischer, sports editor of the *Chicago American*. "I've seen them all. On the basis of his performance against Minnesota, far from the worst defensive team in the country, I think Simpson is the greatest."

Simpson dealt with a leg bruise just fine in a 189-yard effort against Northwestern. McKay gave serious thought to not playing him. He "blamed" the writers for his decision to use his star rather than listen to their backbenching.

"He approaches a hole like a panther," Northwestern coach Alex Agase said after his team's 24–7 loss to USC. "Then, when he sees an opening, he springs at the daylight."

"Simpson's the greatest back in college and the greatest I've ever played against," said Northwestern linebacker Don Ross.

"He's better than [Leroy] Keyes—although we have to meet Keyes and Purdue next week," said Wildcat end Mark Proskine.

Game three was another interesting matchup with the emerging Miami Hurricanes, led by the irrepressible Ted "The Stork" Hendricks. *Sports Illustrated* thought it an interesting enough intersectional game to give it major coverage. Fans numbering 71,189 showed up at the Coliseum to see it.

Stories about Hendricks were already becoming part of his lore. He apparently enjoyed "dismantling" cars. He was unable to even catch O. J., though. The USC star had studied game footage of Hendricks's wild, arm-flapping style, and his desire to penetrate before a runner could get out in the open. O. J.'s studiousness paid off in a 163-yard performance. His two touchdowns fired an easy Trojan win, 28–3.

Sogge, the man everybody thought just "handed off to O. J.," showed that he had an arm (after all, he was a baseball catcher) by hitting on a variety of efficient passes. O. J. still had thirty-eight carries and felt pain from his hips to his feet.

Stanford was ranked eighteenth behind sophomore quarterback Jim Plunkett. A crowd of 81,000 people showed up at Stanford Stadium. Stanford's players had "O. J. Who?" and "Squeeze O. J." painted on their helmets.

The walk from the locker room into the stadium runs a gauntlet past Stanford rooters who take free verbal shots at the opposing team. Their commentary is often biting and obviously partisan, but for the most part just part of the game. A disturbing trend, however, began to develop during O. J.'s year. It would continue into the 1970s. Stanford fans began to use racial epithets.

"N——r lover," some yelled at Coach McKay, because he had as many black athletes on his team as anybody in the country. It was a disgusting "performance" coming from a student body and fan base at one of the country's top academic institutions. It was further shocking considering the fact that, with the war at full throttle, Stanford had made its anti-American sentiments well known, establishing itself as a "liberal" institution.

The whole ugly scene was a carryover from the 1920s and '30s, when USC had passed Cal and Stanford as the dominant West Coast power. Jealousy and recrimination had always marked the Berkeley and Palo Alto schools' attitude toward their southern neighbor. As USC continued to become the dominant "glamour school" in the state, if not the nation, those left behind found that class envy and lies were easier to toss about than genuine praise for a great program. McKay was incensed. He developed a personal disgust with just about anything to do with Stanford after that. To the credit of the Stanford players, who like athletes at Cal are not representative of the student body in general, there were no reports of racial epithets on the field.

O. J. carried *forty-seven times* for 220 yards to just shut 'em up.

"I guess O. J. Simpson showed us on a couple of those runs why he's the man," said Stanford tight end Bob Moore after O. J.'s three touchdowns led Troy to a 27–24 win over the Indians.

The adrenaline of the crowd taunts and the atmosphere no doubt combined with O. J.'s "homecoming" to his native Bay Area to elevate his game and shake off his injuries.

"I felt kind of squeamish running early in the game," he said, "but I felt better as the game wore on."

"I think what probably happened is we ran the injury out of him," said McKay. "If we had only run him thirty times he'd probably still be hurting."

Inexperienced writers listening to this looked at each as if to ask, "Is this guy serious?" The older L.A. corps just shrugged it off as a McKay quip with a touch of sarcasm. The polls after the game installed the Trojans back into the number one slot in which they had finished 1967.

"We knew that Simpson would be coming at us, but there was nothing we could do about it," said Washington coach Jim Owens after O. J.'s 172-yard effort in a 14–7 USC win. "He is one of the greatest backs ever to play football. Because of his size and speed, he probably improvises better than any runner I've ever seen."

Oregon managed to hold O. J. to sixty-seven yards, but USC won at Eugene, 20–13.

Games at Oregon and Washington have always been a little bit of a problem for USC, especially when played late in the season. Fog, rain, mud, and crowd noise often mark the contests, making life difficult for a favored team playing a scrappy underdog.

"O. J. doesn't like playing against a quick team like ours," said Oregon's George Dames.

O. J. classily gave full credit to the Ducks and their speed.

"When I would get ready to turn the corner, somebody would come up from behind to throw me down," he said.

"O. J. Simpson probably is the greatest back of our time," said California coach Ray Willsey after Simpson ran for 164 yards and two scores in a 35–17 victory before 80,871 at the Coliseum. "USC beat us by twenty points without him last year, so I guess we're about forty down this year going in."

Cal was making a bit of a comeback after a decade in the doldrums, despite the fact that half the student body at Berkeley in those days equated athletic competition with *bourgeois capitalist pigs!* Lineman Ed White was an All-American who would star for the Vikings, and the Golden Bears roughed O. J. up. He had a bruised thigh, a twisted knee, and a sprained ankle when the game was over.

"You name it, and I've got it," he stated. O. J. said that Cal hit him harder than any team he had ever played. "Maybe it's time to retire," he added with a smile.

Oregon State, led by Bill "Earthquake" Enyart, came to L.A. in a game that would decide the Pacific 8 Conference championship. Enyart scored first and it was 7–0, Beavers. Sogge controlled a game-tying touchdown drive in the fourth quarter. O. J. broke the defensive battle with a forty-two-yard run capped by a Ron Ayala field goal to put Troy ahead for the first time, 10–7.

USC held. With seven minutes remaining O. J. broke a forty-yard touchdown run for a 17–7 lead. That was the winning score in the 17–13 win. O. J. had forty-seven carries, including an incredible twenty-one in the final quarter (despite the L.A heat, his injuries, and obvious fatigue) for 138 of his 238 yards.

Oregon State coach Dee Andros said afterward that not only was USC deserving of the Rose Bowl berth they earned that day, but also of the number one ranking. The next week it was UCLA. This time it was all Trojans. O. J. carried forty times for 205 yards, caught three Sogge passes, and scored three times. He broke six school records and two NCAA marks, including the season rushing record with one regular season and one Rose Bowl game still left to play. The 28–16 win made USC 9–0, firmly in the number one spot. Joe Theisman and ninth-ranked Notre Dame were headed to the Coliseum the next week.

This game was indicative of what the rivalry is all about. Just when one team thinks they have the other's number, things turn around. Having beaten the Irish soundly in South Bend, unbeaten and riding high toward back-to-back national championships, led by a record-breaking Heisman horse; why, the Trojans were just full of themselves!

Parseghian had a tremendous team, as usual. Without a bowl game in their future, their hopes for a national title hinged on beating USC, and then in turn the Trojans beating Woody Hayes and Ohio State on New Year's Day.

The Irish gladiators held O. J. to fifty-five rushing yards. Theisman (who changed pronunciation of his name from *Thees-man* to *Thys-man* as part of a school PR campaign to promote his candidacy for the rhyming Heisman) made his first bid for the award.

A sophomore, Theisman started slow by getting intercepted, but quickly shocked Troy and their fans by turning the affair from a USC coronation into an upset-in-the-making. He led Notre Dame on three touchdown drives and a 21–7 halftime lead. The tables of 1964 were turned, but one thing remained the same: a patented second half USC comeback, something that McKay and his school were becoming known for and would expand upon in the next two decades.

The star for USC was not O. J., but Sogge, who stepped up and made short passes when he had to in rallying his team to a 21–21 tie. It was enough to drop Troy to number two heading into the Rose Bowl. Woody Hayes's Buckeyes, a tremendous sophomore-led team with no losses or ties, took over the top spot.

"Deep down in my heart," Theisman said after the tie, "I think we should have won it. We had them on the run."

"I'd rather play until midnight," said McKay. "I just don't like a tie."

O. J. expressed a desire for "sudden death overtime," which in those days was used only in pro football play-off games. It had resulted in incredibly exciting affairs, most notably the 1958 NFL title game between the Colts and Giants at Yankee Stadium, and the 1962 AFL championship between the Oilers and Dallas Texans (later Kansas City Chiefs), played on a Houston high school field.

O. J. was rewarded with the Heisman Trophy, but his career ended in disappointment when Woody Hayes and Ohio State defeated the Trojans, 27–16, in the Rose Bowl. Ohio State won the national title, with USC placing fourth in the AP and second in the UPI polls.

O. J. played on teams filled with talent. His greatest teammate was Ron Yary, a late bloomer who had not thought much about college at Bellflower High School. Yary was 6'6", 285 pounds when USC recruited him out of Cerritos J.C. He chose Southern California because they were "much more organized, the athletes are better, and I felt I wanted to play with that type of people. That's why I decided to go to SC."

Yary had been a defensive end, but McKay saw something else in him. He had him slim down to 255 for his junior year, putting him at offensive tackle. Yary did not like the grind at first, but he fit the position like a glove. Yary earned consensus All-American honors in 1966 and 1967. In his senior year he won the Outland Trophy and the Washington Touchdown Club's Lineman of the Year award.

"He was our quickest lineman," said former USC line coach Rod Humenuik. "For pulling and trapping, Ron has the speed to get in front of the ball carrier.

"O. J. Simpson made most of his yardage running behind Ron Yary.

"The boy is a very versatile football player. He had some great days for us. His best game was probably against Notre Dame's 270-pound defensive tackle, on his back all day and we won, 24–7."

"Ron Yary is athletic, which is hard to find in a big man," said Dave Levy, the ex-assistant who was also an assistant athletic director during that time. "Lots of kids in college are big, but not athletic. A lot of young men can't handle their growth. He has great physical attributes. I've been here since 1960 and I don't think we've had any linemen as good as he is. He has great size, strength, speed, aggressiveness, and a professional attitude toward work. We think he could play offensive guard because he can pull like a small man."

Yary was the first player selected in the entire 1968 NFL Draft, by the Minnesota Vikings. He was the first offensive lineman taken number one in thirty years. Yary told the Minneapolis press that his college career had prepared him for the NFL because he had participated in a lot of "pressure games." He certainly was prepared. Yary became a perennial All-Pro on teams that always went to the play-offs.

Yary played in four Super Bowls and is a member of the College and Pro Football Halls of Fame.

The Trojans had so many players go into the NFL during O. J.'s career that it was a remarkable accomplishment for McKay to keep the ball rolling year after year. After the 1966 team had five players drafted, the 1967 team had *eleven players* chosen. An unbelievable *five players* were taken in the first round, which of course included Yary going first, followed by tackle Mike Taylor (tenth to Pittsburgh), Rossovich, running back Mike Hull (sixteenth to Chicago), and receiver Earl McCullough (twenty-fourth to Detroit). All of these players had success in professional football.

Adrian Young was picked by Philadelphia and played until 1973 for several teams. Dennis Crane went to the Redskins, Gary Magner to the Jets, Ralph Oliver to the Raiders, Steve Grady to the Broncos, and Jim Ferguson to the Saints.

O. J. had to say good-bye to all of these stars, yet he was able to lead the next year's team to within a few fumbles of a second straight title.

His senior team, the 1968 Trojans, had eight players picked. O. J. was of course the first player chosen, making USC the first school to ever give the draft its first selection two years running. Tight end Bob Klein was the twenty-first pick of the first round by Los Angeles, and would have a fine pro career. Bill Hayhoe went to Green Bay. The Saints went for Bob Miller and Jim Lawrence. Jack O'Malley was drafted by San Francisco, with Wilson Bowie going to Detroit.

16

"THIS HERE'S WHAT A FOOTBALL PLAYER LOOKS LIKE"

Bryant never said, "This here's what a football player looks like." It never happened. But it should have.

FORMER ALABAMA QUARTERBACK SCOTT HUNTER, 2005

In 1970 USC traveled to Alabama and played the Crimson Tide at Birmingham's Legion Field. USC, with an integrated squad, defeated the segregated Crimson Tide. When it was over, USC's players were utterly drained, physically, emotionally, by the pressure valve being lifted, the turf, and the late-summer humidity. Outside of surgery, military training, and, of course, actual combat, they had just engaged in one of the most debilitating human exercises imaginable. They celebrated in fits and starts, and were doing so when Bear Bryant entered their locker room.

Bryant's appearance caused more than a few eyes to follow him as he made his way into the room. Craig Fertig saw him, shook his hand, and welcomed him. The two spoke for a few moments. Fertig had an expression on his face that said, "You want *what?*"

The players watched this exchange. "What's goin' on?" a few asked.

Then Fertig straightened up. Bryant hung back as Fertig walked over to where McKay was. Something *was* going on. A small drama of some kind.

"Coach Bryant wants to borrow Cunningham," Fertig told McKay.

"What do you mean, 'borrow' him?" asked McKay.

Then Bear approached McKay, as the Trojans looked on. "Coach, could I borrow Sam Cunningham?" he asked.

"You mean for the remainder of the season?" quipped McKay. "Go ahead and take him."

Bryant smiled as if to say, "Just give me an inch, Coach, and I'll take a mile."

McKay summoned big Sam Cunningham. He introduced Bryant to Sam and told him that the Alabama coach would like for Sam to go with him for a few minutes. Cunningham had no idea what was going on, either, but it seemed on the up and up.

Bryant thanked McKay and left with Cunningham. On McKay's instructions, Fertig went with them. Cunningham, bare chested, followed Bryant out the door.

Bryant thanked Cunningham for coming with him. Fertig accompanied them, thinking that maybe some kind of sociological history was about to be made. The fact that Sam was black could not escape Fertig's attention.

What happened next is in dispute. Some say they entered the Alabama locker room. Some say the exchange happened in the crowded hallway between the visitors' and home lockers. Some say it never happened. The following story, which may not be 100 percent accurate, is nevertheless rooted, like most myth and lore, in truth.

They entered the Alabama locker room. The mood was one of utter demoralization and despondency. Cunningham was instructed to stand on a bench. He towered above the all-white Crimson Tide. He was still sweaty. He had deep bruises. There was still blood on his pants.

Bryant allegedly started off by referring to Sam as "this ol' boy," but corrected himself by changing his description to "this man," or, according to others who claim to have been in the room, began the speech by gathering his team's attention by starting off with, "Gentlemen . . .

"This is Sam Cunningham, number 39," Bryant told his team as they sat and looked *up* to Sam. "This man and his Trojan brothers," a term Bryant believed in and did not use lightly because he knew and understood Marv Goux's sincerity when he talked about "Trojan pride" and loyalty. "This team just ran us right out of the Legion Field," he said—just as Goux had said they would.

Bryant is said to have told them to raise their heads and "open your eyes" because "this here's what a football player looks like." Those words would symbolize everything that had happened. It would be what everybody would remember about that night.

The coach instructed every one of his players to shake the stunned Sam's hand. There was no hesitation.

Scott Hunter, who had been humiliated but would come back strong like the champ he was, led the way. "Sam, you're a [heck] of a running back," he (allegedly) said.

As Cunningham stood shirtless in the middle of the room, he was the perfect example of grace, pride, and class, at that moment a vessel of God. Each player shook his hand, most looking him in the eye. There were smiles, gentle ribbing, and a lot of congratulations. Bryant had *sanctified* this moment, and as the billboard on the highway from the airport had demonstrated, the man walked on water around this neck of the woods. The Alabama players did not feel humiliated anymore. Many began to understand that they, too, were part of something.

The Legion Field locker room scene has been touted as Holy Grail within the Trojan family for decades and by many others, including linebacker John Papadakis and possibly Cunningham, who has remained somewhere between vague, coy, sure it happened, or sure it did not, depending on whom you ask (and this includes Southern sportswriters and former USC teammates).

Hunter, who allegedly complimented Sam in the locker room, insists none of it happened—not the Bryant speech and certainly not his handshaking. Hunter's attitude, some contend, is "negative," but a lengthy interview with him revealed that this is entirely untrue. Hunter says that the event did not happen but that "it should have." He had been to Vietnam on an all-star tour with black players, was happy to see integration, and expressed great admiration for Dr. Martin Luther King, Jr., because he recognized that Bryant's words mirrored the civil rights leader's.

"If I admired this man [Bryant]," Hunter says, "and he's saying the same things as Dr. King, then do I pick and choose, and not admire King? No."

Told this, Craig Fertig, who previously thought of Hunter as "negative" and "sour," could only say, "Wow, that changes my whole interpretation of Scott Hunter."

Nevertheless, as Hunter expressed, whether it happened exactly that way or not, *it should have!*

Talking to the Alabama players and the coaches, sportswriters, others—nobody remembers this Bryant speech about Cunningham being "what a football player looks like." The *Mobile Press-Register's* Neal McCready tried to clear this up. As for Cunningham, he told McCready, "I don't want to be the one who said it didn't happen."

Craig Fertig was not in the Alabama locker room. A couple of coaches said it did not happen. Alabama assistant coach Clem Gryska, an honorable man, had a very good point, and so did Scott Hunter. They both said, "The players were ready for integration." Kenny Stabler said as far back as the 1960s, the *players* had no objection. But what would have been the point of bringing Cunningham into that locker room?

Something happened, but not in the way it is described . . . generally something is there on which the legend is based, but it is almost never exactly that way. But there is always a nugget or kernel of truth. Why would not a single Alabama player say it happened? Somebody would say it happened.

Jerry Claiborne, one of Bryant's assistant coaches, is credited with having said, "Sam Cunningham did more for civil rights in sixty minutes than Martin Luther King had done in twenty years." But Marv Goux also said it. He said Cunningham had done more to integrate the *South* in *three hours* than Martin Luther King had done in twenty years.

As for McKay, he repeated the "Cunningham did more than King" remark many times before his death in 2001. McKay normally did not qualify the remark, as in "Jerry Claiborne said it" or "Marv Goux said it"; he just repeated it, as have numerous others until it has become a football article of faith.

Back in his own locker room, Cunningham is supposed to have told two other sophomores what Bryant said about him. The whole affair had by then taken on a religious tone, as if the words spoken and actions taken were Gospel, those who heard and saw witnesses. As for USC's "Wild Bunch" lineman Tody Smith, he was all smiles. A black kid from Texas, he had brought a gun to Alabama out of fear for his life, but had at the last second left it at the hotel. Nobody in the state was more relieved than he was.

THE GREATEST COLLEGE FOOTBALL TEAM OF ALL TIME
(1972 Edition)

Divided by race, a "team of destiny" comes together through Christian Fellowship,
forming the nucleus of the greatest team of all time

History records that an integrated team of happy warriors traveled to Birmingham and "taught Alabama a social lesson" in 1970. Like so much of history, this is not entirely true.

The 1969 Trojans were known as the "Cardiac Kids" because they pulled out game after game with last-minute comebacks. They were undefeated and won the Rose Bowl over Michigan. They defeated UCLA, 14–12, when quarterback Jimmy Jones hit Sam Dickerson in the back of the end zone with a desperation fourth down heave. The teenage Pete Carroll sat in the stands that night.

That 1969 team was led by a defensive line known as "The Wild Bunch," so named after Sam Peckinpah's violent Western of the same name. They were also led by Jones, a black quarterback, a fairly rare thing at that time. With Jones's and the team's success, a sense of complacency came over the Trojans. To outsiders, it looked like USC was a successful "social experiment," orchestrated by a modern-day Moses of Progressivism, John McKay. Somehow, USC had learned how to get it right where others had failed.

It was a facade. In truth, the team was divided by race. First, black players carried guns to Alabama. Defensive lineman Tody Smith planned to have one on the field in Birmingham, but at the last minute reportedly decided not to. When the game was a success, all seemed well.

But over the next two seasons (1970–1971), the players and even the press "took sides." Increasingly, white players favored white backup quarterback Mike Rae. The black players stood behind Jones. When the team went 6–4–1, failing to get to the Rose Bowl in both seasons, the racial problems threatened the program.

"There was 'house n——s and field n——s,'" said running back Anthony Davis, who had just entered the program. "A lot of black players took exception to McKay. He liked a certain kind of black players: quiet guys. I was militant, dated white girls. McKay didn't like that. He spoke to me maybe eight times the whole time I knew him, but I was too good to keep off the field. He needed me. But a lot of us wondered about him being friends with a supposed racist like Bear Bryant. We thought he put the black players in harm's way going to Alabama."

Prior to the 1971 game at Notre Dame, a little-known Trojan offensive lineman named Dave Brown asked Coach McKay if he could arrange a Fellowship of Christian Athletes (FCA) "demonstration."

With his team at 2–4, facing an undefeated Irish squad, the Catholic McKay agreed, "as long as it's voluntary."

According to Brown, "a lot of guys became Christians that day." Black Christians like Rod McNeill, Charles Young, Manfred Moore, Sam Cunningham, and Jones found common ground with Brown, linebacker John Papadakis, and other teammates.

That week, Troy traveled to South Bend and dismantled the Irish, 28–7. That group would not lose for two years. They became the 1972 Trojan national champions. From the 1972 team, thirteen players would be All-Americans.

The 1972 Trojans were the greatest collegiate football team in history. This was a source of frustration to the Nebraska Cornhuskers, whose 1971 national champions had been accorded that status after destroying Alabama in the Orange Bowl. But 1972 saw the end of their thirty-game unbeaten streak when UCLA, led by Mark Harmon, upset them in the season opener at the Coliseum. Harmon, the son of Heisman winner Tommy Harmon, would go on to acting fame. By season's end, the pundits were fairly unanimous in their estimation that, as good as Nebraska had been, McKay's charges were even better.

Previous competition for the "all-time best" spot came from the Trojans themselves (1928, 1932), Army (1945), Notre Dame (1947), Oklahoma (1956), and Ohio State (1968). Since 1972, the 1987 and 2001 Miami Hurricanes have drawn mention. Many felt the 1995 Nebraska team surpassed the '72 Trojans. Of course Pete Carroll's 2004 team can be compared, and the 2005 squad would have earned the "title" had they finished number one. No less an authority than legendary commentator Keith Jackson, who should know, always insisted that the best he ever saw was the 1972 team.

Writers, unaware and probably unattuned to the meaning of Dave Brown's Fellowship of Christian Athletes meeting the year before, called the back-to-back 6–4–1 seasons a "mystery virus," teams of "certain Rose Bowl quality" that proved "enigmatically disappointing," according to Ken Rappoport's *The Trojans: A Story of Southern California Football*.

The season opened at War Memorial Stadium in Little Rock, Arkansas. The Razorbacks were fourth in the country, USC eighth. Arkansas had come close to a national title shot before losing to Texas, 15–14, in 1969. Coach Frank Broyles was at the height of his great career. Quarterback Joe Ferguson was a star who would be a fine player with the Buffalo Bills. With integration, the Hogs were now a complete football program. But press reports before the game foretold a possible USC win. It was stated that USC possessed twenty pro prospects to Arkansas's four. USC, dressed in their road whites, looked enormous in pregame drills. A Razorback scout stated that when his team lined up against Troy, each would face "the best player he's ever seen."

Six-point favorite Arkansas struck first to lead 3–0. An audience of 54,461 fans went Hog wild. Memories of mediocrity crept into the minds of the Trojans. USC fumbled the kickoff, but shakily managed to recover. A defensive struggle ensued, with Arkansas holding USC in a goal line stand before Lynn Swann returned a punt thirty-five yards to set up Mike Rae's twenty-six-yard field goal to make it 3–3 at the half.

Rae hit Edesel Garrison for forty-three yards in the third quarter, then ran it in himself from the 5 to put USC ahead, 10–3. Sophomore Richard "Batman" Wood intercepted a Ferguson pass, setting up McNeill's run to make it 17–3. McNeill added an eighteen-yarder. Then Cunningham went in from 17 to ice it, 31–10.

Wood became an instant Trojan legend when he made an incredible *eighteen tackles* in addition to breaking up passes, one interception, and two quarterback sacks.

"I know we have the quickest and fastest defense in the country," said Wood. "I'm not worried about the national championship. I just want to go to the Rose Bowl three years in a row."

Mike Rae, *finally* installed as the starter, directed three touchdown drives. He now was one with a little bit of job security.

"They kept us off-balance all night, run or pass," said Broyles. "Their offense was as strong physically as any we've ever faced, and Wood destroyed everything we tried to do."

Arkansas's hopes for a national championship were transferred to Southern California. On the basis of the impressive road win and Nebraska's loss to UCLA, they vaulted all the way to number one.

USC returned home to dismantle Oregon State, 51–6. McNeill ran for 111 yards. Every player who suited up played. They passed for 316 yards and ran for 354 (670 total). McNeill scored three times. Charles Young caught a thirty-seven-yard touchdown pass. Pat Haden and J. K. McKay were impressive when the "scrubs" proved to be as talented as the starting eleven. After two games, Rae was completing 70 percent of his passes. McKay was already saying they were the best offensive team he had ever coached.

"They're much quicker, have greater overall size, and their quickness just stuns you," said Beaver coach Dee Andros when asked to compare them to the 1967 national champions. "They are a bunch of great athletes with one overpowering factor: their aggressiveness on both offense and defense."

Sophomore tailback Anthony Davis, known universally as "A. D.," scored twice in a 55–20 thumping of Illinois. Rae hit Garrison from midfield. He later directed an eighty-yard drive, culminating in Davis's first touchdown run of his career. Later Rae hit McKay for a thirty-one-yard score. In the fourth quarter, linebacker James Sims returned a punt thirty-five yards into the end zone.

"We really didn't play very well and I don't know why," said McKay. "We were slow on defense and uninspired on offense."

Asked why he was slow to go to the air, McKay said that his philosophy was to shove the other team around first in order to establish dominance, rather than pass right off the bat, therefore allowing his team to become "pacified."

Michigan State came to town next. Spartan coach Duffy Daugherty "says he has his best team since 1966," McKay told the media. Daugherty was touting defensive back Brad Van Pelt as the best player in the country. Tight end Billy Joe DePre, guard Joe DeLaumielleure, and linebacker Gail Clark all would be drafted high. Then Swann ran a punt back ninety-two yards to power the 51–6 rout of the Spartans at the Coliseum. McNeill scored from the 8. Rae hit McKay from the 9. After taking a 21–6 halftime lead, Wood intercepted a pass, running it back twenty-five yards for a score. Haden came in, nailing Moore and Swann for touchdowns. Allen Carter strolled in from twenty-one yards out. In nineteen years at East Lansing, it was Daugherty's worst loss. After four games, fourteen Trojans had scored.

The following week was the one McKay had been waiting for: Stanford, the so-called Harvard of the West, who McKay derided as the "Radcliffe of the West."

"They're the worst winners I've come up against," McKay said of the 1970–1971 Stanford victories over his team, which propelled them to two straight Rose Bowls. "They've shown no class against us. I'd like to beat them by 2,000 points."

McKay checked his harshest words for Stanford, calling them on their "intellectual snobbery." In the interview with this author years later, he revealed the intemperate, bigoted racial remarks from Stanford's "enlightened" student body had "made my blood boil." Especially, he said, in light of the fact that "conservative" USC had provided many opportunities for blacks while "liberal" Stanford held on to their lily-white status long after the point of courageous action had come and gone.

"People tend to think of Stanford players as being more intellectual," McKay told the press the week of the game. "I don't place much credence in that. But Stanford felt we were nothing but jocks, and when they could beat us at our own specialty that made them *far* more superior than we were."

"Today the Cards host a team that has never been able to keep football in perspective . . ." read Stanford's student newspaper on the day of the game. "If they lose, maybe football will die." The writer of that screed, now probably a "voice of conscience" at the *New York Times* or *Newsweek*, would have done well to investigate Dave Brown's FCA meeting of one year prior.

McNeill, an extremely erudite and articulate fellow, disputed this concept of Trojan football, stating to the media that social problems of the past decade had given his teammates a "new awareness" that football was not all important. "We also enjoy playing chess and reading poetry," he said.

It is also worth noting that USC's backup quarterback would become a Rhodes' Scholar and his pal, the coach's son, a corporate attorney. This may have impressed the Stanford elite, but the fact that several of USC's black players would become ordained ministers no doubt would have been "proof" that they were a "simple breed."

"Forgive them, Father," as Jesus once said, "for they know not what they do."

Politics, religion, and the post-1960s collided with football at Stanford Stadium on October 7. That same day, the Oakland A's were beating the Detroit Tigers in a play-off baseball game across the bay. The unbeaten Cardinal (a Native American tribe was "occupying" nearby Alcatraz at the time, so Stanford, in solidarity with their cause, ended decades of tradition to become a color, or a tree, or somethin') gave Southern California their toughest game of the year, but it was never really close as the Trojans prevailed, 30–21, before 84,000. In an otherwise "perfect" season, McKay was frustrated that his team was unable to beat "Radcliffe" by the appropriate "2,000 points."

"It was the worst game we've played," said Swann, who caught five passes, one for a touchdown. "I still don't think we've paid Stanford what we owed them. Two years ago up here their fans and players made very snide remarks, degrading us and our school. The fans did it again this year. There's a changing attitude among college football players today, and I don't think those remarks help it along. I don't want to hate anybody."

Swann, a man of consummate polish, intelligence, and class, let it go at that instead of coming right out and repeating the fact that Stanford "fans" openly called him and his wonderful black teammates "n———s."

The Pittsburgh Steeler superstar, a product of a Catholic high school, certainly knew how to separate football from life, and in 2006 brought his conservative Republican credentials to the election for Pennsylvania governor. Charles Young, Manfred Moore, Sam Cunningham, Rod McNeill, Swann, and many other African American players on that 1972 team—not to mention the first-class white guys and noble coaches—made up not just the best football team ever seen up until that time. The thirty-four years that have passed since that year reveal a remarkable group of guys who made grades, graduated, and forged professions in the law, education, the arts, politics, the clergy, the media, and pro football. Stanford is a fine school and does not deserve to be painted in a single brush stroke because of a few bad apples, but those bad apples calling these wonderful guys "n———s" were pizzants of unimpressive quality.

McNeill's first quarter fumble had helped Stanford score first, 7–0. Rae and A. D. took over on a touchdown drive to tie it. When Stanford kicked a forty-nine-yard field goal to give the Cardinal a 10–7 lead, it was the last time in 1972 that USC would trail in a game. USC held Stanford to sixty-four yards rushing in the second half. Troy led by 30–13 before Stanford scored, then converted a two-pointer to make it look closer. Davis scored two touchdowns, but the game's last play had added to the intense feelings between the schools. With thirty points on the board and the game won, USC tried a failed touchdown pass.

"I guess they just wanted to beat the s—t out of us," Stanford coach Jack Christiansen said. A war of words ensued in the press between McKay and Christiansen after that. Those close to McKay said there was no love lost between the two.

"I can't say we've ever played a helluva game against Stanford," said Dave Levy. "We've never been able to get our guys to take them seriously."

The term Student Body Right accurately described the end sweeps Davis ran behind. Cunningham, Rae, and Young keyed the victory over Cal, 42–14. With so many easy wins, Pat Haden was getting plenty of opportunity to gain experience.

Washington had quarterback Sonny Sixkiller. They were ranked eighteenth, but their star was hurt and they lost 34–7. In the first half they had minus-seven yards total offense as Troy built a 20–0 lead. Cunningham scored in the first quarter, followed by Davis with a spectacular forty-four-yard romp. Rae kicked two field goals. A. D. scored again in the second half, as did Cunningham. Washington barely averted the shutout by scoring late.

Against Oregon (the only game they were "pushed," said Pat Haden) USC won 18–0. The rain fell on the slippery artificial turf, and at the half it was 0–0. USC fumbled six times, but A. D. was good when he had to be. He gained 206 yards, scoring twice. Cunningham added a third. None of the PATs were converted. The defense was spectacular, with cornerback Charles Hinton picking off two of their four interceptions.

"The only thing different about Davis's runs was that he didn't fall down," said McKay. "I'd rather play in the mud than on those carpets when it's wet. What they ought to do with those carpets is take them out and burn them."

The press started to focus on Davis, who like Reggie Bush in the 2000s was becoming a national star but was not even the starting tailback yet. Davis's brash personality made him a perfect quotemeister. McKay smiled when he thought about the young man now dubbed "A. D."

"I coach 'em not to get tackled," McKay joked.

With Davis finally in the starting lineup, Washington State fell, 44–3. A. D. ran the opening kick back sixty-nine yards, setting up a twenty-three-yard field goal. Rae ran eleven yards and Davis three to make the score 17–3. Overall, A. D. had 195 yards on thirty-two carries. Linebacker Charles Anthony, with thirteen tackles, was voted defensive player of the game. Cougar quarterback Ty Paine was held to eight of nineteen for eighty-five yards.

"USC isn't the top team in the country," joked Washington State coach Jim Sweeney. "The Miami Dolphins are."

The win over Washington State set up a major confrontation with UCLA, who had traveled to Seattle and lost to a healthy Sonny Sixkiller and Washington, 30–21.

Mark Harmon had steered the Bruins into the Rose Bowl picture. They were now using a veer offense under Coach Pepper Rodgers, similar to what Alabama had used to beat Troy in 1971. UCLA was extremely talented, fast, and athletic. If it were not for USC, they would have been a very big deal—a Rose Bowl team, maybe a contender for the national championship.

A huge crowd filled the Coliseum on a hot November evening. *Sports Illustrated* duly noted that the L.A. crowd left behind more trash than any crowd in any stadium in America, a reference to their propensity for alcohol consumption during night contests.

Rae engineered a first quarter drive culminating in a field goal. After holding UCLA's veer, USC drove again. A. D. swept around end for thirty yards, 10–0.

A UCLA touchdown drive and a Davis fumble had the Bruins back in the game, 10–7, but UCLA missed a game-tying field goal try before Wood took over. He chased down James McAlister and harried poor Harmon badly. With the outside lanes shut down, UCLA had to go up the middle. "Batman" Wood was there every time.

Rod McNeill capped an eighty-yard drive with a one-yarder to make it 17–7. Rae led a ninety-six-yard third quarter march, capping it with a keeper to make it 24–7. USC shut it down offensively for some strange reason, but Wood kept dominating, finishing with eighteen tackles. Harmon was a pitiful three for nine for thirty-eight yards. Davis gained 178 yards on twenty-six carries, almost a seven-yard average.

Press reports played on USC's multitalented athleticism, restating the oft-used description of the Trojans being able to win "at two or three different sports at once." UCLA was derided as "the best your taxes can buy." In the socially conscious early 1970s, political differences between schools began to emerge, playing themselves out as part of the football rivalry.

"It was funny how unemotional we were," said A. D. "We were high, sure, but we weren't in a frenzy the way I always thought USC was supposed to be for UCLA."

The 24–7 score did not do justice to USC's utter domination. They toyed with the Bruins in the manner of a cat killing a mouse at its own pace.

"Gentlemen," McKay said, "I'd like to announce that the Rose Bowl no longer belongs to Radcliffe. I don't care what happens the rest of the year because we're going home."

"I guess USC's the best team I've ever seen, period," said Rodgers. "There isn't anything they don't do well on offense or defense, and they know they can do it, and they do it."

McKay noted that his team had run the table in the polls, number one from the opening game to date, and that his pal Bear Bryant was second. McKay said he voted for Alabama out of deference to his friend, but "don't blame me for all those other dumb guys voting for us."

Despite averaging thirty-eight points a game coming in, some UCLA players actually admitted later to being scared of USC. McKay was no doubt fibbing when he said he did not care about the rest of the season. Two weeks later Ara Parseghian and

Notre Dame were looking for revenge. They had not beaten McKay since 1966, when of course McKay said "a billion Chinamen could not care less who wins," and was supposed to have also vowed "never to lose to Notre Dame again."

Since then he had *not* lost to Notre Dame. In the past two seasons his underdog charges had knocked Notre Dame out of the hunt for a number one ranking. Ranked tenth, the Fighting Irish had lost only to Missouri and were already Orange Bowl–bound. Notre Dame may have thought 1972 at the Coliseum was revenge time. They discovered, to borrow another McKay-like Politically Incorrect term that Asians could take offense to, that they did not have "a Chinaman's chance in hell" against Southern Cal.

Alabama, Bear Bryant's perennial contenders, completely recovered from their segregationist doldrums, had been undefeated until losing to rival Auburn, 17–16. USC was installed as a fourteen-point favorite over Notre Dame with a clear path to the school's seventh national title.

"Notre Dame has improved defensively," McKay told his charges. "Their multiple offense will include many things our defense has never seen. And they certainly are bigger than anybody we've played. They weigh their guys only as freshmen. They've got guys inside on defense who are well over 270. It's difficult for most college guards to block them."

A review of USC's 1972 wins reveals a team averaging a little over forty points a game, posting one shutout, usually winning by about thirty. It was never close. But what is most impressive is that in several of their games, they held it back a little instead of laying it on thick. The UCLA game was an example. The 45–23 victory over Notre Dame was another.

Anthony Davis became the legendary "Notre Dame killer" that day in front of 75,243 sun-soaked Los Angelenos. Many recall his game two years later, but his 1972 sophomore performance is very possibly the finest college football game any individual has ever played. He broke five school records, including most touchdowns in a game (*six*), touchdowns in a quarter (three), points (thirty-six), longest scoring kickoff return (97 yards), and kickoff return yardage in season (an astonishing 468). He had 368 total yards, rushing for 99 to finish the season over 1,000. The numbers are only part of the story. He ran back two kicks, a 96-yarder in addition to a 97-yard return.

Davis opened the game with the 97-yard kickoff return for a touchdown. With USC leading 6–3 in the first quarter, A. D. scored from the 1. Then Dale Mitchell recovered Erick Penick's fumble at the Irish 1, setting up another Davis score from the 5 to make it 19–3.

Tom Clements passed to Willie Townsend to make it 19–10 at the half. Davis scored early in the third quarter from four yards out after a Charles Hinton pass interception. The two-pointer failed but the 25–10 lead looked safe. Two Notre Dame interceptions and some Irish heroics gave them the false sense that they were back in the game.

After stomping Notre Dame, USC got cavalier on the sidelines. It was a situation

Brice Taylor was USC's first
All-American in 1925. He was
of African American and
Cherokee descent, born
without use of his left hand.
USC led the way in the area of
opportunity for black athletes
long before the rest of the
country integrated.
*Courtesy of the Amateur Athletic
Foundation of Los Angeles*

Marcus Allen was USC's fourth
Heisman Trophy winner in 1981
and a member of the 1978 national
champions. He played in the same
backfield with 1979 Heisman
winner Charles White. USC is one
of the only schools to have
"Heisman teammates." Others
include USC (Matt Leinart and
Reggie Bush, 2004–2005) and Army
(Doc Blanchard and Glenn Davis,
1945–1946).
*Courtesy of the Amateur Athletic Foundation of
Los Angeles*

Ronnie Lott is one of the great legends of football, an All-American at USC who helped lead San Francisco to four Super Bowl championships.
Courtesy of the Amateur Athletic Foundation of Los Angeles

Howard "Head Man" Jones won four national championships between 1928 and 1939.
Courtesy of the Amateur Athletic Foundation of Los Angeles

John McKay (center, holding cigar) won four national championships between 1962 and 1974.
Courtesy of the Amateur Athletic Foundation of Los Angeles

O. J. Simpson, the 1968 Heisman Trophy winner, is considered by some to be the greatest college running back of all time.
Courtesy of the Amateur Athletic Foundation of Los Angeles

"Jaguar Jon" Arnett may well have won USC's first Heisman Trophy had a West Coast recruiting scandal not set the program back in 1956.
Courtesy of the Amateur Athletic Foundation of Los Angeles

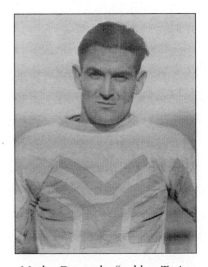

Morley Drury, the "noblest Trojan of them all."
Courtesy of the Amateur Athletic Foundation of Los Angeles

Traveler, USC's mascot since 1961.
Courtesy of the Amateur Athletic Foundation of Los Angeles

Mike Garrett (right) and
Craig Fertig (left) teamed
up to beat Notre Dame
20–17 in 1964.
Courtesy of the Amateur Athletic
Foundation of Los Angeles

The 1962 national champions were Coach John McKay's first, and USC's first since 1939.

Courtesy of the Amateur Athletic Foundation of Los Angeles

Larry Smith coached USC to
three straight Rose Bowls
(1987–1989).
Courtesy of the Amateur Athletic
Foundation of Los Angeles

Safety Mark Carrier was an All-
American and winner of the
Jim Thorpe Award before a
career with the Chicago Bears.
Courtesy of the Amateur Athletic
Foundation of Los Angeles

Todd Marinovich was a symbol
of lost potential.
Courtesy of the Amateur Athletic
Foundation of Los Angeles

Tim Ryan was an All-
American lineman at USC and
star of the Chicago Bears.
Courtesy of the Amateur Athletic
Foundation of Los Angeles

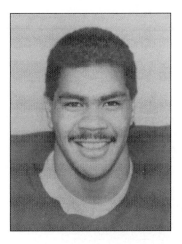

Junior Seau is considered
one of the greatest
linebackers in history.
*Courtesy of the Amateur Athletic
Foundation of Los Angeles*

The 1931 Trojan national championship team that beat Notre Dame 16–14 in the first game
played at Notre Dame Stadium. They are pictured wearing bowlers and fur coats in
Chicago prior to their triumphant return back to Los Angeles.
Courtesy of the Amateur Athletic Foundation of Los Angeles

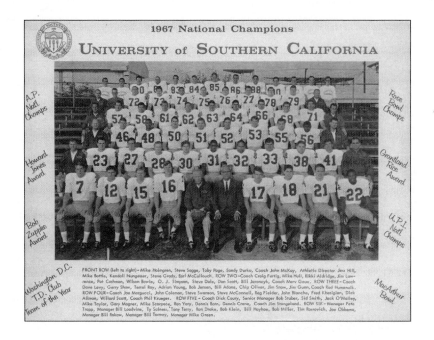

Mort Kaer, known as the "Red Bluff terror," carries the ball.
Courtesy of the Amateur Athletic Foundation of Los Angeles

USC's Song Girls, considered the "gold standard" of college cheerleaders,
are shown during a 1974 TV appearance.
Courtesy of the Amateur Athletic Foundation of Los Angeles

Legendary USC announcer Tom Kelly with 1972 All-American Sam "Bam" Cunningham.
Courtesy of Tom Kelly

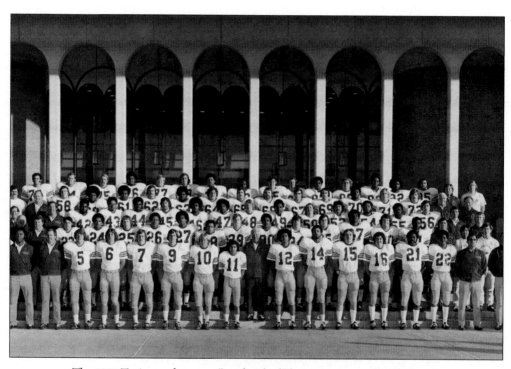

The 1973 Trojans, who were "sandwiched" between two national champs (1972, 1974).
Courtesy of Mrs. Patricia Goux

The 1972 USC national champions, still considered the greatest college football team in history.

Courtesy of Mrs. Patricia Goux

The undefeated 1969 Trojans.

Courtesy of Mrs. Patricia Goux

Marv Goux (left) and
Dave Levy. Levy was the
"favorite" to succeed John
McKay until John
Robinson was chosen.
Courtesy of Mrs. Patricia Goux

John McKay's staff in 1972 included Dave Levy (top, third from right), Craig Fertig (top, second
from right), John Robinson (top, far right), Wayne Fontes (bottom, far left), and Marv Goux
(bottom, second from left). They are pictured before the College All-Star Game vs.
the Super Bowl Champion Miami Dolphins.
Courtesy of Mrs. Patricia Goux

John McKay and his staff in the early 1970s.

Courtesy of Mrs. Patricia Goux

84-Z delay. McKay confers on the sideline during the comeback from 17–0 down to beat Notre Dame 20–17 at the Coliseum in 1964.

Courtesy of Mrs. Patricia Goux

The "Wild Bunch," USC's famed defensive front of 1969. They were named after the Sam Peckinpah movie of that year starring Ernest Borgnine and William Holden. Al Cowlings (far left) drove O. J.'s white Bronco in the infamous "slow speed chase" of 1994.

Courtesy of Mrs. Patricia Goux

Dave Brown (right) and teammate Cliff Culbreath.

Courtesy of Dave Brown

A little-known offensive lineman, Dave Brown,
organized Fellowship of Christian Athletes
meetings. USC's "team of destiny" found
inspiration through Dave's efforts before beating
Notre Dame in 1971, then carried that into the
1972 national championship season.

Courtesy of Dave Brown

Jeff Prugh covered USC and UCLA sports,
then later covered politics in the post-
segregation South of the late 1970s.

Courtesy of Jeff Prugh

Sam Dickerson caught
Jimmy Jones's pass in the
end zone to miraculously
beat UCLA 14–12 in 1969.
High school student Pete
Carroll was in attendance
that day, watching USC play
for the first time.

Courtesy of Sam Dickerson

Sam Dickerson as a San
Francisco 49er.
Courtesy of Sam Dickerson

Tom Kelly with Trojan legends John McKay, John Robinson, and Marv Goux.
Courtesy of Tom Kelly

somewhat similar to their "where's the party" attitude when they led Wisconsin, 42–14, in the 1963 Rose Bowl. McKay was smiling and joking. The players were thinking about USC coeds and the Rose Bowl the next month.

They let Notre Dame back in it, 25–23, but no sooner were the Irish eyes smiling when A. D. ran his second kick back to give them a dose of reality. After Notre Dame kicked out of bounds trying to keep the ball away from him, Cliff Brown tried again. This time A. D. gathered it in at the 4, headed straight upfield into the blocking wedge, squeezed through, and made for the left sideline. He evaded one good shot. From there he was off to the races.

"Whichever way they go I go the other," he explained.

In the end zone, A. D. went into his patented "knee dance."

"Both kickoff returns were practically the same," he said. "On both a wedge opened up on the left. On the second I faked in, and then out, then back in again. One guy just caught my leg when I started that one, and I broke two tackles along the way. I have three accelerations. One when I get the ball. One when I get to the line and one when I get open."

"Davis is the greatest I've ever seen on kickoff returns in college," noted Parseghian.

When Southern California led 32–23, the 75,243 began to chant, "We're number one!" In the fourth quarter, A. D. ran it in *again*, from the 8 for touchdown number six. Cunningham wrapped up the scoring with a one-yard leap to make it 45–23. Had McKay let A. D. score, it would have tied an NCAA record.

"I've never seen a greater single day shown by an individual than Davis gave today," said McKay. "I know he could have tied the record by scoring one more touchdown, but we don't worry about NCAA records."

In 2006, however, A. D. still held some bitterness over not getting his shot.

"He kept me from breaking that record because he didn't like my militant attitude," was his blunt assessment.

"Hollywood never dreamed up anything like this afternoon's tingling drama that catapulted artistic Anthony Davis, a stubby Southern California sophomore, to instant stardom out here in the land where stars are born," wrote the *Chicago Tribune*.

"Supported by perhaps the finest football team in Southern California's championship history, Davis masterfully played a six-touchdown role as the Trojans whipped Notre Dame. Seldom, if ever, has one done so much to entertain so many," concluded the *Tribune* in Churchillian fashion.

The MacArthur Bowl, the national championship trophy, was given to USC. McKay admitted that he would finally switch his vote to USC instead of Alabama.

"This is the best football team I've coached at Southern California," he said.

"This is probably the best balanced football team that Southern California has ever had," added Parseghian, still reeling from his worst-ever Notre Dame loss.

"We gave them everything we had but they're just a superior football team," said Notre Dame athletic director Ed "Moose" Krause. "I feel sorry for Ohio State."

The UPI awarded the title to USC. The AP was waiting until after the bowls. McKay was a bit peeved that titles had been awarded to teams like Alabama in the 1960s, among others, prior to their losing bowl games, but he knew that for a team to be a legitimate winner, they had to emerge from the bowl victorious. A loss to Ohio State would wipe out the whole season and he understood it.

In the pre–Rose Bowl media hoopla, McKay simply disregarded all the usual disclaimers of his team's prowess.

"This team has the best people I've ever had," he said. "We've played a tough schedule, and nobody has come close to beating us."

Ohio State had lost to the same Michigan State team that USC had beaten, 51–6, but Woody's boys beat Michigan to earn their way back to Pasadena. The Big 10 had finally lifted their ridiculous "no-repeat" rule. In addition, 1972 was the first year that freshmen were eligible. The Buckeyes had a good one, running back Archie Griffin.

Once the official pregame luncheons were under way, McKay found a way to pacify Hayes with praise, sort of.

"If our defense isn't better than it was against Notre Dame we'll be in trouble," he said.

"It remains to be seen whether they'll be able to do anything against our defense," said A. D. "I know I can't in practice. To be in the game with us, you have to be a balanced team and I don't know if they can pass that well."

"If the right play is called against the right defense, there's no way to stop us," said Lynn Swann.

"They can run on just about anyone," said Charles Hinton. "The Big 10's kind of a rough league with all those 'three yards and a cloud of dust' offenses. The Pacific 8 relies more on finesse."

McKay went so far as to say that some of Ohio State's players who had been on the roster of the Buckeyes' 1968 team, which had beaten O. J., 27–16, would not even make this Buckeye team—a claim that seems to have little merit but served to puff up the opposition.

"They've got everything," said Hayes. "They're probably as well balanced a team as has ever stepped on the field. They have great team speed, both on offense and defense. They are faster than Michigan. Faster than us, faster than anybody. They're a lot like Jackie Robinson. Baseball men said he could beat you more ways than anybody else. That's exactly the way Southern Cal is."

It was quite apropos that Sam "Bam" Cunningham, who started his career so spectacularly against Alabama, would end it as the headliner against Ohio State. Sam is a Trojan legend, a Hall of Famer and an all-time great, but his career is overshadowed by some of his more flamboyant teammates and events. Not on New Year's Day, 1973.

The first half was close, though. Swann caught a ten-yard pass after Charles Phillips recovered a fumble on the Buckeye 38. Ohio State tied it up after a fifty-six-yard drive. Some felt Ohio State had even outplayed USC.

"McKay got scared a little of Woody Hayes and changed our offense, our blocking schemes, in the first half," said offensive lineman Allan Graf. "It was 7–7, nothing was working. So he said, 'Aw, what the heck,' and changed back to what we'd been doing, and we came back to blow 'em away, 42–17."

USC scored the first five times they had the ball in the second half. Cunningham scored four times, which included his patented "over-the-top" tumbles into the end zone.

"Cunningham had thirty-four yards going over the top, so I look over at Woody in short sleeves," McKay said on *The History of USC Football* DVD, in an interview he had recorded some years earlier. "It's cold and miserable, I just want to get out of there, so I just go like this [motions over the top] and that's what he did. I won't tell you what he did to me, but it wasn't nice."

Rae completed eighteen of twenty-five for 229 yards, six to Swann and six to Young. Davis rushed for 157 yards, but Cunningham was named Player of the Game.

"I owe Sam something," said McKay. "He was a great runner, but I made him a blocker for three years. He's the best runner I ever ruined."

John Bledsoe gave Ohio State a little dignity with a touchdown late to finish it at 42–17.

"Is there anybody else the Associated Press would like us to play?" asked McKay. The Bears, the Jets, the Eagles . . . there were a few NFL teams that probably were not as good.

Hayes could not say anything bad about USC when it was over.

"Yes, they are the best college football team I've ever seen," Hayes admitted. "Because of their tremendous balance. You can run on them some, as we proved, but in the second half, they passed us right out of the park. At halftime I thought we played them fairly even but I thought the key play was a third-and-eighteen pass to Swann. We could never stop them after that. Their passing attack was very good. We couldn't stop it, but eleven other teams couldn't either."

"We stuck it to a team that was supposed to be great," said A. D. "If Ohio State is the third best team in the country, and we beat them like this, we must be unstoppable."

Media pundits said USC was not only number one, but numbers "two through three," as well. That was how great the discrepancy was between the Trojan dynasty and the rest of college football in 1972. Very few collegiate teams have ever swept through their schedule the way USC did.

USC had "the best people I've ever had," said McKay. "We've played a tough schedule and nobody has come close to beating us. The only one who can say this is the best team I've ever had is me. And I've just said it."

The national media took McKay's assessment one step further, positing the notion that it was not USC's best team ever, but rather the best team ever, *anywhere*. McKay would eventually make this same statement. He was still saying it when interviewed by this author in 2000. At the time, McKay still hedged his bets, though.

"I wouldn't want to say about it being the best of all time," said McKay. "But I don't think any team has been deeper than us in backs. We have great receivers. We do a lot of things. We have a lot of people. You can't believe how good a quarterback Pat Haden is, and he didn't even get to play much this season." Then he thought about it some more.

"I've never seen a team that could beat it," he stated.

Prior to the game, Hayes had endeared himself to the West Coast press corps by telling his players, "There are some real a———s out here and not one of them wants you to win. Just be darn careful what you say. Just tell them how darn good they [USC] are and let it go at that."

The Buckeye players were complete gentlemen, but not so Woody. He allegedly slugged an *L.A. Times* photographer on the field before the game, causing him to be sued. Hayes's frustration apparently had grown out of the fact that, while the Big 10 had won twelve of the first thirteen Rose Bowls, they had dropped eight of the previous thirteen. The loss in 1973 marked their fourth straight defeat in Pasadena.

Further post–Rose Bowl analysis was filled with superlatives such as "USC has personnel like Kuwait has oil." Washington State coach Jim Sweeney's earlier comment that "USC isn't the best team in the country; the Miami Dolphins are" was repeated. Miami would finish the NFL season as the only unbeaten Super Bowl champion ever. Superlatives describing Rae, Young, tackle Pete Adams, defensive tackle John Grant, linebacker Richard "Batman" Wood, as well as Davis, McNeill, Cunningham, Swann, and others, had a sublime quality to them. The general feeling was that words alone could not accurately depict how much better they were than not just the 1972 competition, but the 1869–1971 competition.

They captured both polls as the first two-poll unanimous selection, as well as the Bob Zuppke Award presented to the "best team playing the toughest schedule."

Tight end Charles Young was a unanimous All-American. The 6'4", 228-pounder was being called the best college tight end ever. He had revolutionized the position in the style of the Colts' John Mackey. A first round pick of Philadelphia, he played for the Eagles and Rams before helping Bill Walsh's San Francisco 49ers win the 1982 Super Bowl. After finishing his career with Seattle, he settled in the Pacific Northwest, becoming an ordained minister. Three of his beautiful daughters ("Charle's angels") ran track at USC. In 2004 he was inducted into the National Football Foundation's Hall of Fame.

"I only averaged one and a half catches per game," said Young in 2005, "but I was still a consensus All-American. That's because I averaged twenty yards a catch. That was the greatest team in the history of college football. We were the most well balanced team on offense and defense ever. I'm not sure the 2005 Trojans are even better than the 2004 team, but I think that if we had played them, we would have shut them out until late in the third quarter."

The great Sam "Bam" Cunningham was ironically underrated during his Trojan days. Because of his game against Alabama, however, there are very few USC athletes whose name is now more recognizable, and whose star shines more brightly thirty-four years later. Sam was the kind of running back who could have put up enormous numbers at another school where he would have gotten the ball thirty-plus times a game. But he sacrificed his touches and his body, as Young did at the tight end position, as a blocking fullback. Others (Clarence Davis in 1970, A. D. in 1972) got the glory. Sam never cared. He just wanted to win.

Despite not having gaudy personal statistics, Cunningham was rewarded with a 1972 All-American selection in his senior year. The captain of the all-time great '72 squad, Sam was the eleventh pick of the 1973 draft by the New England Patriots. He played in New England with two former rivals, Alabama's John Hannah and Stanford's Jim Plunkett. He retired after a productive career in 1982. He was inducted into the USC Athletic Hall of Fame in 2001.

Defensive tackle and defensive end John Grant was an All-American in 1972, too. The Boise, Idaho, native played for Denver from 1973 to 1979, including their 1978 Super Bowl loss to Dallas.

Offensive tackle Pete Adams was an All-American, then drafted in the first round by Cleveland, where he played for two seasons.

Two sophomores made All-American. A. D. was an honorable mention selection in 1972. Linebacker "Batman" Wood was a first team pick. In addition to A. D. and Wood, Lynn Swann, Booker Brown, Artimus Parker, Steve Riley, and Charles Phillips, all members of the 1972 squad, would make All-American over the next two years.

Ten 1972 Trojan seniors were drafted. Edesel Garrison went to the Oilers. Mike Rae became a fixture as Ken Stabler's backup in Oakland, which garnered him a 1977 Super Bowl ring when the team beat Minnesota at the Rose Bowl. Defensive tackle Jeff Winans was chosen in the second round by Buffalo. The New England Patriots chose Allen Gallaher. Karl Lorch (Miami) and Michael Ryan (Oakland) rounded out the draft class.

As if to symbolize how good USC was—in fact many honestly thought they *were* of NFL caliber—the January 1973 Super Bowl was played at the Coliseum. The team Jim Sweeney said *was* better than USC, Miami, won it over former UCLA quarterback Billy Kilmer and Washington. It was the second and last Super Bowl at the venerable Coliseum. The Pro Bowl would be played there each year throughout the decade until it was shifted to Honolulu.

Forty-one additional Trojans would be drafted off the 1973–1977 teams, most of whom were associated with the 1972 squad in one way or another. Aside from starters and backups, this includes recruits, freshmen, red-shirts, and five-year players. Notable names include Lynn Swann, Steve Riley, Rod McNeill, Booker Brown, James Sims, Manfred Moore, Artimus Parker, Anthony Davis, Charles Phillips, Bill Bain, Richard Wood, Allen Carter, Jim Obradovich, Pat Haden, Marvin Cobb (also a baseball player), J. K. McKay, and Bob McCaffrey.

STUDENT BODY RIGHT

"We became madmen."

RUNNING BACK ANTHONY DAVIS AFTER THE 1974
USC–NOTRE DAME GAME

It was not a sporting event, it was a Roman orgy. USC was not a football team, they were Patton's Army moving through the Low Countries, Grant taking Richmond, the Wehrmacht during the Blitzkrieg.

For SC coach John McKay, it was not about coaching, it was about destiny.

"If I was in control," he says, "we would have scored more than six points in the first half."

For Trojan fans, it was not a game, it was a sighting. It was Fatima, Lourdes, and the Burning Bush combined.

For Notre Dame coach Ara Parseghian, it was the Seventh Circle of Hell, *The Twilight Zone,* "Chef's head" in *Apocalypse Now.*

For the Irish, it was their worst disaster since the potato famine.

It was a seventeen-minute Southern California earthquake, epicentered at the Los Angeles Memorial Coliseum on a fall Saturday in 1974. It was felt as far away as South Bend, Indiana, and the aftershocks reverberate to this day.

The Notre Dame Fighting Irish were the defending national champions. En route to an undefeated 1973 season, they had smoked Southern Cal at South Bend. Notre Dame gave up 2.2 yards per rush and eight touchdowns in their previous 1974 games, and victory over SC would put them in a position to finish number one again. SC was playing for the top slot, too. A national television audience tuned in to the biggest game of the year, and 83,552 filled the Coliseum.

A typical SC–Notre Dame game.

In the first half, Notre Dame outclassed USC in every way, breaking out to a 24–0 lead, and their fans were in Full Gloat.

SC managed a touchdown on a swing pass from quarterback Pat Haden to tailback Anthony Davis with ten seconds left in the first half, but the extra point failed. 6–24.

"I told them that if Davis runs the second half kickoff back for a touchdown we would win the game," said McKay. Over the years, McKay's remarks were changed to "Davis *will* run the second half kickoff back for a touchdown," but like everything else that day, his words are now legend and myth.

At halftime, McKay "informed" his team that "'we're behind.' Two math majors raised their hands and said, 'Yeah.'"

According to Craig Fertig, McKay also informed special teams blocker Mosi Tatupu that "there's no rule in this game against blocking" for A. D. on the second half kick return.

The first seventeen minutes of the second half were the most exciting in college football and Los Angeles sports history.

Kickoff to Davis, who runs it 102 yards for a touchdown; two-point conversion fails. 12–24.

Haden to J. K. McKay for thirty-one yards, followed by Davis for a six-yard touch-down scamper, kick good. 19–24.

Kevin Bruce recovers a Notre Dame fumble, two long Haden pass completions, Davis four yards, touchdown, then Davis dives in to complete the two-point conver-sion. 27–24, SC. 6:23 gone in the quarter. Madhouse.

Marvin Cobb returns a punt fifty-six yards for Troy, Haden to McKay. 34–24, 9:23 gone in the third.

Charles Phillips intercepts Irish quarterback Tom Clements's pass, Haden hits McKay from forty-four yards out, period ends, 41–24.

Bruce recovers another fumble, Haden to Shelton Diggs, sixteen yards. 48–24.

Phillips's third interception is returned fifty-eight yards for a touchdown. Seven-teen minutes after it started, 55–24.

McKay normally stood calmly amid the bedlam, arms crossed like a commuter waiting for the 5:30 to Larchmont. This time, he lost control, hugging Haden (who lived in his house his senior year at Bishop Amat High), his son, J. K. (Haden's best friend), and Davis, all at the same time. None of the players weighed more than 183 pounds.

"There have never been three smaller kids who have done so much so often," he said, managing to sound like Winston Churchill.

Up in the broadcast booth, Ohio State coach Woody Hayes must have felt like a Prussian military commander with a binocular-view of Napoleon's Italian Campaign, knowing he would have to face them down the road. The USC rooting section started chanting, "Woody, you're next!" in reference to the upcoming Rose Bowl.

With thirteen minutes left, the Trojans had conquered Ireland, but before they could "roll over Austria, Poland, and Denmark," as *Sports Illustrated* stated it, McKay pulled his starters in favor of Vince Evans and Rob Adolph.

Toward the end, McKay just turned to Fertig and said, "Damndest thing I ever saw." On *The History of USC Football* DVD, McKay exclaimed, "I have no idea what happened. But I guarantee I was there, and I clapped."

Davis proved himself the best college football player in America that day, but because it was played on a late date, ballots for the Heisman Trophy were mailed prior to his performance. Ohio State's Archie Griffin won it instead.

The game left Notre Dame at 9–2. Southern California was not as phenomenal in their New Year's Day game with the Buckeyes. In keeping with the comeback theme, though, Haden combined with McKay and Diggs to bring his team down the field for a touchdown and a two-point conversion, good for the 18–17 victory, a 10–1–1 record, and the national championship. In those days, not only was USC unbelievably good, but they were as exciting as any team ever.

Parseghian never coached after that season. Rumors have it he sees a therapist to combat visions of a white horse constantly running around a field.

■ ■ ■

The flawed Trojans—*not* the greatest team of all time, *not* as good as the '72 team— had captivated America's fans and, just as important, its poll voters. They were awarded their eighth national championship. It was McKay's fourth, which at this point gave him one more than his friend and rival, Alabama's Paul "Bear" Bryant.

USC could make a strong argument that they were the greatest collegiate football tradition in history. It was close, but they were still second . . . to Notre Dame. Alabama, Nebraska, and Oklahoma were knocking on the door. Michigan's and Ohio State's stars were fading a bit.

A. D. was a consensus All-American. He would go on to be elected to the National Football Foundation's College Hall of Fame. An analysis of Heisman winner Griffin and runner-up A. D., revolving around A. D.'s game against Notre Dame and a comparison of the two players' performances in the Rose Bowl, reveals that A. D. should have been USC's third Heisman winner.

This set of circumstances resulted in the voters holding their votes back until after the last of the rivalry games, which are sometimes played as late as December, in order to get the clearest picture of the "best player in college football." In those days, ballots had to be mailed. Today, the Internet allows for instant voting.

THE TRADITION OF TROY

The smooth transition from King John McKay to Prince Robinson leads to the completion of college football's most dominant two-decade run

John Robinson had in fact been groomed for the job. McKay's departure to pro doldrums in Tampa Bay was shocking to his players and the alumni, but it had been discussed and was being worked on for some time. Robinson had come into the program in 1972, but in 1975 he was sent to Oakland where he was given an unusual job, that of de facto assistant head coach of the Raiders.

There are rumors that McKay got into it with an influential alum, but Robinson's hiring, at least on the surface, had all the appearance of an event that had been planned well ahead of time. Many felt Dave Levy was the deserving heir apparent, but the telegenic Robinson was chosen, possibly because of his public relations skills as much as his football expertise.

Robinson grew up in the San Francisco suburb of Daly City. His childhood pal was John Madden. Madden had gone to Jefferson High, Robinson to Serra, a Catholic school in San Mateo that is legendary for producing famous sports figures, among them Angel shortstop Jim Fregosi, Oriole pitcher Wally Bunker, USC wide receiver Lynn Swann, Patriot quarterback Tom Brady, and Giants' superstar Barry Bonds.

Madden played at Cal Poly San Luis Obispo. His teammate was Ted Tollner, who coached at USC from 1983 to 1986. The team suffered a terrible tragedy when their plane crashed on a road trip, but Madden and Tollner survived. Madden spent the rest of his life avoiding airplanes at almost any cost.

Robinson went to McKay's alma mater, Oregon. He met McKay when he played under him from 1954 to 1957. After that, he got into coaching.

"I was very interested in coaching, even as a player," Robinson said. "I asked John McKay a lot of questions."

Robinson was an assistant coach at Oregon from 1960 to 1971. His star rose, leading him to USC, where he became McKay's offensive coordinator from 1972 to 1974.

Being associated with the 1972 and 1974 national champions gave him imprimatur in that era, similar to Norm Chow in the 2000s.

An "arrangement" was made, whereby Robinson was "sent" to Oakland to tutor under his pal Madden for a year or so. The 1975 Raiders were a talented squad with Kenny Stabler, Clarence Davis, and Fred Biletnikoff, but they suffered a disappointing season. The previous year they had looked to be Super Bowl–bound, but Pittsburgh knocked them out in the AFC title game. The '75 Raiders made it to the AFC championship contest, but lost in freezing conditions on Pittsburgh's artificial turf against the famed "Steel Curtain" Steeler defense.

The following year they did attain, as their venerable broadcaster Bill King liked to call it, the "Promised Land," but Robinson was not part of it.

After McKay's resignation, Robinson was brought in. It was a seemingly seamless transition for a guy groomed for the job in Los Angeles and Oakland. USC President John Hubbard called Robinson from a phone booth at the New York airport in October 1975.

"Hubbard was on the run somewhere when he got hold of me," Robinson said. "He said he couldn't talk, but the job was mine if I wanted it. I simply said, 'Yes.' The next week I was hired. I wasn't even interviewed."

Robinson had challenges and blessings. His blessing was Ricky Bell. His challenges were recruiting and Vince Evans. Robinson hired Paul Hackett to work with Evans.

HERITAGE

Alabama redux, when legends played

1978. Legion Field, Birmingham, Alabama. A day game in September, hot and muggy. National television. Two undefeated teams, the winner would have the inside track at finishing number one.

As Marv Goux would say, "The best of the West versus the best of the East." Eight years prior, in a game that by no means had been forgotten in 'Bama, John McKay's Trojans waltzed into Birmingham for a night game against the Crimson Tide. Southern California was cocky, arrogant. Maybe the greatest program ever assembled over a nineteen-year period (1962–1981). They featured a black sophomore fullback from Santa Barbara named Sam "Bam" Cunningham. Phenomenal black athletes, some from the South, had long been a staple at USC. Their first All-American in 1925 had been a black man.

Coach Bear Bryant's Alabama team was 100 percent white when USC walked into their house in 1970 and administered a whuppin', led by Cunningham with two touchdowns.

Now, in 1978, the men of Troy were back. This time, they were led by a new coach, John Robinson, and he had a team that was possibly more talented than the best of McKay's juggernauts. SC had won the national championship in 1972. In '74 spectacular comebacks against Notre Dame and Ohio State propelled them to the crown.

All-American tailback Charles White led USC in '78. Anthony Munoz opened his holes. Junior quarterback Paul McDonald had as much brains and ability as Pat Haden. Cornerback Dennis Smith succeeded Dennis Thurman as the second straight All-American to come out of Santa Monica High. A young safety named Ronnie Lott was hitting people with the force of a major earthquake.

Alabama was not their father's Tide. This time, they came to play with black athletes. Extremely talented ones. Lots of them. The era of the USCs and Michigan States picking off the Bubba Smiths of the South was over. Now Alabama, Tennessee, Florida State, and the others would reap the harvest sown in their backyards. For this reason, USC no longer enjoyed that quiet advantage that nobody really wanted to talk about in 1970. They would have to play it even up in the other guy's stadium.

It was no contest. White ran for 199 yards and a couple touchdowns. The Trojans dominated from the first snap, taking the huge crowd out early, and the final score, 24–14, did not reflect Southern California's superiority.

A few weeks later, the Trojans had a letdown. It was one of those radio-only Saturday night games against a tough Sun Devil squad, fired up to prove themselves in the new Pacific 10 Conference. In L.A., sports fans making the disco scene at the Red Onion or Flanagan's missed Tom Kelly's broadcast of ASU's 20–7 upset win.

That was it, though. The rest of the conference fell like Eastern Europe under Stalin. Terry Donahue's UCLA Bruins could play anybody else even up in 1978, but against their rivals they were boys facing men.

Then came Thanksgiving weekend.

With Alabama already having been knocked off, the game, played on an overcast day at the Coliseum, before a full house in an electric atmosphere, promised to be for the national championship. In 1977, Joe Montana and the green-shirted Irish derailed SC's winning streak in front of a more-deranged-than-usual Notre Dame crowd. That earned them an eventual national title, but the victory was an exception during that era. In those days, USC beat Notre Dame like a redheaded stepchild.

Mays going all out. Brando emoting. Reagan communicating to the camera. Some people are naturals, and anybody lucky enough to have been at the Los Angeles Memorial Coliseum that day could recognize that Montana had it, too. Absolute charisma. Undeniable magic.

Still, in the beginning, USC moved Notre Dame off the line with ease, Lott was in Montana's face, White ran crazy, and McDonald threaded passes like a southpaw surgeon. Well into the third quarter, SC led by three touchdowns.

Then came Joe! If you were there, you saw Montana wake up the echoes and single-handedly silence the home crowd. He was everything that he would be against Dallas, or Cincinnati, or Denver. He was the best I ever saw.

Still, those were halcyon days at the University of Southern California. They got the ball back with about a minute on the clock, and McDonald moved them up the field. With two seconds left, Frank Jordan, a history major from Riordan High School in San Francisco, calmly broke Joe Montana's heart with the game-winning field goal, 27–25. Montana walked off the field, a defeated warrior bathed in the kind of respect reserved only for the rarest of champions.

In an anticlimactic Rose Bowl game, Southern California toyed with an outmanned Michigan team, holding the score down like Ali letting his opponent save a little self-respect.

THE USC TROJANS

When the sun set in Pasadena on New Year's Day to the chant of "We're Number One," it seemed a foregone conclusion that USC had indeed captured the national championship. They were 12–1 in a year that saw no undefeated teams. Alabama's one loss had come at the hands of SC.

THE HALLOWED SHRINE

Camelot in L.A.

Whether or not the 1978 USC–Notre Dame game was better, or more exciting, than the "1974 A.D." game can be argued. It was certainly a high for Coach Robinson, and a low for Dan Devine, who replaced Ara in 1975. The Irish may have *Rudy*, but the Trojans are happy to settle for Frank Jordan. Just as he had done against UCLA a year earlier, Jordan kicked a game-winner with two seconds left.

Jordan was a Catholic kid who grew up in San Francisco's Irish Sunset District. He went to Riordan High School. His younger brother, Steve, would kick field goals for Troy, as well. Jordan would eventually go to work for New York Life in San Francisco, but he fancied himself a historian. He wrote screenplays about World War I. This author once met with him in proposed collaboration of a movie script. The partnership did not blossom, but eventually, through the circuitous route known in Hollywood as "development hell," a movie about this subject—America's Argonne Offensive—was produced on A&E, starring Rick Schroder.

If one visits the clubhouse at San Francisco's Harding Park Golf Course, they cannot miss the signed color photo of Jordan being mobbed by his teammates after the momentous win over Notre Dame.

"We came out the first part of that game and just took it to 'em," said Paul McDonald. "We had a huge lead in that game; I can't remember what the score was but Joe Montana was maybe two for eighteen in the first half and couldn't hit the broad side of a barn. I was thinking, *Who's this guy? He's supposed to be a good player?* Comes out in the second half and throws for 300 yards, brings 'em all the way back, they go for two, they're ahead 25–24, they go for two at the end—*don't get it!*

"I had hurt my ankle the first series of the game. Bob Golic, their linebacker, rolled up on my ankle. They taped it up so I said, 'Put me back in, see if I can play.' The next series I threw a touchdown so I said, 'I'm fine,' but by the end of the game my ankle was killing me.

"And I got the offense together on the sidelines and I said, 'Hey, guys, we're not gonna lose this game.' All we have to do is go down about fifty yards, kick the field goal to win the game and get out of here. We only had one timeout, so we tried to save that timeout. I rolled into the short side of the field, and nobody was open, so I backpedaled, guy was coming right at me, so I threw it, and I threw it—I knew I had to throw it to stop the clock—and it hit one of their linemen's thigh pads, and of course they thought it was a fumble, and they were ecstatic, their bench emptied, they're jumping up and down thinking they won the game, but the official called incomplete pass. Because the ball, my arm was going forward. Next pass we completed a forty-yard pass to Calvin Sweeney, next play Charles White goes off tackle for another eight, we go on the field with two seconds left and kick a field goal to win the game."

Montana's performance was bravura. He was as good in a noble defeat as any college quarterback ever has been, exceeded perhaps only by his incredible comeback effort against Houston in the Cotton Bowl a little over a month later.

"I came there in '72, and through '80, the winner of that game either won the national championship or came in second," recalled Robinson, referred to in SC circles as J. R., "so both teams were nationally ranked, so the winner was probably gonna win the national championship or come very close to it."

The noise of the crowd when Jordan kicked that field goal was absolutely deafening. Men and women kissed in the aisles, nearly making love to each other. Complete strangers hugged like lifelong lost pals. Fathers and sons found meaning. The emotion, all the incredible pent-up pressure of the national championship, the eternal struggle of the Notre Dame game . . . with everything riding on it, this was a true "winner take all" scenario.

Montana, after doggedly wearing down his adversaries all game, glumly boarded a plane back to Indiana with his beaten, dejected team. On that plane, he met a stewardess. A relationship blossomed and she became his wife, although it ended in divorce.

■ ■ ■

The Trojans had a "vacation game" in Hawaii. They actually trailed for a while against the Rainbows before overcoming their sunburns and hangovers in a 21–5 win.

Unlike 1974, when the Notre Dame game presaged an equally dramatic Rose Bowl, this time around the game against Michigan was workmanlike. McDonald threw a touchdown pass to Hoby Brenner. With 7:29 to play in the second quarter, the Trojans had the ball on the Michigan 3. Line judge Gilbert Marchman ruled that White's dive into the end zone was a touchdown.

It was USC's fifth straight Rose Bowl victory, 17–10. White finished with ninety-nine yards. Wolverine quarterback Rick Leach was spectacular in the second half when the

Trojans tried to go conservative, almost to their chagrin. White and Leach shared Player of the Game honors.

Very possibly, USC lost the AP version of the national championship by not putting fifth-ranked Michigan away. Alabama beat unbeaten, number one–ranked Penn State in a strong showing. Despite having beaten the Tide with an impressive win on their home field, USC had to split the title. It was a reverse of the 1966 vote, when 'Bama—unbeaten, untied, and a bowl winner—had been denied the title, which went to once-tied Notre Dame via the "Catholic vote" and the "antisegregation vote." Segregated Texas's 1969 win, with President Nixon's endorsement, takes something away from the argument that the pollsters voted entirely with social pathos in that era, however.

USC could also look to its 17–10 win over UCLA with a tinge of regret. Leading 17–0, they had barely hung on to win 17–10. Impressive blowouts over the Bruins and Wolverines, both within their range of capability, had not happened when they went a little bit too conservative, which was one of the few complaints anybody could think to attach to Robinson's record, at least up until that point. Their second half complacency had nearly cost the Notre Dame game, as well.

With Alabama now completely integrated and rolling like a juggernaut—these were Bear's best teams—the jowly man in the hound's-tooth fedora was suddenly a sentimental favorite. Alabama's share of the 1978 national championship can be attributed in very large measure to the personal charisma of Bear Bryant. In doing the right thing, whether he was late or early to the dance, Bryant had become a national figure and an adored one at that.

Oddly, USC found itself again victims of their own good works. They had of course helped open the door to integration in 1970, only to be surprised by a 'Bama team with black players in 1971. Their role in social progress was again "rewarded" in '78 when the voters went for the man they had helped make progressive.

"That's what you get," John McKay had wryly told Craig Fertig when he had seen John Mitchell sprinting downfield on the opening kick of the 1971 SC-'Bama game in L.A.

It was the end of the regular season four-game arrangement with Alabama. Oddly, the visitors won all four games between the two storied programs in the 1970s.

"Many people said, 'Hey, you can't make it through that kind of schedule,'" said Robinson of the 1978 season, which included wins over Alabama, UCLA, Notre Dame, and Michigan. "They said our schedule was a mankiller. Well, we had some men that it couldn't kill."

Shared national championship or not, for many 1978 represented the highest point in USC football history until the Pete Carroll era. The aura and mystique of Trojan football reached epic proportions. The question of who was the better traditional, historical team, USC or Notre Dame—or Alabama—was very much up in the air, with USC supporters holding plenty of ammunition in support of their argument.

"It was an amazing time, we had great assistant coaches there, we had well known people who were eager," recalled J. R. "It was like a Camelot to a lot of people."

Indeed, "Tailback U." was now "Quarterback College." McDonald was brilliant on the field as well as off. He was the latest in a string of quarterbacks, from Jimmy Jones to Pat Haden to Vince Evans and now himself, who had created a new paradigm at the position for Troy. Assistant Coach Paul Hackett introduced complexity to the offense that heretofore had not existed.

Hackett later became USC's head coach. He did not succeed, but he is due his share of credit. He was one of the minds who created the concept of the West Coast offense, concepts built on the coaching of Sid Gilman, Marv Levy, and Paul Brown. He would go to San Francisco to help perfect it (and Joe Montana) under Coach Bill Walsh in the 1980s.

"One of Paul's greatest strengths was his ability to throw to a variety of receivers, to find the open man," Hackett said of McDonald. "He never made up his mind on the man he was going to throw to until the last possible moment. He didn't get excited."

White finished the 1978 season with 1,859 yards rushing, but Oklahoma's Billy Sims captured the Heisman Trophy. White would not win "two or three Heismans," but he did have a chance to win one, plus a national championship, and come within a whisker of a second, as well as three Rose Bowl victories. White made All-American in 1978.

TAILBACK U.

Marcus Allen makes it four Heismans at Heritage Hall

The 1979 Trojans may have been the greatest college football team *not* to win the national championship. They were unbeaten and featured the Heisman Trophy winner, Charles White. They also featured, like the 2004–2005 Trojans, Heisman winners in the same backfield. Fullback Marcus Allen would win the award in 1981. Only a 21–21 tie with Stanford denied Troy back-to-back national championships.

Ronnie Lott and Anthony Munoz were superstars. In 1981, USC defeated Oklahoma in a thrilling, comeback 28–24 win at the Coliseum. Life was *goooooood!* Allen was doing things nobody—not O. J., Tony Dorsett, or White—had done. He continued his record-setting rushing pace in a 56–22 win at Oregon State. Unranked Arizona came to town for Homecoming. With Allen running through the Wildcats, USC led 10–0 at the half. USC's boys and girls repaired to the beer aisles to talk things over until they started to hear groans and cheers from inside.

Arizona schools—both A-State and U. of A.—would give USC their fair share of troubles in their first years in the Pacific 10 Conference, and this was one of those days. In a game horribly reminiscent of the 21–21 Stanford tie in 1979, USC's offense shut it down (Allen gained yards but they could not punch it in). Arizona quarterback Tom Tunnicliffe, a local product from Burroughs High School in Burbank, engineered Arizona's second half comeback all the way to a 13–10 upset. Nice Homecoming . . .

The Trojans traveled to South Bend, where Allen dominated. They prevailed over Notre Dame, 14–7, followed by easy wins over Washington State and Cal. At that point the third-ranked, 8–1 Trojans, featuring the sure Heisman winner, looked to have the inside track at the national championship. It was a year of upsets. All the usual suspects were down. The Clemson Tigers opened that season over powerhouse Wofford. They were unbeaten, but it looked unlikely that they would make it all the way.

Every year USC fans look at the schedule. If they see a game in the Pacific Northwest in November they say, "Uh-oh." Especially if the game is at Washington. Unpredictable weather (read: pouring rain) and artificial surfaces create balls and shoes that take funny bounces. So it was on November 14 in Seattle, where 47,347 watched the Huskies knock Southern California out of the Rose Bowl and the national championship, 13–3.

USC found themselves in the role of spoiler against UCLA, who were strong with Tom Ramsey having replaced Jay Schroeder (who was concentrating on baseball) at quarterback. Ranked fifteenth, the 7–2–1 Bruins had the inside track at the Rose Bowl. Nothing seemed to make sense when Washington State upset Washington, but it would not matter to UCLA if they lost.

Allen came in with a gaudy NCAA record 2,123 yards and seven 200-yard games. Quarterback John Mazur found that the *L.A. Times* and sportstalk radio, a relatively new phenomenon that found its best niche in commuter-crazy Los Angeles, was tougher on him than OU with two seconds to go. He was still hanging on to his job when the UCLA game came around, but freshman blue chipper Sean Salisbury and backup Scott Tinsley seemed to be reliable alternatives.

When Mazur passed, it was usually to Marcus, who had twenty-five receptions coming in. The two teams got it on, up and down the field, but six Southern Cal turnovers seemed to be their undoing through three quarters. The Bruins were ahead, 21–12. Allen just pounded and pounded and pounded until USC went ahead 22–21 with 2:14 to go on his five-yard run. When USC cornerback Joe Turner intercepted Ramsey with 1:19 on the clock, it seemed to be over except for a flag thrown on SC linebacker August Curley, charged with roughing the passer.

UCLA drove to the 29 before calling on kicker Norm Johnson with four seconds left and Southern California holding on by the skin of their teeth. Nose guard George Achica etched his name in the marble annals of Trojan memory by breaking through Dennis Edwards and Charles Ussery to block the forty-six-yard try, returning the Victory Bell to Figueroa and Jefferson. Curley awarded his firstborn son to Achica, and is still seen washing his car on Sundays.

Allen rushed for 219 yards on forty carries. It was USC's eleventh win over UCLA in fifteen seasons, and redemption after the ignominious 1980 loss in "The Probation Bowl," in which Marcus had been held to only seventy-two yards.

A new era had come to college football by 1981. No longer were Pac 10 teams restricted from going to non–Rose Bowl games. The growth of various bowls created an extravaganza of postseason pageants.

The Fiesta Bowl in Tempe, Arizona, once a sleepy game for the Western Athletic Conference winner (usually Arizona State) to host, was now a major New Year's Day game. With USC heading to the desert to play traditional power Penn State, the team they had beaten in the first game ever played in the Rose Bowl Stadium (1923), the game looked to be a national marquee matchup between Allen and the Nittany Lions'

Curt Warner. With Washington "backing in" to Pasadena, the glamour of that game seemed to dim.

Not so. Washington won the Rose Bowl to uphold the honor of the conference. USC entirely failed on their end. Allen fumbled the ball away on USC's first possession. A crowd of 71,053 saw Warner demonstrate that on this day at least he and Joe Paterno's team were superior to the Trojans, 26–10. USC never scored an offensive touchdown. Chip Banks's twenty-yard interception return was their only one. Robinson brought in Salisbury, but any promise he held would have to be unveiled on another day. At 9–3, USC finished twelfth (AP) and thirteenth (UPI).

It was a strange year, one in which USC had beaten Notre Dame on the road, beaten UCLA, and played on New Year's Day, and their record-setting tailback won the Heisman. But the loss to Penn State was a devastating one, leaving their supporters with an uneasy feeling. There was no outward hint that the empire was on the verge of collapse.

Allen was of course the brightest of bright spots. Coming out of Lincoln High School in San Diego, he had been a quarterback who led his team to the CIF-San Diego Section title.

"I think they made me quarterback because they felt I was the team leader," said Allen, who also played baseball. "I was no passer of distinction."

The USC coaches switched him to running back when they saw him up close. In his freshman year he replaced an injured Charles White versus Michigan State and almost broke a touchdown run.

"I'd broken for about fifteen yards and there was one man between me and the goal line," he said. "Then I cut back on the wrong foot, slipped, and I was the loneliest man on that football field."

He played fullback as a sophomore and tailback as a junior.

"He made the switch without a murmur," said John Jackson, an assistant coach of the running game. He broke his nose in a scrimmage, but rushed for 649 yards.

"I don't think I ever recovered from that introduction," he said. "My nose has been put back together like a puzzle. But playing fullback made me more aggressive. However, I was just looking forward to getting back to tailback."

Nicknamed "Young Juice" for his physical resemblance to O. J., he employed a similar style in the open field. He was the second leading rusher in the nation as a junior through ten games, but missed the 20–3 win over Notre Dame with an eye injury.

When Allen broke all the national rushing records, earning the 1981 Heisman, combined with his good looks and natural charm, he became an iconic figure at Troy.

The captain of the 1981 team, Allen set sixteen NCAA records and was the first collegian to break 2,000 regular season yards. He won the Walter Camp and Maxwell trophies, averaging 212.9 yards a game in his senior year. In 1982 the Raiders, in the process of moving from Oakland to L.A., made him their first pick. In 2010 John Robinson joined Allen in the College Hall of Fame.

RESURRECTION

*Pete Carroll arrives to establish the greatest half-decade dynasty
in college football history*

From 1983 to 2000, the University of Southern California football program spiraled downward. They maintained the status of a marginal college football power, but were far below the standards of the game's elite.

USC went to some Rose Bowls. Under Coach Larry Smith, they challenged for the 1988 national championship. Quarterback Rodney Peete came close to winning the Heisman Trophy that year. They played big games and had great players, but the program was not close to the standards set by Howard Jones, John McKay, and John Robinson.

USC lost to Notre Dame every year from 1983 to 1993, tied the Irish in 1994, then lost again in 1995 before finally ending the agony in 1996. They lost to UCLA every year from 1991 to 1998. They experienced the terrible disappointment of Todd Marinovich, who was supposed to lead them to glory but instead led them down the tubes.

It was apparent that USC's fall in football coincided with its rise as a first-rate academic institution. By 2000, when USC was named the "Hot School" and the "School of the Year" by the Kaplan College Guide and the *Time*/Princeton Review, they were more likely to be rated in the Top 25 for classroom excellence than for football excellence.

Why did this happen? There were various reasons, but the loss of Marv Goux is as good an explanation as any. Goux departed prior to the 1983 season, which was the departure point between USC greatness and mediocrity, with no parachutes to soften the landing.

One could even call it a "Goux Curse," although Marvie would hate this assessment. Despite shabby treatment from the college in the wake of his role in the school's early 1980s probation scandals, he loved Southern California throughout. But it was not until Goux's death in 2002 that USC regained its form.

His funeral, coming just prior to that season, marks in many ways the beginning of USC's resurrection. At that memorial service, his lovely granddaughter, Kara Kanen, a USC student, urged USC's future football teams à la Knute Rockne.

"To the Trojans," she said, "remember to 'win one for the Goux.'"

Over the following years, the Trojans took that advice to heart . . . and then some!

■ ■ ■

Prior to World War I, the best college football was played in the Ivy League by Harvard, Yale, and Princeton. "Out West," Michigan took to the game in a big way, too.

In the aftermath of World War I, California's Wonder Teams were the top power in the nation. In the succeeding years, until World War II, Notre Dame, Southern California, Alabama, and Minnesota led the way.

Michigan, Ohio State, and Oklahoma joined the party in the 1940s and 1950s. Traditional powers USC, Notre Dame, and Alabama reasserted themselves, dominating the landscape of the 1960s and 1970s.

After Southern California defeated Notre Dame for the fifth year in a row in 1982, they could point to their recent dominance of the Fighting Irish, their national championships, their Heisman Trophies, and assert that if there was such a thing as an Associated Press–style "All-Time Top 25" poll of the best programs in history, it would read:

> Notre Dame
> Southern California
> Alabama
> Oklahoma

When John Robinson announced that he was stepping down; when he and Marv Goux departed for the Los Angeles Rams; when the school was hit by a series of NCAA sanctions; when a long losing streak to Notre Dame began, the possibility of closing that narrow gap between number one Notre Dame and number two USC evaporated.

Had that "All-Time Top 25" poll been taken at the end of the 1992 season, USC would have fallen at least to third. Alabama caught them as the all-time bowl leader in victories when they defeated Troy in the 1985 Aloha Bowl. Glory again reigned in Tuscaloosa when the Crimson Tide captured the 1992 national championship.

Over the next decade, a series of new teams boldly stepped forward, challenging "old school" programs like Notre Dame and USC, now derided as Yesterday U. Miami, Florida State, Florida, even Virginia Tech, competed with the likes of traditional powers Penn State, Nebraska, and Michigan for national supremacy. The best football was no longer played in the Pacific 10 Conference. The Southeastern Conference, the Big 12, that's where it was at.

As USC goes, so goes the West. They represent a gold standard in the conference, like the Yankees in baseball. The fall of the Trojan Empire created an egalitarian landscape in which Washington, Washington State, Arizona State, Arizona, California, and Stanford, like "breakaway republics" from the Old Soviet Union, felt they had the right to freely challenge the vacated throne.

When Oklahoma, under first-year coach Bob Stoops, finished number one, that mythological "Top 25" poll was in need of reshuffling. Notre Dame still tenuously held to the top spot, but USC had tumbled further. Oklahoma was by now challenging Alabama for number two, for the chance to play in that fictional "BCS Game of the New Millennium."

USC still had enough history; there was still enough respect for its traditions, its Heismans, its white horse, and its dramatic finishes to keep them in the top four or five. But Michigan, Nebraska, even Miami . . . a few more years of losing and Troy's statues would have to be mothballed, or sent to the Smithsonian as part of an "ancient sports history" exhibit, complete with old men telling wide-eyed youngsters about A. D. and McKay and Charlie White.

"The gleaming trophies that were a lineage of Troy were beginning to tarnish," said narrator Roger Birdsall in *The History of USC Football* DVD, produced in 2005.

USC is a school of glamour and mystique. This imprimatur of supernatural glory rings forth like the entreaties of Trojan warriors who battled ancient Greece. The ancients were inspired by the beautiful "face that launched a thousand ships," the legendary Helen of Troy. Advocates of the modern Troy feel this gives them license to invoke Biblical imagery on its behalf.

"The Trojan Nation prayed for the Second Coming of McKay, and just days before Christmas in the year 2000, the university introduced the man who would be Savior," said Birdsall on *The History of USC Football* DVD.

TRADITION RESTORED

Under a new savior, Carson Palmer wins the Heisman; by the end of
2002, the Trojans were the nation's best team

Pete Carroll was the third or fourth choice at USC. A California native and former pro coach, he fell into the job when Mike Riley, Dennis Erickson, and Mike Bellotti turned Athletic Director Mike Garrett down.

His daughter was playing volleyball for the Women of Troy, so Carroll was spending time around the school. He had moved to Los Angeles because the South Bay area of L.A. was the home of his wife, Glena. After following him from one end of America to another for some twenty-seven years, he owed it to her to move to a place of her choosing for once. As the daughter of a USC graduate, Glena had grown up a Trojan fan, which influenced daughter Jamie's decision to go to school there. As a young man, Carroll had attended games at the Coliseum, rooting for USC.

"I was a Trojan fan when Sam 'Bam' Cunningham helped integrate football in Alabama," Carroll told his hometown newspaper, the *Marin Independent Journal*, in the 1980s. "I had SC pennants hanging in my room."

When the coaching job opened up in 2000, Carroll was naturally interested. His hiring stirred little enthusiasm, however. By that point, few coaches really would have been viewed as difference-makers at USC, a school derided as "Yesterday U." In his first year, Carroll was 6–6. His team lost to Utah in the Las Vegas Bowl. But they rallied from a 2–5 start to win their final four regular season games. A "turning point" victory at Arizona seemingly saved them from disaster. They shut out UCLA. They lost at Notre Dame, 27–16, but each of the other five defeats was by less than a touchdown.

There was a strong sense that 2002 would be a make-or-break year at USC. Despite the loss in the Las Vegas Bowl, Carroll had some people excited that perhaps he could right the ship. However, other coaches had gotten the fans' hopes up in the past, only to let them down.

The Associated Press ranked Troy eighteenth coming in. The main source of optimism came via reports that Norm Chow was making major progress with Carson Palmer. One of the most celebrated high school quarterbacks California has ever produced, in four years he had shown sparks of brilliance interspersed with terrible glimpses of Sean Salisbury.

In the 2002 season, the unbeaten Ohio State Buckeyes played the unbeaten Miami Hurricanes in the so-called BCS national championship game at the Fiesta Bowl in Tempe. In that game, Ohio State won an uninspiring, defensive struggle, ending Miami's thirty-four-game winning streak and their hopes for back-to-back titles. The rules are the rules. USC plays by them, but the fact is that in the last seven games of the 2002 collegiate football season, the USC Trojans were far and away the best team in the land.

Had there been a play-off, USC would have won it in 2002. As good as their successive national championship teams of 2003 and 2004 turned out to be, it is not inconceivable to say that USC in the last seven games of '02 would have very possibly beaten them. They became a juggernaut like few teams the game has ever seen. That a team could improve so much so quickly—from getting blown out for three quarters against Kansas State and handing victory to Washington State—is a testament to what happens when Pete Carroll's coaching is allowed to reach full fruition.

Thanksgiving weekend, 2002, the college football world—ESPN's *GameDay*; the talking heads on Fox Sports and the networks; the Lee Corsos, Kirk Herbstreits and Craig Jameses—suddenly was saying that the best team in the nation was not Miami or Ohio State, but USC. Furthermore, the Heisman winner was their supposedly washed-up red-shirt senior, the guy who did not even make his school's media cover: Carson Palmer.

Palmer and USC decided to take it not to the next level, but to levels both he and his school may not even have thought were possible. The Trojans ventured to Pasadena to take on a solid 7–3, twenty-fifth-ranked UCLA squad before 91,084.

Tab Perry fumbled early. USC recovered. Palmer hit Kareem Kelly from thirty-four yards out sixteen seconds into the game. In the early days of the series, when UCLA was establishing itself as a school and a football team, USC beat them by some enormous margins. However, the 52–21 trouncing they put on the Bruins in their house may have been the most impressive single performance in the history of the City Game (until the 2005 thrashing). Palmer's "watch-me-win-the-Heisman" performance may be more impressive than Bush's "watch-me-win-the-Heisman" '05 effort. Palmer dominated the Bruins in an unstoppable offensive extravaganza.

Mike Williams caught six passes for sixty-six yards. Kelly caught four for ninety-four, Keary Colbert four for eighty-four. Palmer had four scoring strikes. Justin Fargas scored a touchdown. Hershel Dennis made a thirty-eight-yard run. The defense was spearheaded by Mike Patterson, Antuan Simmons, and Matt Grootegoed. Keneche Udeze made four stops for losses with two sacks.

If there was any doubt in anybody's mind, Palmer secured the Heisman Trophy the next week before 91,432 at the Coliseum in a totally devastating 44–13 annihilation of seventh-ranked Notre Dame. His numbers were nothing less than gaudy: thirty-two of forty-six for 425 yards and four touchdowns. The contrast for Notre Dame coach Ty Willingham's offense was embarrassingly dramatic. Irish quarterback Carlyle Holiday was held to 70 yards in the air. Fargas ran for 120 yards and added 41 on receptions. Williams caught ten for 169.

Linebacker Mike Pollard made six stops, while his partner Melvin Simmons had seven tackles. Darrell Rideaux and DeShaun Hill had interceptions.

USC moved up to number five in the final regular season rankings. They beat UCLA and Notre Dame in the same season for the first time since 1981 (the first time in back-to-back games since 1978), when Marcus Allen had won the school's fourth Heisman. The combined sixty-two-point margin of victory over their two rivals was the largest in USC history. Troy was the co–Pacific 10 Conference champion for the first time since 1995.

Palmer made it Heisman Trophy number five when the Downtown Athletic Club of New York anointed him in their ceremony shortly after the Notre Dame game.

"It's such an honor, it's indescribable to me, it's unlike any other award," said Palmer in *The History of USC Football* DVD. "Because of the closeness of the people who've won it in the past, and the respect for the people who've won it and just for the Heisman Trophy itself, and I still can't believe it to this day, to be put into that group of people; it's just incredible to be included with all the past winners, so to this day I still have to pinch myself and feel blessed to have been in a position to be there."

The 10–2 Trojans were invited to the Orange Bowl against number three Iowa. They featured a quarterback who had been touted for the Heisman himself, Brad Banks. All-American safety Troy Polamalu pulled up lame just before the game, but nothing was going to stop Troy (the team). Palmer left no doubt that he was the best player in college football with a spectacular aerial show, hitting Kareem Kelly with a sixty-five-yard bomb to set up Justin Fargas's touchdown.

After going in to the locker room tied at 10, Palmer led Troy to thirty-one unanswered points in a display of utter domination. It removed any question regarding Palmer (although in actuality no questions were being asked). After the lackluster BCS championship game between Ohio State and Miami (in which neither team seemed willing to win the game), the Trojans convinced almost everybody that the best team in college football actually was USC.

Iowa was the ninth AP-ranked team that USC beat. Their 2002 schedule was judged by the computers to be the hardest in the country. It was their eighth straight thirty-point effort, a school record and a remarkable statistic. USC gained 550 yards on offense. It was their ninth straight 400-plus total yardage effort.

Palmer was twenty-one of thirty-one for 303 yards, earning MVP honors. Mike Williams set an NCAA freshman record for receptions (eighty-one), receiving yards (1,265), and touchdowns (fourteen). His improvement since the Kansas State and Washington State debacles directly correlated with the team's—and Palmer's—success. Matt Grootegoed had six tackles.

USC finished fourth in the polls. They averaged 35.8 points a game while allowing an average of 18.5.

Palmer, who along with safety Troy Polamalu was the team captain in 2002, set or tied thirty-three Pac 10 or USC total offense and passing records. Aside from the Heisman, he earned the Johnny Unitas Award as the nation's best senior quarterback; the Pop Warner Award for MVP on the West Coast; *The Sporting News* Player of the Year; the conference co–Offensive Player of the Year; and team Most Valuable Player award. He finished fourth in NCAA history in passing yards (11,388) and first in conference history in total offense (11,621) and passing (11,818). He made it into the USC Athletic Hall of Fame in 2003, and was the number one pick in the entire draft by Cincinnati. Signing a multimillion-dollar bonus, Palmer became a starter in 2004. In 2005 he led the Bengals to their first play-off appearance since 1990 while coming into his own as one of the NFL's finest signal-callers. He's a genuinely nice guy, and the reports from Cincinnati are that he is a community leader and one of the most popular athletes the city has known in years.

"IT'S A GOOD DAY TO BE A TROJAN!"

Carroll establishes a new paradigm to coaching football

One of Pete Carroll's favorite expressions, with which he often exhorts his team in the locker room just before taking the field, is "It's a good day to be a Trojan!" Perhaps it is because he rooted for USC as a kid, or because his wife's father was a Trojan, or because his daughter chose to play volleyball for the Women of Troy before he took over as head coach; whatever the reason, Pete has never been a mercenary coach. From the very beginning, when he asked Charles Young, "What is the essence of the University of Southern California?" and spoke weekly with Marv Goux on that very subject, he has always understood the special nature of USC. He embraced it in 2001. When he restored a grand tradition in 2002, the university embraced him.

USC had tradition in Alabama. Carroll ingeniously made the most of it. He invited Sam "Bam" Cunningham and John Papadakis, two of the players from the 1970 team that had beaten Alabama at Legion Field, helping to ease the way for integration. They flew with the team, rode the bus, roamed the sidelines, and spoke to the team prior to the 2003 opener at Auburn.

Inspired by this link to their storied past, USC took the field with a mission. Darnell Bing intercepted a Jason Campbell pass. Offensively they played ball control, driving on Auburn until they reached their five-yard line. Then . . .

Sophomore quarterback Matt "Leinart threw a touchdown pass his first throw, his first play, so we were under way, and he was totally at ease right away, totally in command," said Carroll on *The History of USC Football* DVD.

There were 86,063 fans. Very few were Trojan supporters. The weather was hot and steamy, but in front of a national CBS audience, USC quickly took the crowd out of the game. They never let them in, shutting out *Sports Illustrated*'s "number one team in the nation," 23–0.

Mike Williams caught Leinart's initial toss for the score. The defense simply shut down Carnell Williams (40 yards), Ronnie Brown (28), and Campbell (121 yards). USC dominated the turnover game. In truth they could have won by a bigger margin, but chose to keep things simple for their young quarterback.

"He had fun playing the game, and we beat a very good Auburn team is what we did," recalled Carroll. "We were very fortunate to beat them at the time, and then things just started going and we put together wins one after another and put together a great season."

In the first game of what indeed became a great season, Leinart was seventeen of thirty for 192 yards, mostly working short yardage in Chow's updated version of the "West Coast Offense." Williams caught eight passes for 104 yards. Dennis rambled for 85.

Unheralded linebacker Lofa Tatupu established his "presence with authority," as Nuke LaLoosh in *Bull Durham* once said, by making twelve tackles, including two sacks, three and a half for losses. Jason Leach and Patterson starred. Tom Malone's punts established field position all game.

It made USC 3–0 all-time in Alabama (1970, 1978, and 2003), moving them to number four in the polls going into the Brigham Young game at the Coliseum.

A crowd of 75,315 came to see Norm Chow's alma mater take on USC. SC took an impressive early lead, let the Cougars get back into it, then pulled away at the end for a 35–18 win.

Williams caught a short pass for the first score. Leinart hit Keary Colbert on a patented Chow play called "catch-and-run," which took advantage of the receiver's speed and open field abilities. An Omar Nazel interception return made it 21–0.

USC was dormant in the second and third quarters while Brigham Young pulled back into it. When the score was 21–18, panic began to descend. This was the kind of game the Trojans lost in the past ten to fifteen years. Momentum lost, mistakes piling up, compounded by penalties and turnovers.

The success of 2002 looked to be old news. A national title looked not just to be in jeopardy, but not within this team's ability to achieve. But a Pete Carroll team is a second half team, a fourth quarter team, a well-conditioned team.

Leinart led a drive, ending with a nice eighteen-yard touchdown toss to Williams. After a BYU fumble, SC scored again to make the final tally more impressive. It was not an outstanding game, but Tatupu and Grootegoed *were* outstanding. Will Poole intercepted a pass. Malone's punting earned him Pac-10 Special Teams Player of the Week.

Williams caught ten passes for 124 yards. Freshman Reggie Bush got his first carry ever. Leinart completed nineteen passes for 235 yards. Chow let him open his game up more.

With an eleven-game winning streak going back to the loss at Washington State in 2002, USC was heavily favored at Cal. They were shocked, losing 34–31 in three overtimes.

"We came out after not playing well at the beginning, came roaring back after halftime to tie it, but just for whatever reason had just a couple plays that just didn't allow us to win," Carroll said on *The History of USC Football* DVD. "We missed a field goal that day, an extra point, we fumbled on their two-yard line and went into overtime; the kinds of plays where if they don't go well for you against a team that's pumped up and you get upset. The great thing about that game wasn't that we lost but that we've not lost since [until 2006]. It didn't knock us off pace or knock us off course."

In an interview with Brian Curtis of College Sports Television prior to the 2005 season, Carroll reiterated that "the best thing about that game is that we haven't lost since."

The coach learned another valuable lesson: go for the win, not the tie. Two years later at Notre Dame, that lesson proved the decisive factor in a Trojan victory.

■ ■ ■

Napoleon once instructed his generals that "if you take Vienna, *take Vienna!*" There was to be no fooling around for Carroll's Trojans, either. Not after the Cal loss. If Troy hoped to have a chance at the national championship, they could not afford another slip.

So it was when Carroll's number five Southern California Trojans entered South Bend like Napoleon invading Austerlitz, destroying the Irish with no mercy, 45–14, before 80,795 at Notre Dame Stadium. "Touchdown Jesus" signaled for USC all day long.

USC compiled 551 yards in total offense against a statistically strong Irish defense. Leinart engineered five drives of eighty yards in compiling 351 yards and four touchdown passes. Williams and Colbert combined for seventeen receptions and 232 yards, with one touchdown each.

Reggie Bush asserted himself with 89 yards on the ground. LenDale White added 75. Defensively, Simmons, Bing, Tatupu, Patterson, and Udeze spent most of the afternoon on Notre Dame's side of the line, making tackles for losses in a spectacular display.

In Seattle, Leinart completed four touchdown passes, two to Bush. The USC offense showed new wrinkles from Chow, who was now convinced that the young quarterback had come of age. Running backs were now receivers. Defensive coordinators have been shaking their heads ever since. Multiple splits, alignments, stunts, and every kind of play-action, short or long, mixed in with running and unconventional play calling, has marked the USC offense. Like a baseball pitcher who throws breaking balls on fastball counts and fast balls on breaking ball counts, Chow would mix it up, throwing on first down, running when the defense looked for the pass. More important than the plays called, however, was the talent. USC was loaded like few teams ever get loaded. Now they were clicking on all cylinders.

Leinart finished nineteen of twenty-nine for 351 yards with four TD strikes (and no interceptions) in earning conference Offensive Player of the Week honors. Bush had 270 all-purpose yards. Dennis rushed for 98. Poole, Udeze, Frostee Rucker, and Jason Leach spearheaded the defensive effort. The final score: Trojans 43, Huskies 23.

THE USC TROJANS

Fans numbering 82,478 came to the Coliseum for number six Washington State, but USC's defense stopped them cold while making more big plays on the offensive side of the ball. "Wild Bunch II" forced four Cougar turnovers behind the inspired play of Nazel, Udeze, Patterson, Dallas Sartz, Rucker, Bing, Shaun Cody, and Leach.

White rambled for 149 yards. Colbert caught nine passes for 80. USC won going away, 43–16.

When the "Super Station," WTBS, opened their broadcast of the USC-Arizona game on November 15, they showed highlights of the 1978 Trojans interspersed with the 2003 version, while running the sound track of Led Zeppelin's Robert Plant singing, "Been a long time since I rock and rolled." The lead announcer then stated that it had indeed been a "long time"—twenty-five years—since USC's last national title, but that the current edition was making a strong bid to do just that.

When USC crushed Arizona in Tucson, 45–0, the "Super Station's" studio analyst, Brian Bosworth, said now second-ranked Troy was the best team in the country. The former Oklahoma star was asked about his Sooners, who behind quarterback Jason White were unbeaten, had won each game by huge margins, and were ranked number one.

The Bos looked like a deer caught in the headlights of an oncoming car. He tried to correct himself, as if he had "forgotten" about Oklahoma. Call it a faux pas or a Freudian slip, but he was a man who had seen enough football in his day to know that USC was, indeed, the best team in the land, loyalty aside.

Leinart passed for 292 yards while holding back. John David Booty and Brandon Hance got some snaps. It was a game USC could have won 70–0, which is what Oklahoma was doing to some opponents in 2003. But Carroll was establishing himself as a coach who does not run it up. Late in games, he would play it close to the vest, often choosing to walk off the field instead of making a last-ditch try at the end zone.

Williams caught eleven balls for 147 yards; Bush returned a kick 58 yards. The defense was impenetrable. At 9–1, Southern California was right where many preseason prognosticators thought they would be.

26

KINGS OF L.A.

Carroll, Leinart, Williams, and Bush: L.A.'s new royal family

When UCLA entered the Coliseum, 93,172 fans watched the modern version of Christians being eaten by lions. USC scored on offense, defense, and special teams. UCLA, like Notre Dame, does not benefit from the kind of "hold the score down" mentality that sometimes permeates Carroll's game management. In the rivalry games, USC pulls out all the stops to the delight of their fans. The game marked the fifth straight win over UCLA. USC decided to crush all memory of the Bruins' 1991–1998 winning streak into nonexistence. Or, as Marv Goux once said, "The indecencies of those people over there" were avenged to the satisfaction of all.

After four possessions Southern Cal led, 30–0. Troy went through UCLA in the manner of Patton's tanks rolling through the Low Countries. Cornerback Ronald Nunn tackled UCLA quarterback Drew Olson in the end zone, forcing a fumble that was picked up for a touchdown by Kenechi Udeze. Later, a Marcell Allmond tackle of Olson forced another fumble, which Mike Patterson picked up and ran fifty-two yards for a score.

Bush earned conference Special Teams Player of the Week, returning a kick ninety-six yards and officially entering the pantheon of Trojan lore. Leinart methodically hit twenty-three passes out of thirty-two attempts for 289 yards (273 in the first half), with Williams snaring eleven for 181. UCLA managed all of 11 yards on the ground, committed four turnovers, made thirteen frustration penalties, and saw Olson get sacked six times.

Carroll, almost as if he felt sorry for UCLA, or wanted to preserve the notion that the rivalry still featured real competition, *did* call off the dogs a bit in the fourth quarter with reserves, including appearances by Brandon Hance and John David Booty. Final score: Trojans 47, Bruins 22.

USC fans were less "sorry," chanting "five more years" as the teams left the field.

Oklahoma was still unbeaten, but to all observers of the college football scene, USC had the earmarks of being the nation's finest team, with little doubt. Two weeks later, that doubt was erased when the Trojans vaulted into the number one position in both the Associated Press and *USA TODAY*/ESPN polls, utterly annihilating Oregon State, 52–28, at the Coliseum.

Oklahoma lost in ignominious fashion to Kansas State in the Big 12 title game, making it easy to decide who was number one entering the bowl season. In the final regular season game, Leinart tossed five touchdown passes, with Williams and Bush (who was now regularly catching the ball almost as much as he was running it) grabbing two each. Beaver quarterback Derek Anderson was able to throw for over 400 yards, but Oregon State, after opening the game with a touchdown, never got close after that.

Leinart's twenty-two of thirty-eight game for 278 yards set conference records for touchdown passes (thirty-five) and consecutive passes without an interception (212 before a first quarter pick). Williams established a season touchdown mark (sixteen). Tatupu made fourteen tackles. The game also helped USC set a school and conference average home attendance record of 77,804.

Ranked number one in both polls, Southern California advanced to the Rose Bowl against Michigan.

"I'm not looking for the money," Carroll told *USA TODAY*. "I'm not looking for the hype. I'm not looking for a one-shot deal."

Pete Carroll was looking to make history. He took a giant step in that direction when Southern California won the national championship in the Rose Bowl. It was a manner befitting the Trojans, just as eight of the previous nine SC national champs had done (the 1928 champs did not play in the Rose Bowl). It marked the ultimate goal of a Pete Carroll team: beat UCLA and Notre Dame, win the conference title, win the Rose Bowl, and finish number one. With the history would come all the things he was not looking for: the hype, the money, the "one-shot deals."

There are few teams that have the unique chance to win national championships at "home," which is what USC calls the Rose Bowl—their "winter residence"—despite the fact that UCLA rents the building in the fall.

"We've prided ourselves on doing well in all areas of the program," said Carroll of the 2003 national championship on *The History of USC Football* DVD. "The tension mounts when you see the position you're in at the end of the year, and it's a great challenge to programs to continue to perform at a high level. We had opportunities to go against great football teams. The year before against Iowa, a marvelous game in the Orange Bowl, and then that great matchup against Michigan in the Rose Bowl that was a marvelous experience. They had a phenomenal team, experience at every spot, draftable players at every position on their football team, and we played a really solid game against a great team, so we earned our way; it was a great finish against a great team, to do that, to win right here in Southern California and to achieve that national championship status right here at home was really a great deal for us."

"Guys stepped up," said Leinart. "Keary Colbert stepped up big time in that game.

Mike Williams did his part; the offensive line did great. We ran the ball when we needed to, and I just got the ball to the open receivers, so it was a memorable moment for me. I remember after the game, earning MVP honors and holding the sword up to 'Conquest' and kind of doing it to the fans after the game, it was definitely great."

"USC came out of it, they got to stay home, they got to play in the Rose Bowl, which they love," said Steve Bisheff of the *Orange County Register*. "It helps their recruiting; they bring all their recruits to the Rose Bowl. It helps their recruiting locally and in state in talent rich California, playing in the Rose Bowl, winning the Rose Bowl is a great thing for recruiting. You know, they had the best of both worlds."

USC indeed was the national champion and the "people's champion," as ESPN's Michael Wilbon said on *Pardon the Interruption*. They did it the way they had done it all season. The big question was, Who would have won a game between Palmer's 2002 Trojans and Leinart's 2003 version? Both teams, in their stretch runs from October through November and on into the bowl season, had been as good as any team has ever been. Since halftime of the fifth game, October 4 at Arizona State, the 2003 Trojans were a juggernaut.

The Rose Bowl seating capacity had been reconfigured, and the stadium no longer held 100,000 people. The 93,849 who saw the Trojans beat Michigan, 28–14, had one of the hottest tickets in L.A. sports history. In the game, Leinart threw three touchdown passes and caught another. The defense recorded nine sacks.

Michigan came in fourth, led by quarterback John Navarre and running back Chris Perry. Many pundits thought they, not LSU or reeling Oklahoma, who played a lackluster, dull, I-don't-know-how-to-win Sugar Bowl, was the second best team in the country. When USC was finished with them, however, they were just another badly beaten foe. The truth is, it was like so many games Pete Carroll has coached: not as close as the score. USC could have won 45–14—or by more. There was a sense that USC dictated and dominated to such an extent they were essentially just writing the game story according to their whim.

It marked USC's twenty-first victory in twenty-nine Rose Bowls, the most wins and the best percentage of all Rose Bowl teams. SC led 21–0 until late in the third quarter. Cody blocked an early Wolverine field goal. Four plays later Leinart had USC in the end zone with a twenty-five-yard aerial to Colbert.

After a Tatupu interception, White took a short pass in for the score. Later, Colbert made a spectacular forty-seven-yard grab and score. USC went to Chow's bag of tricks when Williams pulled up and passed *to Leinart* for the last touchdown. Leinart earned the MVP award on the strength of his twenty-three of thirty-four, 327-yard, three-touchdown afternoon. Colbert and Williams were unstoppable. USC put up 410 total yards.

Tatupu added twelve tackles. Poole made two quarterback sacks. Udeze had three more. The game added to USC's all-time records for overall (946,482) and average attendance (72,368).

According to tradition the team came before the cheering student section and put

THE USC TROJANS

their fingers up in the "V for Victory" sign (which is *not* a peace sign; rather it is what Dwight Eisenhower and Winston Churchill did when addressing crowds while leading the Allies to *victory* and *conquest* over Nazi Germany). The band played "Conquest!" Single digits were raised to shouts of "We're number one!"

Carroll accepted the Rose Bowl trophy and told the multitudes that his team "just won a national championship." USC and their fans left the Rose Bowl having won their tenth national title since 1928, and their first since 1978. If USC did not have a loss on their record, the 2003 Trojans may very well have gone down in history as the greatest team ever, instead of just one of them.

"We've had a fantastic season," said Carroll. "I think these guys should be rewarded accordingly, and I think they will be."

"Everybody knows who the people's champions are—it's the USC Trojans, baby," said Omar Nazel.

Michigan coach Lloyd Carr agreed that USC was the deserving national champion. The *USA TODAY* headline, "Trojans render Sugar Bowl meaningless," told the entire story.

"It's over," it read. "The team ranked number one, decisively, in both the Associated Press and the *USA TODAY*/ESPN Coaches' Poll, won its high-profile bowl game, decisively, on New Year's Day" to capture the national title.

"If you look at the polls, there is no controversy. The number one team in the land—USC—has successfully completed its run to the mythical national title," and "the true game for the national championship occurred Thursday night in Pasadena."

USC scored four touchdown passes on a defense that previously allowed five all year. They gave up fifteen sacks; then nine to USC. Various coaches throughout the country were quoted in *USA TODAY* saying the very idea of somebody other than USC being the national champion was "a joke." The article said evidence of USC's national championship was self-evident because "people watched the game." It was like a crime committed on videotape. No witnesses are necessary. Simple observation of it renders knowledge that it is.

Res Ipsa Loquitur.

USC celebrated its title knowing that only Colbert was graduating among their offensive skill players (although Mike Williams would declare for the draft). Just three senior starters would be leaving on defense. They ranked second nationally, allowing just 61.1 yards a game.

Sports Illustrated featured Matt Leinart scoring on his touchdown *reception*, trumpeting the 2003 national champions with the headline, "USC's the one!"

Five 2003 Trojans made All-American. They included wide receiver Mike Williams, offensive tackle Jacob Rogers, defensive end Kenechi Udeze, punter Tom Malone, and quarterback Matt Leinart.

"LEAVE NO DOUBT!"

The 2004 Trojans make their bid for history

In tune with the campaign theme of a hotly contested election to be decided in a little over two months, ESPN's assessment after the 2004 opener versus Virginia Tech in Landover, Maryland, was "Bush carries Southern California."

Reggie was asked about having to "replace" All-American Mike Williams, who was ineligible after declaring for the NFL Draft.

"Just his presence on the field was felt by the defense and he's a big weapon out there, so I had to step up and be a leader on this team and go out there and make plays and be a weapon all across the board," Bush said on *The History of USC Football* DVD.

"Step up" he did. Bush caught three long touchdown passes from Leinart in a very hard-fought, comeback, 24–13 win. Considering all the hoopla, it was probably just the thing the team needed to get their minds right. Bush had 258 all-purpose yards (127 on receptions, 60 on punt returns, 44 on kickoff returns, 27 on rushes).

Tatupu intercepted a pass to put USC in position to score. Bush scampered thirty-five yards in the first quarter. Leinart struggled while Virginia Tech answered with a field goal and a touchdown to go into the locker room leading 10–7.

"We struggled at times but Reggie being the big player he is made big plays," recalled Leinart. "I just kind of got in a groove. I struggled in the first half a little bit. We were off our timing a little bit. It was loud; I remember it being super loud, like 80,000 or 90,000 people there were for Virginia Tech, so it was definitely a hostile environment, and I really believe that that game really prepared us for the whole game to do what we did. Playing a team like that that early, battling back from halftime, playing a championship caliber team playing in a BCS game that only had two losses the whole year, so it definitely helped us the rest of the year."

Virginia Tech was still winning late in the third quarter when Bush pulled in a fifty-three-yard bomb to put Troy ahead, 14–10. The stubborn Hokies came back with a field goal to narrow it, 14–13, in the fourth quarter. The Trojans did not secure it until

Leinart hit Bush on a twenty-nine-yard scoring strike. After Ronald Nunn's fumble recovery, Ryan Killeen iced it with a forty-one-yard field goal to make up for a first half miss.

Patterson and Bing were defensive standouts. All in all, Carroll and his team were happy to get out of Landover with their winning streak still going. They had trailed, they had not beaten the spread, and the question of whether they were truly the best team ever, better than the 1972 Trojans, was very much in doubt.

There was no reason to believe the Stanford game would pose any troubles. The Cardinal under Coach Buddy Teevens had some talented players, but not in USC's class. Instead, quarterback Trent Edwards looked like Joe Montana for a half. USC had to pull out all the stops.

Before half the crowd was even in the stadium, USC drove down the field to score on a twenty-three-yard Killeen field goal. Kevin Arbet intercepted a pass, returned it sixty-six yards, and Smith caught a two-yarder for a touchdown to make it 10–0 USC. The Trojan fans who made the traditional Bay Area trip probably thought they were in for a trouncing. Maybe they could score 60 or 70? Maybe they could find a bar and watch the second half on WTBS? Maybe head up to San Francisco and see what's cookin' there?

As it turned out, USC and Stanford fans were stuck to their seats until the end. Troy needed every minute of this one to leave with a victory. After USC's fast start, Edwards engineered four straight scoring possessions. Stanford pulled out all the stops, including a fake field goal. Holder Kyle Matter, the guy many thought was better than Leinart when they were both Southland blue chippers in 2000, scampered eleven yards for the touchdown.

Trailing 21–10, Leinart led USC on a drive to pull close by halftime. Bush broke a tackle and went in from the 17. USC breathed easier. Stanford got the ball with seconds left. They decided to run out the clock. Somehow J. R. Lemon broke an eighty-two-yard touchdown score to make it eleven again, 28–17, at the half.

Instead of panicking, Carroll just told his team, "Let's go take this piece by piece by piece and put this game back in our control. In the fourth quarter, that's when we're gonna get this done."

Stanford received the kick to start the second half. USC stiffened. Leinart led a methodical scoring drive to make it 28–24. Carroll solved Stanford's offense. In the fourth quarter, Bush returned a punt thirty-three yards, running all over the field. USC drove inexorably until, with a little over six minutes to go, White hugged the ball into the end zone to put Southern California ahead, 31–28.

Stanford was held again. Leinart controlled the game from then on out. USC got down within sight of the Stanford goal. They could have scored to make it more impressive, but chose not to chance a fumble or interception. When the clock allowed it, Leinart just went to his knee. USC left with a win. They would not come up for air until a few days later.

"It was crazy, it was intense," Leinart said in the locker room.

"I just asked for thirty minutes of heart," Lofa Tatupu said he told his mates at the half. "That's what we got."

"That was probably the most meaningful win of the season for us, because that was the game when we solidified who we were and what we were all about," Carroll said on *The History of USC Football* DVD.

Given two weeks to prepare for a home game against Jeff Tedford, Aaron Rodgers, and number seven Cal, it seemed the Trojans were on their way. The Golden Bears were unbeaten, but had a game at Southern Mississippi postponed until the end of the season because of a hurricane. Their early schedule was tepid.

Cal's special teams botched a punt. Patterson recovered a fumble. USC followed those opportunities with a touchdown and field goal to make it 10–0 after a quarter. It looked like Southern Cal's day.

Fans numbering 90,008 were on hand on a perfect, sunny afternoon. The game was nationally televised. ESPN's *GameDay* crew did their show from the Coliseum. The hype was lived up to when Rodgers stormed California back. He led them on a drive resulting in a field goal. USC came back with a thirty-nine-yard field goal by Killeen. Rodgers got the ball back and hit Geoff MacArthur, a former L.A. prep star at Palisades High, for a touchdown. USC managed to squeeze a forty-two-yarder out of Killeen with only three seconds left in the half to make it 16–10.

The teams traded touchdowns in the third quarter; Leinart to Dwayne Jarrett from sixteen out followed by Cal's Marshawn Lynch with a two-yard run. It was 23–17 USC entering the fourth quarter.

Bush ran a kick back eighty-four yards, but Leinart was intercepted. On the game, White was held to fifty-two yards on the ground, Bush a mere twenty-three. Cal's J. J. Arrington ran for 111 yards. Leinart was fifteen of twenty-four for just 164 yards.

Rodgers completed an NCAA record twenty-three straight passes, but Carroll's defense kept him to short yardage, 267 total. Rodgers outplayed Leinart, putting his name in the Heisman conversation. Cal outplayed USC, but Tedford did not outcoach Carroll. The game was won by a "bend but don't break" defense. They gave Rodgers a little but would not yield a lot. They were strong in the all-important "red zone," and SC's special teams made the difference.

When it was all said and done, it was defense at the goal line that won the game. With 1:47 to play, Rodgers had Cal on the USC 9, first-and-goal. Manuel Wright sacked him. Rodgers, despite completing twenty-three straight earlier, could not get it in the end zone when it mattered. On a fourth down play for all the marbles, Rodgers's pass into the end zone could not connect with well-defended receivers. Southern Cal had a desperate 23–17 win.

Lost in the hoopla over Rodgers's great performance was the fact he was sacked five times and lost two fumbles. It was the highest-rated Cal team to play at USC since 1952, when Pappy Waldorf's number four Bears lost, 10–0. It reminded people of the

1951 game, when USC and Frank Gifford traveled to Berkeley, beating number one–ranked Cal, 21–14. It was the first time since 1968 that both teams were ranked when they played each other.

"Obviously there was a lot of hype going into that game," said Leinart on *The History of USC Football* DVD. "It was kind of a revenge game for us; I wasn't really thinking like that but inside of everyone else including the coaches we just wanted that game bad, and I just remember it was a battle from the get-go. I mean we got on 'em early, we got up 14–0 or seven or something like that, and the defense was playing good, but the one thing was they kept the ball so often and kept the defense on the field so long, and we kept going three-and-out, four-and-out, and the defense was getting tired and all that, and it came down to the last series of the game—back and forth, back and forth—and then four plays on the nine-yard line. With a potent offense like that, with a smart offense, it's like, this is gonna be tough. I remember just sitting on the sidelines just thinking to get ready for a two-minute drill and try to score and get the game, but our defense; the first play we had a chance, the second play, now get down to the third and fourth play, you're getting down, it's critical, the two biggest plays of the year, and we stop 'em."

DYNASTY!

The greatest back-to-back national champions ever

The Trojans had held the number one spot in the AP and *USA TODAY*/ESPN polls since the preseason. They had in fact been ranked number one since the end of the 2003 regular season, through the bowls, and on into 2004. They were approaching the all-time record of twenty straight AP number one rankings, held by Miami from 2000 to 2002, followed by Notre Dame from 1989 to 1990, and then by the 1972–1973 Trojans (seventeen).

Notre Dame arrived, and 92,611 sat in a slight drizzle. It was a night game at the Coliseum, nationally televised on ABC. For the second time ESPN's *College GameDay* broadcast from outside the stadium.

If there was any doubt Matt Leinart was deserving of the Heisman, like Palmer in 2002 he sealed the deal with his best game ever against Notre Dame. He hit five touchdown passes and 400 yards on twenty-four of thirty-four passing in a dominating 41–10 trouncing. It "left no doubt" who the best team in the land was, at least until the bowls. It was USC's twentieth straight win and twenty-first in a row at home. They were 11–0.

After fiddling around for a while, as occasionally was their wont, SC scored thirty-eight straight points. Dwayne Jarrett caught two scoring strikes. By this point in the season, people were calling White and Bush "Thunder and Lightning." Bush scored on a sixty-nine-yard pass, catch, and run. USC had 488 total yards. Tatupu, Grootegoed, and Cody stopped Notre Dame and their quarterback, Brady Quinn, all day.

In USC's last home game of the season, they set a season record for attendance, with a Pac 10 per-game record average of 82,229.

The UCLA game showed that Leinart's Heisman competition would not just be Oklahoma's Jason White and Adrian Petersen. Reggie Bush would be one of his main rivals for the award. On December 4 before a sold-out Rose Bowl crowd of

88,442 and another national television audience, Bush put himself on the cover of *Sports Illustrated* with two dazzling touchdowns and 335 all-purpose yards, including 204 on the ground. Bush went down in USC-UCLA history along with O. J. Simpson. He made 65-yard and 81-yard touchdown runs. He added 73 yards on six catches, 39 on kickoff returns, and 19 on two punt returns. His combination of running and kick returning was reminiscent of Anthony Davis's great 1972 and 1974 games against Notre Dame.

USC had a total of 477 total yards. White rushed for 75. Leinart connected on twenty-four of thirty-four for 242 yards. Dwayne Jarrett caught five passes. Lofa Tatupu made ten tackles. UCLA's Drew Olson was twenty of thirty-four for 278 yards. His touchdown pass to Marcedes Lewis late in the game created some Trojan tension, though. Visions of an onside kick followed by a "Miracle in the Arroyo Seco," which Bruin fans could talk about until 2099, did not happen. USC won, 29–24, to remain number one heading into the BCS national championship game.

"You knew it was a tough game; they played us a lot harder," Bush said on *The History of USC Football* DVD. "We didn't expect 'em to come out and play us as hard as they did, but it was a great game from the start to the end and it was a part of history. It sent us on our way to the national championship."

The next week the "perfect season" got more perfect. Ranked number one in both polls from the preseason to the end of the regular season, USC was also ranked first in each of the BCS computer rankings that surface after seven weeks.

They would face Oklahoma, number two in both polls every week, as well as in the BCS computers. The FedEx Orange Bowl would feature two unbeaten, untied teams with storied traditions.

In addition, an added element created extra excitement. The five Heisman finalists at New York's Downtown Athletic Club included two Trojans (Leinart and Bush) and two Sooners, quarterback Jason White and freshman running back sensation Adrian Peterson.

As if there was not enough serendipity in the room, the fifth contender was Bush's teammate from Helix High School in La Mesa, California: Utah quarterback Alex Smith.

Smith was a junior, expected to come out early for the NFL Draft. At that point, many felt Leinart would do the same. The general feeling among experts like Mel Kiper Jr. was that if this occurred, Leinart would go number one with Smith number two or lower.

In the end, Leinart won the Heisman balloting in a landslide. This meant the winner, the runner-up (Peterson), and four of the top five finalists would face each other in the national championship game on January 4 in Miami.

There have been many great games played over the years. Some would live up to the hype; some would not. When it came to pregame expectations, the 2005 Orange

Bowl was far and away the most anticipated, built-up game ever played by college teams.

Leinart, who along with Carroll, Bush, and the team was walking on water in Los Angeles, somehow managed to stay focused.

"I really accepted that award as part of the team," Leinart said modestly on *The History of USC Football* DVD. "Obviously it's mine and I get recognized, but I don't think I could have done it without my teammates, and I think any passing quarterback will tell you that they needed their guys around them to do that. I think it will mean more to me when I get older, but it's just a very special thing to be a part of, not a lot of people can do it, there's only been seventy-two winners. Not a lot can say they're part of that. It's definitely changed my life, but I think it's gonna mean more to me in twenty or thirty years, when I'm looking back, because now I'm a kid and it's just a reward I got this past season."

Oklahoma coach Bob Stoops could see it all unraveling when his own players started to open their mouths, thus providing perfect bulletin board material for Troy. Defensive end Larry Birdline of OU said that "beyond Bush they're an average team . . . Leinart's definitely overrated."

Of Taitusi Lutui, Birdline mispronounced his name as *Pitooie*, saying, "He's strong, but he may not be as strong as other guys I've seen. If God blesses me with three sacks, so be it."

USC wore home red, Oklahoma road whites. USC was favored to win by only a point and a half to two points. Before the game, in the privacy of a meeting room, fiery Assistant Coach Ed Orgeron dispensed with diplomacy while looking at video clips.

"He ain't gonna block Mike Patterson," Orgeron said of Sooner center Vince Carter.

When the game started, Leinart tried to draw Birdline out with verbal taunts. Alex Holmes blocked him with one arm.

"I was blocking him with one arm and telling him, 'You're not going anywhere, buddy,'" said Holmes. When USC went up 45–10, Holmes asked Birdline, "Is he still overrated?"

For the record, USC beat Oklahoma 55–19, behind the performance of game MVP Matt Leinart, who was eighteen of thirty-five for 332 yards and five touchdowns. The statistics of the game do not lie. The greater meaning of what happened at Pro Player Stadium is that USC achieved Carroll's admonition to "leave no doubt!"—that they were without question the finest team in the land. Beyond, the Trojans reached for and made a bid for history; they put themselves on that short list of teams who must be mentioned when historians argue, "Who is the best single-season team ever?"

Furthermore, when combined with the 2003 juggernaut (not to mention the 2002 "best in the country if there had been a play-off" team), Troy established themselves as the best back-to-back national championship team of all time.

USC trailed a few teams at times during the season. They got more than "pushed," which was the word Pat Haden used to describe the best any opponent could do against the 1972 Trojans (arguably the Stanford game, 30–21, and the Oregon game, 18–0). SC had not beaten the spread every time. They had to rally against Stanford, hold off Cal. An honest assessment of this team may possibly reveal that the '72 Trojans and 1995 Cornhuskers are better. Maybe.

The harder argument would be to find a *dynasty* greater than Carroll's Trojans from 2002 to 2004. Frank Leahy's Irish in the '40s, Bud Wilkinson's Sooners in the '50s, Howard Jones's 1930s Thundering Herd. It is a short list. USC can make a valid argument with any of them. Alabama fans would point to their "back-to-back national championships" in 1964–1965. Pointing out that the '64 Tide lost their bowl game ends that argument with a loud slam of the door. The 1978–1979 Tide makes a better case.

A crowd of 77,912 people were at Pro Player Stadium; a national audience tuned in to ABC. What *they* saw was the greatest team most of them ever have or ever will see. As they scratched their heads walking out, the realization that the team was still quite young and mostly returning in 2005 made them realize they had seen something unprecedented.

ESPN analyst Lee Corso, rumored to have been around since the days of Amos Alonzo Stagg, simply declared USC's win over OU "the greatest game I have ever seen any college team play!"

This was USC's eleventh national championship. It was only the second team to hold the number one ranking from the preseason through the bowls, and the sixth to hold it from game one to the bowls. They were the tenth team to win repeat AP national championships, but only eight of those were legitimate, either claiming titles when the polls were taken before bowl games they lost, or teams on probation. The "real" repeaters were Minnesota (1940–1941), Army (1944–1945), Notre Dame (1946–1947), Oklahoma (1955–1956), Nebraska (1970–1971), Alabama (1978–1979), and Nebraska (1994–1995).

Prior to the AP, USC had done it in 1931–1932, and Alabama from 1925–1926. Minnesota also made a claim.

The fifty-five points tied the most ever allowed by Oklahoma, who four years earlier sat atop the college football world while USC was 5–7. Now, the chasm between their 12–1 record and USC's 13–0 was as wide as the Grand Canyon. They would not recover easily.

SC scored thirty-eight points off OU turnovers. Steve Smith caught three scoring passes. Incredibly, OU had USC worried early when White drove them ninety-two yards for the first score to make it 7–0, Sooners. Southern California just came right back down the field until Leinart hit Byrd, who made an absolutely spectacular one-handed catch for a thirty-three-yard strike to even it up. SC scored twenty-eight unanswered points.

Trojan safety Josh Pinkard recovered a botched Oklahoma punt. LenDale White just ran it in from the 6 to make it 14–7. Jason Leach then intercepted a Jason White pass. Leinart nailed Jarrett on a fifty-four-yard bomb. 21–7. Cornerback Eric Wright picked White. Three plays later Leinart hit Smith from the 5. 28–7, 9:17 to play in the half.

Oklahoma managed a field goal, so USC just responded by scoring on four plays, with Leinart hitting Smith for another one of those one-handers from the 33. After Grootegoed recovered a fumble, Ryan Killeen made a forty-four-yard field goal with three seconds left to send Troy into the locker room leading 38–10.

The game was over. The only "bad" news for Southern California was that they won so convincingly, people looking for competition did not see much of their second half, which was as impressive as the first.

The Trojans took the ball down the field on their first third quarter possession, until Leinart hit Smith again from the 4. After holding Oklahoma, they got it back and set up a forty-two-yard Killeen field goal. Unrelenting, they stuffed the Sooners, got it back, and marched down the field in five plays. White powered it in against a helpless Sooner defense.

USC went to their reserves, the ultimate insult. The Trojans gained 525 total yards, averaging 8.3 a play. They had no turnovers. White rushed for 115 yards on fifteen carries, Bush for 75 yards and 149 all-purpose yards. He made two catches for 31 yards.

Lofa Tatupu made twelve tackles, Darnell Bing ten, and Grootegoed had seven. OU's White threw three interceptions, making some yards against fourth quarter reserves. Adrian Peterson was held to eighty-two yards.

"This a great moment for the University of Southern California for us to get an opportunity like this, and cash it in," Carroll said. "Hard to believe now, but we took this step by step.

"I just want to see if we can keep doing well.

"When you look back and someone says you got a record here or there, that's cool, but that's not what we're doing here. We're just trying to do well."

"Immediately after USC had taken a 28–7 lead over Oklahoma, the scoreboard operator posted an announcement for Sooner fans interested in drowning their sorrows: 'Alcohol sale ends at the end of the third quarter,'" wrote T. J. Simers in the *L.A. Times*.

The Orange Bowl was a star-studded event. Snoop Dogg, who showed up at a USC practice during the regular season, was there, along with SC grad Will Farrell, basketball star Shaq O'Neal, Carson Palmer, and others. Simers joked that it was a "reunion of the Simpsons: Jessica, Ashlee and O. J."

Ashlee Simpson performed, uh, poorly in a halftime show that did nothing to help her image after a lip-synching fiasco on *Saturday Night Live*. Her sister and her husband were of course Leinart's cool friends. USC kept their fingers crossed that the "third" Simpson, O. J., a Miami-area resident, would not make his presence publicly known.

The former Heisman winner's image had not improved in the years since his 1995 trial. A civil court subsequently found him responsible for the murders and ordered him to pay restitution to the family. O. J. succeeded in protecting his assets. He was living a golf course lifestyle in South Florida, showing no remorse, and granting occasional interviews in which he said he still wanted to find "the real killers."

The good news was that he was old news. The team created headlines on the field, pushing the O. J. talk to the back burner.

Tom Malone was chosen as an All-American after averaging forty-nine yards a punt, but was denied the honor of leading the nation in that category because the team hardly *needed* to punt, so he missed qualifying by five kicks.

Leinart was, of course, a consensus All-American, his second selection, and Reggie Bush was also a consensus pick.

Matt Grootegoed, chosen USC's co–Most Inspirational Player and captain, made All-American, too. He signed with the Tampa Bay Buccaneers and then went to Miami.

Ryan Killeen went to the Detroit Lions; Lee Webb and Jason Mitchell to Jacksonville; Alex Holmes to Miami; Jason Leach to San Diego; and Kevin Arbet to Tampa Bay.

GOIN' HOLLYWOOD: THE GREATEST COLLEGE FOOTBALL PLAYER EVER

Matt Leinart becomes the most hyped college athlete in history

The first big "recruit" of 2005 was Leinart. The NFL experts were in virtually unanimous agreement. If he declared, he would be the very first pick in the upcoming NFL Draft. To the surprise of some—but not all—Leinart chose to stay! When he did that, he turned himself into a hero on campus and in Los Angeles, an athlete of legendary status.

Carroll hugged Leinart. The 2005 national championship seemed all but assured. Backup QB John David Booty, to his credit, was classy and supportive of his teammate, even though it meant that his big shot at starting, which he would have to earn in competition with Mark Sanchez, would be pushed back to his junior year, 2006.

USC had the best recruiting class in the nation in 2003 and 2004—its '04 class was said to be the best ever, at the time. The February 3, 2005, issue of *USA TODAY* announced that Tennessee and Nebraska had the top recruiting classes of the new year. However, Allen Wallace of *SuperPrep* rated USC third behind Tennessee and Michigan, while Tom Lemming of ESPN.com rated USC third behind Nebraska and Tennessee. Wallace did not have Nebraska in his top five.

Student Sports and some other recruiting analysts revised the rankings as the fallout of recruiting season took place: players not getting into school, changes of heart, late signees. By the time the preseason magazines started coming out in May and June, USC was again considered to have had the best recruiting class in America, for the third straight year. It was an unprecedented accomplishment which reflects on what may be Carroll's greatest strength.

Of the returning players, Matt Leinart was of course the headliner. He entered the season with a chance to break all of the USC career passing records, become the second player ever (Archie Griffin of Ohio State did it from 1974–1975) to win two Heismans, plus win the Davey O'Brien and Maxwell Awards (he had won the 2004 Walter Camp Award). He was again a *Playboy* magazine preseason All-American selection, going for a third All-American season.

Leinart, the returning team captain, shared 2004 Pac 10 co–Offensive Player of the Year honors with Bush after having won that award outright as a sophomore.

Michael Wilbon of ESPN's *Around the Horn* openly said if he repeated a Heisman-winning national championship campaign, Leinart would have to go down in history as "the greatest college football player who ever lived."

He was featured in every possible spot and commercial, promoting college football on CSTV, interviewed with Bush on the *Best Damn Sports Show Period*, and quite simply continuing to be the most hyped amateur athlete anybody had ever seen.

His name was continually linked with more Hollywood actresses and models. He needed a bodyguard to walk the campus. He was, along with Carroll and Bush, a guy who reached the very top of L.A. celebrity status.

His decision to turn down NFL millions engendered some criticism, but most applauded the value he placed on loyalty, USC, Carroll, his teammates, and the college experience. It was an incredible endorsement of USC, worth as much to the school and the program in terms of revenue, prestige, recruiting, and goodwill as his on-field performance.

"The things I value at this school are more important to me than money," he said. "I realize the money I could have made if I had gone to the NFL, but I wanted to stay in school. I wanted to be with all my friends and teammates, living the college life and going through the graduation process. All those things make up my college experience and I didn't want to give that up. . . .

"Being in college is the best time of my life. . . . There is something special going on at USC that I didn't want to give up. . . . I'm having fun here. It's all a part of growing up, all part of being a kid, and I wasn't ready to pass that up. . . . A lot of people said they didn't envy me being in that situation. In a way, it was a great position to be in, but on the other hand it was one of the biggest decisions of my life. . . . There's still a lot of motivation for me to play college football. . . . I realize that some say there's really not much more I can accomplish. But I can get a lot stronger physically and mentally. Another year of experience can only help. It's not about the awards. It's not about trying to win another Heisman. It's really about trying to win a third national championship and getting better as a player. . . .

"The next level is business. I'm playing for passion and for the love of the game. There's nothing like this right here. . . . Sometimes I just kind of look around and think it's cool being in the position I'm in. Yeah, life is pretty cool."

As for his celebrity status, Leinart said, "It's crazy. I get linked with people because they're celebrities I've hung out with. It's kind of sad that I can't go hang with them without getting my name in the paper. I just want to hang out. I don't want to be in all the magazines. That's not who I am. . . . When I go out, it's all over the TV. That's the thing about celebrity life. You never know who's watching you. You just have to be really secure in what you're doing. . . . I'm a normal guy, just like any other twenty-one-year-old college student. Really, there's nothing special about me. . . . It's hard to trust a lot of people and know what they're after."

Leinart reflected on the 2004 Heisman Trophy.

"I remember when Carson was sitting up there and won it," he recalled. "He said his heart was beating out of his chest. Mine was about to do the same thing. . . . I just kind of dropped. My legs were weak. My heart was beating twenty beats a second. It was probably one of the greatest feelings I've ever had in my life. . . . I was a fat kid, cross-eyed, and other people made fun of me. So I'm extremely honored. . . .

"But when I got home, I put the trophy away and acted like nothing had happened. I was still the same guy. I let my team know that I thanked them. Then, I continued to work hard. . . .

"I feel like I still have so much more to accomplish. . . . I'm still the same person and act the same. All my friends treat me the same, as a goofball. They still could care less. . . . I remember talking to Jason White after he won and him saying how winning the Heisman changes your life completely. . . . My life has changed drastically. A few years ago I was a nobody. To me, I'm still a nobody, but in the eyes of a lot of people I'm a role model, which I take pride in. It's been an incredible journey so far."

Leinart had a huge target on his back. He was no longer the unknown sophomore playing in his first game at Auburn.

"I love it," he said, and he meant it. "I love having pressure on my shoulders. I've been having pressure my whole life. This is a spot where we want to be as a team. We like being on the national stage where everybody's watching us. . . . I've got great players around me. Our system works, obviously. We recruit the best players every year. We have backups who are awesome.

"I'm not the most physically gifted kid. I'm not going to scare anybody with my arm or with my running ability. But I feel like my mind sets me apart. And my accuracy.

"I'm laid back. But I expect perfection. I'm very hard on myself. . . . On the field, I have a cool confidence. I've never been arrogant. I could care less about awards. I just want to win. . . . I don't like being in the spotlight. I just like playing. Obviously, you're going to be the hero or the goat when you're the quarterback. But I'm kind of a more roll-with-things kind of person. . . . As a person, I'm pretty boring. I play video games. That's my favorite hobby. . . .

"If you told me when the 2003 season started that I'd do what I did, I never would have believed it. . . . The season I had, that the team had, I think no one really expected that. It was a dream come true. It was kind of surreal in a way. . . . I learned a lot from Carson Palmer on how to lead a team. He was the same all the time, never nervous, always calm under pressure. And that's kind of how I've been. . . . The way

Carson carried himself, even when he was getting ripped by everybody, I really admired that. I tried to be the same way. . . . And with all the talent around me, it would have been hard not to be successful."

Leinart was asked about the "turning point" game of his sophomore year, when he played in second half pain (as Paul McDonald had done in the 1978 Notre Dame thriller) to beat Arizona State in the desert heat.

"I was trying not to limp, but I was in a lot of pain," he said. "Sometimes, you've got to play through it. . . . The guys realized I was willing to do everything, even though I was just doing my job. . . . I really didn't realize it that much at the time. But then I read the next day that some of the guys said they wanted to play for someone like that. I thought, 'Wow, these guys really have my back.' That was a huge turning point. . . .

"Mike Williams had my back from day one. He was constantly in the newspapers saying I was the man. When one of the best players in the country is saying, 'This is our guy. He's going to lead us wherever we go,' that gives you great confidence."

Leinart was down the depth chart his first two years. Obviously, it was Palmer's job, but Leinart appeared to have made little impact or good impression in his redshirt and second-year freshman seasons.

"My attitude was a big part it and that needed to change," he admitted. "It was tough working all the time and not playing. There were times when I really didn't care and didn't want to be there. . . . I was upset with myself. In high school, you're the man. You come here, and it's a reality check. . . . I wondered if this was what I really wanted to do. And I was down on myself, too. . . . But it seemed like as soon as Carson Palmer left, everything changed. I realized I couldn't be that way anymore. I had to grow up and become a leader. . . . Once I got comfortable in the system and running the offense, I just never looked back, and here I am today, confident, knowing the system like its my own and just very capable of running it."

Football fans might listen to Leinart's analysis of his maturation process and think that he is exaggerating the growth it took to get to where he is. After all, he was talented, a huge high school star in a system designed to produce college players, and ultimately even Heisman winners (John Huarte having played for Mater Dei in 1960). However, Trojan football historians need look no further than their not-all-that-distant past to see just how difficult the role can be.

"Matt Leinart had an even more impressive season in 2004 than Carson Palmer had in 2002 when he won the Heisman," wrote Steve Dilbeck of the *Los Angeles Daily News*. "Leinart also had a better year than in 2003, when he finished sixth in the Heisman."

In fact, many argued that sophomore Leinart was better in 2003 than fifth-year Heisman winner Palmer in 2002.

"He put up equal or better numbers, despite losing his top three receivers and despite playing behind an almost all-new offensive line. . . ." Dilbeck went on. "The most dramatic thing about Leinart might be his consistency. . . . And the way he takes advantage of all the talent around him is Palmeresque."

"In the celebrity-driven culture of Los Angeles, it's been suggested that Matt Leinart might be L.A.'s new leading man," wrote Kelly Whiteside of *USA TODAY*. "Though as unassuming as a movie-set backdrop, Leinart has Central Casting qualities. A Heisman Trophy–winning quarterback for the two-time defending national champion Trojans, with boyish good looks and big-lug charm, Leinart's got everything going for him."

"Go ahead, pick a fantasy," wrote Matt Hayes of *The Sporting News*. "Dream it up. You know what? Matt Leinart has got you beat. And the ride is just beginning. Come on, who among you wouldn't want to switch places with this guy? A hip quarterback at a private Los Angeles university with a stars-aligned, bathe-in-the-glory-of-it-all lifestyle. He looks like a Ken doll, a 6-5 statue glowing amid one of the most storied programs in the history of college football. . . . Leinart could be one of the biggest college football stars in decades. He already is the king of the city that's fashionably late. . . . But he isn't who you think he is. It's touchdowns and titles and Tinseltown on the surface. It's just plain Matty inside."

"Matt's got the world in his hands," said Reggie Bush, who Leinart said would have gotten his vote for the 2004 Heisman, and was fairly sure to get it in 2005. As a past winner, Leinart earned voting privileges while still in college. In fact, his jersey number (11), while not officially retired, was unveiled along with the other Heisman numbers: Garrett's 20, O. J.'s 32, White's 12, Allen's 33, and Palmer's 3, in the peristyle of the Coliseum at the home opener with Arkansas.

"Early in his career, he knew the system, he knew what was going on, he impressed the coaches that way," said Carroll of his star quarterback. "But he really didn't deliver the ball well. He didn't throw the ball hard. He was kind of a touch guy. . . . He just improved steadily. His strength just became tremendous strengths for him, his smarts and his awareness and his poise. . . . He's very comfortable with everything that we're doing. Nothing fazes him."

"THE PRESIDENT"

The "Lightning" to LenDale White's "Thunder"

While Leinart was the team's MVP as a 2003 sophomore, following that up with a Heisman campaign in 2004, it was Reggie "The President" Bush who earned the team MVP award for 2004. Entering the 2005 campaign, all the other awards—Heisman, Maxwell, Unitas, O'Brien—promised to be less competitive than this singular honor, which spoke volumes about what Pete Carroll had built in Los Angeles. In addition to being an almost-guaranteed New York finalist for the 2005 Heisman, Bush also was a Doak Walker Award contender with a chance at breaking various USC records.

The backfield combo of LenDale White and Bush had come to be nicknamed "Thunder and Lightning." Bush was the "Lightning." As a sophomore, he had finished fifth in the nation in all-purpose running yards (179.2 a game). His 2,330 all-purpose yards were the most by a Trojan since Marcus Allen. He averaged 10.1 yards each time he touched the ball. In addition to finishing fifth in the Heisman vote, in which he was a finalist in New York City, Bush was named the 2004 College Player of the Year by the Touchdown Club of Columbus. He was a consensus All-American and, along with Leinart, the conference co–Offensive Player of the Year. When the 2003 national champions visited the White House, the real President Bush singled Reggie out for his last name.

He earned Freshman All-American and all-conference honors in 2003 after coming out of Helix High, where the local prep media alternated between calling him the best high school football player to come out of San Diego since Marcus Allen, or the best high school football player *ever* to come out of San Diego.

That is quite a compliment. Aside from Bush and Allen, Ricky Williams, Rashaan Salaam, Junior Seau, Terrell Davis, and Cotton Warburton played high school football in San Diego County.

"I expect great things out of myself," said Bush, a deeply religious young man from a strong, tight-knit family. "I expect to make great plays, great moves. In my mind, I can never be good enough. . . . It just comes with the territory of making the most of what God has given you. I'm just trying to make the most out of a blessing I was given. . . ."

"To do it all" was how he saw his role. "My favorite role is to get the ball in my hands. Any way I can do that. I just like getting the ball in my hands and making a play for my team. . . . Ever since I started playing football it just felt right. It just felt like something I loved to do. I just loved being able to entertain the crowd and to go out there and make plays happen. It was fun at the same time. . . . I have to know a lot more about the playbook than the other players. But that goes with the territory and I love it. . . .

"I don't really look at other people's moves and copy them because, when I'm on the field, I'm not going to remember them. It's just something that has a lot to do with instinct and vision and all those running back aspects that you have. You put them all into a basket, and you just use them on the field and go out there and make plays. . . .

"I'm a competitor," he said of splitting time with LenDale White. "I love having the ball in my hands. . . . What's important is winning. . . . It's a little tough for a running back to get into a rhythm when you're not in there getting all the reps and feeling the defense. But we did it the whole season and when you got in there you had to take advantage of it . . . . There's no jealousy on the team at all. We're all out here pulling for each other and trying to make each other better. . . .

"The hard part has been learning to wait for my opportunity. They can't double- and triple-team me the whole game. If they do, that opens up opportunities for the other guys and, once that starts, I know I'm going to get my chance. . . . I feel if I ran the ball thirty times, I could definitely do some damage. But it's a different situation and it's working out. . . .

"Off the field, I'm quiet. On the field, I'm probably the exact opposite of that. Split personality on and off the field."

After finishing as a finalist for the 2004 Heisman, Bush just said, "I'll be back next year." The *real* speculation immediately began; would he come back in 2006, either to claim his first or *second* Heisman, and maybe a fourth national title? The talk about Leinart being the best collegiate player ever could easily switch to Bush holding that lofty position.

"A punt return is almost freedom of speech" was the way Bush described what many felt was the most exciting part of his game. "You get to go out and do whatever you want. It's not a set-up play. You go out and catch the ball and do something for your team. I do what I want. You can't get in trouble. I just get to go out there and express me, my athleticism, my personality, the type of player I am. . . .

"You have to stay humble and do everything the right way. You have to represent the team the right way. . . . I don't mind all the attention. But it makes me hungrier. It makes me want to do bigger things."

"He's the best running back I've seen since Tony Dorsett," said Stanford play-by-play announcer Ted Robinson.

"If you've got a linebacker covering him, you might as well start singing their fight song" was Washington State coach Bill Doba's interesting observation of defending Bush.

"Every time Reggie touches the ball, anything can happen. . . ." said Leinart. "He's an awesome weapon. . . . A lot of people think he's an outside runner, but he's tough. He can run in between the tackles. . . . When he first came to USC, he was running all over our first defense in fall camp, cutting back, reversing his field. We knew he was special. Anytime he has the ball, something special can happen. It's unbelievable what he can do."

MR. WHITE

A superstar laboring in the shadow of more heralded teammates

Where Bush was "Lightning," six-foot, two-inch, 235-pound powerhouse LenDale White, his alternate at the tailback position, was "Thunder." White was All-American, All-State for three years, and the Gatorade Colorado Player of the Year as a senior at Chatfield High in Denver. He gained a state record of 7,803 yards as a four-year starter (the first three at Denver's South High).

As a 2003 freshman, White ran for 754 yards, earning Freshman All-American, All–Pacific 10, and Pac 10 Freshman Offensive Player of the Year honors.

In 2004 he made All–Pac 10 and Collegefootballnews.com's Sophomore All-American team.

Despite his reputation for "running inside the tackles," White insisted, "I'm shifty, but I have the power when I need it. I used to be a scatback, but I got to USC and gained some weight."

White actually was the starter in 2004, although Bush started in the Orange Bowl against Oklahoma. White, with the exception of one reported flare-up that may not have happened or been overblown, accepted his sharing role as a complete team player.

"There's not even competition between us," he said of Bush and, in 2003, Hershel Dennis. "Our competition is how we can push each other to be our best. . . . All of the tailbacks here believe we're great, and great as a group. . . .

"We were the tailback. It's like there was no special tailback and there was no main tailback. We all just went out there when we got our chance and just tried to make things happen. All of us were capable of doing it. We had fast guys, big guys, quick guys. We were all special in our own types of ways. When they called on us, we all cheered for each other. It was like a family to me. . . . When I saw them doing well, I wanted to do well, so they helped me elevate my game."

Still, White envied Bush in one respect.

"I want to line up wide and go deep, too, just like Reggie," he fantasized. "That's my dream, to have Reggie at tailback and me catch a bomb."

"White is the thunder and has drawn comparisons to bruising backs from Jamal Lewis to former USC great Ricky Bell. . . ." wrote Todd Harmonson of the *Orange County Register* early in White's career. "He is a tackle-breaking bulldozer who delivers punishment with a try-to-stop-me grin. It's too early to anoint White as the next great tailback at USC, but his quiet confidence and thunderous running style are enough to inspire Trojan imaginations. Fans with decent memories compare him to Ricky Bell. Offensive linemen who must make their blocks point to Justin Fargas. . . . Off the field, White is the fun-lover who raves about seeing Beyonce at the BET Awards, adds tattoos the way he does yards and always seems to be laughing." Mel Kiper Jr. predicted that White would be selected late in the first round of the 2006 NFL Draft should he choose to come out. However, the tantalizing possibility remained that in '06, with Leinart graduated and Bush drafted number one, White would be USC's marquee name, very possibly its eighth Heisman Trophy winner, and incredibly a member of *four national champs in four years*!

(Unfortunately, White turned down the spotlight that eluded him when he declared for the '06 NFL Draft, and all the best hopes and predictions just barely missed coming to fruition.)

THE GREATEST COLLEGE FOOTBALL TEAM OF ALL TIME
(2005 Edition)

The most publicized college sports team ever sets out to
do things never done before

The USC Trojans entered the 2005 season shooting for a string of superlatives that included:

1. Passing Notre Dame as the greatest collegiate football tradition ever.
2. Becoming the greatest single-season team ever.
3. Becoming the greatest half-decade dynasty of all time.
4. Quarterback Matt Leinart becoming the best college football player in history.
5. The Leinart-Bush duo passing Army's Mr. Inside and Mr. Outside Blanchard-Davis combo to become the most ballyhooed teammates ever.

Bush, Leinart, and White had a supporting cast to outdo all other supporting casts. Without Leinart or Bush, White would have been a Heisman candidate coming in. If not for all the big stars, players like Dwayne Jarrett and Steve Smith may well have entered into that discussion. If all the prep hype was to be believed, third-year sophomore John David Booty just might have been draped in glory had he won the job back in 2003.

Junior safety Darnell Bing, he of Garrett's number 20, helped anchor the secondary in 2005. The *Parade* All-American from Long Beach Poly had been a 2003 Freshman All-American and a 2004 All–Pac 10 selection. In 2005 he asserted himself in the Jim Thorpe Award discussion.

"I know what Mike Garrett meant to this program," he said of the number. " . . . I just have to show that I'm worthy of wearing number 20. Mr. Garrett said that if I don't do it, he'll take it back."

"He's got a golden horseshoe in his pocket," Carroll said, referring to Bing's natural "luck." "Sometimes there are safeties who are like that."

Jeff Byers, the 2003 Gatorade National Player of the Year at Loveland High in Colorado, entered 2005 with question marks. In the classroom he was right on the mark with a B-minus average. As a 2004 freshman, it might seem incongruous, but despite earning the starting job at season's end, making Freshman All-American and Freshman All–Pac 10, he had not pushed Ryan Kalil out of the center's job. This was, in fact, a testament to Kalil and to the high competition at SC, not any indication that Byers was a disappointment as a true freshman.

However, he had hip surgery that kept him out of spring practice. His injuries prevented him from entering the year on the active roster. Instead, Carroll planned to red-shirt him.

"I knew when I came here that USC has the most talented players in the country," said Byers, who as a Colorado lineman at Southern Cal followed in the large footsteps of Tony Boselli. "I get my eyes opened every day."

"He has very high expectations for himself," said Carroll.

The 6'3", 260-pound senior tight-end-who-plays-like-a-wideout, Dominique Byrd, enjoyed a spectacular, if sporadic, junior year. He starred in the Orange Bowl, but missed the first four games with an injury. Amidst all the talent he did not get as many touches as he otherwise might have.

Battling small-scale injuries, Byrd was a Mackey Award candidate in 2005. The All-American from Breck High in Minneapolis interned for Minnesota Senator Mark Dayton. He seemed philosophical about life.

"I believe that my injuries were blessings in disguise," he said. "I think everything happens for a reason, and it was just time for me to mature as a person."

Freshman tailback Michael Coleman was part of the spectacular 2005 recruiting class. He had entered school in the spring. A *Super Prep* All-Farwest, All-Southern Section, and San Bernardino County Player of the Year in 2004, the 6'1", 235-pound Coleman played quarterback at Arroyo Valley High, but was switched to running back where he showed phenomenal promise. His speed and size seemed to be a younger combination of Bush and White. His quarterback-to-running back transition could not help but remind people of Marcus Allen.

Fred Davis, the 6'4", 225-pound wideout-turned-tight end, two-time prep All-American, and prized 2004 recruit from Ohio, hoped he could make an impact his sophomore year after an unfortunate missed-meeting episode, costing him a trip to Miami.

Another high school All-American, tailback Hershel Dennis from Long Beach Poly, also looked to find some redemption in a disappointing career that had seemed so promising when he starred as the starting tailback on the 2003 national champions.

Another former track standout, Dennis got off to a bad start when police were called to his apartment. A girl complained about his actions prior to the 2004 campaign. No charges were filed, but he had been suspended, played rarely, then hurt himself, missing the Orange Bowl.

In 2005 he was still recuperating from torn knee ligaments, but had buckled down, kept his mouth shut, and stayed with the program with a legitimate chance at being a big part of the 2006 team as a fifth-year senior.

"He's in this for the right reasons, knowing the team can accomplish something," said Carroll.

"It was difficult," Dennis said of his up-and-down fortunes at USC. "I have to believe things will work out for me. God has good things planned for me. . . . I wanted to stay a team player, support my teammates, and help out any way I could."

So, too, would 285-pound sophomore defensive tackle Sedrick Ellis. The All-American from Chino entered 2005 looking to start at nose tackle.

The 6'5", 265-pound sophomore defensive end Lawrence Jackson, a consensus prep All-American and two-time CIF-Southern Section first teamer at Inglewood High, was a 2004 Freshman All-American.

"He's a specimen—big, fast, and strong," said Shaun Cody of Jackson. In addition, Jackson was known as a contrarian, a debater who philosophizes "about stuff the average person doesn't think about."

The 6'5" wide receiver Dwayne Jarrett, a sophomore in 2005, was New Jersey's Offensive Player of the Year, a *Parade* All-American, and considered to be the top prep receiver of 2003 at New Brunswick High School. He followed that up with a spectacular rookie year, earning Freshman All-American and all-conference honors.

"I wasn't used to being away from home," Jarrett said of his first year in Los Angeles. "It was a shock to me. In the first couple of weeks of camp, it was like, 'Oh, man. I don't like it here.' I talked to Coach Carroll a lot. I told him, 'I'm not sure this is the place for me.' But I got through it. It made me a better person."

"That's not Mike Williams? That's not Lynn Swann? That's not Keyshawn Johnson?" marveled Keith Gilbertson. "Jarrett is the next great one. He's tremendous. He's a lot like Keyshawn and Mike—tall and rangy and really, really good."

"He is extremely talented," said Carroll. "If you watch him on the field, you see he is just so natural and so gifted. He is all we could have hoped for. We were hoping to find someone to fill the Mike Williams role. Dwayne can do all the things that Mike can do."

"He's reminiscent of Mike Williams in the height, the athleticism, and just the way they make plays and create mismatches," said Leinart. "But Dwayne might be more athletic."

Six-foot, six-inch, 300-pound junior offensive tackle Winston Justice returned to the field in 2005 after a student conduct violation. Justice was an All-American and the

L.A. Times Southern California Lineman of the Year at Long Beach Poly in 2001, a Freshman All-American in 2002, and All–Pacific 10 in 2003.

He trained with Mike Tyson at a Hollywood boxing gym during the off year.

"It was hard," he said. "But life goes on. . . . I learned a lot about certain situations during my time off. I learned you can't take things for granted because they can be taken away from you. . . . I feel more mature now."

Justice considered moving on to the NFL, where he most likely could have forged a career, but chose to be part of something special again.

Junior center Ryan Kalil won USC's Courage Award in 2004, holding on to the job coveted by the heralded Jeff Byers.

"He's the type of kid you dream of," his father, Frank Kalil, said of his son, an All-American at Servite High School in Anaheim. "He's a throwback. He doesn't drink or smoke. And I'd always hear him playing Sinatra in the bedroom."

Junior linebacker Oscar Lua, 240 pounds, had made a great impact since his freshman year, receiving little fanfare amid his heralded teammates. Growing up rooting for ex-Trojan and Charger All-Pro Junior Seau, Lua was an All-American, All–Southern California, and All–Southern Section pick at Indio High, located in a desert community east of L.A. He also hit .485 with eleven home runs, earning two-time All–Desert Valley League honors in baseball.

The 6'6", 365-pound senior offensive tackle Taitusi Lutui dominated his Orange Bowl matchups. An All-State selection at Mesa High near Phoenix, he earned All-American kudos at Snow J.C. in Utah.

Married with a child, he said his parents "brought us to this country for a purpose" from the Tongan Islands.

Senior punter Tom Malone could have entered professional football, but the 2004 All-American, All–Pac 10, and Ray Guy Award semifinalist wanted to stick around. He was a *Playboy* magazine preseason All-American in 2005 after leading the nation in punting (without full credit because the offense was so good he did not get enough attempts to qualify in '05).

Malone was an All-American in his sophomore year (2003) and a Freshman All-American and all-conference in 2002, after an All-American career at Temescal Canyon High School in Lake Elsinore, California. A political science major, Malone had enough credits to graduate had he chosen to do so. Instead, he was bidding to be a rare three-time All-American.

"Tom Malone is college football's vanity plate, the chocolate truffle at the end of five courses," wrote Mark Whicker of the *Orange County Register*. " . . . He's an indulgence on a team that never punts."

The 305-pound junior offensive guard Fred Matua was All-L.A. City Section at Banning High School in 2000, All-American in 2001, Freshman All-American in 2003, and Sophomore All-American in 2004.

His uncle played at USC. Assorted other relatives played and coached at high levels.

"When he first came in, he was a wild man," said Shaun Cody of Matua.

"He's a player with a defensive temperament" on offense, said offensive line coach Tim Davis.

Safety Josh Pinkard had been All-American at Hueneme High on the Ventura County coast.

Sophomore tailback Desmond Reed, who if it were not for Bush and White would have been a national figure already, earned All–Pac 10 honors in 2004 after an All-American career as running back and defensive back at Temple City High in the San Gabriel Valley.

"Desmond Reed is the best kept secret in college football," said Leinart.

The 6'3", 220-pound sophomore linebacker Keith Rivers (wearing the famed number 55 of Seau and other linebacker stars) was simply the best player at his position in the 2003 recruiting class after an All-American and three-time All-State career at Lake Mary High in Florida.

A Freshman All–Pac 10 pick playing alongside Matt Grootegoed in 2004, Rivers was "really fast and tough," said Carroll. "He has an unusual body in that he can strike guys in a small space and unload on them." He was beginning to remind some people of Richard "Batman" Wood and Charles Phillips of 1974 national championship fame.

The 6'3", 260-pound senior defensive end Frostee Rucker was a typical example of Carroll's democratic system. He earned a place at the table through hard work, outplaying more heralded blue chippers. Rucker had not been an All-American at Tustin High, although he was a CIF-Southern Section Division VI first teamer and Golden West League MVP. He went to Colorado State, then transferred to USC when he realized that he had the chops to play with the very best.

The 6'4", 260-pound sophomore defensive end Jeff Schweiger entered 2005 with high expectations. Austin Murphy of *Sports Illustrated* predicted that USC would anchor defense of their national championship around his defensive leadership. Schweiger was one of the very highest-rated All-Americans in the nation as a senior at Valley Christian High School in the San Jose area.

Junior wide receiver Steve Smith was one of the most heralded prep athletes in America at Taft High: a track star, All-American basketball player, three-time All-State receiver, L.A. City Section MVP, and 2002 *Parade* All-American. He made numerous big catches in his freshman and sophomore years, entering 2005 on the Biletnikoff and Maxwell watch lists.

"I didn't feel any pressure replacing" Mike Williams and Keary Colbert, said Smith.

As the season approached, the natural talk about "three-Petes" became inevitable, along with the ridiculous notion that the school could not market the theme "three-Pete" because former Laker basketball coach Pat Riley had patented the term—a peculiarly "only in L.A." oddity.

It was the most loaded, talented, hyped collegiate football team of all time; prep

All-Americans *everywhere* . . . a Heisman winner, Heisman contenders, All-Americans, Lombardi, O'Brien, Unitas, Maxwell, Biletnikoff, Ray Guy candidates . . . The only thing that could stop USC was USC.

The chance to win an unprecedented third straight title, something no team had ever done, and to do it at the Rose Bowl, added to the "perfection" of the situation.

"It's an exciting challenge to be the returning national champion, and we look forward to dealing with everything that goes with that," said Carroll. "We'll handle it well. Our approach will be the same as it always is. Our goal always is to win the Pac 10 and the Rose Bowl."

USC had eleven first team All-Americans, two of three Heisman winners, winning twenty-two straight and thirty-three of the last thirty-four over the previous three years.

"We're really proud of our recent accomplishments," said Carroll. "But we view those now as things in the past. All indications are that we have been able to move forward. Our focus is on the 2005 season."

Fourteen starters returned (eight on offense, five on defense, the punter) along with seventy-five squadmen (fifty-eight of whom had seen playing time, forty-nine lettered, and twenty-eight on the two-deep chart). Twenty-four players started in the past. Nineteen new scholarship players joined the roster.

"We have grown comfortable with being in this environment, with all this attention on us," said Carroll. "We've been there. We went through the whole season last year as the nation's number one team. We deal with that kind of thing as we do with everything, by going about our business in a normal fashion. We aren't concerned with the hype and the future. We'll just try to prove our worth week to week. I love that kind of challenge. We have to see if we can do it.

"In previous years, we've shown the ability to deal with the loss of great players. I'm confident we have the personnel who will seize their opportunities and step up, especially among our new and our younger players. This kind of an annual challenge is what makes college football so fun."

Leinart came in with gaudy numbers: 65.3 percent completion rate, 3,322 yards, thirty-three touchdowns against six interceptions in 2004. His seventy-one career touchdowns in two years was one behind Palmer, who needed the better part of five seasons. He was 25–1 as a starter with a twenty-two-game winning streak.

"Matt Leinart's decision to return for his senior year really sent a message about him as a person and how much fun it is to play college football," said Carroll. "He has two outstanding seasons under his belt now and is in such command of our offense. He's a gifted quarterback and a true team leader. We expect him to pick up right where he left off."

Aside from Leinart, Carroll had "Thunder and Lightning"—Bush and White.

"With LenDale White and Reggie Bush, we have an unusually effective combination of running backs," said Carroll. "LenDale packs a punch on every down. He's the engine of our offense. Reggie creates problems wherever he lines up because of his speed and elusiveness, so teams always have to pay extra attention to him. He has the potential to score every time he touches the ball."

In a private phone conversation with this author in March 2005, Pete Carroll expressed more than his usual optimism and confidence. Of the Orange Bowl blowout, he said, "We were so confident. I just knew that our program couldn't be beat. What we've got here, it works, they've bought into it, and honestly the Sooners couldn't beat that. There was no doubt left by the time that game came around."

Just as in 2004, every single magazine and poll chose USC as the preseason number one prediction. The Associated Press gave them the highest number of preseason number one votes in the poll's seventy-year history, with Texas a distant second. USC entered the 2005 campaign having been ranked number one by the AP for seventeen straight polls. Miami held the record from 2001 to 2002. Notre Dame in the late 1980s was second at nineteen. USC was tied with itself (the 1972–1973 Trojans) for third. If they could be number one for the first four polls, another big-time college record would fall.

USA TODAY/ESPN also ranked them first. *Athlon Sports College Football* magazine was typical of the plethora of publications gushing about the supposedly unbeatable Trojans. Featuring Leinart on the cover with Oklahoma's Adrian Peterson (Leinart and Bush, sometimes together, dominated all the covers), they rated USC first.

As if USC's number one–ranked team was not enough, *Athlon* rated their cheerleaders as the "best" in the country, too. When you're hot, you're hot!

Speaking of beautiful girls, *Playboy* featured the "Girls of the Pac 10" in 2005. In their college football preseason edition, USC was again their pick to win the national championship. A nice photo of Leinart was accompanied by a story in which Matt talked about his weekly lunch at Togo's with his dad.

"Nothing fancy, but it's become a ritual," Leinart told Gary Cole. "The last time I missed our Tuesday lunch, we lost to Cal. We're not going to miss another one. . . .

"I'm watching a lot more film this year. I want to be better prepared. . . . My favorite day of the week is game day. I'm not nervous, just excited. It's the greatest feeling in the world."

The *Playboy* coaches' interview was with Carroll. Asked about Leinart's return, Carroll responded, "A lot of other people were surprised, but I can't say I was. Matt said all along he wanted to stay in school. I knew his situation here was a good one. And knowing how supportive his parents were about his decision, I wasn't surprised at all."

Of the players replacing Cody and Patterson, he said, "While I think it will be difficult for us to be better than we were last year," he remained optimistic.

Sports Illustrated, notorious for their bad preseason college football predictions, had hit it right on the button with USC in 2004. The Trojans were their pick again in '05, followed by Texas, Florida, and Michigan.

Bush graced their cover with the headline, "Gamebreakers, REGGIE BUSH, He's One of Those Unstoppable Players. Can He Keep USC on Top?"

"Sometimes I go back and watch myself [on tape]," Bush told Austin Murphy. "To be honest, I'm not really conscious of what I'm doing while I'm doing it. Even after that, I don't really remember what I did."

"You can do everything right, be in perfect position to stop him, and Bush will hurt you," Murphy wrote of the defenders' mind-set facing Bush.

S.I. promoted Texas as the Trojans' top national challenger, and their talented quarterback, Vince Young, as the main Heisman contender in season-ending show-downs with USC, Leinart, and Bush. Their preseason All-American predictions were Leinart, Bush, and Darnell Bing.

The rest of America's college football world looked at the monopoly of attention USC was getting. They wanted nothing more than to knock them off their high horse. The accolades continued. *The Sporting News College Football* preseason edition: Leinart for Heisman, USC number one. Every paper, daily, weekly, and monthly, saw it that way.

ESPN the Magazine featured Leinart literally riding on Bush's back: "ON BOARD FOR MORE." Inside was color photo after photo of the two with their male model smiles.

The Yankees, of course, had been down this path. Maybe Joe Montana's 49ers. Nationally, USC was getting as much ink as the three-time Super Bowl winners from New England, and half of their star power came from *their* GQ quarterback, the California "golden boy" Tom Brady. The Red Sox were huge in New England and nationally, but in a quirkier, sect-like way.

There were others, but few others, and nobody from the college ranks.

"When you enter into this velvet-rope level, you have to handle the tricky tentacles of fame," wrote *ESPN the Magazine*'s Bruce Feldman. "After winning the Heisman, Leinart got to cherry-pick the late-night talk-show circuit. He chose Kimmel (Nick was a guest, too). Even Malone, the punter, now has a web site touting him for the Heisman."

Indeed, L.A. talk radio seemed to be Trojan radio 24/7, without exaggeration. There was KMPC 1540 "The Ticket," a derivative of the old Gene Autry–owned Golden West Radio Network. They had gone through a series of genre, ownership, and management changes since the "Singin' Cowboy's" death. Formerly found at 710 AM, they now had a new physical location, as well: Santa Monica, with improved signal wattage.

Petros Papadakis, Fred Roggin, Dave Smith, John Jackson, and others poured forth constant USC interviews, tidbits, opinion, and analysis. They were not the only ones. Various stations popped up all over the AM sports dial: Fox Sports Radio, ESPN Radio,

The Sporting News Radio networks. A lot had changed since 1997, when USC had their broadcasts on an FM station that starts to fade when one drives into Orange County.

"If USC pulls off a three-Pete," former quarterback Rodney Peete was asked on ESPN Classic, "will they be the greatest team of all time?"

"I think so," replied Peete. "In today's era, with the competition, the scholarships, the national level of the game; yes, they'd have to be."

USC entered 2005 as the sixth back-to-back national champion to enter the third year ranked number one.

"I think it would be monumental, especially in this day and age," said Washington State coach Bill Doba.

"I don't think 'these days' has anything to do with it," said Carroll.

"I think winning three in a row is tougher to do today," said Ara Parseghian. "You look at the number one and number 25 teams now, and there's just not as much difference as there used to be."

CSTV's Brian Curtis also pointed out a hugely relevant fact, which was that since 1990 the best players usually left after their junior years. Of course the best players usually play for the best teams. USC had retained Leinart, yes, but lost Williams as a *sophomore* and then Lofa Tatupu, both All-Americans. The common wisdom was that juniors White and/or Bush would leave after 2005, but they would cross that bridge when they came to it.

"We didn't really pay any attention to the polls back then," said Johnny Lujack, Notre Dame's 1947 Heisman Trophy winner. "I don't recall the players or coaches ever even talking about the polls. We were just thinking about winning the next game. At the end, they just said we were number one."

Two-time champion Notre Dame opened the 1948 season number one, but a season-ending tie with Southern California allowed Michigan to sneak in. The Irish finished second (9–0–1). 1955–1956 champion Oklahoma started 1957 at the top, but a 7–0 loss at Notre Dame ended their forty-seven-game winning streak and hopes for a "three-peat." They finished fourth (10–1).

The 1966 Alabama Crimson Tide, still ranked first, claimed two straight titles coming in (despite losing their 1965 bowl game to Texas after the "final" polls), but the "Catholic vote" gave it to the Irish, with Michigan State second, both with their tie against each other. 'Bama finished third (10–0).

Nebraska (1970–1971) opened the 1972 campaign number one with a thirty-game unbeaten streak (going back to a 1969 season-opening loss to USC, interrupted also by a 1970 tie with the Trojans). They must have been cursing the Golden State when UCLA ended their dream for a third one with a 20–17 win at the Coliseum. The Cornhuskers finished fourth (9–2–1), although Johnny Rodgers won the Heisman.

The 'Huskers again opened in the poll position in 1996 after two straight titles from 1994 to 1995, but finished sixth at 11–1.

Curtis pointed out that many title strings had been accomplished in Major League baseball, the NBA, and the NHL, while UCLA had won seven straight in basketball from 1967 to 1973. With only a dozen games in a college football season and no play-off, a single slip, injury, bad bounce, bad call, or bad day can do a team in.

"Plus, there's the pressure of being in Los Angeles," wrote Curtis. "The Trojans are in the second biggest media market in the country, surrounded by the Dodgers, Angels, Lakers, Clippers and Kings, yet they still have the focus almost entirely on them during football season, with no NFL teams in sight. The myriad media outlets are hanging on USC's streak."

"I don't think there's any question it can be a distraction," Carroll said. "It's our greatest challenge to maintain that focus."

Curtis mentioned Leinart's name being "romantically linked to some pseudo-star in that celebrity-craving town," but he was handling all the attention with ease.

THREE-PETE

The Trojan Nation embraces the new "America's Team"

Sportstalk host Jim Rome advised that there was "no reason" why Carroll and his team could not win five or ten national titles in the manner of John Wooden's basketball dynasty at Westwood. There was plenty of pride with no sign of any fall.

With one week to "recover" from their vacation on the islands, which came in the form of a total 63–17 domination of Hawaii, the Southern California Trojans returned to a fawning student body, a fawning press, a fawning city. The newspapers were filled with daily missives about their latest comings and goings, usually at the expense of the page six Bruins, and truth be told, to the consternation of the town's Hollywood celebrities, suddenly sharing their spotlight and sex appeal with a bunch of college guys living in dorms and run-down South-Central apartments called The Bean (Leinart's digs).

Coach Houston Nutt brought the Arkansas Razorbacks to town. They lost to USC in the 1972 opener and again in 1973, but knocked Pat Haden and the Trojans down, 22–7, in the first game of 1974. The Trojans won the national title in '72 and, despite the '74 loss at Little Rock, did it again that season. Nutt was a ball boy on the Razorback sidelines in the two games played at War Memorial Stadium.

On Friday Nutt's team walked through the silent Coliseum. It had the same effect as Notre Dame Stadium and Yankee Stadium, thrilling and simultaneously intimidating visiting teams. The "ghosts" of Gifford and White; Hornung and Montana; Ruth and Mantle seem to manifest themselves before them, reminding them that they are in the presence of greatness, and *they will have to play against it!*

In the case of the Coliseum, images of more than just USC and college football reverberate when one stares at the Olympic torch, the replica jerseys. It is, without a doubt, the most famous of all stadiums, precisely because of the diversity of its events: two colleges, two pro teams, Super Bowls, Pro Bowls, high school play-offs, soccer, college track, two Olympics, the Dodgers, the All-Star Game, the World Series, rock concerts, religious revivals, military homecomings . . . and of course monster truck shows!

"Lot of history here in this stadium," Nutt said. "You always hear about it and see it on TV. It makes it that much more special to tee it up here."

A crowd of 90,411 showed up for the home opener September 17. McKay's teams in their greatest glory would have drawn 60,000 or 70,000 tops for an unranked, early-season, nonconference foe.

The atmosphere on campus, on the walk past the Rose Garden, in and around Exposition Park, and in the Coliseum, resembled a paradigm shift in USC football. The essence of the program had changed. There was intensity and a fervor surrounding the team that never existed before, with the exception of really big games.

Gimmes like Arkansas previously produced expectant alumni who took the victories as an article of faith; and relatively apathetic student bodies as interested in beer and the opposite sex as the game, which if not close by the third quarter meant license to pursue the opposite sex over by the beer lines.

But in the last few years, under Carroll, the game-day campus came to look like Mardi Gras. *Best Damn Sports Show Period* did its Friday show in front of Tommy Trojan. The bookstore filled with lines of consumers buying every possible book, pennant, and T-shirt; girls' sexy half-shirts, guys' baggy shorts; "SC gear everywhere; on cars, mail boxes, in the office . . ." as Jim Rome said.

The old Coliseum seemed to literally come to life as never before, its ghosts dug up, memories relived in an exciting new combination of tradition and modern. A giant video screen produced graphic replays, highlights, constant scores, new features, and amenities.

The sound system seemed to reverberate as never before, a gong or drum sound echoed each third down defensive "hold 'em" situation, with a fan response that would have been ignored in the pre-Carroll era.

When the baritoned P.A. announcer intoned that the "2003 and 2004 national champion USC Trojans" were taking the field, the crowd reacted in a way that cannot be described as quite Southern in its rabidity, but rather something new in the West, or at least in L.A. It seemed like a rock concert.

The 2004 national championship banner was unveiled. Leinart's number 11, while not retired (yet), was hung with care alongside the five other Heisman jerseys.

The game? Oh yes, they played a game. It was an extension of the Honolulu festival. Bush touched the ball. Thus, Bush scored after a seventy-six-yard run.

The offense waited around a little bit, handed Bush the ball a second time . . . and Bush scored from the Arkansas 29.

In the first quarter, USC had the ball a total of one minute, 32 seconds. In that time they ran off four touchdown "drives" to lead 28–7.

"USC scores so fast, it just messes you up," said Houston Nutt.

"I definitely think we're starting to send a message about this offense—that we've got a lot of weapons," Bush said. "For the teams that are going to be playing us, you just better be ready."

Ya think, Reggie?

By halftime it was 42–10. Carroll emptied his bench after three quarters. They came out to play like kids on the last day of school.

USC had 745 yards in total offense. Leinart just handed it off and made a few passes when called on, not wanting to embarrass one of the country's most prestigious college football traditions, and a Southeastern Conference foe to boot. He passed for 264 first-half yards seemingly without effort, resulting in 429 overall yards on thirty-two plays. On the night he was eighteen of twenty-four for 381 yards, plus a 17-yard touchdown scramble of his own. The final score: Trojans 70, Arkansas 17.

Bush rushed eight times for 125 yards (15.6 a carry).

The Arkansas game started after 7 p.m. With all the scoring it lasted long into the night. Many left, departing for dinner, drinks, and revelry at the Pacific Dining Car, the House of Blues, Dublin's, Barney's Beanery, the Rainbow, Hennessy's, the Saddle Ranch, and all the myriad hot spots that dot the city from the beaches to the edge of the Hollywood Hills.

Hours after the game ended, as people settled into their cars to head on home after a long Saturday that was now well into Sunday, they turned on 1540 "The Ticket," only to hear John Jackson still fielding phone call after phone call from the Trojan Nation. The callers could not get over what was going on in the City of the Angels. Some freshman who had gotten into the game late and showed great moves. Comparisons between who was better, Jarrett or Smith; Smith or Williams. The team MVP? Bush. Heisman? Leinart.

"But LenDale White's better than Bush," somebody would call in and say.

"Is this the greatest Trojan team ever . . . ?"

"The greatest college team ever . . . ?"

"Better than the 49ers or the Texans even . . . ?"

"Is Carroll the best coach ever . . . ?"

"Better than McKay . . . ?"

It when on like that into dawn's early light, until fans could wake up on Sunday, shake off their hangovers, and gorge over the feast of color photos and running commentary in the Sunday *Times*, the *Register*, the *Daily News*; all describing what had not been a game but a pageant.

A week later, USC traveled to Eugene to take on the twenty-fourth-ranked Oregon Ducks (3–0). A capacity crowd of 59,129, par for the course whether the Trojans were at home or on the road by now, filled Autzen Stadium.

When Oregon went up 13–0, as Oregon State had done in the Corvallis fog a year earlier, concern marked the Trojan sideline. As good as they were, could they be *vulnerable*? Sports is a crazy thing. There is no such thing as a lock, or at least when you think there is, some "absolutely unbelievable, phantasmagorical" thing happens, to quote ex-Oakland A's announcer Monte Moore.

All the hubris, pride, and arrogance endemic to the preseason hype, to what was now four years of almost-uninterrupted success and glory—which was turning out not to be all that fleeting—it had a way of building itself into a tight ball of pressure. On the road, in front of a capacity crowd of hostiles, it can strangle a team. There was another truth made apparent to observers of Carroll's Trojans: like a great pitcher who has to be knocked out early or not at all, Troy was a team that, if they were to be had, could only be had on the road early, in September or October.

Not so this day.

Oregon struck early with Paul Martinez's thirty-seven-yard field goal.

Leinart's pass was intercepted by Aaron Gipson in the end zone and returned thirty-eight yards. Oregon drove to the USC 36. Quarterback Kellen Clemens hit Demetrius Williams for the touchdown to make it 10–0.

Oregon held. Martinez hit a forty-eight-yarder to make it 13–0. Los Angelenos watching on the tube began to squirm.

But Leinart calmed everybody down, manufacturing two second quarter drives. The first ended with a nineteen-yard touchdown pass to Bush. After holding Oregon, SC pushed into field goal range for Mario Danelo's thirty-six-yarder just before half-time. It allowed Carroll's team to go in with momentum and confidence. Every Oregon fan and player was now on their heels.

USC made the field their personal fiefdom in the second half. Leinart led a long drive culminating in an eleven-yard strike to Jarrett. Clemens and his team suddenly looked befuddled. USC scored on White's one-yard bull rush, then followed up with a six-yard Leinart-to-Jarrett touchdown catch with two Ducks draped all over the receiver to put it out of reach, 31–13.

Oregon went to highly regarded quarterback Dennis Dixon out of San Leandro, California, but nothing mattered. Bush scored from the 11. The once huge, screaming crowd, now totally out of the game, booed and streamed out of the stadium. White later scored, closing it out at 45–13.

"History has shown we're a really good second half football team and particularly good in the fourth quarter," said Carroll. "We count on that."

Leinart, twelve of twenty-five in the first half, finished twenty-three of thirty-nine for 315 yards and three touchdowns.

"We know you can't win a game in the first three quarters," he said. "It's how you finish."

Bush caught a scoring pass, ran for another, and gained 122 yards rushing plus 43 by air. Jarrett caught eight for 94 yards and two touchdowns. White had 11 yards and two scores.

"We were slowly and slowly rolling and once we got the train moving there was no stopping us," said Bush.

Clemens was fifteen of thirty for 168 yards and a touchdown for Oregon.

"Kellen got a little dinged," said Oregon coach Mike Bellotti. "He answered our questions on the sideline, but I don't think he was the guy we've had out there playing for us. He was a little out of it there in the third quarter."

"They were getting tired, definitely, toward the end of the game," said Bush. "I think we really outprepared them and outconditioned them."

Be careful what you wish for.

Pete Carroll said he and his team "embraced" all the attention, defending the national title, "guys being mentioned for Heismans." Of course he cited as one of his driving theses the whole aspect of USC being a "private university, Hollywood, the weather," all the things that made it special, but could also make it a pressure cooker.

Being number one in Tuscaloosa or Lincoln is not the same as being number one in Los Angeles. Only Notre Dame carries as much baggage, what with its "national" reputation, its ghosts, and the hopes of Catholics from Dublin to Detroit.

But this USC team had taken on so much. They rejected nothing. They decided they could run an undefeated table while doing handstands. Nobody said that Leinart was messing up because he was hangin' with Nick and Jessica when he should be studying film. He and Bush were playing at a solid Heisman level.

But when Troy fell behind, 21–3, at Arizona State, all bets were off. Best team ever . . . Dynasty . . .

Fans numbering 71,706 yelled, screamed, and stomped. The stifling midday heat was 100 degrees with no abatement, giving special meaning to the name Sun *Devil* Stadium.

Maybe it was all hype. Or maybe it was just a chance for the Trojans to show that they were not only a great team, but also a team of heart, of guts, of great will.

Most teams quit, die, wilt. Not just teams of lesser ability, but lesser moral fiber, or character, or will to win—choose your description. The landscape is littered with lesser lights, unimpressives—the Cals, the Stanfords—all the teams that never had what it took to challenge Troy and its right to the throne.

What USC had, what few teams have had over the years; what the Irish, Tide, Sooners, and Nittany Lions have had—maybe a small handful of others—is what everybody wants but nobody wants to pay for. Peace without a price. The sports version of appeasement. Victory in a bloodless skirmish.

Faced with a guerrilla war against a skilled tribe of desert terrorists who knew every inch of the terrain, Pete Carroll's troops still relied on the fact they had the better training, the better men, the better leadership. In the end it would pay off.

The pundits in their suits, sitting in their air-conditioned studios, oblivious through years of the soft life, had no idea what Chris Carlisle had put these so-called Hollywood Trojans through since 2001.

"I don't think they can come back," said Kirk Herbstreit of ESPN.

Terry Richardson got Arizona State out to a quick 7–0 lead, exposing USC's special teams weaknesses on an eighty-four-yard punt return. Quarterback Sam Keller, one of those former highly rated prepsters who looked at USC and saw a school that had chosen the Palmers, the Leinarts, the Bootys, and the Sanchezes ahead of him, took his revenge out on Troy. His passes were precision-perfect, his receivers swift and sure.

Leinart and the Trojans looked as if they were lying in bed the night before when somebody came by and said, "Hey, let's go to Martini Ranch." They looked as if they had snuck out of their hotel rooms for a night on the town in nearby Scottsdale, which is world-renowned for its nightlife and *Girls Gone Wild* atmosphere. They looked as if they had spent the night drinking Long Island Ice Teas, as if the last half-dressed party chick had not left until the team bus was pulling up. They looked as if they were paying for their sins in this awful heat, their heads pounding amid this terrible noise, their pride battered by those *very good* Sun Devils who, by the way, looked like they had all been tucked in safe and sound by nine.

"They didn't try anything fancy in the second half," said Arizona State coach Dirk Koetter. "They just ran the two tailbacks at us."

It looked like the old days. Tailback U . . . Student Body Right. Simpson, Charlie White, Allen on a sweep, only their names were Bush and *LenDale* White. In the third quarter, Southern California decided to separate the boys from the men. No more screwin' around. Time to go to work.

After White's thirty-two-yard scamper and Bush's twenty-four-yard scoring run, Arizona State, a team that had not trailed all day, entered the fourth quarter with a 21–17 lead, but felt more like a guy who just busted open an indoor bee hive, only to realize the room was locked.

USC capped a scoring drive in the fourth quarter with a one-yard touchdown by Leinart to make it 24–21, but the Sun Devils were worthy foes. Keller led them back into the end zone to regain the lead at 28–24.

From there, it looked like a replay of the last drive of the 1980 Rose Bowl. Substitute numbers 5 and 21 (Bush and White) for number 12 (Charlie White). They ran it wide. They ran it up the gut. They just ran and ran and ran.

The Sun Devils suddenly felt their own Apache sun, unable to stop Geronimo's daredevil raids. Carlisle's better-conditioned athletes turned the fourth quarter into *their party*.

A thirty-four-yard burst by Bush gave USC the lead, 31–28, with a mere 3:44 left. That was followed by a forty-six-yard explosion by White to secure it, 38–28, although the talented Keller had no quit in him. The possibility of a late Sun Devil touchdown and onside kick remained until almost the end.

When it was finally secure, the TV cameras found White on the sidelines. He smiled the smile of champions, raised his fingers in a V like Churchill at Yalta or Ike at the Rheims schoolhouse, and said, "Too dominant."

Dominant or not, most Trojans did not come up for air until after Sunday church services.

White finished with 197 yards on nineteen carries. Bush was good for 158 yards on seventeen attempts. USC outrushed fourteenth-ranked ASU, 373–68. The win, SC's twenty-sixth straight, broke Pac 10 and school records.

"We just pounded the football in the second half," said Carroll. "It was a beautiful job by the offensive linemen, a beautiful job by Reggie and LenDale."

"They came out and fought hard for a couple of quarters," White said. "Here at SC, we 'finish.' It's not about how the first and second quarter ends or the third; it's about how you finish in the fourth quarter."

Keller was twenty-six of forty-five for 347 yards and two touchdowns, but his five interceptions were proof that if one "lives by the sword, they die by the sword." Oscar Lua's second quarter pick was a key turnaround at a time when Troy was reeling.

"We very well could have won that game, and I think they were scared, too, at a lot of points in that game," Keller said. "A few bad plays by me, if they don't happen, we win the game."

He failed to add that "scared" does not mean "defeated," at least not at USC.

Despite Bush and White taking most of the credit, Leinart did not hurt his Heisman chances. He completed twenty-three of thirty-nine for 258 yards, but most important, as opposed to Keller he had no interceptions. His management of the game when the team trailed, his steady leadership as they inexorably crept back into it, was masterful.

David Kirtman was spectacular, catching seven tosses for ninety-seven yards. Jarrett caught seven for ninety. Leinart took a vicious, unsportsmanlike late hit that drew blood and gave him a concussion.

THE FOUR HORSEMEN OF SOUTHERN CALIFORNIA

Outlined against a blue, gray October sky, the Four Horsemen rode again. In dramatic lore, they are known as famine, pestilence, destruction and death. These are only aliases. Their real names are Stuhldreher, Miller, Crowley and Layden.

SPORTSWRITER GRANTLAND RICE, 1924

Outlined against a blue, gray October sky the Four Horsemen rode again. In dramatic lore they are known as famine, pestilence, destruction, and death. These are only aliases. Once named Stuhldreher, Miller, Crowley, and Layden, the gladiators of the New Millennium are men of youth, color, and American diversity. Their real names are Leinart, Bush, Jarrett, and White. These new Four Horsemen of Southern California came to the land of destiny riding their famed white steed, Traveler, that dreaded Coliseum sight of Irish past. They relegated the old Notre Dame ghosts to their place and time, a time when the only color was white, myths were protected, lies told as Truths. They formed the crest of the South Bend cyclone before which another Fighting Irish team was swept over the precipice at Notre Dame Stadium on the afternoon of Saturday, October 15, 2005. A crowd of 80,795 spectators peered down upon the bewildering panorama spread out upon the green plain below.

These fans observed the changing of the guard, the team of the New Age, the University of the Twenty-first Century. For the better part of the previous century *their* team held that loftiest position on the grid landscape. No more. Their ancient rivals arrived at their house of worship, paid homage to their shrines, and honored their traditions.

Their skill, class, and guts emanated like water pouring forth upon a barren valley, informing all whose eyes saw that Truth, when witnessed in an American arena, is never misunderstood.

The Truth of October 15, 2005, in that most perfect of settings, was that the Trojans of Southern California had taken over from the previous title-holders, the Fighting Irish of Notre Dame, the lofty moniker Greatest Collegiate Football Tradition of

All Time! They did as their legendary old coach, Marv Goux, advised countless legions to do. They did as Goux's beloved granddaughter asked them to do. Four games in four years had passed since Kara Kanen advised that future Trojans "win one for the Goux!"

For four years now they took on the Irish at home and away. Each time they left them heartbroken in noble defeat. On this day, they would take more than a shillelagh back to Heritage Hall. There was no plaque, no crystal football, nothing inscribed.

There was only pride and knowledge that what they did secured for them everlasting glory. Legends were made. Expectations had been met. Eighty years of excellence had not only been lived up to but exceeded by a new generation. They took the foundation laid brick by brick by decades of Trojans, erecting a higher statue than ever before.

A modern Lancelot led them, for indeed the times he was living in were those of a Camelot quality. His name is Leinart. The similarity to "Lion Heart" is not insignificant. It is, rather, cosmic, for he does not lace his cleats in a land of mere mortals. He is part of something ancient and utterly sacred. The standards this tallest and sturdiest of the new Horsemen set under that blue, gray October sky, with the wheat of an Indiana harvest swirling about like so much stardust, are standards that nobody will ever be expected to meet. To strive for, but not to meet.

The second new Horseman's name is Bush. On a field of play where eighty-one years ago he would have been invited to leave, this stepson of a preacher man stepped up and took a nation, a Trojan Nation, and with his loyal partner with the "Lion Heart" he thus moved mountains on the flat Midwestern plains.

The third new Horseman's name is Jarrett. A babe in the woods, a child desperate to return to his Jersey roots rather than accept the challenges that God graced him with the ability to meet, he did meet them on the green plains of South Bend. He met them; soft of hands and swift of feet did he meet them as he raced through the gauntlet set forth before him. His was a moment of mystery and wonder, a Shakespearean marvel: "There are more things on Heaven and earth, Horatio, than can be dreamt of in your philosophy."

Finally, in the "most Gracious" Shakespearean of seasons, did the fourth new Horseman emerge. His name is White, a famous last name and one he lived up to, as he had taken the previous man's number, 12, and turned it around: 21. In the glare of the spotlight, Mr. White did what makes him splendid. He sacrificed for his team. His name will not be synonymous with the glory and memory of this challenge met under the watchful eye of "Touchdown Jesus," but his mates knew that they would not have been there without his sacrifice.

Thus was history made. Leave no doubt? Thus is the statement made.

■ ■ ■

> Sometime, Rock, when the team is up against it, when things are wrong and
> the breaks are beating the boys—tell them to go in there with all they've got
> and win just one for the Gipper. I don't know where I'll be then, Rock. But
> I'll know about it, and I'll be happy.
>
> NOTRE DAME FOOTBALL COACH KNUTE ROCKNE'S
> APOCRYPHAL DESCRIPTION OF FORMER IRISH STAR
> GEORGE GIPP'S DYING WORDS

On a cold November 1920 afternoon in Evanston, Illinois, Notre Dame's first All-American, halfback George Gipp, sat shivering under a blanket on the bench as his teammates controlled Northwestern. He had a sickly complexion. He was racked by pain. He coughed violently. Coach Knute Rockne was looking ahead to the big game the following week against Michigan State.

According to a teammate, the star player had fallen behind in his gambling debts. The rumor is that his bookies promised to forgive what he owed if he would sit out the Northwestern game. For three quarters, Gipp did just that.

For reasons that can only be speculated on, Gipp then ignored his respiratory problems, coming off the bench in the fourth quarter to throw a couple of meaningless touchdowns. The scores extended Notre Dame beyond the spread.

In the wake of that game, Gipp was hospitalized. Less than a month later he died of strep throat and pneumonia. Coach Rockne visited him one last time.

"I've got to go, Rock," Rockne says the twenty-five-year-old Gipp told him. "It's all right. I'm not afraid."

Eight years later at Yankee Stadium, an injury-depleted Irish team trailed at halftime against heavily favored Army. Rockne gathered his team together in the quiet locker room. He told them Gipp once asked a favor of him. Rock told his breathless team that the dying Gipp had said to him: "Sometime, Rock, when the team is up against it, when things are wrong and the breaks are beating the boys—tell them to go in there with all they've got and 'win just one for the Gipper.' I don't know where I'll be then, Rock. But I'll know about it, and I'll be happy."

Notre Dame rallied to defeat Army, 12–6. Over the years it became "common knowledge" that the story was fabricated by Rockne. Rock died tragically three years later in a plane crash. He insisted it was true. There is so little chance that it is true that, for all practical purposes, it can simply be stated that it is false.

However, like so much Notre Dame malarkey, it lived on just as the "Four Horsemen" story had. Grantland Rice did indeed write those words, but it was a heads-up Notre Dame PR man who found four horses from nearby stables, then photographed the four star players on them, thus creating the imagery to go with the words.

Nobody would argue that Notre Dame is a great tradition, a tradition of great teams and great players. But while so much of Notre Dame's storied legacy is legitimate, much of it is built on the strength of fables such as Rockne's "win one for the Gipper," or the overinflated, flowery words of Rice.

USC, ironically the "Hollywood school," had built their tradition on the solid foundation of actual accomplishment, not myth and lore—at least not in comparison with the Irish. The 2005 game was thorough proof of just that.

USC was not tested; they were outplayed. But championship teams do what championship teams do. On the game's final play, Leinart pushed into the line, then did a spin move that looked like something he learned in a Tuesday night ballroom dancing class. With three seconds left, he found a seam, and might have gotten a push of momentum from Bush, which may or may not have been an uncalled penalty, to score the winning touchdown. Number one USC escaped with its twenty-eighth straight victory, 34–31 over the ninth-ranked Irish. The game more than lived up to expectations. It was the greatest game in the history of the storied rivalry that goes back to 1926. Depending on one's perspective, and considering the pressure, the stakes, and the atmosphere, it may have been the greatest football game ever played, college or pro. It was watched by the largest TV audience of any regular season college football game in a decade. To say it meant the rivalry was revived was as obvious as saying Pamela Anderson possesses sex appeal. The college football world, increasingly complaining about Trojan hegemony, now saw a reason to tune back in.

"You gotta believe you're going to win the way that happened," Carroll said.

Notre Dame came in 4–1. They broke out their Kelly green jerseys. Before Leinart's dive, they and their fans thought victory was theirs. Trailing 31–28, there was enough time for one pass play from around the 5. The southpaw Leinart rolled to his left. He could pass for a game-winning touchdown, throw an incomplete pass, or run out of bounds. Options two and three would stop the clock and probably set up a game-tying field goal to send it to overtime. Instead, Leinart went for a fourth option, one fraught with consequences bathed in glory or cloaked with agony.

Leinart, Carroll, and the Trojans did not want to go to overtime. They were beat up, exhausted, hurt. Leinart was decidedly not right. He was shook up, his head in cobwebs. LenDale White inadvertently stepped on his back after Leinart fell *leading a block* for Bush early in the game. Former USC quarterback Pat Haden, announcing the game for NBC, said over and over again that he was not right. Sideline camera shots showed him sitting silently, in pain, head in his hands. One shot showed the Mater Dei graduate making a small, quick sign of the cross.

He needed every ounce of strength and inspiration he could muster. Overtime was not a good option. Too tired, too beat up. They played for a tie at Berkeley in 2003. The ball had not bounced their way. It was, to quote George Patton, victory "or let no man come back alive."

When Leinart scrambled from inside the 5 and headed toward the goal line, not the sideline, he committed himself. If he could not make it, USC had no time-outs. The clock would expire to an agonizing 0:00. The field would explode in Irish green and the kind of rabid football happiness that only Golden Domers are capable of. USC would have to slog their way through the mess to their losing locker room and their losing flight home, facing the rest of their probably Rose Bowl–less season.

The 6'5", 225-pound Leinart, who turned down multiple millions to do all of this for free, built up momentum and launched himself toward the end zone. For a split second it looked like he might make it, but a wall of Notre Dame defenders sacrificed their bodies, meeting him at the line. It is not an exaggeration to say Leinart was stopped *one inch* from the end zone. It was close enough that the referee could have seen him in. All he needed was to have the ball cross the plane. It was that agonizingly close.

In a desperate effort to do just that, Leinart one-handed the ball toward the end zone, hoping the pigskin, if not his body, would cross that plane for the six points. Brady Quinn basically did the same thing on his touch score just two minutes earlier.

But Leinart was stopped short by a phalanx of defenders, led by Corey Mays. The referee was right there. He saw it correctly. USC wanted his arms to go up, but they did not. The ball, precariously held in Leinart's hand, could not withstand the pressure of the defenders who made themselves into a veritable Irish wall. The ball was knocked out of Leinart's hand and sent flying . . . out of bounds.

Had Leinart not fumbled the ball out of bounds, the clock would have ticked down. They would have lost. Had he fumbled and it was recovered in bounds by USC, time would have expired. It was a lucky break.

In the USC broadcast booth, announcer Pete Arbogast saw clearly what happened. He knew the ball went out of bounds with three seconds left, stopping the clock and giving USC the ball wherever the referee spotted the ball's plane going out of bounds. However, the clock continued ticking, probably because the clock master did not see the fumble amid the bodies and confusion. But Arbogast calmly assured listeners that the clock stopped and the refs were on top of it.

TV viewers, on the other hand, only saw the clock tick down to 0:00. For Trojan fans, it was like watching a car crash. Notre Dame fans, most of whom did not see the ball pop loose, just saw the clock tick to zero. They rushed the field. Coach Charlie Weis raised his hands in victory.

But Carroll knew what happened. He ran down the sideline. The officials, to their credit, saw it correctly. After clearing the field and holding a conference, they put seven seconds back on the clock. Leinart probably lost close to a yard via the fumble. He had been stopped inches away, but the spot after the fumble placed it on the 1.

Some pundits would later say the spot favored USC, that it should have been the 2 or the 3, but no postgame film verified this. Others said that the ball was fumbled out of the end zone, and should have resulted in a game-clinching touchback for Notre Dame. That argument does not hold weight. If the ball was fumbled in the end zone, then it would have meant Leinart crossed the plane, which is all he would have needed to score. But he did not.

The clock stopped, but Leinart and USC had to make a decision. They could spike it and take their time instead of the quick formation required with no time-outs, although Leinart would not be able to go to the bench to confer with Carroll. In terms of confusion and player decision-making, it had all the earmarks of the 1931 game. Howard Jones did not trust Johnny Baker to make a game-winning field goal. He missed an extra point and Troy was down a point because of it.

But Orv Mohler and Baker had been practicing field goals all year. They knew he could make it. On that day, when they lined up Notre Dame thought they would run a regular play, but they quickly formed into field goal formation. Baker kicked it true. Troy escaped with the 16–14 win.

In 2005, the teams lined up as Leinart approached the line. Carroll could be seen making the "spike it" motion. Apparently it was a deke. In the NFL, Miami's Dan Marino approached the line against Carroll's Jets, looking to spike the ball to stop the clock, luring the Jets off-balance before throwing a touchdown pass.

Leinart looked at the stack of Notre Dame defenders. The play called was a sneak. He turned to Bush.

"What should I do?" he screamed. *"I don't think I can make it, Reggie; what should I do? You think I should go for it?"*

"GO FOR IT, MATT!!" yelled Bush.

Then the Irish crowded the line. Bush had second thoughts.

"NO, NO, NO, NO, NO!!" he screamed. Leinart never heard him.

Leinart took the snap, heading into the line. It was not even close. He had no chance to muscle through the pile. But it was all in one place. He pirouetted. The ball was precariously held halfway tucked against his shoulder and halfway in the air, where it could be swatted away. He somehow found a hole. Bush rushed into the fray and was right up Leinart's back.

It is a penalty to "push" a ball carrier on one's team forward. Replays were not totally conclusive. Bush's action was part of the natural body contact that happens when twenty-two behemoths crowd into one area a few feet wide. With the game safely won, Bush was happy to take credit, though.

"I used all 200 pounds of my body to push Matt in," he said.

In the previous confusion of the time clock, Carroll's son, Assistant Coach Brennan Carroll, approached the officials. TV cameras showed him making a "time-out" signal with his hands. Critics said he was calling a time-out the team did not have, similar to what basketball player Chris Webber did in costing Michigan an NCAA Final Four championship game some fifteen years earlier. But it was not a correct assumption. Carroll was not calling time-out, just making the time-out sign to indicate to the officials that the time *should already* have been called.

The "Bush push" did not appear to be what got Leinart in, either. It was his footwork and drive. A penalty would have been outrageous. In the end it was Leinart who propelled the final drive and the phantasmagorical ending, but it was Bush who had kept his team alive for four quarters, running for 160 yards on fifteen carries with three touchdowns. It was his fifth straight 100-yard game. Arbogast and Paul McDonald were appropriately excited. Pat Haden seemed stunned. An ending this extraordinary required the unique talents of Bill King, who called dramatics for the Oakland and Los Angeles Raiders in the most eloquent, descriptive manner possible. Tragically, King died of complications from hip surgery in a Bay Area hospital a few days later.

The field goal, according to Carroll, was not an option.

"We did *not* want to have to keep playing them in overtime," he said.

"I just saw it; I thought it was there and I just wanted to get in," Leinart said. "I didn't want to spike the ball so I made the choice, and they were looking down from up above and we got in. That was all that mattered."

Brady Quinn gave Notre Dame a 31–28 lead with 2:02 left, rolling and then running to his right end for a five-yard touchdown, extending his right arm across the goal line with the ball in a manner somewhat similar to what Leinart would try a couple minutes later. SC may have won the game on Quinn's touchdown, curiously enough. Had he not made it, the clock would have ticked away while Notre Dame lined up. They likely would have scored, but too much time would have passed for USC to be able to get it back and drive. As it was, USC had the necessary two minutes to run a "two-minute drill."

But it was not a "smooth" two-minute offense.

Bush returned the kickoff twenty yards to the USC 25. Leinart was deep in his own territory, where the crowd is loudest. In the history of Notre Dame Stadium, *never* were the echoes awoken quite so loudly. Leinart threw incomplete on first down. He was sacked by defensive lineman Trevor Laws for a nine-yard loss on the next play.

Faced with a third-and-eighteen, Leinart split the difference with a pass to Bush. The hope was that Reggie would break it after the catch, racing down the field for a first down, maybe get out of bounds. But Bush was tackled just short of a ten-yard gain.

There was one minute, thirty-two seconds left. Fourth-and-nine, ball on the USC 26. The game was all but over. USC fans were virtually relegated to a smile and the consolation that it had been a great ride. If it had to end, this was the fitting place for it against a worthy foe.

The crowd was beyond comprehension: a wall of sound desperately pounding their noise into Leinart's ears. His signals could not be heard—an audible could not be called. Leinart brought the Trojans to the line. In the huddle he had exuded confidence. Desperate confidence, but the hope that sprung from years of pulling games out of the fire, from Mustang League to Mater Dei to now.

But Leinart's heroics had not led Mater Dei to victory in that 31–28 loss to De La Salle in 2000. He had done all he could do, but the game-tying kick had failed. Now, a kick could again tie, but Leinart wanted to control his team's destiny. He and his coach wanted a touchdown.

Leinart looked at the Notre Dame defense. Something was not quite right. To the horror of USC fans from Maine to Manhattan Beach, *Leinart called an audible!*

He's calling an audible. Nobody can hear him.

But Dwayne Jarrett was ready for it. He was paying attention. He was focused. They practiced with noisemakers, and they had a system. They tuned the crowd down and let time slow down, let their God-given skills take over. Pat Haden said the same thing about the final winning plays of the 1975 Rose Bowl. Leinart could have looked to the sidelines in deference to the clock. Charlie Weis had what was called the "Two Tampa" defense in place. It was designed as a prevent: nothing long, nothing over the middle, narrow it to the lanes.

Leinart decided to throw into the heart of it, knowing that Jarrett, the child from New Jersey who wanted to go home a year earlier, had the speed to beat his man.

"*Nobody* throws a pass like that into a 'Two Tampa' defense," said Weis.

But Leinart did. A *perfectly thrown* half-floater, half-bullet that *threaded the needle* directly into Jarrett's hands, right on the numbers, just before the outstretched hands of Irish defenders, including cornerback Ambrose Wooden, who only needed to touch it, deflect it, block it, screen it off, blur Dwayne's vision, obstruct him; but could not.

Jarrett got it, his hands as soft as a child's, the ball nestled into his grasp. Now he had *momentum* up the field. He ran and ran and ran, sixty-one yards, finally dragged down by Wooden, saying penitence with every step, at the Notre Down 15.

After Leinart called his own number a few plays later to win the game, he sat on the bench with his helmet still on, looking exhausted.

USC trailed at the half, 21–14, after Tom Zbikowski's sixty-yard punt return gave the Irish their first lead. Zbikowski? Nobody with a Polish name like that ran kicks and had speed in the modern game any more, did they? He was a throwback to those kinds of names who starred for Notre Dame throughout its history, but as Slim Pickens might have said, "What in the wide, wide world of sports is goin' on here?" Who was gonna take the field next, Bronco Nagurski?

Bush tied the game with a forty-five-yard touchdown romp early in the third quarter, giving rise to Trojan hopes that the second half juggernaut would roll from there. It was not to be.

Notre Dame kept up the pressure on D. J. Fitzpatrick's field goal to make it 24–21. USC was held. The Irish came back. USC bent but did not break. Quinn's third down pass was wide on a short try for a sure first down, forcing Fitzpatrick to try a field goal that would still keep Troy within a touchdown instead of down by ten. When the kick missed from thirty-four yards out, it gave life to Southern California.

The fourth quarter droned on, the crowd wild, fervid, rabid. The ghosts echoed and groaned; shrill, screaming, frantic. Trailing by three, USC drove down the field. It

THE USC TROJANS

was mostly Bush. The playbook was straight out of the 1980 Charles White Rose Bowl. Reggie was up to the challenge.

Down to the 9 the Trojans moved, until with a little over five minutes left he went around the left corner for a touchdown. The kick made it 28–24, USC. The first thought in every Trojan mind was that they had given Quinn and Weis too much time. It was followed by the conviction that if truly they are the national champions, then they stop the opposition right now, as they had done to Aaron Rodgers a year before.

The kick pinned Notre Dame on their own 13. Eighty-seven yards to go. An Elwayesque challenge. Then it was Quinn's turn to carve a place in the Notre Dame shrine. He brought out a big, sharp knife for the occasion. With it he cut an eighty-seven-yard swath through the Trojan defense, to quote Patton, "like s—t through a goose." He completed all three of his passes, scoring with 2:02 left, but as mentioned his score came, for Notre Dame now, too early.

He finished nineteen of thirty-five for 264 yards.

When USC failed to stop Notre Dame, they realized that they failed to live up to the national title challenge, the same one Cal had posed in '04. Notre Dame deserved it. That thought was then immediately replaced by eighty years of collective memory: Johnny Baker, Nave-to-Kreuger, Fertig-to-Sherman, Ayala, Jordan, A. D., McDonald, White, Haden-to-McKay, Fred Cornwell, Keyshawn. Oh, yes, the ghosts of Trojan Men, a storied past, were not residing only in the blue, gray shadows of the South Bend autumn. They traveled from L.A. and points north, east, and south, wherever the soul of this most storied and legendary program, the *one* program that had the chops to match Notre Dame's gloried history, had given pleasure and thrills to a million fans across a Fruited Plain.

What USC did in those two minutes, two seconds surpasses all the previous names. It was Caesar entering over Rome, surrender on the Missouri, Ike with his two pens. It was USC at the very height of their glory. Like Daniel in the lion's den, Christ upon the cross, they entered that most perilous of enemy territory, emerging triumphant over the most implacable of foes. For Carroll's Trojans, and Trojans of generations long removed from this day, no matter how many national championships lay in their future—and Jim Rome's "five or ten" looked very possible at that moment— well, none of it could be more dramatic or perfect than what had happened on those green plains.

TEAM OF THE DECADE

USC replaces Notre Dame: the best football tradition and
athletic program of all time

The Notre Dame game changed things perceptibly. A seismic shift had taken place.

USC, already the "Athletic Program of the Twentieth Century," also passed Notre
Dame as the "College Football Tradition of the Century." Not just the twenty-first
century. As Muhammad Ali says, "The greatest . . . *Of ALL TIMES!*"

Acronym: G.O.A.T.

But they had trodden on this hallowed ground before. After dominating the Irish
in the late 1960s, 1970s, and early 1980s, winning multiple national championships and
Heisman Trophies, Southern California seduced themselves into believing that by
1982 they had surpassed the mythological bar of all-time greatness dividing them
from their ancient foe.

If indeed for a brief period this was true, it was just that: brief.

1983 to 1996: thirteen straight years without beating Notre Dame. Notre Dame:
one national championship and eighteen straight number one AP rankings from 1988
to 1989. USC: zip. Notre Dame: one Heisman Trophy winner. USC: zip.

■ ■ ■

USC followed the Notre Dame game with a series of easy wins in which they polished
their statistics and place in history. Then Fresno State came to town.

"Fresno may be the best team we've played all year," said Carroll. The game,
scheduled for a 7:15 start at a sold-out Coliseum on Fox Sports TV, promised to be a
major challenge. In many ways, it was the true "battle of California." The cultural and
social significance of the game was the subject of John Branch's article in the *New York
Times*.

Twenty thousand Bulldog faithful caravanned the three and a half hours from
Fresno to Los Angeles. The theme of the game for Fresno State coach Pat Hill was
"acceptance," both of his sixteenth-ranked team and his beleaguered city.

"Everyone says, 'You have nothing to lose,'" said Hill. "We're trying to establish ourselves. We have a lot to lose."

The game was billed as the "biggest in the program's history." One man secured nine hundred tickets and reserved eighteen motor coaches—the self-dubbed "Red Wave"—for the pilgrimage.

"Ever since I've been here, this is the type of game we want," said senior quarterback Paul Pinegar, the latest NFL prospect in the tradition of Trent Dilfer, Billy Volek, and David Carr. "A big game against USC where we can show the nation who Fresno State is."

Actually, that was already an accomplished act. Fresno State may bill itself as the "little engine that could," but the secret was long out. They are a first-rate program that competes year in and year out on a national basis.

It was Dilfer who put the program on the map when he led Fresno State to a stunning 24–7 Freedom Bowl victory over Troy in 1992. Oddly, this was an event that gave mighty USC some motivation for revenge, rather than the other way around.

The validation for Fresno supporters was more about the city than the program. Their athletic department—not just football but other sports—had all the respect they could ask for. Fresno the city does not. Three hours from San Francisco, a little further than that from L.A., two hours to the ocean, an hour-plus from Yosemite, Fresno is just *there*. It is a valley town, hot in the summer, foggy in the winter. Agricultural smog hangs heavy over the fertilized farm fields where migrant laborers dot the countryside, observed by motorists passing through on Interstate 5 and Highway 99.

"It is a city in the middle of nowhere, yet enticingly close to everything," wrote Branch. "And, especially this week, the same can be said of its football team."

"Play on the road, play as tough a schedule as we can, and try to go undefeated," said Coach Hill. "I don't know any other way" to break into the BCS party.

Since 2000, Fresno State had gone 10–7 against BCS competition. They were 5–5 versus ranked opponents. They had beaten Colorado, Wisconsin, and Kansas State in regular season games; Georgia Tech, UCLA, and Virginia in its previous three bowl games. They had played at Tennessee and Oklahoma.

"That's what's so great about our program," said senior defensive end Garrett McIntyre, "the opportunity to play this kind of schedule, the 'anyone, anywhere, anytime' philosophy that Coach Hill talks about."

Fresno State entered the Coliseum having won fourteen of fifteen games, outscoring opponents by an average of 46–16. Their only loss in 2005 came at the hands of tenth-ranked 9–1 Oregon, by 37–34. They had "blown" that one. Otherwise, the USC game could have been for the right to play for the national championship.

They ended Boise State's reign in the Western Athletic Conference. They built enthusiasm in the central valley to a simmering boil. Hill admitted his roster was filled with blue-collar types rejected by the likes of USC. He tapped many prospects from the Southland and the Bay Area, but also had a large recruiting base to draw from. Metropolitan Fresno consists of some one million people. Clovis West High School long established itself as one of America's greatest sports schools. Pro baseball scouts stated that Fresno-area high schools had the finest collection of stadiums in the nation; most schools had well-constructed, lighted, minor league–style facilities. Basketball arenas and football stadiums were equally impressive. Despite its "strip mall" reputation, great wealth was long settled in the San Joaquin Valley.

"Fresno State football is the biggest thing to hit the valley since irrigation," wrote Steve Dilbeck of the *L.A. Daily News*. In an effort to coalesce the support of the entire Sac-Joaquin Valley, the Bulldogs emblazoned a giant "V" for "valley" on the back of their helmets.

The area *supposedly* suffered from a self-imposed inferiority complex with roots that stretched all the way back to John Steinbeck's ode to Socialism, *The Grapes of Wrath*. Regional self-promoters dubbed it "California's Next Frontier," but the "nagging, self-deprecating worry is that Fresno is as close to being forgotten as it is to being found," wrote Branch.

His words were read with a grain of salt, though. After all, he was with the *New York Times*, that arbiter of elitism that looks down upon the "red state" politics of Middle America, which Fresno embodies. As for Fresno, the truth is, they were less concerned with what the *New York Times* thought of them than they were with simply going forth and producing excellence, as the rest of Middle America consistently does.

They played on the road against the best for years, but this game, versus Southern California at the Coliseum, was their greatest challenge—ever. That was all well and good, of course; Fresno State takes on all comers. But so does USC. For years, when Southern teams rarely traveled outside their region, USC traveled to Austin, to Dallas, to Durham, to Atlanta, to Little Rock.

In 1970, when the NCAA added an eleventh game, Troy accepted Alabama's offer to play at Birmingham. They could have played Rice, Tulane, or Navy, three of the weak sisters who regularly made up Notre Dame's schedule in those days. Instead they created a home-and-home arrangement against the legendary Bear Bryant's program at a time in which the Tide was embarking on a period of their greatest success.

In 2000, the Trojans were offered the choice of playing their TBA (to be announced) game against one of the state schools in California (not Fresno). They decided instead to travel to New York and take on Joe Pa's Penn State Nittany Lions. UCLA took the local option. 'Nuff sed.

A look at the 2004 media guide shows no mention of Fresno State in their "future schedules" (2005). Fresno was looking for a game. They called up the "mighty" LSU Tigers, offering to travel to Tiger Stadium in Baton Rouge. LSU declined. They went for Appalachian State, whose mascot might as well have been a faded 1960s poster of Bobby Kennedy with a look of concern amongst po' white trash who, according to him, were starving because of Republican insensitivity.

Fresno called USC. Let's see, thought Mike Garrett and Pete Carroll. Who can we schedule? Well, how 'bout those Sacra-tomato Hornets? Busy? Hey, those animal husbandry majors from Cal Aggies looked pretty good, but of course they would go on to beat Stanford, so nix that. UOP perhaps? Pete's alma mater opened the 1991 season at Berkeley, only to have Cal hang seventy on 'em.

"Fresno State still holding on line two."

Uh, geez, what about Alabama–Birmingham? Louisiana–Monroe? Wofford? Central Florida? All teams the so-called big boys of the Southeastern Conference liked to schedule.

"Pat Hill on lines two *and* four, Mr. Garrett."

. . .

"Oh sure, Pat. Come on down . . ."

"Fresno State? Yeah."

Picture Joe McCarthy wiping sweat off his brow after getting called to the carpet by Ike.

"Why not? The Bulldogs. Go, dawgs. Sure, why not Fresno State? Easy trip. Gas stations on the Grapevine'll 'preciate the business."

So it was decided that TBA in 2005 might just mean "The Best Anywhere."

At least that is what it seemed like on a sultry mid-November evening at the Coliseum.

As Keith Jackson never said, *"Whoa*, Nellie."

What 90,007 saw—and *maybe* 65,000 of those people were Trojan fans—was nothing less than . . .

UN—*BE*—LIEVABLE!!!

It was insane. Was it the greatest game ever played? More dramatic than the Notre Dame game at South Bend one month earlier? Okay, probably not. But it was a masterpiece. A struggle between a mongoose and a cobra; the lion and the bear . . . a scrappy Bulldog and a mighty Trojan warrior who used every weapon at his disposal, stabbing and killing the damn mutt, but *it would not die.*

The whole thing had people scratching their heads. Where's the home field advantage? It was part of the larger picture of USC football. Here is a team that plays the best schedule in college football year in and year out, and had been doing it since Howard Jones was their coach. But when 'Bama played at Legion Field, or LSU hosted Georgia, or the Domers were on the green plains of South Bend, every single time *those* teams played on *their* home fields, they had home field advantage.

But USC? Oh, nooo. Can't have that. Bring 20,000 or 30,000 nutsoid Bulldog fans, why don'cha? Plenty of hotel rooms. Every year they played UCLA, and is that ever really home field advantage? Half a stadium full of Bruins? When Notre Dame comes a-callin', is *that* home field advantage? Every Catholic from Barstow to Brentwood shows up. They steal a high school band from Sherman Oaks and let them play their songs. It's blarney and guys dressed like Father Guido Sarducci every ten yards.

So Pat Hill could talk about playin' "anybody anytime," but USC was that anybody and this was the time, on November 19. The game? It was a donnybrook. USC played a great game and barely won, which is everything that needs be said of Fresno State. They did not back down an inch. They were not intimidated one iota. They came to play, to strap it on.

So, the question was begged, is USC really the "greatest team of all time"? Tough question after this one, and yet, despite all the obvious evidence that they were not that good, still, *they were*.

Napoleon valued luck in his generals. There is no question that Pete Carroll and his team seemed to reside under a lucky star, yet luck is the "residue of design." It would be inaccurate to characterize their ultimate victory as lucky. It was well earned.

The greatest *offensive* team ever? Yes, that they were. In comparing USC to the other contenders, however—the 1972 team, the 1995 Nebraska juggernaut, Notre Dame in 1947 . . . the usual suspects—well, all the normal criteria would point to these other teams. The '05 Trojans were a team with a vulnerable defense, wracked by inexperience and injuries. Manuel Wright had lost his eligibility and was toiling in the NFL. Eric Wright was kicked off the team.

Dallas Sartz? Injured. Terrell Thomas? Injured? Keith Rivers? Gimped up early against Fresno. USC supporters looked at Fresno, and like Butch turning to Sundance asked, "Who *are* those guys?"

Standing all alone on its 2005 merits, no, USC was not the greatest single-season team in history. But something else was at play here. Something Leinart said after the Notre Dame game: "This team just doesn't know how to lose." This team needed to be judged in ways most teams are not judged. The winning streak, the number one ranking that now threatened to stretch into a third calendar year. A third national title, OU's forty-seven games looming just up the road. Everybody gunning for them on all cylinders.

The real question needed to be asked: would any of these other teams of destiny want to play these people? Would McKay's guys from thirty-three years in the past *really* beat this Leinart/Carroll/Bush triumvirate? Charles Young said the 2005 team was not as good as the 2004 team, which was not as good as the 2003 team, and would "not score on us until late in the third quarter." But he said it with laughter in his voice. Tree is too smart to really believe that blarney.

Other teams might have better defenses, better stats, better this and that. But would they *beat* this team? Texas had won more impressively throughout the season, just as the 2003–2004 Sooners had, but look what had happened when Oklahoma strapped it on in Miami! This was the overriding factor.

Carroll would have two weeks to get ready for UCLA. Drew Olson had thrown for over *500 yards* the previous week against Arizona State. Every USC fan filing out of the Coliseum, walking past the "John the Baptist" guy who has preached salvation at the Rose Garden to Coliseum crowds forever; all of them were thinking about Olson shredding them on December 3.

But Carroll, the defensive guru, would come up with *something*. And if they could survive the UCLA test, then he would have a month to study the Longhorns, just as he had done with Bob Stoops's team. Vince Young was tough. You betcha. But was he Joe Montana? Jason White had *numbers* for two years, and he also had Adrian Peterson's 1,900-plus yards, yet Troy stuffed 'em.

So, on a neutral field, would Beano Cook's hallowed Golden Domers of 1947, with Johnny Lujack and Frank Leahy, really be a team that could, adding it all up, beat the 2005 Trojans? In the new era, the era of weights, diet, training, *integration?*

Same with Bud Wilkinson's Sooners and their non-facemask helmets. Tom Osborne's Cornhuskers, fresh off a schedule that included eleven games against Kansas State: were they really better?

No, even though Fresno revealed a USC defense that was as vulnerable as a sixteen-year-old girl jilted by her first boyfriend. The Trojans remained on course to be the greatest collegiate football team ever. The intangibles of greatness were still in their corner.

But even SC fans were frustrated by the inability to knock each opponent around like a rag doll. There is arrogance in those circles, to be sure. A self-righteous feeling that only a traditional Trojan stomping will do.

At a summer 2005 USC alumni banquet featuring Carroll and Garrett as speakers, one older USC graduate turned to a younger one, remarking, "Gee, last year sure was great, wasn't it?"

"Yeah," the younger man hedged, "but I just wished we'd won by bigger margins."

The older alum just turned to the table and said, "Now he's the kinda guy who'd say we didn't win World War II by enough."

Patton coulda taken Bastogne sooner . . .

Why're those Marines pussyfootin' around at Iwo Jima for? Hurry up.

That kind of thinking.

The Fresno State game? Oh, yeah. USC 50, Fresno State 42. Mario Danelo's field goals were huge. It reminded many of the 1963 Rose Bowl, when Troy withstood a furious rush from Ron VanderKelen to beat Wisconsin, 42–37, and capture the national championship. But the big story was "The President."

Many people say that the single greatest game ever played by a college football player was Anthony Davis against Notre Dame in 1972. Perhaps the best competition for that comes from A. D. two years later. But Reggie Bush was superhuman against Fresno State. Maybe better than A. D. had been.

513 all-purpose yards. 294 yards on just twenty-three carries. Two touchdowns. Three receptions for 68. 151 on kick returns. Second all-time in NCAA Division I history for all-purpose yardage. Broke A. D.'s old school record of 368 in 1972. But the numbers do not tell the whole story.

On this night, Bush was so unstoppable, so unreal, that he won the Heisman Trophy. Matt Leinart, the golden boy with the Hollywood friends, would be in New York and deservingly so. So would Vince Young. The UCLA game would be played on national TV and would give everybody one last chance to shine. This game was played on Fox cable. It ran so late many West Coast papers did not have it, so the impact of Reggie's performance may have been diminished, but not by those who observed it.

Bush had spoken of "not having an 'S' on my chest," but he sure did look like Superman against the Bulldogs. If Leinart could actually beat this guy out for the Heisman Trophy (and he was planning to vote for his teammate), then he would really earn the moniker "greatest college football player ever."

The moment that stood out occurred in the fourth quarter. USC supporters with historical knowledge were comparing Reggie in their minds to Mike Garrett's 1965 game versus UCLA. On that afternoon, Garrett rushed for well over 200 yards, but committed key fumbles, allowing UCLA to rally late and win. It cost Mike his chance at a Rose Bowl. More than a few Bruin players said they were near tears at this development.

Bush *never* fumbles. Just as people committed this thought to their consciousness, and as some even made mention of it—like talking about a pitcher throwing a no-hitter in the eighth inning—it was jinxed. With about ten minutes remaining and USC holding on to a tenuous 41–35 lead, Bush stood at the goal line receiving a Bulldog kickoff. He fielded the ball, ran it out, got hit around the 18, and fumbled! Fresno State's Jason Huss scooped it up. Wendell Mathis rambled eighteen yards on the next play to put them up 42–41.

Stu Nahan likes to talk about the "look in his eyes" when describing O. J.'s 1967 run to beat UCLA, but Juice had nothing on Bush. Reggie was a man possessed. He was the Royal Air Force protecting London. The Third Army picking up 100 miles a day in early 1945.

Bush ran and ran and ran, but the big play was a pass. Leinart, starting at his own 11 after a penalty on the kick, recognized a winner when he stood right next to him. He called Bush's number. The pass was a little side pattern. The run after the catch, a Norm Chow specialty, went for forty-three yards to the Fresno State 21. Leinart engineered Troy to the 2. Then the big man, LenDale White, bulled in to make it 47–42. A two-point conversion failed. Nobody felt safe yet.

Three plays later, Lawrence Jackson sacked Paul Pinegar, a fourth-year senior starter who was magnificent in the manner of VanderKelen. But Jackson's blast caused a fumble. Brian Cushing recovered, but SC stalled. They could not convert a touchdown that would ice it. Danelo's twenty-six-yard field goal split the uprights, however, making it an eight-point game. Fresno State would have to score a touchdown and a two-point conversion, then outscore USC in overtime.

Nobody at the game or watching on the tube doubted their ability to do just that!

Fresno State started with 3:06 left on the clock. Pinegar drove them to the USC 25. Memories of Aaron Rodgers in 2004 stirred the crowd. Then Darnell Bing, bidding hard for the Jim Thorpe Award, intercepted Pinegar's pass into the end zone, returning it to the SC 40 to secure victory, just like Willie Brown had done when he picked VanderKelen in 1963.

The game started off in Fresno State's favor. Pat Hill deferred the opening kick, something almost nobody ever does. He gambled that his team could hold USC, take the ball down the field, and then have it to start the second half. His strategy was picture perfect.

Troy came out throwing, just as they had with Cal. Spread the Bulldogs out, then go to the run. Leinart threw a variety of passes, short and long, sideline and over the middle. He connected with a few. It looked like the usual Trojan plan. He hit Jarrett perfectly in the end zone, but the sophomore dropped the ball. Fresno State held.

USC punted. Pinegar drove them through the Trojans as if they were admiring spectators. 7–0, Fresno State.

Why'd we schedule these guys? What's wrong with U.C.–Davis? Aren't the New Mexico Lobos available?

It was not about a USC letdown. Leinart & Co. were on top of their game, although Matt tried a frustrating number of fade passes, mostly to Jarrett. They failed as they had against Cal. It was a low-percentage play that Mike Williams, and even Jarrett, previously made look easy somehow: a soft toss, usually on the sidelines or in the corner of the end zone, requiring the receiver to outjump one or two or three DBs. The play could work if the receiver was spectacular and could keep his feet in bounds. It was hard to intercept and could result in pass interference against the defense. But Hill, and other defensive coordinators in past weeks, knew about it. It was not working.

Leinart avoided mistakes. USC moved the ball. The running game picked up steam. But Fresno had the breaks going their way, along with sky-high emotion. Two Bulldogs fumbles did not cost them. One went out of bounds; another was picked out of the air and converted into a touchdown. Hill's team played ball control. They had studied Charlie Weis's playbook.

Pinegar had 203 yards and two touchdowns in the first half. Leinart threw for about half that, but he drove Troy late in the second quarter. Danelo, with little riding on his shoulders before this night, made a key field goal after Carroll seriously considered trying a fourteen-yard pass play with six seconds left. It was 21–13 when the teams went to the locker room. The atmosphere was similar to the one USC dealt with against Stanford in the 2004 game at Palo Alto. Hill's team would get the ball to start the third quarter.

If Pinegar could engineer a touchdown drive to make it 28–13, then the panic button might have to be pressed. But Josh Pinkard and Scott Ware stepped up, tipping passes to stop Fresno State. Over the next six and a half minutes, it looked like the 1974 game with Notre Dame. USC scored three times. Bush's forty-five-yard scamper was beyond the ability of this author to accurately describe. It looked like a high school play, with overtones of O. J.'s "23-blast" against UCLA in 1967. Bush appeared to be a grown man playing with boys; juking, outrunning, criss-crossing the field, leaving eleven Bulldogs holding their collective jock straps.

Leinart just went to him. Bush picked up chunks of yardage in spectacular form, all the yards Matt would need to pad his Heisman numbers. The quarterback was all too happy to give them up. Every time Bush touched the ball, he was a truly legitimate threat to break a touchdown no matter where USC was on the field. It was impossible but he was doing it!

Interceptions by Brandon Ting and Bing totally stopped the Fresno State momentum. After Steve Smith's six-yard touchdown reception, the score was 35–21 in favor of USC. Fresno's supporters seemed to just settle back and wait for the inevitable. The Trojans and their fans figured the rest of the game was going to be a victory parade. Oh, how wrong they were.

With victory within reach, Carroll decided to get aggressive. He threw a variety of blitz packages at Fresno State. The Bulldogs' offensive line controlled the line of scrimmage, protecting Pinegar. He had all day to spot receivers. His linemen resembled the 1976 Raiders.

Pinegar drove his team relentlessly down the field, then hit Paul Williams from twenty yards out to make the score 35–28. Fresno held. Tom Malone punted, but Adam Jennings returned it fifty-seven yards. The USC kick defense was porous all night. But when Scott Ware intercepted Pinegar's pass at the goal, returning it thirty yards, it set up another unreal dash by Bush: fifty yards for the touchdown.

Surely it was over now, 41–28 late in the third quarter. *Au contraire.*

USC was held, which to the Fresno faithful seemed a miracle in and of itself. Pinegar brought his team back, hitting Joe Fernandez for a six-yard TD to make it 41–35. He reminded people of Montana on this field in '78. That was when Bush fumbled the ensuing kick. After Mathis's scamper, the Bulldogs had scored fourteen points in twelve seconds. It was beginning to sound like the "Heidi game," the improbable 1968 encounter between the Jets and Raiders.

Bush's subsequent catch-and-run, and USC's ability to withstand the onslaught, was, despite a weak defense and bad special teams, highly impressive. There was no sense that Fresno caught Troy off guard. Rather, Fresno looked to be a team that could beat anybody in America on this night, including Texas. In some ways they looked like Texas Tech the night they beat Cal in the 2004 Holiday Bowl: unstoppable. Yet, somehow, Carroll's team found a way to pull it out.

The game had some parallels to the 1937 USC-UCLA game, when the Bruins' Kenny Washington passed and passed and passed, to USC's fourth quarter "distraction," according to Ken Rappoport's *The Trojans: A Story of Southern California Football*.

"Washington's passing helped the Bruins score two touchdowns in the fourth quarter and brought them to the fringe of another," wrote Rappoport. "The Bruin rally threw the Coliseum crowd into a frenzy and had [Howard] Jones on the edge of nervous exhaustion."

Substitute: Pinegar for Washington and Carroll for Jones. Then add the 1937 postgame meeting between Jones and UCLA coach Bill Spaulding. Spaulding visited the Trojan locker room, knocking on Jones's closed office door.

"Who's there?" a voice asked.

"Bill Spaulding."

"What do you want?"

"Tell Howard he can come out now. We've stopped passing."

Hill, he of the walrus moustache and gruff valley demeanor, had Spaulding's ghost shadowing him. Carroll probably felt like Apollo Creed after his first fight with Rocky.

Mathis rushed for 109 yards on twenty-three carries. A comparison of the statistics, between Leinart, Bush, and Pinegar, was telling. On the surface, it would appear Pinegar outplayed Leinart: twenty-seven of forty-five for 317 yards and four touchdowns versus Leinart's twenty-two of thirty-three for 200 yards and one touchdown. Undoubtedly, the numbers favored Bush, too: 294 yards on the ground, just for starters.

But Bush, while garnering some Heisman support, did not win the award outright, at least not yet. First, Leinart had zero interceptions. He also absorbed some big hits without fumbling. Pinegar fumbled and threw four costly picks.

The key was still Leinart's leadership: his steady game management and ability to direct the team in the "red zone." He did not always score touchdowns, but he gave Danelo the chance to kick two key field goals. He did not turn the ball over deep in his own territory nor near his opponent's goal.

Furthermore, he was unselfish. He had a hot hand in Bush. There was no hogging the ball for numbers. Many of Bush's yards were yards Leinart would have passed for if needed. It was a well-oiled machine based on experience, veteran savvy, and respect. It does not get better than that in sports. Leinart did not need to put up Andre Ware or Ty Detmer numbers to maintain his status as the "greatest college football player of all time." He still was. Whether he would win the Heisman or even team MVP honors was a larger question, which says all one needs to know when assessing the 2005 USC Trojans.

Several Fresno State players were quoted saying that USC was the best team of all time, but of course this needs to be taken with a grain of salt. This concept made them look good, to be sure. Furthermore, none of the Bulldogs were known to be college football historians.

Matt Leinart made no bones about it: Bush deserved the Heisman and would have his vote. There was not a hint of jealousy or covetousness in him. Still, Leinart's lobbying on behalf of his teammate, while admirable and perhaps influential, was not going to dissuade a fair number of voters from favoring the senior quarterback.

Bush earned National and Pac 10 Player of the Week honors for his 513-yard performance against Fresno State. It was the third Pac 10 Player of the Week honor of the 2005 season for Bush. He was previously recognized for his efforts against Oregon and Notre Dame. The second time he was honored by *The Sporting News* (also Notre

Dame) and The Master Coaches Survey. Two other Trojans—Leinart and White—previously earned Pac 10 Offensive Player of the Week honors in 2005.

Fox Sports's *Best Damn Sports Show Period*, which is filmed in L.A., had over the last several years taken on the flavor of a USC sideshow, especially after bringing in former Trojan quarterback Rodney Peete as one of its hosts. They liked to film the show in front of Tommy Trojan on occasion. The night before Thanksgiving, they turned the USC–Fresno State game into an instant classic, replaying it in its virtual entirety, interspersed with breathless interviews with Carroll and Bush.

Pete looked exhausted, unable to explain the last game, or the whole run for that matter. Bush was more matter-of-fact.

"I expect to do great things," he said, meaning his unreal performance was just part of the game plan. If *Best Damn Sports Show Period*'s replay was not enough, viewers could switch over to Fox College Sports and watch it again, complete with appropriate amazement from Fox sportscasters Petros Papadakis and Barry Tompkins. It was all Trojan football all the time well past midnight!

Junior fullback Brandon Hancock and junior twin safeties Brandon and Ryan Ting were named to the 2005 Pac 10 All-Academic first team. Junior tight end Nick Vanderboom made Pac 10 All-Academic honorable mention. Hancock earned a 3.91 grade point average while majoring in communications. Ryan Ting sported a 3.90 GPA and Brandon Ting was at 3.76, both as American studies and ethnicity majors. Hancock, a member of Phi Beta Kappa (the nation's oldest honor society), was a 2003 CoSIDA Academic All–District VIII first team and Pac 10 All-Academic first team selection. Hancock and Ryan Ting also made the *ESPN The Magazine* Academic All–District VIII first team. Both Tings made the 2004 Pac 10 All-Academic second team, while Vanderboom made honorable mention.

"FIGHT ON!": THE MIGHTY EMPIRE OF TROY AND ITS QUEST FOR ULTIMATE GLORY

Bush wins the Heisman, and USC finally meets its match in the Rose Bowl

UCLA was due at the Coliseum for the annual bloodletting known as the City Game on December 3. As in the 1967 matchup, it would be for much more than just the Victory Bell. At 9–1, the Bruins were one loss (at Arizona) away from being in a position to play for a shot at the BCS Rose Bowl. They were playing an eleven-game schedule, which says something about the difference between USC and their crosstown rivals.

The Trojans *always* play their full allotment of twelve regular season games. The Bruins do not. In past years, they had eschewed the extra game or chosen to play a weak sister instead of a strong opponent. On occasion it was USC who picked up the extra game versus the strong opponent. USC is a program that simply does not avoid challenges. UCLA is what it is.

That said, Karl Dorrell's team posed a major challenge. In the back of their minds, if Texas and a few other teams could be upset, they were hoping that a win over the vaunted Trojans might just possibly vault them into national championship contention; if not in the BCS, then perhaps in the AP.

A few days prior to the game, Jim Rome interviewed defensive end Lawrence Jackson. Rome had stated on many occasions that USC athletes are the best interviews in college sports, if not all sports. He was totally impressed with their intelligence and personality, to a man. But Jackson was a cut above.

A mere sophomore from Inglewood, Jackson was a philosophy major. He sounded downright Socratic in speaking to Rome: soft-spoken, thoughtful, spiritual.

"I'm always impressed with USC guys," Rome said of the interview, "but Lawrence Jackson just took it to a new level. He's quoting philosophy, he's a team leader even though he's still young, he was just a great interview and a great guy. . . .

"You know," he went on, "a lot of people get down on USC. They're the team you love to hate. They're like the Yankees, but I have to tell you, their players are not like that. It's the fans, the alumni. They're a touch arrogant, you know, with the pom-poms in the mailbox, the bumper stickers, the SC gear, but the players are not that way. They're humble, they're good guys, and it's gotta come back to Pete Carroll."

Discussion continued regarding USC's place in history; in particular, whether their offense was the greatest ever. Ned Miller was in his fiftieth year compiling press box statistics of Trojan games. He was amazed that Troy had amassed more than 700 yards in each of their first three home games.

"That's just incredible," Miller said. "You just don't get numbers like that."

"They're the best-balanced offense that I can ever recall," said Kent Stephens, curator of the College Football Hall of Fame in South Bend, Indiana. Entering the UCLA game, SC was leading the nation in offense with an average of 571.3 yards per game, while scoring 48.8 a game. They had already become the first team ever to feature a 3,000-yard passer, two 1,000-yard rushers, and a 1,000-yard receiver, with Steve Smith a mere 100 yards from getting to the 1,000 mark, too.

"You don't want to throw all your eggs in one basket," said Carroll.

Assistant Coach Lane Kiffin was asked who had the greatest offense ever.

"It's like arguing religion," he said. "You, you never get anywhere."

Still, what was very impressive was the fact USC was averaging more than 100 yards per game more than the 1979 team, the previous school record-holder. Leinart's numbers were significantly better than his Heisman campaign of 2004: 66 percent completion rate, 3,217 yards in the air, twenty-four TD passes, and even six rushing touchdowns.

Of Reggie Bush, former Oklahoma coach Barry Switzer said, "He's the best back since Barry Sanders came along. Him and Leinart get all the publicity, but White is also a stud."

According to Stephens, the 2005 Trojans were in a very elite class of offensive teams that included Army (1944–1945), Oklahoma (1971), Nebraska (1983), Houston (1989–1990), and Nebraska (1995).

"This is such a huge game," said UCLA's Maurice Drew. "With the schools being so close together, you see each other everywhere. Every time you go out, you have a chance to see [a USC player]. There's a lot of stuff going into this rivalry and on top of that, a share of the Pac 10 championship is at stake and a lot of bowl ramifications.

"We're just so anxious to get out there and play. They've had a week off and we've had three, so we're more refreshed and ready to play. Guys are tired of hitting each other. . . . We're ready to get after them."

Former UCLA coach Terry Donahue was planning to attend his first USC-UCLA game since he had coached in it one decade earlier. His NFL duties with the 49ers had directed his attentions elsewhere in the succeeding years.

"Really looking forward to it," he said. "Obviously, USC has a great team, but anything can happen in that game and I definitely think UCLA is capable of winning. I'll be rooting for the Bruins, as I've done for so much of my life."

Six-foot three-inch, 225-pound Drew Olson was now considered a top pro prospect. He entered the game leading the nation in passing efficiency (172.47), with thirty touchdowns against only three interceptions (a school record) to go along with 2,909 yards.

"Reggie Bush just might be the best college runner I've ever witnessed, although I'm not quite old enough to have seen Red Grange or Ernie Nevers," wrote Doug Krikorian.

Carroll had been conferring off and on with former UCLA basketball coach John Wooden, and now he was faced with a similar challenge to the one the "Wizard of Westwood" had faced: maintaining a dynasty over a long time.

"We try and keep the guys at an even keel, and not let them get too high or too low," said Carroll. "We don't prepare any differently for any game, and try to practice the same hard way week after week."

"Reggie Bush is so popular right now," said comedian Alex Kaseberg, "President Bush has asked a genealogist to determine if they somehow are related."

Bush "reminds [me] of Gale Sayers, who, I recall, scored six touchdowns against San Francisco [in 1965]," recalled Charles White on radio station 570. "I haven't seen anyone close to that. Reggie is awfully close."

Saturday, December 3 blew in clear and sunny, one of those unbelievable Southern California days that leave the rest of the world in awe. It had rained slightly the day before. The breezes were up, but that served only to clear the air of any smog on a cloudless, Pacific blue afternoon.

From the Coliseum press box, the view was nothing less than spectacular. To the east, the San Gabriel Mountains stood proud, although they had yet to be draped in their winter snowcaps. Straight ahead lay the downtown skyscrapers, tall and majestic. Just to the left of that, the Hollywood Hills. The Hollywood sign was clearly in view. Considering USC's near-total hold on the City of the Angels, it seemed apropos to send a construction crew above Lake Hollywood to install a giant "USC" underneath the iconic Hollywood symbol. Actual homes in the Hollywood and Beverly Hills could be picked out. To the west, the tall buildings of the Miracle Mile and Century City could easily be seen.

From the veranda adjacent to the press box, the view stretching across the basin spread out from behind the Coliseum's shadows was equally impressive. As the day droned on, with the early-setting December sun descending behind the Palos Verdes Peninsula into the Pacific and the Golden West, the whole image was utterly surreal. It was a dream day—for the Trojans. Right from the very beginnings, it was a day of total *Conquest!* The old "half USC, half UCLA" nature of the City Game was no more. It was obvious just walking to the stadium, and especially once inside it, that this was

SC's house. It was a sea of cardinal and gold, reminiscent of Nebraska's "Big Red." A small, quiet contingent of UCLAns bravely clung to their little corner of the Coliseum. The Trojan Nation were the Allies; 92,000-strong (completing USC's sixth sellout in six home games and eleventh of twelve overall) descending on the Normandy Beaches. Their opponents: a beaten, doomed crew. After Troy's beyond-imagination 66–19 thrashing, there was nothing left but to send out condolences, because USC took no prisoners! All the drama was in the pageantry, the ceremony, the symbolism.

ESPN's *GameDay* made the peristyle end of the Coliseum college football central. The Hollywood sign was not the only glitz shining down on Trojan Land. It was fitting that a who's who of celebrity glitz and glamour came to see the best show in town. USC graduates Tom Selleck and Henry Winkler were in attendance. Kirsten Dunst graced the sidelines. Sexy Fox sideline reporter Leeann Tweeden had gone to Westwood and given the Bruins about five minutes. The rest of the week, including pregame and during the game, she spent high-fiving the Trojans, doing push-ups with SC's male yell leaders, and genuflecting in front of their players. USC's guys were given enthusiastic greetings from Miss Tweeden after each successive fumble recovery, touchdown, mind-numbing tackle, or long-yardage catch. For the numerous high school recruits, it was the final clincher, if in fact any doubt still remained, that the choices came down to USC, SC, Southern California, or Southern Cal. Who could blame them?

As is tradition, USC's seniors were introduced to the crowd prior to the game. Remarkably, they made up a relatively small portion of this still-young team, which of course reinforced the realization that Trojan dominance promised to continue strongly for years to come.

But Leinart was a senior, the last to be brought out of the tunnel. A sensitive type anyway, he had predicted heavy emotions. The previous year, he had teared up just watching his friend and teammate from Mater Dei, Matt Grootegoed, do the same thing. All 92,000 fans stood and gave him a prolonged standing ovation, acknowledging that here was perhaps the greatest of all Trojans, the most successful quarterback, maybe the finest player, ever to play the collegiate game. Here was a guy who was beyond legend and myth, a man who, along with Reggie Bush and a few of their teammates over the past four years, had not only lived up to but in some cases gone beyond the achievements of Drury, Simpson, White, Allen, Lott. The best of the best. Guys that Heisman winners and Hall of Famers could look *up* to and admire!

Leinart had finally met his match. He lost it. He began to bawl uncontrollably, which simply endeared him to the hearts and minds of America even more. Because of his late entrance, Leinart had been hanging back in the tunnel, instead of warming up on the sideline. It was a rare faux pas, something Carroll and his staff had not taken under account.

As the team captain, Leinart then had to wipe his tears and meet the referees and the Bruin captains at midfield for the opening coin toss. UCLA won and deferred, meaning SC received . . . and Leinart would have no time to make practice tosses in the end zone.

That meant the usual aerial bombardment that marked the Norm Chow-Lane Kiffin era was replaced by the most potent ground attack since Patton's infantry. Most pundits felt Reggie Bush was the Heisman favorite entering the day. Earlier, Texas quarterback Vince Young, who, along with Leinart, was Bush's main competition, had led the Longhorns to a stunning 70–3 victory over Colorado in the Big 12 championship game.

Young had his supporters, but Leinart was the defending Heisman winner, the glory boy of Troy, the face of the dynasty. If he could have a huge game on this national stage, particularly if Bush were not at his best, he still could become the second two-time Heisman winner ever (Archie Griffin of Ohio State having done it in 1974–1975). After the first possession, however, it was obvious that it was not Matt's day. It was Reggie's. Instead of one two-time winner, the program would boast two teammates playing together as back-to-back winners, a feat not seen since Army's Doc Blanchard and Glenn Davis ("Mr. Inside and Mr. Outside") in 1945–1946.

With Leinart still "a mess," his arm not warmed up and his head in the clouds, USC went to the run on their first seven attempts from scrimmage.

"We planned on them coming out trying to run because, why wouldn't they?" said UCLA linebacker Wesley Walker. "That's football if you want to win. Run the ball on offense and stop the run on defense."

"From the beginning of the game we thought, 'OK, we can do whatever we want to do against these guys,'" said Bush.

That was precisely what Troy did. They dictated and dominated. With Bush carrying the ball, USC moved straight down the field. On their eighth play from scrimmage, Leinart sailed a pass. He was off and would be throughout the first half and even into the second half before regaining some semblance of his usual form. But it did not matter. The concept that USC could win in as thorough a manner as conceivable, on a day in which Matt Leinart had the worst game of his career, said everything about Trojan football.

Was it Bush's best game of his career? Possibly. The Fresno State game had provided a highlight reel of spectacular plays and gaudy statistics, but against UCLA Bush was even better, if that is possible.

With the USC superstar leading the way, Troy ran the field and kicked a field goal. They held Olson. Then Bush ran three times for forty-six yards. Leinart, not untracked but finally loose, hit Dwayne Jarrett from eight yards out to make it 10–0. By the time UCLA had run its thirteenth offensive play from scrimmage, it was 24–0, all with Leinart out of sync!

USC finished the game with ninety-five offensive plays, thirty more than UCLA, averaging 7.1 yards per snap. USC gained 679 yards in total offense. Marcus Cassel and Jarrad Page of UCLA made twenty-five "tackles," which were really little more than pulling somebody down after a long gain or getting carried by somebody five or ten yards along with the rest of the team until another first down marker was moved up-field. Bush and LenDale White were more likely to fall down from exhaustion than actually get tackled.

USC secured its place as the greatest college football team ever. Of course, this lofty title would not stand if they lost to Texas in the BCS Rose Bowl, but if the Long-horns would fall, USC would be in a league all of their own. While Leinart did not make his name on this day, he managed to improve in the second half to finish with twenty-one completions out of forty tries for a decent 233 yards, no interceptions, and three touchdowns. His place as the greatest player ever, while arguable, was still viable.

It was Bush who vaulted into a new pantheon of Trojan, and college football, history. He had 228 yards at the half. There was talk of beating Ricky Bell's record of 347. Bell had set the NCAA record against Washington State in 1975. Carroll went to the pass in the second half, ostensibly to get Leinart back in rhythm, and also to prevent an unnecessary injury to Bush. He finished with 260 yards on twenty-four carries, a 10.0 average. Like so much of USC's season, the only thing preventing him from running for as many yards as he chose to run for was the decision not to try it.

LenDale showed no ill effect from a shoulder bruise, averaging even more yards (11) than his partner (fourteen carries for 154 yards). Bush made a spectacular, leaping thirteen-yard touchdown run and later a ten-yard TD scamper to send Troy into half-time with a 31–6 lead.

Fox Sports's John Jackson stopped Pete Carroll on his way into the locker room. He was asked what, if anything, his team needed to do in the second half. The coach could have been ebullient, lighthearted, and carefree. Instead, his eyes blazed.

"We gotta come out *freaking smokin'* to start the second half," he all but raged. He was not going to let this get away, like the Fresno State game had almost gotten away.

USC legend Ronnie Lott was at the game, but did not have a ticket. Like so many Trojan alumni, he had a sideline pass, but he had his young son with him. Apparently, there was a rule of some kind that did not allow children of that age on the sideline, probably for insurance or legal purposes. So Lott watched the first half from the tunnel entrance.

Carroll saw Lott as he was entering the locker room. He stopped to speak to the player he had once coached in New York, and when he learned of his predicament he invited Lott and his son into the locker room.

Later, Lott told a USC alum named Wayne Hughes what transpired in there. Hughes, an Oklahoma native, is the founder of Public Storage. A billionaire, he was at the time contemplating producing a film about the 1970 USC-Alabama game in which his friend, Sam "Bam" Cunningham, had run roughshod over the Crimson Tide, thus effectuating the end of segregation.

The day after the game, Hughes's aide, David Rothenberg, relayed what Lott told him, which was that Carroll had entered the locker room like a wild man. He threw a chair against the wall and went into a rage, ensuring that complacency not set in. According to Hughes, Lott said that in all of his many years in football, from high school in Rialto to USC to the San Francisco 49ers, he had never seen such a fired-up team. He had never seen such eyes, such fierce competitiveness. Lott had said that he observed the team prior to the 2005 Oklahoma Orange Bowl, and that on *that* occasion they broke new ground in terms of readiness; but this was something else, something beyond that.

The summary of this is that, when focused, the 2005 Trojans were simply unbeatable within the normal scheme of things. Nobody is actually "unbeatable." Human weakness makes such infallibility impossible. But they were as close to it as any collegiate football team ever had been. UCLA was mere highway fodder. The Bruins trotted out for the second half like it was a Monday practice. USC came out with fire in their shoes.

"We heard a lot of criticism after giving up forty-two points," said Brian Cushing, referring to the Fresno game. "We wanted to turn that around. It sparked us to play better. I think Coach Carroll took it personally."

Leinart never found his groove, but he stopped sailing his passes, finding some semblance of rhythm in the second half.

"I probably let my emotions get to me a little bit, but I'm happy with the way I played, especially in the second half," said Leinart. "The team did well. That's all that matters."

"When [Bush] is spinning and juking and all that and I come in and try to beat up on you, that definitely takes a lot of energy off the defense," said White.

"I'm disappointed and embarrassed," said Olson, sounding just like Jason White after the Orange Bowl. USC totally bottled up Olson and Maurice Drew, leaving no doubt about their defense at this crucial point. UCLA came in with one of the most vaunted offenses in the nation, but had been stuffed at every turn.

White had made a nice nineteen-yard touchdown run to make it 17–0 early in the second quarter. UCLA's Kahlil Bell fumbled a squib kickoff, and after USC recovered, it set up a Bush touchdown run. Leinart hit Fred Davis with a fifteen-yard scoring strike in the third quarter. Rey Maualuga then forced an Olson fumble. Justin Wyatt snatched it and rumbled thirty-eight yards for the score. Leinart hit White on a scoring pass, and LenDale added an eight-yard run.

"It couldn't have been sweeter," said Carroll in the understatement of the day. "There's no question about what's going on. This is what we're all about."

In the postgame locker room, it was revealed that Leinart was "so emotional, teary and crying," said Carroll. "He was a mess. . . . He was trying to maximize the moment, and he did."

His teammates, seeing his state of mind and combining that with his first five pass attempts (all incompletions), came to him one after the other to calm him down and tell him he was the best QB in the nation.

"It was an unbelievable experience," Leinart said. "Something I'll always remember."

It was Bush's day all the way.

"He ran so fast past us sometimes, it was amazing," said Fred Matua. "He was flying around out there like he was Superman, like he was playing acrobatic football or something. I was like the fans; I was like, 'Wow.'"

"You hear the oohs and aahs, and all you want to do is get up and look like you're blocking somebody," said center Ryan Kalil.

"I'm running down the field, and I see a guy on the other team who Reggie just faked into the ground, and I always lean down and have words for him," said Matua. He told the fallen Bruins, "'I've seen this all year; I know how you feel.' I'm like, 'Dude, you might as well go to the sideline, because you don't have a chance.'"

"The way they run the ball, I've never seen anything like that," said Olson.

"We've done it with a little bit of flair, a little bit of drama," said Carroll. "This game was an exclamation point."

"How easy was it on a scale of one to ten?" Bush said. "It was a ten."

It was a game so thorough and so complete that it reminded some historians of the 1929 drubbing (76–0). The loss was so devastating that, even though there is no actual prospect of it happening, its effect was such that taking five years or so off from the rivalry (as the Bruins had done in the early 1930s) was really a better bet than continuing to subject themselves to this kind of beating.

Over the next week, USC was treated like royalty. Bush and White were guests on the *Best Damn Sports Show Period*.

Ushers at a UCLA basketball game were instructed not to speak of the football score, like apparatchiks getting instructions on Stalin's latest revisionism.

An ESPN recruiting analyst said seven of the nation's top ten prospects, all five-star blue chippers from outside of Los Angeles who were not considered to be in Troy's orbit, had shifted to USC, leaving old commitments. They were actually calling USC, not vice versa.

"Let me tell you something," said *Long Beach Press-Telegram* sports columnist Doug Krikorian, who has seen 'em all, "when USC gets focused, *nobody* can beat 'em. They have the best offensive line in college football history. All eleven offensive starters can play in the NFL right now. Reggie Bush is the greatest running back in history. Matt Leinart is the most successful college quarterback ever. What more can you say?"

"Reggie Bush will be the number one pick in the draft," said Mel Kiper Jr. "Matt Leinart will be number two. LenDale White will be drafted in the late first round if he comes out."

Kirk Hirbstreit talked about Bush on the *Jim Rome Show*.

"I saw Bush at the 2004 Rose Bowl, when he was a freshman," he said. "I said then and there he's the best player I ever saw. I sought him out on the field after that game and told him that."

Talk about all-time greatest teams was in the air. USC was now the prohibitive favorite to replace their own 1972 version. The unbeaten Indianapolis Colts were on pace to unseat the Miami Dolphins, another 1972 juggernaut of the pro variety, as the only unbeaten NFL team since the AFL-NFL merger.

"Forget about the Dolphins and Colts," wrote Gene Wojciechowski of ESPN.com. "If Indy beats the Jaguars, Chargers and Seahawks, then we'll talk. Until then, we ought to be naming babies, buildings and freeways after the greatest dynasty this side of Ming.

"The USC Trojans. . . .

"Since Oct. 6, 2003 . . . USC is 45-1. Freaks.

"In those 45 victories, only five were decided by less than a touchdown. 33 of those wins were decided by 20 points or more.

". . . The Trojans are on such a championship roll, they have their own parking space at the White House Rose Garden. The only downside to this remarkable run is having to hear the Trojan Marching Band play 'Conquest' 11,000 times per game."

USC had "taken every opponent's best body blow (Notre Dame and Fresno can tell you about that, too). If nothing else, you have to respect the streak, respect USC's inner resolve and respect a loaded roster that, by January 4, will feature—for the first time ever—two Heisman Trophy-winning teammates playing in the same game. The two stiff-armers: Matt Leinart and Reggie Bush.

"Nothing against the '72 Dolphins—or the '05 Colts if they win out—but a third consecutive USC national title, a second consecutive unbeaten season and a 35-game victory streak is at least the equal, if not superior, to an NFL single-season 17–0 or 19–0 record."

USC had beaten the last sixteen ranked opponents they had faced. They had beaten UCLA seven straight times. In the Carroll era, they had defeated Notre Dame four straight times, Auburn twice, Cal four out of five, Iowa, Oregon twice, and Oregon State four times. In their thirty-four-game winning streak, they had beaten Arizona State four times, Michigan, Virginia Tech, Arkansas, Fresno State, and Oklahoma once apiece.

"They've done it despite injuries, early defections to the NFL, graduation, coaching departures and the law of averages," wrote Wojciechowski. They had done it in the age of the BCS, the television age, the age of cable, Fox Sports, ESPN, the Internet, big money, gambling, steroids, total integration of whites, blacks, Pacific Islanders, even Chinese Americans (two of whom, the Ting brothers, were significant defensive contributors to Troy). They had done it in the age of the newest coaching techniques and training and diet methods; in an age in which the best coaches were spread throughout the land, lending a sense of egalitarian fairness to competitive sports at all levels and in all regions. They had done it when the best juniors leave for the NFL, and they had the best juniors (in Mike Williams's case, the best sophomore). They had done it amid the white-hot glare of a Hollywood spotlight; no college sports team had ever attracted so much attention, all in the media capital of the world.

There was simply no comparing the 1947 Irish, the 1956 Sooners, not even the

1995 Cornhuskers or the '72 Trojans. Nobody was a match for this team if they could survive number two Texas.

■ ■ ■

By the end of the evening on Saturday, December 10, it was almost too much. Even for Trojan fans. Almost.

Reggie Bush left the competition behind, as was his and his team's usual custom, in winning USC's seventh Heisman Trophy. This tied Troy with Notre Dame for the most Heismans. If they could beat Texas, it would push them ahead of the Irish for the most national championships, 12–11.

More impressively, it was USC's seventh Heisman since 1965. During that span, Notre Dame had won one. Since 1962, USC had won seven national titles (going on eight?). The Irish in that time span: three. The advent of the modern era had clearly delineated a new champion, a new "America's Team" of collegiate football, a new standard of excellence. USC now possessed the greatest tradition in the game's long history. There was no real argument worth making anymore. It was no longer a barroom argument. It was now looking more and more like established fact. The numbers did not lie.

In the biggest landslide in Heisman history, Bush was announced as the seventy-first winner of the Heisman Trophy during a nationally televised show from the Nokia Theater in New York. He defeated a small field: Leinart and Texas quarterback Vince Young, with the highest percentage of votes ever.

"It's truly an honor to be elected to this fraternity of Heisman winners," Bush said. "To think I've been in college for three years and this is the first time I've been invited to a fraternity."

He won all six regions and was named on a record 99 percent of the ballots. Only USC's O. J. Simpson (855 first-place votes in 1968) had more than Bush (784). It was a much bigger landslide than the one the real "President" and his party had won by a little over a year earlier.

"His play shows why he's the best player in college football," said the unselfish Leinart, who voted for Bush the second straight year. Leinart had voted Young second and left the third spot blank. "Playing big in big games and being a leader in big games. He's the perfect description of the Heisman Trophy."

"The decision to come back changed my life," Bush said to Leinart in accepting his award. He also had a nation choked up when he tearfully acknowledged his "father," who adopted him at age two.

"You didn't have to do that," Bush said as the lay preacher from San Diego mouthed the words "I love you" on camera. "It takes a man to do something like that."

"He's going to be one of the best ever," said Mike Garrett, who was among the past Heisman winners in attendance. "He looks like another Gale Sayers."

It was impossible not to make the comparison between Blanchard and Davis. For the first time, Heisman teammates would play in a game together. "Mr. Inside and Mr. Outside" had not played in a bowl game after Davis won the award in 1946.

Reggie also made it clear that he had not decided whether to turn pro or not, although most felt it was a fait accompli. Still, USC athletes were proving themselves to be so special, such fine people off the field as well as on, so clearly different from the rest of the field, that the prospect of Bush doing what Leinart had done was not totally out of the realm of possibility.

Young showed little grace and was unable to hide his disappointment, a factor that the pundits speculated about over the next weeks as the Rose Bowl approached.

"Bush is the new Barry Sanders," said Emmitt Smith on Stephen A. Smith's *Quite Frankly* on ESPN.

■ ■ ■

The weeks leading up to the Rose Bowl were filled with greater hype and anticipation than any collegiate sporting event in history, more so even than the ballyhooed 2005 USC-Oklahoma Orange Bowl.

Texas came in with a 12–0 record, averaging more than fifty points per game, with one of the nation's best defenses. Young, the star of the 2005 Rose Bowl when he led the Longhorns to a stunning 38–37 victory over Michigan, was the face of their team. As great as he was, it was felt that it would be too much for him to carry Texas on his shoulders alone. USC, also averaging fifty points a game, was installed not only as a seven- to eight-point favorite, but was anointed as the greatest offensive team ever as well as the greatest college team in history. ESPN ran a series of polls and "fantasy games," using computers and expert analysis, comparing the Trojans to the greatest teams ever. It was "determined" that indeed the 2005 team was the best ever assembled.

The Longhorns arrived in Los Angeles amid all the Hollywood hoopla. Day after day, on TV and radio and in the papers, they were subjected to pagan idolatry heaped upon their opponents, as if Texas were the Washington Generals, set up as opponents for the Harlem Globetrotters to trounce. The pressure to live up to their star billing worked on USC, and spurred Texas to establish their own place in history.

On Wednesday, January 4, 2005, in the "ring of fire" known as the Rose Bowl in Pasadena, the Longhorns did just that. Vince Young played what may have been the greatest game any player has ever played. That is what it took to break USC's hearts.

USC in its history has played a number of games that might be considered the "game of the century" or "the best college football game ever played." The 1931, 1974, and 1978 Notre Dame games come to mind because of what happened on the field, but they were great mostly from USC's point of view.

The 1988 Notre Dame game and the 2005 Oklahoma Orange Bowl were steeped in pregame hype, but failed to live up to the billing. The 1967 UCLA game was unique in many ways and may have been the best college game ever played, considering everything, but the 2006 Rose Bowl topped them all. It was the greatest game of all time.

In 1975, the Boston Red Sox defeated the Cincinnati Reds, 7–6, in twelve innings in game six of the World Series. Many historians consider it the best baseball game ever. In that game, Cincinnati's Pete Rose, who aside from being a great player was a great fan of the game, told Boston catcher Carlton Fisk that it was just plain fun to play in a game of that magnitude. Despite losing, Rose felt it was an honor and a privilege just to be a part of it.

After Vince Young sprinted nine yards for a touchdown with nineteen seconds remaining to give Texas the 41–38 win and the national championship, those Trojans who were able to put it all in perspective felt the same way Rose did. Considering the setting, the spectacle and pageantry, the magnificence of Young, the fight of Texas, and the fact that Pete Carroll's team left it all on the field, there was nothing left to do but give Texas credit while absorbing the knowledge that they were part of something more special than any previous contest.

Win or lose, it was an honor just to be a part of it.

Yes, USC lost more than just a football game. Their place in history was more than merely the '05 national title. A laundry list of records and accomplishments, most of which would have separated them from Notre Dame and Alabama, clearly delineating them as the greatest of all traditions, became suddenly a closer call when Young crossed the goal line.

It was reminiscent of the 2003 BCS Fiesta Bowl, when Miami's thirty-four-game winning streak and quest for a second straight national title were lost in an overtime loss to Ohio State. The defeat left sports historians in further awe of the great John Wooden, whose UCLA basketball team had managed to win seven straight NCAA titles and ten of twelve. Jim Rome had openly predicted that Carroll's dynasty could put up those kinds of numbers. Instead, it was shown just how difficult a task it was, despite the fact Troy had made it look somewhere between easy and probable. Thus, USC fell far short of the kind of sustained run that Wooden's Bruins had managed.

Symbolically, USC failed to win its twelfth national championship, which, aside from pushing them from the eleven-all tie with Notre Dame, would have surpassed UCLA's eleven hoops championships and equalled the twelve won by the Trojan baseball team over the years. In an eerie coincidence, Rod Dedeaux, who coached eleven of those baseball titles between 1948 and 1978, died at ninety-one the day after SC's loss. USC also remained far behind their twenty-six NCAA track titles.

Also lost was the quest for an unprecedented third straight title; their attempt to break Oklahoma's forty-seven-game winning streak; the end of their thirty-three-week record of AP number one rankings; the chance for returning seniors to win four national championships in as many years; and possibly Matt Leinart's claim to be the "greatest college football player of all time." It initially put in some jeopardy Reggie

Bush's "lock" as the number one pick in the 2006 NFL Draft, but as Draft Day approached the "Vince Young to Houston" consensus began to die down, with the original prediction—Bush number one and Leinart number two—appearing to be the most reasonable probability.

Up until the Rose Bowl, it had seemed that Bush would be chosen first by the Houston Texans with Matt Leinart set to go second. Young suddenly became the focus of discussions on whether the Texans should take the Houston-bred Longhorn quarterback.

Whether Young would actually usurp Leinart's spot in the draft was very much a possibility. Even the most ardent Trojan fan had to admit that had the Heisman voting taken place after the Rose Bowl, it may have been Young, not Bush, who would have walked away with the statue. At the very least, Young had used the "loss" of the award in December to spur his great effort in January.

In the days after the game, the media awaited word that the junior Bush would indeed declare. They also wanted to know the decision of junior LenDale White, USC's best player in the Rose Bowl, whose performance did two things: seemingly make him a surefire high first-round pick if he would come out, or (with Young out) the favorite for the '06 Heisman on a USC team figured to be ranked number one in the preseason, should he stay.

There were strange omens surrounding USC after the loss. Aside from Dedeaux's passing, the great Carson Palmer injured his knee four days later in an AFC play-off game with Pittsburgh.

For those looking to compare the game with past battles, the 1969 Rose Bowl seemed as good a comparison as any. In 1968, USC was the defending national champion. O. J. Simpson won the Heisman Trophy. Unbeaten Troy was favored to win the Rose Bowl and repeat. They were anointed with all the bells and whistles that come with sports glamour in L.A.

Their opponents, the Ohio State Buckeyes, had a chip on their shoulder, something to prove. They did just that, upending Southern California, 27–16. It was a battle between numbers one and two for the national title, won by the underdog. O. J. had a spectacular touchdown run but committed a key fumble, contributing to their defeat. In 2006, Reggie Bush had a spectacular touchdown run, but his key fumble also contributed to defeat. O. J. was later drafted number one, accompanied by a plethora of highly drafted teammates. Bush was favored to also get picked first with an even greater number of fellow first-round teammates.

Getting back to the John Wooden comparison, the game held some similarities to the 1974 Final Four matchup between UCLA and North Carolina State. Substitute Matt Leinart and Reggie Bush for Bill Walton and Keith Wilkes, then Vince Young for David "Skywalker" Thompson. USC, like the Bruins thirty-two years earlier, held the lead late in the game. Victory, firmly within their grasp, was allowed to slip away, and with it the chance to sail in uncharted waters of sports greatness.

Yes, USC did allow victory to elude them. Mostly, they had nobody to blame but themselves. There were numerous mistakes and strange plays: an ill-conceived Bush lateral and a fumble lost, fumbles not recovered; interceptions against and an interception not made; questionable penalties called and not called; spotty spotting, technical malfunctions, poor clock management, ill-chosen time-outs, coaching decisions that lacked the famed Carroll "good luck" touch; two fourth down efforts that failed with critical results; failure to wrap up tackles, to prevent Texas from getting out of bounds at crucial times while the Trojans went out of bounds when they needed the clock to run; and a handful of plays that went the Longhorns' way by a matter of inches, any one of which probably would have given Troy victory, only if . . .

So yes, USC made errors that cost them victory, just as they had done with Ohio State in 1969, and just as UCLA had done with North Carolina State in 1974. They committed many unusual errors and mental failures. For those who saw the game in person, ESPN Classic's TV replay three days later was a bitter pill to swallow because it revealed multiple mistakes that went against Troy time and time again, usually by a matter of inches that the fan in the stands could not see.

There had been a sense that USC could not lose. Leinart himself had said, "This team doesn't know how to lose," after the Notre Dame game. They had won for so long, usually in dominating fashion, that defeat seemed foreign. There was a sense that this was a team of destiny, that their coach lived under a lucky star. They had dodged bullets, in South Bend mostly. In the back of some nervous Trojan minds, there may have run the uneasy thought that if all their good luck turned around, they could be upset, but Carroll was so full of confidence and bravado, the team wrapped in such glory, that this unease was quickly dispelled. As White had said at the end of the Arizona State game, they were just "too dominant."

There was that carryover effect from the UCLA game, too. Such a perfect day, all the way around; a sense that the championship had been won that day without proper regard for the fact that Texas had beaten Colorado by a bigger margin than USC beat the Bruins.

As Trojan fans lingered at the Coliseum on December 3, while the band played "Tusk," the song they had earned a gold record for playing in concert with Fleetwood Mac, their cheerleaders gyrating, fans dancing in the stands, victory so secure within their consciousness, they truly could have used one of Caesar's slaves whispering to them that "all glory is fleeting," in an effort to bring down the hubris.

Despite all of that, however, they led by twelve with six and a half minutes to go. They had it won. They could not stop Young and Texas. In the end, the credit must go to the Longhorns and their fabulous quarterback. Furthermore, the credit must go to the Texas defense, which was better than USC's. Defense wins championships. USC had won in 2003 and 2004 on the strength of that very axiom. Despite having all their star power, all their historical baggage that, after everything was said and done, left them nineteen seconds away from being the "greatest collegiate football team of all time"; in the end their defense was exposed and it was all ripped away from them.

For the record, it was a clear, warm day in the Arroyo Seco. Recent snows had capped the nearby San Gabriel Mountains. The setting was as spectacular as ever, confirming the notion that the Rose Bowl, the "Granddaddy of 'em all," is truly the finest college football setting in America.

Fans arrived early. Alumni of both schools engaged in a mutual admiration society. They were polite, well dressed, their children well behaved, their women equally beautiful. Because it was the BCS national championship game, it was played at night, so temperatures cooled a bit, but it was pleasant throughout. After a fly-by, a parachute jump, and the "Star-Spangled Banner" sung by LeAnn Rimes, the realization came to one and all that a football game was to be played.

It started out USC's way. Texas won the toss, electing to defer. USC would have done the same, choosing to get the ball first in the second half. After holding USC it looked like Texas made the right pick, but it was all for naught when the ensuing punt was fumbled on the return, giving Troy the ball in Texas territory.

Matt Leinart drove the Trojans to the Texas 4, when on a fourth down try White barreled in for the touchdown. Young was forced to watch USC get two separate possessions before he could take a snap. Texas looked out of their league at first; the fumble, a terrible late hit after Leinart was well out of bounds, and the failure to stop USC were just the beginning. Young was unable to sustain a drive. USC came roaring back, but on another fourth-and-one in the Texas "red zone," Leinart's footing failed him and Texas held. Had he made it, the Trojans likely would have scored to make it 14–0.

Events following that lend to the uneasy conclusion that but for mental errors, Troy might well have gone up 21–0 or even 28–0, putting the game away and setting up a dispiriting rout, à la the Oklahoma game of a year earlier.

This included Bush, who after catching a short pass romped down the field, only to try an ill-advised lateral to an unsuspecting teammate deep in Texas territory. Texas recovered the loose ball. Also included was an end zone pass by Leinart intended for Dwayne Jarrett. The ball was caught by a Texas defender, seemingly out of bounds, but the replay went the Longhorns' way. The Bush lateral and the Leinart interception took what probably would have been fourteen points off the board for USC.

The swing was momentous. It erased Trojan momentum and gave Texas—their players, their fans, and especially Mr. Young—the confidence that they were still in the game and might be able to stay there.

In the second quarter, still smarting from mental errors, USC stalled while Young led his team on three scoring drives: nine plays (fifty-two yards) and a field goal; seven plays (eighty yards) and a touchdown (point-after missed); and four plays (fifty-one yards) capped by a thirty-yard scoring run by Ramonce Taylor. The second touchdown was controversial. The machine that normally reviews plays was briefly malfunctioning. The fact that Young's knee was down before he made an illegal upfield lateral was not reviewed.

USC found themselves totally on their heels. Down 16–7, they mounted a drive to close out the first half. Tentatively, they worked their way into scoring position, but Leinart was sacked twice. Questionable clock management eliminated any chance at a touchdown strike. Mario Danelo came in for the field goal.

If Danelo missed, with Texas getting the ball to start the second half, USC was beginning to consider the reality of a 23–7 deficit before getting the ball in the third quarter. Stopping Young was already a major problem. When Danelo hit a forty-three-yard field goal to close it to 16–10, USC went in to the locker room happy to be within a touchdown. Considering that their mistakes had wiped out an additional two or three potential scores, it was a tremendous psychological blow and a major challenge for Carroll. Instead of a replay of the OU victory, they felt like Davy Crockett at the Alamo.

Texas on the other hand was thrilled. They had dodged bullets, overcome early mistakes, then clicked on all their cylinders. They were playing beautifully on both sides of the ball and, most important, Coach Mack Brown's team now *knew*—despite any pregame false confidence—what they had previously only suspected: they could beat Southern California!

But Carroll had become the best halftime and second half coach in the nation. His team was known for finishing, and they came out in the third quarter looking like the 2005 national champions.

After holding Texas, Leinart drove Troy sixty-two yards on seven plays, with White bulling in to make it 17–16. White was establishing himself as USC's star on a day in which Bush was off, and for unexplained reasons not getting as many carries—a point that would be debated. Leinart, shaky at the beginning, settled into a rhythm and was fabulous.

But the defense was not. Young answered the call, driving Texas back for a score. Trailing again, 23–17, the Trojans knew they were in for a major test, and their response was fantastic. Leinart drove them on a methodical seventy-four-yard drive, mixing runs and passes with White scoring again. USC 24, Texas 23. The next possession seemed to swing things back to the Trojans. Texas was held and USC scored another touchdown to lead by eight, 31–23.

Young came back, but after driving deep into USC territory, they were unable to get into the end zone, settling for a field goal to make it 31–26. A slight edge had been gained by Troy, with the ball back in their hands and a chance to close. They seemingly did. Leinart hit Jarrett with a high pass, which he caught and then stretched into the end zone. Two Texas defenders collided and hit the ground hard. They had to be carried off the field. The Texas bench was down, heads hanging, but Coach Brown exhorted his team to stay up. Young danced and skipped to the delight of his team's fans, showing no pressure.

Jarrett's straining touchdown grab had the strange effect of working against USC, however. Had he not made the score, Troy would have been at the 1 or 2. A couple of plays would have eliminated about forty or fifty precious seconds, meaning that they would have been kicking off, leading by twelve with about six minutes or less left, instead of the 6:42 that did remain.

With USC leading 38–26, the atmosphere was muted. There were, statistically, more USC fans than Texas supporters, but from the minute one arrived at the Arroyo Seco, the sight of burnt orange colors dominated the atmosphere.

Texas fans seemed to consider victory a faraway proposition. They knew USC was almost unbeatable and many said as much. But as the game developed and the Trojans could not put the Longhorns away, the team and their supporters gained confidence. They were well behaved, respectful, and polite, but they *were* loud. They cheered, filling the air with down-home Texas homilies and shouts of encouragement.

USC fans, on the other hands, sat on their hands—to the extent that there was any sitting in a stadium that took almost every play on its feet. But USC was supposed to win. So much was riding on it that their fans, if not their players, were taking on a "hold 'em" mentality: just six more minutes, who cares how, just finish with more points and spend another off-season bathed in glory.

It was not to be.

Bush had finally broken out of his after-fumble funk with a twenty-six-yard touchdown run to put his team up by 31–23, but in the end Carroll went to White to close it out. LenDale was up to the task, but it was not enough.

Texas followed with a seventeen-yard Young touchdown run to make it 38–33 with 4:02 left. USC did what John Wooden always warned against—what his team did in losing to North Carolina State when victory seemed to be theirs in 1974—they "did not play to win; they played not to lose," as Wooden put it.

A Trojan scoring drive would have clinched victory at that point. With White carrying the ball, USC drove into Texas territory. One completed pass unfortunately led to USC going out of bounds, stopping the clock when time needed to keep ticking away. White carried close to a first down, but fumbled. USC recovered but the ball was put further back than the carry had taken it. With a little over two minutes left, the fate of the game rested on Carroll's decision to go for it on fourth-and-a-little-over-one on the Longhorn 45. A first down would allow them to run out the clock.

The talk radio mavens had every answer the next day, but the "play not to lose" mentality was not part of Carroll's gamble. The "Monday morning quarterbacks" advised that Carroll should have let White block and Bush run. Use Bush as a decoy. Roll out and hit Dominique Byrd for two yards. Instead, White took it right up the gut. At first it looked like he might get it. He had momentum, but Texas won the national championship by stopping him with a brick wall of defenders. The crowd hummed, not sure. A measurement was taken. USC fell inches short, and the Texas faithful went wild.

Later, Carroll said he went for it because it was his gambling style and that his team could not stop Young whether he started on his 20 or his 45. He was right. But the past was now past. The defense that Carroll knew "couldn't stop Young" now had to. Everything rested on it. Beleaguered, tired, beaten all day by the Texas superstar, they stepped up and made plays.

Brandon Ting broke up a pass, but he knocked it down instead of making the interception like he had done against Fresno State.

Harrying Young, they forced him into a third-and-long situation. He completed a pass, but All-American Darnell Bing's facemask penalty did them in. Instead of fourth down and about seven to go at midfield, Texas had a first down well into USC territory with the clock stopped and enough time to get it done.

On several plays, Young evaded capture. He and his receivers carried USC tacklers out of bounds, stopping the clock. Young completed a pass to the 14. It was just like the 2004 Cal game, but the superiority of Young over Aaron Rodgers was apparent. At first, it looked like Southern California's defense would prove heroic in the style that befitted the Pete Carroll era. Texas moved up to the 9, third and five. A pass into the end zone was broken up.

With nineteen seconds left, Young faced a fourth-and-five. He could get a first down to the 4 and had time-outs, but it would be a narrow margin. He called the same play that had failed on the previous try, dropped back, and to USC's credit saw no man open. Then he went with his instincts and started to run. For a brief second it looked like a defender could get him. The historical memory conjured up Johnny Lujack stopping Doc Blanchard in 1946; the Tennessee Titans falling half a yard shy against the Rams in the 2000 Super Bowl; even the noble Permian effort that falls just short in the paean to Texas prep football, *Friday Night Lights*.

But Young was too quick. Six feet, five inches, between 230 and 240 pounds but fast, he was not to be denied. He could outrun his defenders. He could juke them, Bush style. Or he could bull past them with sheer power. On this play, he basically juked and ran, untouched. Young had the first down and then ran into the corner of the end zone to make it 39–38 with nineteen seconds remaining. Texas hearts soared. USC felt something they thought they would never feel: despair.

With twelve USC defenders on the field, a time-out was called as Young lined up for a two-point conversion. Bad clock management had bedeviled them all game, and this was the last insult, although it was an on-field call, not Carroll's. Young converted easily anyway, making it 41–38.

Bush ran the kickoff back, then took a shovel pass from Leinart into Texas territory. The pundits later speculated that Danelo, who had put several balls in the back of the end zone on kickoffs, should have attempted a sixty-yard desperation field goal try.

Leinart rolled to his left. With no time-outs he had only the sidelines and missed Jarrett. The dream was over.

"We've been winning for so long, somebody had to lose," White said.

Carroll, Leinart, Bush, and his team showed class, as did the fans on both sides. Leinart and Bush ventured into the Texas locker room to applaud this fearless team. There was immediate consensus that not only had the game surpassed the hype, but that it very well may have been the finest, most exciting football contest, played at the highest level by two great teams, of all times.

With one nine-yard run, Vince Young had erased the mantle of "greatest collegiate football team of all time" from USC, and now opened up a new discussion: how good was Texas? The answer is that the 2005 Texas Longhorns are one of the greatest football teams in history. In the top five, at the very least.

■ ■ ■

White finished as USC's all-time career touchdown leader. Bush and White passed Blanchard and Davis for most combined teammate TDs. Jarrett broke the single-season USC touchdown record.

Bush was named 2005 Pac 10 Offensive Player of the Year. Carroll was voted conference co–Coach of the Year (along with UCLA's Dorrell). Nine Trojans—including six on offense—made the All–Pac 10 first team. It was Carroll's second such honor in his five years at USC. In all, twenty-one Trojans made All–Pac 10 first team, second team, or honorable mention.

It was the second consecutive Pac 10 Offensive Player of the Year honor for Bush. He shared the 2004 honor with Leinart. Bush became just the fifth player to win the offensive award in back-to-back seasons, joining USC's Charles White (1978–1979), Stanford's John Elway (1980–1982), Washington State's Rueben Mayes (1984–1985), and Leinart (2003–2004). Bush was the first non-quarterback in twenty years to win it consecutively.

It was also the fourth year in a row that a Trojan was the conference Offensive Player of the Year. Quarterback Carson Palmer started the streak in 2002, the year he won the Heisman.

Leinart made the All–Pac 10 first team for his third straight year, just the second quarterback ever to do so. Bush and Leinart were joined on the first team by wide receiver Dwayne Jarrett and three offensive linemen, guard Taitusi Lutui, tackle Sam Baker, and center Ryan Kalil.

On defense, safety Darnell Bing and ends Lawrence Jackson and Frostee Rucker were first team selections. USC's second team All–Pac 10 picks were tailback LenDale White, offensive guard Fred Matua, and safety Scott Ware. Bush also made the second team as a punt returner.

Nine other Trojans were recognized as honorable mention All–Pac 10ers: placekicker Mario Danelo, defensive tackles Sedrick Ellis and LaJuan Ramsey, offensive tackle Winston Justice, fullback David Kirtman, linebackers Oscar Lua and Keith Rivers, wide receiver Steve Smith, and cornerback Justin Wyatt.

Bush, Leinart, Dwayne Jarrett, Darnell Bing, Taitusi Latui, LenDale White, and

Sam Baker were all named to the Associated Press All-American team. Bush was the AP Player of the Year. Leinart won the Johnny Unitas Award as the nation's best senior quarterback.

Bush won the Doak Walker Award as the nation's top running back as well as the Walter Camp Award as the best player. The Pigskin Club of Washington, D.C., named Bush its Offensive Player of the Year. He made the 2005 Football Coaches, Football Writers, Walter Camp, ESPN.com, SI.com, and CBSSportsline.com All-American first teams. Leinart was named the "Sportsman of the Year" by *The Sporting News*.

Reggie was USC's team MVP (for the second consecutive year) and won USC Player of the Game versus Notre Dame, co–Player of the Game versus UCLA, Co-Lifter and Jack Oakie "Rise and Shine" (for longest run) awards.

Bush, Leinart, Jarrett, and Lutui were named to the Football Coaches All-American first team. That made 139 Trojan All-American first teamers. It was the first year since 1931 (and only the second time ever) that USC has had four offensive players named to an All-American first team.

Leinart became just the second USC player ever to be a three-time All-American first teamer, joining linebacker Richard Wood (1972–1974).

Entering 2006, Carroll was 54–10 in five seasons, but wait. Of those ten losses, only one was by more than seven points (27–16 at Notre Dame in 2001). Eight of them were on the road or in a bowl game. In 2001 he lost to Kansas State (home, 10–6), Oregon (road, 24–22), Stanford (home, 21–16), Washington (road, 27–24), and Utah (Las Vegas Bowl, 10–6).

In 2002 he lost to Kansas State (road, 27–20) and Washington State (road, 30–27 in overtime). In 2003 he lost to California (road, 34–31 in three overtimes). In 2006, he lost to Texas (Rose Bowl, 41–38). That is ten losses by a total of forty-five points. Take away the Notre Dame defeat and it is nine losses by thirty-four, an average of less than four points per loss!

In other words, with luck and a few good bounces, Pete Carroll's record could have been 63–1. If so, he could have had four or five national championships, not two. If his 2001 team had won all those close games, finishing 10–1 at the end of the regular season, they might have gotten the nod over once-beaten Nebraska to play against Miami in the BCS Rose Bowl. Once-beaten Oregon was barely edged out.

In 2002, both losses were by the slimmest of margins, so obviously if Troy were 12–0 (with the toughest schedule in the nation that year), they would have finished ahead of both Miami and Ohio State in the BCS standings going in to the Fiesta Bowl.

In 2003, once-beaten USC was ranked number one by the Associated Press anyway in a season with no unbeatens. The 2006 Rose Bowl loss spoke for itself. Nevertheless, all the "close but no cigar" scenarios could not overshadow reality. Reality, as of January 2006, was that despite their accomplishments, and despite coming close by the slimmest of margins, Carroll and USC had to look at Knute Rockne's Irish of the 1920s, Frank Leahy's Notre Dame teams of the 1940s, and Bud Wilkinson's record at

Oklahoma in the 1950s, and face the fact that they still had work to do.

The fact that Rockne (with the exception of the 1925 Rose Bowl win over Stanford) and Leahy had done it without the hassle of an end-of-the-season bowl challenge, while Wilkinson's Sooners were on probation when they reeled off forty-seven straight, did not assuage Trojan pain. The BCS system, in place since 1998, had created a higher standard. In the past, the number one Trojans would have annihilated Big 10 champion Penn State in the Rose Bowl, while Texas would have beaten some lesser light in the Cotton Bowl, or the Orange Bowl, then offered indignation at the voters' anointing Southern California with their twelfth national championship instead of earning their third (1963, 1969, 2005) fair and square.

While USC could not yet establish clear evidence that they were the best two-year, three-year, short-term, and single-decade dynasty ever, they were clearly contenders. They were now tied with Notre Dame for the most national championships and Heisman winners, with more success and momentum in the modern era than the other great traditions. The failure to close the deal at Pasadena had denied them clear claim to have surpassed all other collegiate records, but the edge was still theirs with plenty of optimism that the next years would provide further opportunity to get those bragging rights.

Any talk of the NFL was dispelled when Carroll signed a long-term contract extension, beginning with the 2006 season. The 2006 Army High School All-Star Game featured more players committed to USC than any other school.

In February 2006, USC landed the number one recruiting class in the country for the fourth straight year (2003–2006). That did not include Jimmy Clausen of Oaks Christian in Thousand Oaks (an L.A. suburb), the younger brother of former Tennessee quarterback Casey Clausen. A 2005 junior, Clausen was thought to be the nation's finest high school player as an underclassman. Reports that he had verbally committed to USC were unconfirmed, but inside sources reported that it was between Southern California and Notre Dame.

■　■　■

It was the prediction of this author that the 2006 Rose Bowl will go down in history as the greatest collegiate football game in history, a game that will mark the times in a manner similar to the 1979 Larry Bird–Magic Johnson Indiana State–Michigan State NCAA basketball title game. The 2005 Trojans were a collection of talent that probably will never be seen, together on one team, in our lifetimes, or at least in our generation. A game featuring the college talents of Leinart, Bush, White & Co. versus a player of Vince Young's attributes, with both teams and all their stars playing at the top of their respective games, is a sports rarity. The prediction here is that, just as Bird and Johnson defined pro basketball in the 1980s after their Final Four matchup, so too will the players from USC and Texas define the NFL over the next decade. 2004–2005 will be remembered as a true Golden Age of college football; the '05 season may well be the best of all time, and this will carry over. Future matches or teammate combinations involving Leinart versus Young, or Bush teamed with Young, or White and Carson Palmer . . . the ghosts of the '06 Rose Bowl will reverberate on the sports landscape for years to come!

TEAM OF THE CENTURIES

College football's all-time greatest dynasty

Entering the 2006 season, the Trojans found themselves in more or less a "tie" with Notre Dame as the greatest of all collegiate football traditions, having equaled the Irish with eleven national championships and seven Heisman Trophies each.

In the 2006 NFL Draft, Reggie Bush was selected number two overall by New Orleans. Two Trojans went among the first ten picks, with Matt Leinart going to Arizona. With the selection of Texas's Vince Young and Michael Huff also among the top ten, that meant four of the top ten had competed against each other in Pasadena. Eleven Trojans were selected in the draft (the school record is fifteen, in 1953). LenDale White's spring injury dropped him to the second round, but the draft still left USC with 67 first round selections, the most of any program in history (with seven of those having played for Carroll).

Almost any college football program in America would consider the next four seasons (2006–2009) wildly successful. There are no actual complaints at USC, but despite monumental achievements, the Trojans were ever-so-slightly disappointing. Thus are the expectations at Troy.

At the end of the 2009 season, however, USC under Pete Carroll had firmly established themselves as the "team of the decade." Close contenders were Florida and Texas, but neither put together the body of work—Heismans, BCS records—quite matching Southern California's 34-game winning streak (2003–2006), three Heismans, 6–1 BCS mark, and two national titles between 2000 and 2009.

Arguably, this was the fourth time (1930s, 1960s, 1970s, 2000s) USC could lay claim to such a "team of the decade" title. On top of that, USC had the best record in the 1920s. Notre Dame could claim to be the best team in two decades (1920s, 1940s). Alabama would certainly argue that they were the best team in three decades USC claims: the 1930s, 1960s, and 1970s. For any number of legitimate reasons Southern California rebuffs those claims.

In 2006 everything seemed to be on track under new quarterback John David Booty. An upset loss at Oregon State failed to derail Troy's inexorable advance to Carroll's third national title. After demolishing Notre Dame, all USC needed was to beat a mediocre UCLA squad, a program that had not defeated them since 1998, in order to advance to the BCS title game. Few games in the history of sport have been as puzzling as the Trojans' flat 13–9 loss at the Rose Bowl that December afternoon. Florida advanced in their place. In truth nobody, including USC, would have beaten the Gators the way they played in destroying an out-manned Ohio State team that had no business being there. However, the Buckeyes would have fallen hard to USC had the Trojans only beaten the Bruins, but alas it was not to be.

Instead, USC wrapped up an 11–2 record and number four ranking with an impressive 32–18 Rose Bowl victory over a one-loss Michigan juggernaut ranked third coming in. Wide receivers Dwayne Jarrett and Steve Smith made All-American along with offensive tackle Sam Baker, center Ryan Kalil, and defensive tackle Sedrick Ellis.

The 2007 season was still more puzzling. Losses to Stanford and Oregon seemingly eliminated Troy from both Rose Bowl and national championship contention, except that everybody else in the country lost, too. Somehow, Ohio State "earned" a second straight trip to the BCS title game, but there remains no logical reason why two-loss Louisiana State was chosen ahead of the Trojans to oppose them. It was the same as the previous season, with LSU running roughshod over the Buckeyes, leaving little doubt that had USC gone to New Orleans instead, they too would have had their way with the Big 10 pretenders.

Again, the Rose Bowl was a beautiful consolation prize, with USC tying the all-time record for points in the hallowed game, blowing Illinois out by 49–17. Ellis, tight end Fred Davis (the Mackey Award winner), linebacker Keith Rivers, and safety Taylor Mays all made first team All-American. A look back at their 11–2 mark and number two final ranking leaves frustration, however. Their record was as good as number one LSU. Indeed, there was nothing to differentiate the Tigers from the Trojans, and most pundits felt that USC would have beaten them, but LSU wore ultimate glory.

It was more of the same the next season. Indeed, the 2008 Trojans were one of the greatest teams in college football history, but a single slip-up denied them the national title. USC threw three shutouts and in five other games allowed a single score. Pundits called them the greatest defensive team of all time. Certainly they were the best since the 1932 Trojans achieved *eight shutouts*.

A look at their scores results in nothing less than astonishment. The succession of blowouts, week after week after week, approaches the dominance of the 2002, 2003, 2004, and even 2005 dynasties. Joe Paterno brought once-beaten Big 10 champion Penn State to the Rose Bowl, and Southern California destroyed them in the manner of a professional squad taking care of a Division III program. In the second half USC's first round prospects eased up a bit to avoid injury, mercifully allowing Penn State to score a few times and avoid utter embarrassment, but what Carroll's team did to Paterno's more resembled Rome salting Carthage.

Nevertheless, there was frustration again. Just as LSU was not better and probably worse than USC in 2007, one-loss Florida had absolutely no legitimate reason to be in the BCS title game over USC in 2008. Even more galling was the choice of Oklahoma, a program USC was so far superior to as to be a joke if not for the Sooners' somehow sneaking past them. When Florida destroyed Oklahoma, certain truths were confirmed. For one, a good idea might have been for Congress to disallow Oklahoma from ever being in another BCS bowl game, so abysmal had they been throughout the decade. The other truth was that Tim Tebow and Florida were impressive in beating the Sooners, but the prospect that they would have beaten the Trojans more resembled no prospect at all! The USC team that beat Penn State on January 1, 2009, was not going to lose . . . to anybody, but they had to settle for a number two final ranking.

Mark Sanchez had a dominant junior season and one of the greatest Rose Bowl performances ever, orchestrating the 38–24 lambasting of the Nittany Lions. Rey Maualuga, Brian Cushing, and Clay Matthews Jr. formed the greatest linebacker corp anybody ever saw. Maualuga, Cushing, and Taylor Mays were first team All-Americans. Sanchez, who probably would have won the 2009 Heisman Trophy had he returned, was drafted in the first round (Jets) along with Cushing (Texans) and Matthews (Packers). An incredible eleven Trojans were drafted.

Between 2002 and 2008, Pete Carroll's team compiled a record of 82–8. This was one better than Miami's 81–9 mark between 1985 and 1993. Since the inception of the modern era in 1919 (after World War I ended), this was the "second best" 90-game mark. Between 1947 and 1955, Bud Wilkinson's Oklahoma Sooners were 82–6–2. However, in those days there was no overtime. Two of USC's losses (Washington State, 2002; California, 2003) had come in overtime, meaning that USC had, in effect, "tied" OU for the best 90-game mark.

Even more insane was the fact that until the seventh game of the 2009 season, Pete Carroll had lost only once (Notre Dame, 27–16 in 2001) by more than a touchdown. As mentioned, two defeats had come in overtime. In other words, but for a few good bounces and lucky breaks, between 2001 and game seven of the 2009 season, the Southern California Trojans easily could have been *108–1 with six or seven national championships!* Between game eight (2001) and game seven (2009), the Trojans could have been undefeated. Between 2001 and 2008, Carroll never lost in November. Between 2002 and 2008, his teams lost only one game at home. USC also surpassed the benchmark all-time .700 winning percentage in its history.

For the better part of seven years, a rumor had swirled around college football circles, and in 2009 it was confirmed. The rumor was that Pete Carroll's Trojans were human beings. The loss of so many All-Americans and first round draftees finally caught up to them. Freshman quarterback Matt Barkley, a two-time *Parade* National High School Player of the Year at Mater Dei, led the team to a 9–4 record with a victory over Boston College in the Emerald Bowl. The possibility that he will follow in Carson Palmer's, Matt Leinart's, and Mark Sanchez's footsteps—a Heisman, a first round draft pick—remains a high probability. USC defeated Notre Dame for the eighth straight time, and UCLA for the tenth time in eleven years. Whether the departure of legendary coach Pete Carroll to the NFL will result in a smooth transition, as did the move from John McKay to John Robinson in 1976, or whether troubles lie ahead, similar to Robinson's controversial move to the NFL followed by the Ted Tollner years, remains to be seen.

New coach Lane Kiffin is a bright young mind with the potential to achieve great things. Entering the 2010 season, USC has compiled a record that clearly demonstrates that they are college football's all-time greatest dynasty. Notre Dame, Alabama, Oklahoma, Ohio State, Nebraska, Texas, Miami, Michigan, and Penn State all have remarkable traditions, but in adding everything up USC's dominance is impossible to deny. The records that determine their lofty all-time number one ranking include the following:

Legacy: national championships, Heisman Trophies

- 11 national championships (1st; tied with Notre Dame, modern era, 1919–2009)
- 7 Heisman Trophy winners (1st; tied with Notre Dame, Ohio State)
- 6 Heisman Trophy teammates: White '79/Allen '81; Palmer '02/Leinart '04; Leinart '04/Bush '05 (1st, tied with Notre Dame)
- 17 number one final rankings, all services (2nd; Michigan 1st, 22)
- 5 UPI national championships (1st; tied with Oklahoma, Alabama)
- AP repeat national champions, 2003–2004 (1st; tied with 10 teams)
- AP number one ranking, pre-season poll to final ranking, 2004 (1st; tied with Florida State, 1999)
- AP number one ranking, regular season poll to final ranking, 1972 (1st; tied with 6 teams)
- 121 national championships, all sports (1st entering 2009–2010)
- 75 NCAA men's sports championships (1st entering 2009–2010)

Polls

- 90 all-time AP number rankings (1st)
- 33 consecutive AP number one rankings, 2003–2006 (1st; USC, 17 weeks, 1972–1973)
- 688 ranked all-time, AP poll (5th; Michigan 1st, 754)
- 44 times ranked all-time, final AP poll (5th; Michigan 1st, 54)
- 7 consecutive top 5 final AP poll rankings, 2002–2008

Records

- 776 all-time victories (6th; Michigan 1st)
- 776–307–54 all-time record (6th; Michigan 1st)
- 34-game winning streak, 2003–2006 (2nd; Oklahoma 1st, 47, 1953–1957; USC 25, 1931–1933)

- 34-game unbeaten streak, 2003–2006 (5th; California 1st, 50, 1920–1925; USC 28, 1978–1980; 27, 1931–1933; 25, 1931–1933; 23, 1971–1973)
- 7 consecutive 11-win seasons, 2002–2008 (1st)

Bowls

- 32–16 all-time bowl record (1st)
- 32 all-time bowl wins (1st; tied with Alabama)
- 48 all-time bowl games (3rd; Alabama 1st, 57)
- 24–9 all-time Rose Bowl record (1st; best record in any single bowl game)
- 6–1 all-time BCS record (1st)

Individual honors

- 153 all-time All-Americans (3rd; Ohio State 1st, 179 entering 2009)
- 86 all-time consensus All-Americans (2nd; Notre Dame 1st, 96 entering 2009)
- 70 all-time *Playboy* Pre-season All-Americans (1st entering 2009)
- 36 all-time College Football Hall of Famers (2nd entering 2010)

Pro football

- 5 all-time number one pro football draftees (1st; tied with Notre Dame, Alabama)
- 74 all-time first round pro football draftees (1st through 2009 draft)
- 5 first round pro football draftees, 1968 (tied for 2nd; Miami 1st, 6, 2004)
- 15 pro football draftees, 1953 (tied for 2nd with Notre Dame, 1945; Notre Dame 1st, 16, 1946; USC, 14, 1975, 1977; 11, 2009)
- 485 all-time pro football draftees (1st through 2009 draft)
- 414 all-time pro football players, approximate (1st entering 2009)
- 2 AP Pro Football Players of the Year; O.J. Simpson, 1973; Marcus Allen, 1985 (3rd; Notre Dame 1st, 5)
- 14 all-time Pro Football Hall of Famers (1st through 2009)
- 98 all-time Super Bowl players (1st through 2005)
- 45 all-time players on winning Super Bowl teams (1st through 2005)
- 2 all-time Super Bowl MVPs; Lynn Swann, 1975; Marcus Allen, 1984 (4th; Alabama, Michigan, Notre Dame tied for 1st, 3 entering 2009)
- 198 all-time Pro Bowl players (1st through 2005)

Traditions

- 1972 Trojans, greatest team of all time
- "Team of the Decade" (1930, 1960s, 1970s, 2000s).
- All-time greatest 20-year dynasty, 1962–1981
- Matt Leinart, greatest college player of all time
- Anthony Davis, greatest single-game individual performance of all time, 1972 versus Notre Dame

- USC 55, Oklahoma 24, 2005 BCS Orange Bowl; greatest single-game team performance of all time
- Texas 41, USC 38, 2006 BCS Rose Bowl; greatest game of all time
- Collegiate Athletic Program of the 20th Century

Notre Dame, USC's traditional ultra-rival both on the field every year and in the overall role of college football titan, has fallen too far of late to hold off USC. In recent years the Irish set an NCAA record for most consecutive bowl defeats with nine (1994–2006), fell to the Trojans every season from 2002 to 2009 (by mostly lopsided margins), and have dealt with continued turmoil. Of their eleven national titles, seven came in years in which they did not even play in a bowl game. USC's titles invariably came with victory in the Rose Bowl over a national powerhouse like Woody Hayes and Ohio State or Bo Schembechler and Michigan, or in the 2005 BCS Orange Bowl over Oklahoma. None came with the taint of illegitimacy, as is the case with two of Alabama's so-called "national titles." The Crimson Tide call themselves the champions of 1964 despite losing to Texas in the Orange Bowl, and the champions of 1973 despite losing to Notre Dame in the Sugar Bowl.

Notre Dame continues to hold off Alabama, probably the third greatest tradition, although the Crimson Tide soared in the late 2000s. However, a number of factors work against 'Bama, not the least being the fact that when Notre Dame set the record for most consecutive bowl losses, it was Alabama's "record" they broke (under Bear Bryant from the late 1960s to the mid-1970s).

For both of these programs, a comparison with USC's incredible 32–16 bowl record, set mostly against the nation's best competition in the Rose Bowl, effectively renders all argument against them lacking in weight or substance.

In addition, USC's athletic department boasts the most national championships overall, including the most in baseball (12), track (26), and tennis (17). In 2000, the department was named "Collegiate Athletic Department of the Century" while Rod Dedeaux was voted "College Baseball Coach of the Century" (1999). The baseball Trojans claim the most big leaguers (90 entering 2005), the most first-round draft picks, the most drafted players, the most professional players, the most World Series players, the most All-Stars, the most Cy Young winners (nine), and the most Rookies of the Year (three). USC also shares the record with UCLA for the most Olympians and the most medallists.

If Matt Barkley can lead USC to their twelfth national championship and earn the school's eighth Heisman Trophy, the question as to whether USC indeed is "number one" will surely be settled. In the meantime, the battle for collegiate football supremacy between Southern California, Notre Dame, Alabama, Oklahoma, Miami, Texas, and the other fabulous traditions will continue to thrill the fans and loyal alumni supporters throughout the twenty-first century. May God bless America, and may the Trojans continue . . . to *"Fight On!"*

BIBLIOGRAPHY

Adams, Bruce. "Cal sees the old USC swagger." *San Francisco Chronicle*, November 13, 2005.

Adande, J. A. "L.A. gets a double treat with Bush and James." *Los Angeles Times*, December 4, 2005.

———. "Return could mean back-to-back-to-back." *Los Angeles Times*, January 5, 2005.

Albee, Dave. "Keeping his lust for life." *Marin Independent Journal*, August 25, 2004.

———. "Coach T handed Carroll first gig." *Marin Independent Journal*, November 11, 2005.

Associated Press. "#1 USC 63, Hawaii 17." September 4, 2005.

———. "USC gets back to normal—scores 51 points." October 23, 2005.

———. "USC defense finally flexes its muscle." October 30, 2005.

Athlon Sports College Football. "Best of 2005." September 9, 2005, 10.

Barra, Allen. *The Last Coach: A Life of Paul "Bear" Bryant*. New York. W.W. Norton & Company, 2005.

Baum, Bob. "Trojans turn the tide on second-half surge." Associated Press, October 2, 2005.

Bisheff, Steve. *Orange County Register*.

Bolch, Ben. "Leinart will take his time." *Los Angeles Times*, January 6, 2005.

———. "For Carroll, Dai is a family affair." *Los Angeles Times*, December 4, 2005.

Boyles, Bob, and Paul Guido. *50 Years of College Football*. Wilmington, Del.: Sideline Communications, 2005.

Branch, John. "Culture, Football Will Battle when Valley Takes on L.A." *New York Times*, November 18, 2005.

Brennan, Christine. "Trojans render Sugar Bowl meaningless." *USA TODAY*, January 2, 2004.

———. "No need for playoff this time." *USA TODAY*, January 5, 2005.

Carey, Jack. "Trojans don't horse around." *USA TODAY*, January 5, 2005.

Chavez, Kevin. "No need for nostalgia for Troy." *San Gabriel Valley News*, January 6, 2005.

Chengelis, Angelique. "USC defense overwhelms Michigan." *The Detroit News*, January 2, 2004.

Chronicle News Services. "Arizona makes USC work for its fifth victory." *San Francisco Chronicle*, October 9, 2005.

Clary, Jack. *College Football's Great Dynasties: USC*. Popular Culture Ink, 1991.

Cole, Gary. "*Playboy's* 2004 Pigskin Preview." *Playboy*, September 2004, 130.

———. "'05 *Playboy's* Pigskin Preview." *Playboy*, September 2005.

Collier, Gene. "Mitchell's tale still twisting." *Pittsburgh Post-Gazette*. September 2, 2004.

Collin, Phil. "Trojans go Carrolling." *The Daily Breeze*, December 20, 2000.

Coyne, Tom. "Notre Dame hopes to rewrite the plot against USC." Associated Press, October 15, 2005.

Curtis, Jake. "USC has offense, schedule to pull off unprecedented feat." *San Francisco Chronicle*, September 1, 2005.

———. "These teams pass—or fail." *San Francisco Chronicle*, September 1, 2005.

———. "Pluck, luck benefit lion-hearted Leinart." *San Francisco Chronicle*, October 17, 2005.

———. "Diverse Trojan offense arguably the best ever." *San Francisco Chronicle*, November 3, 2005.

Dalton, Dennis. *Power Over People: Classical and Modern Political Theory*. Recorded course from Barnard College at Columbia University, New York. Available at www.teach12.com.

Dettlinger, Chet, and Jeff Prugh. *The List*. Atlanta: Philmay Enterprises, 1984.

Dilbeck, Steve. "Trojans' undefeated season leaves no doubt." *Los Angeles Daily News*, January 5, 2005.

Dohn, Brian. "Overshadowing Leinart?" *Long Beach Press-Telegram*, December 2, 2005.

DuFresne, Chris. "Turnovers leave Sooners a shade of crimson." *Los Angeles Times*, January 5, 2005.

———. "BCS obsessed." *Los Angeles Times*, January 5, 2005.

———. "With simple formula and fresh approach, Carroll builds a potential Trojan dynasty." *Los Angeles Times*, January 6, 2005.

———. "Weis leading a rivalry revival." *Los Angeles Times*, October 16, 2005.

———. "Getting to the point." *Los Angeles Times*, December 1, 2005.

———. "Putting the 'C' back in the BCS." *Los Angeles Times*, December 5, 2005.

———. "Rose Bowl hype balloon could burst on game day." *Los Angeles Times*, December 5, 2005.

Dunnavant, Keith. *Coach: Life of Paul "Bear" Bryant*. New York: Simon & Schuster, 1996.

Dwyre, Bill. "More like powdered blue." *Los Angeles Times*, December 4, 2005.

Elliott, Helene. "Trojans put up tough barricade to stop Sooners." *Los Angeles Times*, January 5, 2005.

Farmer, Sam. "49ers to go after Carroll." *Los Angeles Times*, January 6, 2005.

Feldman, Bruce. "Reaction time." *ESPN the Magazine*, August 30, 2004.

———."Wanna see that again?" *ESPN the Magazine*, August 29, 2005.

Fischer, Leo. *Chicago American*, September 29, 1968.

Fittipaldo, Ray. "Experts: USC could be among greatest teams." *Pittsburgh Post-Gazette*, October 26, 2005.

Florence, Mal. *The Heritage of Troy*. JCP Corp, 1980.

Friend, Tom. "Finishing school." *ESPN the Magazine*, July 18, 2005.

Gardiner, Andy. "Tennessee, Nebraska top signing charts." *USA TODAY*, February 3, 2005.

Groom, Winston. *The Crimson Tide: An Illustrated History of Football at the University of Alabama*. Tuscaloosa: University of Alabama Press, 2000.

Hammerwold, Walter. "BCS finally delivers the goods." *Long Beach Press-Telegram*, December 5, 2005.

Harmonson, Todd. "Trojans run hog wild all night." *Orange County Register*, September 18, 2005.

———. "Two heads better for Trojans." *Orange County Register*, December 2, 2005.

———. "BCS will have its perfect game." *Orange County Register*, December 5, 2005.

Harris, Beth. "USC's focus: Limit mistakes." Associated Press, October 10, 2005.

Hayes, Matt. "Trouble for the Trojans." *The Sporting News*, October 21, 2005.

Himmelberg, Michele. "A workplace divided." *Orange County Register*, December 2, 2005.

Hisermam, Mike. "USC's win means a bit of a loss for business." *Los Angeles Times*, December 4, 2005.

Hoffarth, Tom. "L.A. deprived by early start." *Los Angeles Daily News*, January 5, 2005.

Jares, Joe, and John Robinson. *Conquest*.

Katz, Fred. *The Glory of Notre Dame*. Bartholomey House.

Keisser, Bob. "Bam's impact not forgotten." *Long Beach Press-Telegram*, September 12, 2005.

———. "It's an old-school drubbing." *Long Beach Press-Telegram*, December 4, 2005.

Klein, Gary. "Conquest." *Los Angeles Times*, January 5, 2005.

———. "Cardinal and bold." *Los Angeles Times*, January 5, 2005.

———. "USC does the grunt work with ease." *Los Angeles Times*, September 18, 2005.

———. "Leinart's sneak peak." *Los Angeles Times*, October 16, 2005.

———. "Chart breakers." *Los Angeles Times*, December 2, 2005.

———. "Trojans go on a tear." *Los Angeles Times*, December 4, 2005.

Knapp. Gwen. "Finally, BCS gets its 'Magic' moment." *San Francisco Chronicle*, December 6, 2005.

Krikorian, Doug. "Pundits way off on USC." *Long Beach Press-Telegram*, January 6, 2005.

———. "Dennis waiting for his turn." *Long Beach Press-Telegram*, December 1, 2005.

———. "Trojans leave the Bruins Bushed." *Long Beach Press-Telegram*, December 4, 2005.

LeBatard, Dan. "The view from . . . Miami." *Miami Herald*, January 5, 2005.

Los Angeles Daily News. A Tradition Restored. Champagne, Ill.: Sports Publishing, 2003.

McCready, Neal. "Cunningham had impact on 'Bama football." *Mobile Press-Register*, August 2003.

McKay, John, with Jim Perry. *McKay: A Coach's Story*. New York: Atheneum, 1974.

Michaels, Vicki. "Southern Cal loaded for another shot." *USA TODAY*, January 2, 2004.

Modesti, Kevin. "Routing Oklahoma only the start for USC?" *Los Angeles Daily News*, January 5, 2005.

THE USC TROJANS

——. "Everything went right on this night." *Los Angeles Daily News*, January 6, 2005.

Moore, Leon. "Carroll re-energizes Trojans." *USA TODAY*, December 31, 2003.

——. "USC strikes first in title race." *USA TODAY*, January 2, 2004.

——. "Senior Colbert turns in career day." *USA TODAY*, January 2, 2004.

——. "Junior Leinart easily junks Heisman jinx." *USA TODAY*, January 5, 2005.

——. "Carroll's Trojans have talent to maintain prime position." *USA TODAY*, January 5, 2005.

Moran, Malcolm. "Dream season ends with nightmare." *USA TODAY*, January 5, 2005.

——. "Leinart cements legend with late heroics." *USA TODAY*, October 17, 2005.

Murphy, Austin. "Without a doubt." *Sports Illustrated*, January 10, 2005.

——. "Danger is his game." *Sports Illustrated*, August 15, 2005.

——. "College football 2005." *Sports Illustrated*, August 15, 2005.

——. "Can anyone beat USC?" *Sports Illustrated*, October 17, 2005.

——. "Fantastic finishes." *Sports Illustrated*, October 24, 2005.

Murray, Jim. *Los Angeles Times*, November 19, 1967.

——. "Hatred shut out as Alabama finally joins the Union." *Los Angeles Times*, September 13, 1970.

Nadel, John. "USC steamrolls Stanford." Associated Press, November 6, 2005.

Newhouse, Dave. "Leinart outshines Bears as USC cruises to victory." *Oakland Tribune*, November 13, 2005.

Norwood, Robyn. "Spotted fever." *Los Angeles Times*, December 3, 2005.

——. "Trojan defense gives the Bruins no shot." *Los Angeles Times*, December 4, 2005.

Nyiri, Alan. *The Heritage of USC*. Los Angeles: University of Southern California, 1999.

Penner, Mike. "There are no big winners in ABC booth." *Los Angeles Times*, January 5, 2005.

Perry, Jim. "USC loses one of its legends with the death of McKay." *Trojan Tail*, 2001.

——. "Alabama goes black 'n' white." *Los Angeles Herald-Examiner*, September 11, 1971.

Peterson, Anne M. "Oregon overwhelmed by USC in second half." Associated Press, September 25, 2005.

Pierson, Don. *The Trojans: Southern California Football*. Chicago: Henry Regnery, 1974.

Plaschke, Bill. "It's crystal clear—no one can touch this USC team." *Los Angeles Times*, January 5, 2005.

——. "Good from the word 'go.'" *Los Angeles Times*, October 16, 2005.

——. "In run-up to a vote, Bush surely makes his case." *Los Angeles Times*, December 4, 2005.

Pool, Bob. "Rah, rah—boo, hiss." *Los Angeles Times*, December 3, 2005.

Prugh, Jeff. "Trojans fall on Alabama . . ." *Los Angeles Times*, September 13, 1970.

——. "Two black students had enrolled before Wallace showdown." *Los Angeles Times*, June 11, 1978.

——. Excerpt from *The Herschel Walker Story*. Fawcett, 1983.

——. "George Wallace was America's merchant of venom." *Marin Independent Journal*, September 15, 1998.

——. "Anger boiled within Gerald Ford before this football game." *Marin Independent Journal*, August 12, 1999.

Rappoport, Ken. *The Trojans: A Story of Southern California Football*. Huntsville, Ala.: Strode Publishers, 1974.

Ratto, Ray. "USC is the new Notre Dame; the new 'America's Team.'" *San Francisco Chronicle*, October 16, 2005.

Russo, Ralph. "Bush runs off with Heisman Trophy." Associated Press, December 11, 2005.

Schrader, Loel. *Long Beach Press-Telegram*.

Schulman, Henry. "Astros win time to watch USC." *San Francisco Chronicle*, October 16, 2005.

——. www.theuscreport.com.

Simers, T. J. "The Trojans owe it all to good ol' Uncle Pete." *Los Angeles Times*, January 5, 2005.

Sports Illustrated. "Showdown in L.A." November 17, 1967.

——. "USC Trojans." November 17, 1967.

Springer, Steve, and Michael Arkush. *60 Years of USC-UCLA Football*. Stamford, Conn.: Longmeadow Press, 1991.

Stanford Daily. "Putting game in Perspective." October 6, 1972.

Stewart, Larry. "Peete was looking for a special delivery." *Los Angeles Times*, December 1, 2005.

Taylor, Phil. "The Tide gets rolled." *Sports Illustrated*, September 27, 2004.

Thamel, Peter. "Leinart's goal-line dive gives No. 1 USC win in thriller." *New York Times*, October 16, 2005.

Travers, Steven. "When legends played." *StreetZebra*, September 1999. Available at www.streetzebra.com.

———. "Petros Papadakis: USC's player of the month." *StreetZebra*, October 1999.

———. "Is it too early to hype Palmer for the Heisman?" *StreetZebra*, September 2000.

———. "Villa Park wins rivalry game." *Los Angeles Times*, September 25, 2000.

———. "It wasn't a football game, it was a sighting." *StreetZebra*, November 2000. Available at www.streetzebra.com.

———. "Legend: A conversation with John McKay." *StreetZebra*, March 2000. Available at www.streetzebra.com.

———. "Rich McKay." *StreetZebra*, April 2000. Available at www.streetzebra.com.

———. "The eternal Trojan." *StreetZebra*, September 2000. Available at www.streetzebra.com.

———. "The tradition of Troy." *StreetZebra*, 2001.

———. "An unsung hero." *San Francisco Examiner*, May 1, 2001.

———. "He was a legend of the old school variety." *StreetZebra*, June 2001.

———. *Barry Bonds: Baseball's Superman*. Champaign, Ill.: Sports Publishing, 2002.

———. "Orange Countification: The true story of how the GOP helped the South rise again." Excerpted from *September 1970: One Night, Two Teams, and the Game that Changed a Nation*. Lanham, MD: Rowman & Littlefield, forthcoming.

———. *God's Country: A Conservative, Christian Worldview of How History Formed the United States Empire and America's Manifest Destiny For the Twenty-first Century*. Forthcoming.

Underwood, John. "A big sigh of relief in Pasadena." *Sports Illustrated*, January 8, 1963.

USA TODAY. "Shake-up in college poll." October 17, 2005.

Walsh, Bill. "Coaching Key to USC's Success." *Los Angeles Times*, January 5, 2005.

Wharton, David. "USC is better than OK for title win." *Los Angeles Times*, January 5, 2005.

———. "Leinart played conquest in clutch." *Los Angeles Times*, October 16, 2005.

———. "USC bowls over UCLA." *Los Angeles Times*, December 4, 2005.

Wharton, David, and Gary Klein. *Conquest: Pete Carroll and the Trojans' Climb to the Top of the College Football Mountain*. Chicago: Triumph Books, 2005.

Whicker, Mark. "Many questions abound about USC's defense, but does it matter?" *Orange County Register*, September 18, 2005.

———. "Perfect touch." *Orange County Register*, December 2, 2005.

White, Lonnie. *UCLA vs. USC. 75 Years of the Greatest Rivalry in Sports*. Los Angeles: Los Angeles Times Books, 2004.

———. "Bruins outgrow terrible twos." *Los Angeles Times*, December 1, 2005.

———. "Bush run over Bruins' defense." *Los Angeles Times*, December 4, 2005.

Whiteside, Kelly. "Southern Cal could be just warming up." *USA TODAY*, January 5, 2005.

Wieberg, Steve. "What USA's top prep players are thinking." *USA TODAY*, December 31, 2003.

Witz, Billy. "Soon after early lead, OU fell apart." *Los Angeles Daily News*, January 5, 2005.

Wojciechowski, Gene. "USC setting standard for football dominance." ESPN.com (http://sports.espn.go.com/espn/columns/story?columnist=wojciechowski_gene&i%20d=2249925%3E%20&id=2249925), December 6, 2005.

Wolf, Scott. "It's unanimous: USC captures title in rout." *Los Angeles Daily News*, January 5, 2005.

———. "Leinart mum about his future." *Los Angeles Daily News*, January 5, 2005.

———. "Analysis: Can Trojans wins a third title in a row?" *Long Beach Press-Telegram*, January 6, 2005.

———. "USC future is bright if Carroll stays." *Los Angeles Daily News*, January 6, 2005.

———. "Route 66 to Pasadena." *Long Beach Press-Telegram*, December 4, 2005.

Zakaria, Fareed. *The Future of Freedom: Illiberal Democracy at Home and Abroad*. New York: W. W. Norton & Company, 2003.

Zimmerman, Paul. "Parity between Bruins and Troy." *Los Angeles Times*, December 10, 1939.

———. *Los Angeles Times*, November 19, 1967.

Websites

www.aaregistry.com

www.cfrc.com/Archives/Top_Programs_2004.htm

www.lhgames.com

www.msnbc.com

www.rolltide.com

www.trojanreport.com

www.uscfootball.blogspot.com

www.usctrojans.com

www.wearesc.com

Additional DVD

The History of USC Football. Produced and directed by Roger Springfield, Riverbank, Calif.: Warner Home Video, 2006.

Additional Video

History of Notre Dame Football.

Trojan Video Gold. Narrated by Tom Kelly. Los Angeles, Calif.: Tom Kelly Productions, 1987.

Additional documentaries

Songs of Our Success. Hosted by Tony McEwen, 2003.

Sports Century. Bristol, Conn.: ESPN, 2001–2006.

Miscellaneous

Best Damn Sports Show Period. Los Angeles, Calif.: Fox Sports, 2004–2006.

The Jim Rome Show. Sherman Oaks, Calif.: Premiere Radio Networks, 2003–2006.

Rome Is Burning. Bristol, Conn.: ESPN 2004–2006.

Around the Horn. Bristol, Conn.: ESPN, 2003–2006.

Pardon the Interruption. Bristol, Conn.: ESPN, 2003–2006

APPENDIX: ALL-TIME GREATEST COLLEGE FOOTBALL TEAMS

All-Time Top 25

1. Southern California Trojans
2. Notre Dame Fighting Irish
3. Alabama Crimson Tide
4. Oklahoma Sooners
5. Ohio State Buckeyes
6. Nebraska Cornhuskers
7. Miami Hurricanes
8. Texas Longhorns
9. Michigan Wolverines
10. Penn State Nittany Lions
11. Florida State Seminoles
12. Tennessee Volunteers
13. Florida Gators
14. Louisiana State Tigers
15. Auburn Tigers
16. Georgia Bulldogs
17. UCLA Bruins
18. Pittsburgh Panthers
19. Minnesota Golden Gophers
20. California Golden Bears
21. Army Black Knights
22. Washington Huskies
23. Michigan State Spartans
24. Stanford Indians/Cardinal
25. Georgia Tech Yellow Jackets

Greatest Single-Season Teams

1. 1972 Southern California Trojans
2. 1995 Nebraska Cornhuskers
3. 2004 Southern California Trojans
4. 2005 Texas Longhorns
5. 1947 Notre Dame Fighting Irish
6. 1971 Nebraska Cornhuskers
7. 2001 Miami Hurricans
8. 1945 Army Cadets
9. 1979 Alabama Crimson Tide
10. 1956 Oklahoma Sooners
11. 1999 Florida State Seminoles
12. 1987 Miami Hurricans
13. 1968 Ohio State Buckeyes
14. 1986 Penn State Nittany Lions
15. 1988 Notre Dame Fighting Irish
16. 1969 Texas Longhorns
17. 1932 Southern California Trojans
18. 1920 California Golden Bears
19. 1948 Michigan Wolverines
20. 1973 Notre Dame Fighting Irish
21. 1991 Washington Huskies
22. 1928 Southern California Trojans
23. 1924 Notre Dame Fighting Irish
24. 1962 Southern California Trojans
25. 1992 Alabama Crimson Tide
26. 2000 Oklahoma Sooners
27. 1966 Notre Dame Fighting Irish
28. 1976 Pittsburgh Panthers
29. 2009 Alabama Crimson Tide
30. 1934 Alabama Crimson Tide
31. 1901 Michigan Wolverines
32. 1917 Georgia Tech Yellow Jackets
33. 1929 Notre Dame Fighting Irish
34. 1930 Alabama Crimson Tide
35. 1936 Minnesota Golden Gophers
36. 1944 Army Cadets
37. 1946 Notre Dame Fighting Irish
38. 1985 Oklahoma Sooners
39. 1997 Michigan Wolverines
40. 1997 Nebraska Cornhuskers
41. 1998 Tennessee Volunteers
42. 2002 Ohio State Buckeyes
43. 2003 Southern California Trojans

Greatest Single-Season Teams, Chronological Order

1901 Michigan
1913 Washington
1920 California
1924 Notre Dame
1928 Southern California
1929 Notre Dame
1930 Alabama
1932 Southern California
1934 Alabama
1936 Minnesota
1944 Army
1945 Army
1946 Notre Dame
1947 Notre Dame
1948 Michigan
1956 Oklahoma
1962 Southern California
1966 Notre Dame
1968 Ohio State
1969 Texas
1971 Nebraska
1972 Southern California
1973 Notre Dame
1976 Pittsburgh
1979 Alabama
1985 Oklahoma
1986 Penn State
1987 Miami
1988 Notre Dame
1991 Washington
1992 Alabama
1994 Nebraska

1997 Michigan
1998 Tennessee
1999 Florida State
2000 Oklahoma
2001 Miami
2002 Ohio State
2003 Southern California
2004 Southern California
2005 Texas
2009 Alabama

Top Single-Season Teams of the Decades

19th Century: 1893 Princeton
1900s: 1901 Michigan
1910s: 1913 Washington
1920s: 1924 Notre Dame
1930s: 1932 Southern California
1940s: 1947 Notre Dame
1950s: 1956 Oklahoma
1960s: 1968 Ohio State
1970s: 1972 Southern California
1980s: 1987 Miami
1990s: 1995 Nebraska
2000s: 2004 Southern California

By Decades

1900s: Michigan Wolverines
1910s: California Golden Bears
1920s: Notre Dame Fighting Irish
1930s: Southern California Trojans
1940s: Notre Dame Fighting Irish
1950s: Oklahoma Sooners
1960s: Southern California Trojans
1970s: Southern California Trojans
1980s: Miami Hurricans
1990s: Nebraska Cornhuskers
2000s: Southern California Trojans

Dynasties

1. Southern California under John McKay and John Robinson (1962–1982)
2. Alabama under Bear Bryant (1958–1982)
3. Notre Dame under Knute Rockne (1919–1930)
4. Oklahoma under Bud Wilkinson (1948–1958)
5. Notre Dame under Frank Leahy and Terry Brennan
6. Miami under Howard Schnellenberger, Jimmy

Johnson and Dennis Erickson (1983–1992)
7. Penn State under Joe Paterno (1968–1986)
8. Nebraska under Tom Osborne (1993–2001)
9. Oklahoma under Chuck Fairbanks and Barry Switzer (1971–1988)
10. Southern California's "Thundering Herd" under Howard Jones (1928–1939)
11. Ohio State under Woody Hayes (1968–1995)
12. Notre Dame's "Era of Ara" under Ara Parseghian and Dan Devine (1964–1978)
13. Florida State under Bobby Bowden (1993–2000) 14. Southern California under Pete Carroll (2002–2008)
15. Texas under Darrell Royal (1963–1970)
16. California's "Wonder Teams" under Andy Smith (1920–1924)
17. Army under Red Blaik (1944–1950)
18. Minnesota under Bernie Bierman (1934–1941)
19. Alabama under Wallace Wade and Frank Thomas (1924–1937)
20. Tennessee under Bob Neyland and W.H. Britton (1926–1940)
21. Michigan's "point a minute" teams under Fielding "Hurry Up" Yost (1901–1905)
22. Michigan under Fritz Carlisle (1940–48)
23. Washington under Gil Dobie (1908–1916)

Top Two-Year Periods

1. Nebraska (1994–1995)
2. Southern California (2003–2004)
3. Notre Dame (1946–1947)
4. Army (1944–1945)
5. Nebraska (1970–1971)
6. Southern California (1931–1932)
7. Oklahoma (1955–1956)
8. Alabama (1978–1979)
9. Notre Dame (1929–1930)

10. California (1920–1921)
11. Oklahoma (1974–1975)

Top Three-Year Periods

1. Southern California (2003–2005)
2. Nebraska (1993–1995)
3. Notre Dame (1947–49)
4. Miami (1987–1989)
5. Southern California (1972–1974)
6. Army (1944–1946)
7. Oklahoma (1954–1956)
8. Southern California (1930–1932)
9. Alabama (1977–1979)
10. Minnesota (1934–1936)
11. Nebraska (1995–1997)
12. Oklahoma (1973–1975)
13. Alabama (1964–1966)
14. California (1920–1922)
15. Florida (2006–2008)

Top Five- to Six-Year Periods

1. Nebraska (1993–1997)
2. Notre Dame (1943–1947)
3. Oklahoma (1953–1957)
4. Miami (1987–1992)
5. Southern California (1967–1972)
6. Southern California (1972–1976)
7. Oklahoma (1971–1975)
8. Southern California (1974–1979)
9. California (1920–1924)
10. Notre Dame (1973–1977)
11. Alabama (1961–1966)
12. Penn State (1982–1986)
13. Southern California (1928–1932)
14. Notre Dame (1924–1929)
15. Alabama (1930–1934)
16. Minnesota (1936–1941)
17. Notre Dame (1988–1993)

Top Ten- to Fifteen-Year Periods

1. Oklahoma (1947–1958)
2. Notre Dame (1919–1930)
3. Southern California (1967–1982)
4. Notre Dame (1941–1955)

5. Alabama Crimson (1964–1979)
6. Miami (1983–1994)
7. Southern California
   (1962–1976)
8. Nebraska (1990–2001)
9. Florida State (1988–2000)
10. Southern California
    (1928–1939)
11. Notre Dame (1966–1977)
12. Oklahoma (1971–1985)
13. Penn State (1982–1994)
14. Miami (1987–2001)
15. Southern California
    (1920–1933)
16. Nebraska (1970–1983)
17. Alabama (1924–1934)

Top Twenty- to Twenty-Five-Year Periods

1. Southern California
   (1962–1981)
2. Alabama (1960–1982)
3. Miami (1980–2003)
4. Notre Dame (1964–1989)
5. Ohio State (1954–1975)
6. Notre Dame (1919–1939)
7. Alabama (1924–1945)
8. Nebraska (1970–1995)
9. Nebraska (1980–2001)
10. Florida State (1984–2004)
11. Penn State (1973–98)

"Close But no Cigar" (the best teams not to win national championships)

1913 Army
1913 Auburn
1914 Texas
1915 Oklahoma
1916 Pittsburgh
1919 Texas A&M
1920 Notre Dame
1938 Duke
1939 Tennessee
1942 Georgia
1945 Alabama
1947 Michigan
1947–1951 California
1948 Notre Dame
1952 Georgia Tech
1966 Michigan State
1966 Alabama
1968–1969 Southern California

1968–1969 Penn State
1969–1970 Ohio State
1971 Oklahoma
1973 Michigan
1978 Penn State
1979 Southern California
1979 Ohio State
1983 Nebraska
1986 Miami
1994 Penn State
2003–2004 Oklahoma
2005 Southern California
2006 Ohio State
2009 Texas

Longest Major College Winning Streaks, Modern Era, 1919–2009

47—Oklahoma: Started 10/10/53 at Texas, snapped 11/16/57 vs. Notre Dame

34—USC: Started 10/4/03 at Arizona State, snapped 1/4/06 vs. Texas (Rose Bowl)

34—Miami: Started 9/23/00 at West Virginia, snapped 1/3/03 vs. Ohio State (2 OT Fiesta Bowl)

31—Oklahoma: Started 10/2/48 vs. Texas A&M, snapped 1/1/51 vs. Kentucky (Sugar Bowl)

30—Texas: Started 10/5/68 vs. Oklahoma State, snapped 1/1/71 vs. Notre Dame (Cotton Bowl)

29—Miami: Started 10/27/90 at Texas Tech, snapped 1/1/93 vs. Alabama (Sugar Bowl)

28—Alabama: Started 9/21/91 vs. Georgia, snapped 10/16/93 vs. Tennessee (tie)

28—Alabama: Started 9/30/78 vs. Vanderbilt, snapped 11/1/80 at Mississippi State

28—Oklahoma: Started 10/6/73 vs. Miami, snapped 11/8/75 vs. Kansas

28—Michigan State: Started 10/14/50 vs. William & Mary, snapped 10/24/53 at Purdue

25—*USC: Started 10/3/31 vs. Oregon State, snapped 10/21/33 vs. Oregon (tie)

23—**USC: Started USC 10/23/71, snapped 10/27/73 at Notre Dame

*Extended to 27-game *unbeaten streak*, snapped 11/11/33 by Stanford's "Vow Boys"

***Unbeaten streak* (tied UCLA 11/20/71)

Toledo started a 35-game winning streak on 9/20/69 vs. Villanova, snapped 9/9/72 at Tampa.

A *winning streak* consists of consecutive games, regular season, and bowl games, with no ties or losses.

An *unbeaten streak* consists of consecutive games played without a loss, including ties.

Unbeaten Streaks

California had a 50-game unbeaten streak between 1920 and 1925 that included four ties.

Records are sketchy, but Washington had a 63-game *unbeaten streak*, which included 39 straight wins between 1908 and 1914, but it is not considered the modern record due to rules changes and the playing of rugby instead of football.

Georgia Tech had an *unbeaten streak* of approximately 36 games in the 1950s, probably with at least one tie, which was ended by Notre Dame in 1953.

Penn State had an *unbeaten streak* of approximately 30 games from 1968 to 1970.

Nebraska also had an *unbeaten streak* of 32 games, begun after an opening-game loss vs. USC in 1969, interrupted by a 1970 tie at USC, and ending in a season-opening 1972 loss at UCLA.

Miami had a 36-game *regular season* winning streak from 1985 to 1988, ending at Notre Dame, but they had lost the 1987 Fiesta Bowl to Penn State.

Division III's Mount Union College did not lose a game in four years, reaching a 46-game winning streak.

Mount Dora (Division III) won 54 straight from 1996 to 1999.

In Division II, Hillsdale College posted victories in 34 straight games between 1954 and 1957.

Morgan State had the longest unbeaten streak in Division II, winning or tying 54 straight games between 1931 and 1938.

National Champions by Year

1869 Princeton 1–1
1870 Princeton 1–0
1872 Princeton 1–0
1873 Princeton 1–0
1874 Princeton 2–0
1875 Princeton 2–0
1876 Yale 3–0
1877 Princeton 2–0–1
1878 Princeton 6–0
1879 Princeton 4–0–1
1880 Yale 4–0–1
1881 Princeton 5–0–1
1882 Yale 8–0
1883 Yale 8–0
1884 Princeton 9–0–1
1885 Princeton 9–0
1886 Princeton 7–0–1
1887 Yale 9–0
1888 Yale 13–0
1889 Princeton 10–0
1890 Harvard 11–0
1891 Yale 13–0
1892 Yale 13–0
1893 Princeton 11–0
1894 Yale 16–0
1895 Pennsylvania 14–0
1896 Princeton 10–0–1
1897 Pennsylvania 15–0
1898 Harvard 11–0
1899 Princeton 12–1
1900 Yale 2–0
1901 Michigan 11–0
1902 Michigan 11–0
1903 Princeton 11–0
1904 Minnesota 13–0
1905 Chicago 10–0, Stanford 8–0
1906 Yale 9–0–1

1907 Yale 9–0–1
1908 Harvard 9–0–1
1909 Washington 7–0
1910 Harvard 8–0–1
1911 Princeton 8–0–2
1912 Harvard 9–0
1913 Washington 7–0
1914 Army 9–0
1919 Harvard 9–0
1920 California
1921 California 9–0–1
1922 *California 9–0
1923 *Michigan 8–0
1924 Notre Dame 10–0
1925 Alabama 10–0
1926 Stanford 10–0–1, Alabama 9–0–1
1927 *Illinois 7–0–1
1928 *Southern California 9–0–1, Georgia Tech 10–0
1929 *Notre Dame 9–0
1930 *Notre Dame 10–0, Alabama 10–0
1931 Southern California 10–1
1932 Southern California 10–0
1933 *Michigan 7–0–1
1934 *Minnesota 8–0, Alabama 10–0
1935 *Minnesota 8–0
1936 *Minnesota 7–1
1937 *Pittsburgh 9–0–1, California 10–0–1
1938 Texas Christian 11–0 (Heisman: Davey O'Brien)
1939 Southern California 8–0–2, Texas A&M 11–0
1940 *Minnesota, Stanford
1941 *Minnesota 8–0 (Heisman: Bruce Smith)
1942 *Ohio State 9–1
1943 *Notre Dame 9–1 (Heisman: Angelo Bertelli)
1944 *Army 9–0
1945 *Army 9–0 (Heisman: Doc Blanchard)
1946 *Notre Dame 8–0–1
1947 *Notre Dame 9–0 (Heisman: John Lujack)
1948 *Michigan 9–0
1949 *Notre Dame 10–0 (Heisman: Leon Hart)
1950 Oklahoma 10–1
ILLEGITIMATE
REVISED: Tennessee 11–1

1951 Tennessee 10–1
ILLEGITIMATE
REVISED: Maryland 10–0
1952 *Michigan State 9–0
1953 Maryland ILLEGITIMATE
REVISED: Michigan State 9–1
1954 *UCLA 9–0, Ohio State 10–0
1955 Oklahoma 11–0
1956 *Oklahoma 10–0
1957 Ohio State 8–1, *Auburn 10–0
1958 Louisiana State 11–0
1959 Syracuse 11–0
1960 Minnesota 8–2
ILLEGITIMATE
REVISED: Mississippi 10–0–1
1961 Alabama 11–0
1962 Southern California 11–0
1963 Texas 11–0
1964 Alabama 10–1
ILLEGITIMATE
REVISED: Arkansas 11–0
1965 Alabama 9–1–1
1966 *Notre Dame 9–0–1
1967 Southern California 10–1
1968 Ohio State 10–0
1969 Texas 11–0
1970 Nebraska 11–0–1
1971 Nebraska 13–0
1972 Southern California 12–0
1973 Notre Dame 11–0 (AP), Alabama 11–1
ILLEGITIMATE (UPI)
1974 Southern California 10–1–1 (UPI), *Oklahoma 11–0 (AP)
1975 Oklahoma 11–1
1976 Pittsburgh 12–0
1977 Notre Dame 11–1
1978 Southern California 12–1 (UPI), Alabama 11–1 (AP)
1979 Alabama 12–0
1980 Georgia 12–0
1981 Clemson 12–0
1982 Penn State 11–1
1983 Miami 11–1
1984 Brigham Young 13–0
1985 Oklahoma 11–1
1986 Penn State 12–0
1987 Miami 12–0
1988 Notre Dame 12–0
1989 Miami 11–1
1990 Colorado 11–1–1 (AP), Georgia Tech 11–0–1 (UPI)
1991 Washington 12–0 (UPI), Miami 12–0 (AP)

1992 Alabama 13–0
1993 Florida State 12–1
1994 Nebraska 13–0
1995 Nebraska 12–0
1996 Florida 12–1
1997 Michigan 12–0 (AP)
 (Heisman: Charles Woodson),
 Nebraska 13–0 (*USA Today*)
1998 Tennessee 13–0
1999 Florida State 12–0
2000 Oklahoma 13–0
2001 Miami 12–0
2002 Ohio State 14–0
2003 Southern California 12–1
 (AP), Louisiana State 13–1
 (BCS/*USA Today*)
2004 Southern California 13–0
2005 Texas 13–0
2006 Florida 13–1
2007 Louisiana State 13–1
2008 Florida 13–1
2009 Alabama 14–0 (Heisman:
 Mark Ingram)

*No bowl
National champions were selected
 prior to bowl games: AP
 (1936–1964, 1966–1967); UPI
 (1950–1973)

Most Post–World War I National Championships by Team

1. (tie) Southern California (11):
 1928, 1931, 1932, 1939, 1962,
 1967, 1972, 1974, 1978, 2003,
 2004 (seven Heismans). (Note:
 Each USC national
 championship included victory
 in the Rose Bowl, except for
 1928 [did not play in a bowl]
 and 2004 [BCS Orange Bowl].)
1. (tie) Notre Dame (11): 1920*,
 1924, 1929*, 1943*, 1946*,
 1947*, 1949*, 1966*, 1973, 1977,
 1988 (seven Heismans) (*did
 not play in a bowl game)
3. Alabama (10, 8 considered
 legitimate): 1925, 1926, 1930,
 1961, 1964 (lost bowl game),
 1965, 1978, 1979, 1992, 2009
 (one Heisman)
4. Oklahoma (8, post-WWI: 7):
 1915, 1950, 1955, 1956, 1974

 (NCAA probation), 1975, 1985,
 2000 (five Heismans)
5. Minnesota (7, post-WWI: 6):
 1904, 1934, 1935, 1936, 1940,
 1941, 1960 (one Heisman)
6. (tie) Michigan (6, post-WWI: 5):
 1902, 1918, 1923, 1933, 1948,
 1997 (three Heismans)
6. (tie) Miami (5): 1983, 1987,
 1989, 1991, 2001 (two
 Heismans)
6. (tie) Ohio State (5): 1942, 1954,
 1957, 1968, 2002 (seven
 Heismans)
6. (tie) Nebraska (5): 1970, 1971,
 1994, 1995, 1997 (three
 Heismans)

Other National Championships Won by Traditional Modern Powers

Arkansas (1): 1964
Auburn (2, post-WWI: 1): 1913,
 1957 (two Heismans)
Brigham Young (1): 1984 (one
 Heisman)
Florida (3): 1996, 2006, 2008 (three
 Heismans)
Florida State (2): 1993, 1999 (two
 Heismans)
Georgia (2): 1942, 1980 (two
 Heismans)
LSU (3): 1958, 2003, 2007 (one
 Heisman)
Penn State (2): 1982, 1986 (one
 Heisman)
Tennessee (3): 1938, 1950, 1998
Texas (4, post-WWI: 3): 1914, 1963,
 1969, 2005 (two Heismans)
Washington (1): 1991

National Championships by Other Teams

Army (2): 1944, 1945 (three
 Heismans)
California (3): 1921, 1922, 1937
Chicago (1, post-WWI 0): 1905
 (one Heisman)
Clemson (1): 1981
Colorado (1): 1990 (one Heisman)
Georgia Tech (3, post-WWI: 2)
 1917, 1952, 1990
Harvard (6, post-WWI 0): 1890,
 1898, 1901, 1908, 1910, 1912

Illinois (1): 1927
Michigan State (2): 1951, 1965 (lost
 bowl game)
Mississippi (1): 1960
Pennsylvania (2, post-WWI: 0):
 1895, 1897
Pittsburgh (3, post-WWI: 2): 1916,
 1937, 1976 (one Heisman)
Princeton (19, post-WWI 0): 1869,
 1870, 1872, 1873, 1874, 1875,
 1877, 1878, 1879, 1881, 1884,
 1885, 1886, 1889, 1893, 1896,
 1899, 1903, 1911 (one
 Heisman)
Stanford (2): 1926, 1940 (one
 Heisman)
Syracuse (1): 1959 (one Heisman)
TCU (1): 1938 (one Heisman)
Texas A&M (2): 1919, 1939 (one
 Heisman)
Yale (12, post-WWI 0): 1876, 1880,
 1883, 1887, 1888, 1891, 1892,
 1894, 1900, 1906, 1907, 1909
 (two Heismans)

National Champions by Conference Since World War I

PACIFIC 10: 19

USC, 11: 1928, 1931, 1932, 1939,
 1962, 1967, 1972, 1974, 1978,
 2003, 2004
California, 4: 1920, 1921, 1922,
 1937
Stanford, 2: 1926, 1940
UCLA, 1: 1954
Washington, 1: 1991
10 Heismans

BIG 10: 18

Minnesota, 6: 1934, 1935, 1936,
 1940, 1941, 1960
Michigan, 5: 1918, 1923, 1933,
 1948, 1997
Ohio State, 5: 1942, 1954, 1957,
 1968, 2002
Illinois, 1: 1927
Michigan State, 1: 1951
13 Heismans

SOUTHEASTERN: 19

Alabama, 9: 1925, 1926, 1930, 1961,
 1965, 1978, 1979, 1992, 2009
Tennessee, 3: 1938, 1950, 1998
Georgia, 2: 1942, 1980

LSU, 3: 1958, 2003, 2007
Auburn, 1: 1957
Florida, 1: 1996
Mississippi 1: 1960
9 Heismans

INDEPENDENTS: 15

Notre Dame, 11: 1920, 1924, 1929,
1943, 1946, 1947, 1949, 1966,
1973, 1977, 1988
Penn State, 2: 1982, 1986
Army, 2: 1944, 1945
11 Heismans

BIG 12: 14

Oklahoma, 7: 1950, 1955, 1956,
1974 (NCAA probation), 1975,
1985, 2000
Nebraska, 5: 1970, 1971, 1994,
1995, 1997
Colorado, 1: 1990
Texas, 1: 2005
8 Heismans

BIG EAST:

Miami, 5: 1983, 1987, 1989, 1991,
2001
Pittsburgh, 2: 1937, 1976
Syracuse, 1: 1959
4 Heismans

SOUTHWESTERN: 6

Texas, 2: 1963, 1969
Texas A&M, 2: 1919, 1939
Arkansas, 1: 1964
TCU, 1: 1938
5 Heismans

ATLANTIC COAST: 5

Florida State, 2: 1993, 1999
Clemson, 1: 1981
Georgia Tech, 2: 1952, 1990
2 Heismans

WESTERN ATHLETIC: 1

Brigham Young, 1: 1984
1 Heisman

All-Time USC Football Team

OFFENSE (HONORABLE MENTIONS IN PARENTHESES)

QB: Matt Leinart (Pat Haden,
Carson Palmer, Paul
McDonald, Rodney Peete)

TB: O. J. Simpson (Charles White,
Mike Garrett, Ricky Bell, Frank
Gifford)
FB: Marcus Allen (Sam "Bam"
Cunningham)
WR: Lynn Swann
WR: Mike Williams (Keyshawn
Johnson, Erik Affholter, Bob
Chandler, Dwayne Jarrett)
TE: Charles "Tree" Young
OT: Anthony Munoz
OT: Ron Yary (Tony Boselli, Ernie
Smith, Don Mosebar, Pete
Adams, Keith Van Horne, John
Vella)
OG: Brad Budde
OG: Bruce Mathews (Aaron
Rosenberg, Roy Foster, Johnny
Baker)
C: Stan Williamson

DEFENSE

T: Marvin Powell (John Ferraro)
DT: Shaun Cody
DT: Ron Mix (Mike Patterson, Tim
Ryan)
DE: Tim Rossovich
DE: Willie McGinest (Mike
McKeever, Charles Weaver,
Keneche Udeze)
LB: Junior Seau
LB: Richard "Batman" Wood
LB: Clay Matthews (Dennis
Johnson, Chip Banks, Adrian
Young, Charles Phillips, Chris
Claiborne, Rey Maualuga)
DB: Ronnie Lott
DB: Tim McDonald
DB: Troy Polamalu (Dennis Smith,
Dennis Thurman, Joey
Browner, Mark Carrier, Taylor
Mays)

SPECIAL TEAMS

KR: Reggie Bush (Anthony Davis)
P: Tom Malone
PK: Frank Jordan (Ron Ayala)

Offensive Player: Matt Leinart
Defensive Player: Ronnie Lott
Coach: John McKay (Pete Carroll,
Howard Jones, John Robinson)

All-Time Greatest Collegiate Athletic Programs

1. Southern California Trojans
2. UCLA Bruins
3. Texas Longhorns
4. Miami Hurricanes
5. Michigan Wolverines
6. Alabama Crimson Tide
7. Ohio State Buckeyes
8. Florida State Seminoles
9. Stanford Indians/Cardinal
10. Oklahoma Sooners
11. Louisiana State Tigers
12. Tennessee Volunteers
13. Notre Dame Fighting Irish
14. Penn State Nittany Lions
15. Arkansas Razorbacks
16. Florida Gators
17. Indiana Hoosiers
18. Georgia Bulldogs
19. Texas A&M Aggies
20. Oklahoma State Cowboys
21. Arizona State Sun Devils
22. Auburn Tigers
23. Duke Blue Devils
24. North Carolina Tar Heels
25. Syracuse Orangemen
26. California Golden Bears
27. Brigham Young Cougars

All-Time College Basketball Programs

1. UCLA Bruins
2. North Carolina Tar Heels
3. Indiana Hoosiers
4. Duke Blue Devils
5. Kentucky Wildcats
6. Kansas Jayhawks
7. Michigan Wolverines
8. Ohio State Buckeyes
9. Virginia Cavaliers
10. Michigan State Spartans
11. Nevada–Las Vegas Runnin' Rebels
12. Louisville Cardinals
13. Arizona Wildcats
14. Stanford Cardinal
15. West Virginia Squires
16. San Francisco Dons
17. Syracuse Orangemen
18. Maryland Terrapins

All-Time College Baseball Programs

1. Southern California Trojans
2. Texas Longhorns
3. Cal State Fullerton Titans
4. Arizona State Sun Devils
5. Louisiana State Tigers
6. Miami Hurricanes
7. Stanford Indians/Cardinal
8. Florida State Seminoles
9. Oklahoma State Cowboys
10. Florida Gators
11. Mississippi State Bulldogs
12. Texas A&M Aggies
13. Arkansas Razorbacks
14. Arizona Wildcats
15. Georgia Bulldogs
16. Oklahoma Sooners
17. California Golden Bears
18. Fresno State Bulldogs
19. Michigan Wolverines
20. Clemson Tigers

Prep Football

De La Salle H.S. (Concord, Calif.)
Mater Dei H.S. (Santa Ana, Calif.)
Poly H.S. (Long Beach, Calif.)
Moeller H.S. (Cincinnati, Ohio)
Highland Park H.S. (Dallas, Texas)
Washington H.S. (Massillon, Ohio)
Valdosta H.S. (Georgia)
Austin H.S. (Texas)
Carroll H.S. (Southlake, Texas)
St. Thomas Aquinas H.S. (Ft. Lauderdale, Florida)

Prep Basketball

Verbum Dei H.S. (Los Angeles, Calif.)
Crenshaw H.S. (Los Angeles, Calif.)
Mater Dei H.S. (Santa Ana, Calif.)
Cardinal Gibbons H.S. (Baltimore, Md.)
De Matha H.S. (Hiattsville, Md.)
Power Memorial Academy (New York, N.Y.)
McClymonds H.S. (Oakland, Calif.)
New Trier H.S. (Winnetka, Illinois)

Prep Baseball

Lakewood H.S. (Calif.)
Redwood H.S. (Larkspur, Calif.)
Sharpstown H.S. (Houston, Tex.)
Rancho Bernardo H.S. (San Diego, Calif.)
Fremont H.S. (Los Angeles, Calif.)
Serra H.S. (San Mateo, Calif.)
Clovis West H.S. (Fresno, Calif.)

INDEX

BOOKS BY STEVEN TRAVERS

One Night, Two Teams: Alabama vs. USC and the Game That Changed A Nation (also a documentary, *Tackling Segregation*, and soon to be a major motion picture)

A's Essential: Everything You Need to Know to Be A Real Fan!

Trojans Essential: Everything You Need to Know to Be A Real Fan!

Dodgers Essential: Everything You Need to Know to Be A Real Fan!

Angels Essential: Everything You Need to Know to Be A Real Fan!

D'Backs Essential: Everything You Need to Know to Be A Real Fan!

The USC Trojans: College Football's All-Time Greatest Dynasty

The Good, the Bad & the Ugly Los Angeles Lakers

The Good, the Bad & the Ugly Oakland Raiders

The Good, the Bad & the Ugly San Francisco 49ers

Barry Bonds: Baseball's Superman

Pigskin Warriors: 140 Years of College Football's Greatest Games, Players and Traditions

The 1969 Miracle Mets: The Improbable Story of the World's Greatest Underdog Team

Dodgers Baseball Yesterday & Today

What It Means to Be a Trojan: Southern Cal's Greatest Players Talk About Trojans Football

A Tale of Three Cities: The 1962 Baseball Season in New York, L.A. and San Francisco

God's Country: A Conservative, Christian Worldview of How History Formed the United States Empire and America's Manifest Destiny for the 21st Century

Angry White Male

The Writer's Life

From the Frat House to the White House to the Big House